Small Wonder

Books by Walter Henry Nelson

SMALL WONDER
The Amazing Story of the Volkswagen

THE GREAT DISCOUNT DELUSION

THE BERLINERS
Their Saga and Their City

THE SOLDIER KINGS
The House of Hohenzollern

Small Wonder

The Amazing Story of the
VOLKSWAGEN

by Walter Henry Nelson

REVISED AND ENLARGED

With Photographs

BOSTON • Little, Brown and Company • TORONTO

LIBRARY OF CONGRESS CATALOG CARD NO. 79-119031

REVISED AND ENLARGED EDITION

Grateful acknowledgment is made for permission to reprint the following copyrighted material:

"The Beetle Does Float" by Huston Horn, *Sports Illustrated,* August 19, 1963, © 1963 Time Inc.

"The Snob's Guide to Status Cars" by Dan Greenburg. Originally appeared in *Playboy* Magazine; Copyright © 1964 by HMH Publishing Co., Inc. Reprinted by permission of *Playboy* and the author.

The New York Times, © 1936, 1937, 1938, 1963, 1964 by The New York Times Company. Reprinted by permission.

All data from *1963 Automobile Buyer's Guide,* © 1963 Mel Martin Enterprises, published in *Small World* magazine, Summer 1963; reprinted here with permission of copyright holder.

"Some Dreams I've Driven" by Arnold Gingrich. First published in *Esquire* Magazine, June 1966. © 1966 by Esquire, Inc. Reprinted by permission of *Esquire* and the author.

"Porsche" by Ferry Porsche, *Merian,* No. 7, 1958. Reprinted with the permission of Hoffmann und Campe Verlag.

Portions of this book have appeared in *Cosmopolitan, Small World* and *Die Welt.*

Published simultaneously in Canada by Little, Brown & Company (Canada) Limited

PRINTED IN THE UNITED STATES OF AMERICA

Once again, for Rita

Acknowledgments

SMALL WONDER has undergone several revisions since it was first published; this latest revision brings the story up to date as Volkswagen revs up for the seventies. The first thirteen chapters tell the story of the VW's amazing beginning and even-more amazing rebirth after World War II: how a genius at designing cars created his masterpiece and how a genius at producing and selling masterpieces later took over to win millions of customers for the VW. A final chapter has been added to this revision: Chapter 14 tells of VW's "Transition Toward Tomorrow" — and tells why the title of this book will in the years to come no longer seem so very appropriate. The passage of time and the passing of great men like Ferdinand Porsche and Heinz Nordhoff are leaving their mark upon the company which most readers know simply as the corporation producing the world-renowned VW "beetle" or "bug"; under the new leadership of Kurt Lotz, the VW company is turning into a very "big wonder" indeed.

In acknowledging my debt to the many persons who helped me in my researches, it might therefore be appropriate to shift into reverse and to begin with the present, working backwards. At the end of 1969, I revisited the city of Wolfsburg, Germany, in order to meet members of the new management team and to research the last chapter of this book; my special thanks go, therefore, to Dr. Kurt Lotz, head of the worldwide Volkswagen organization (in his capacity as chairman of the Vorstand, or management board, of the parent company, Volkswagenwerk AG). He generously spent hours with me, to answer my questions and explain the chart he had devised to help Volkswagen navigate the challenging years to come. He was as frank in his replies as Heinz Nordhoff had been and just as generous with his encouragement and interest. Others on his Vorstand deserve my thanks as well, as do many department heads and other top executives whose names are too numerous to list here, but most of whose names appear later in the pages of this book.

I am glad that I was able to express my gratitude to Heinz Nordhoff while he was still alive; it was he who told me that the VW story might well have to be written by an American such as myself, as others might have too many axes to grind or skeletons to hide; it was also Nordhoff who was particularly pleased that *Small Wonder* was not a company-sponsored history, but an independent work produced by a freelance writer beholden only to his reader — and to his understanding of the truth. There are not many companies which will make a freelance writer privy to their full stories (and even to some of their "secrets"): Volkswagen, which practically pioneered "honesty in advertising" in the U.S.A. with its bland admission that the beetle might be regarded as "ugly," was an outstanding exception.

I have told the story of VW "like it is"; the fact that I was able to do so is in large part due to the enormous amount of help I received from members of the American VW organization, headed by J. Stuart Perkins, the young, articulate and imaginative president of Volkswagen of America, Inc., at Englewood Cliffs, New Jersey. I am much indebted to Stuart Perkins (whose own career at "VWoA" both encompasses and symbolizes the very growth of which I wrote) for his interest and help over the years, as well as for his readiness to be frank and open in many successive interviews. My special thanks go to Arthur R. Railton, VWoA's Vice President in charge of Corporate Relations, without whom this book would probably never have been written at all, for it was he whom I first approached for information and who immediately put at my disposal all the resources of his department, feeling as I did that here was a story worth telling — and worth telling fully. Baron K. Bates and Herbert W. Williamson, public relations managers respectively of Volkswagen Operations and Porsche-Audi Operations at VWoA, have also been extremely helpful over the years, as have other members of the American public relations staff: Chet Bahn, Mildred De Piano and Tony Weaver.

The press department of Volkswagenwerk AG, Wolfsburg, has been equally as helpful in providing information, advice and detailed data of all kinds; in arranging interviews; in explaining some of the complexities of an increasingly complex international corporation — and in countless other ways. My thanks, therefore, go to the head of that department, Richard Budde; he saw to it that I obtained the data I needed when I needed it. My particular thanks go to his deputy, the tireless and endlessly cooperative Rudi Maletz, whose private office I have often usurped as my temporary headquarters while researching in Wolfsburg. I am also extremely grateful to Dr. Volkmar Köhler, VW's able archivist (and today Wolfsburg's urbane and charming Bürgermeister); he has, over the years, proved an unfailing and unflagging source of information and guided me through the intricacies of the company's history in a manner as generous as knowledgeable.

I cannot list all those without whom this book also could not have been written: the many men in both lofty and lowly positions whose stories I have been able to incorporate into these pages because they were kind enough to sacrifice time in order to make themselves available to me. They include men on the corporate Vorstand and drivers in the company motor pool; they include early veterans and late arrivals, Germans and Americans as well as many of other nationalities, who have helped make VW popular the world over. I am grateful also to Everett Martin, who made available to me notes he had taken during interviews with a number of VW executives some years ago and to whom I am indebted specifically for certain details regarding the earliest years of the VW organization in the U.S.A. and elsewhere. My thanks also go to those in Stuttgart's Porsche organization whom I interviewed at length: Ferry Porsche, Louise Piëch, Ghislaine E. J. Kaes, and Huschke von Hanstein.

What errors there may be in this book are my own, of course; I apologize for them, as I also do for the fact that I may possibly not have included sufficient technical and/or financial data for readers who are especially interested in the VW's technology or in the Volkswagenwerk as a corporate entity. I did not attempt to tell more than seemed to me absolutely necessary about such matters, for to me the story of the Volkswagen and its company is primarily a human one. I wrote of the things which interested me: of a man's long dream to build a "people's car" and of his hard work to realize that dream; of the nightmare of seeing that dream shattered; of the near-miraculous fulfillment of it after World War II; of the dramatic, intriguing events and developments which have taken place since. I have attempted not only to portray the Volkswagen itself, but to present a picture of the men without whom the VW story could never have taken place; I have attempted to tell their own personal stories not only to make these men familiar to the reader, but to show also how the lives of men, as well as their characters and characteristics, can shape a car and a corporation. In short, I wrote for those more interested in men than in machines, in a story of fulfillment more than one of finance; I wrote for all those who have been bemused, amused, or puzzled by that strange little car which so many millions have taken to their hearts—and which became the cornerstone of a great, international multi-line corporation. The Volkswagen on which I lavish most of my attention in this book is, of course, the "beetle"; some day the story of all the cars the beetle spawned may have to be told in greater detail but that day has not yet arrived. The familiar "bug" has turned into an acorn; the oak is growing still.

Contents

The Volkswagen: the car "nobody wanted," except people; its development summarized. How it all began: the early years of its designer, Ferdinand Porsche. His plans for a "people's car" described. His racing- and luxury-car career at Austro-Daimler, German Daimler, and Steyr. The start of his private design bureau. Stalin makes him a tempting offer. The first two Volkswagen prototypes emerge, only to be killed.

The new Reich Chancellor and his interest in small—and big—cars. Ferdinand Porsche meets "the Führer" to discuss racing and the VW. Jakob Werlin, Baron von Oertzen, and the P-car racers. How the German automakers start to oppose the development of a Volkswagen.

The Nazis form a Volkswagen Development Company. VW prototypes are built and tested—to death? Porsche tours the U.S.A., meets Henry Ford, and recruits engineers. How the Nazis plan to finance their schemes by means of an elaborate layaway "savings" program. The search for a factory site. Count von der Schulenburg fights to save his lands. Plans for an "ideal Nazi workers' city" are announced.

Hitler dedicates the factory, names Porsche's

rise from the ruins accelerates. The story of "the Volkswagenwerk miracle" — how the first ten million cars were built. The man who provided the leadership: Nordhoff evaluated.

Early efforts to introduce Volkswagens into the United States. The arrival of Will van de Kamp, Geoffrey Lange, and Stuart Perkins. The controversial, colorful van de Kamp meets those who become VW's American distributors. How it all began and how the end of the beginning is reached.

The arrival of Carl Hahn in the U.S.A. Herman Bruns and the VW service-and-parts policy. The dealer network is built up, requirements set. Sales rise. How VW survived Detroit's "compact" counterattack. Volkswagen and the "black and gray" markets in beetles. Stuart Perkins assumes leadership; his contribution and future challenges analyzed.

Volkswagen's first reaction to advertising: who needs it? How and why it all started and how it got as good as it is. The fight among agencies to get the VW account. Why did VW select the agency it did? Just what is honest advertising really? Some examples of VW ads as illustrative of VW advertising policies. What admen and the public think of the ads. What effect have U.S. VW ads had on advertising in general?

The VW breeds a global "Volkslore." The stories of VWs that float and fly and compete in rallies and races. Who are "typical" VW-owners? Snob-appeal and the development of VW clubs. Volkswagen jokes and anecdotes.

Small Wonder

1

The Years of Preparation

IN MARCH 1948 Henry Ford II seated himself at a conference table in Cologne, Germany, to help decide the fate of the Volkswagen. With him on the "Ford side" of the negotiating table were Ernest Breech, chairman of the board of Ford Motor Company, and the heads of Ford's German and British companies. Across the table sat Colonel C. R. Radclyffe, representing the British Military Government, and Heinz Nordhoff, a German engineer, who had recently been appointed head of the Volkswagen factory.

Nordhoff attended the meeting with mixed feelings. He knew that the British had been trying to give the Volkswagen factory away ever since World War II. Now Henry Ford was being offered the plant, gratis. "Perhaps," Nordhoff thought, "it would be for the best. Perhaps the only hope for this company is to be taken under the wing of a powerful American manufacturer." He had been with Volkswagen only two months and was not yet really confident of the company's future. Production was insignificant and the factory was in ruins.

"It was plain," Nordhoff says, "that Sir Patrick Hennessy, who was head of British Ford at Dagenham, did not want to see Volkswagen come into the Ford family. Perhaps Sir Patrick felt that if VW were combined with Taunus [German Ford], it would make Ford's German subsidiaries too strong."

Finally, Colonel Radclyffe ended the discussion and asked Henry Ford to decide if he wanted to take over the Volkswagen plant. Ford turned to Ernest Breech and asked for his opinion. He received a famous answer.

17

"Mr. Ford," Breech said, "I don't think what we are being offered here is worth a damn!"

The factory nobody wanted was turned over to the Germans. Nordhoff began trying to sell Volkswagens. He had his problems. In 1949 he arrived in New York City to look for American customers for his product. By this time he had developed a fondness for his beetle-like automobile and hoped that others, perhaps even American auto dealers, would share his feelings. He was disappointed; no one took him seriously. His car, according to all the American experts, was just what Ernie Breech said, "not worth a damn."

Not only was the car strange-looking, but its history was suspicious. Nordhoff could hardly expect to sell "a Nazi creation" to Americans four years after the war. The Volkswagen was out of date politically, and its design was out of tune with public tastes. And yet today more than twelve million Volkswagens have been sold in more than one hundred countries, a painful fact for the marketing men of Detroit to face. More than two million Americans have already bought this car, several hundred thousand more Americans buy it each year, and Heinz Nordhoff's company today is one of the world's largest producers of automobiles, following General Motors, Ford, and Chrysler. It is West Germany's biggest corporation, and it stands among the top corporations in Europe today.

How this was achieved, how a bombed-out plant in which cars could be produced only if it didn't rain, could grow into a colossus which builds—and sells—a Volkswagen every eight seconds, is only part of the story.

Nobody had wanted the Volkswagen—except people. Hitler gave the car its impetus, then throttled it with his war. Three hundred thousand Germans fell for his propaganda and started saving for the car, but the Führer was to disappoint them here as elsewhere. He never produced a single Volkswagen for the public, despite his boasts of outproducing Henry Ford.

After the war, what was left of Hitler's preposterously ambitious plant was offered to all comers. The car it now produced in tiny quantities was one no "expert" took seriously. Finally the British had no choice. They had to find someone to run it and give its workers something to do. They turned to Heinz Nordhoff, who took the job only because he was broke and hungry. He also disliked the Volkswagen at first, but came to love it later.

In 1950, Nordhoff showed the factory's production line to a small, chunky old man in a wrinkled suit. Ferdinand Porsche, who recently had been freed after two years in a French prison, had come to see the plant which owed its existence to him.

"Yes, Herr Nordhoff," said Porsche, "that's how I always imagined it." He was finally seeing the fulfillment of a dream which had obsessed him throughout his life. Since the end of World War I, when he was a young auto designer full of visions which no one would share, he had planned a Volkswagen, a people's car. At a time when cars were thought to be only "for the rich and for the very rich," he had dared design for the man on foot or on a bicycle. His idea was rejected year after year. He left one company after another, usually because he was not allowed to pursue his vision. Had it not been for the fact that he built at the same time some of the fastest, biggest, most luxurious, and finest cars in the world, he might have been discredited.

Then Hitler wanted just such a small car, and for his own reasons. He provided Porsche with the means to build his people's car and Porsche perfected the beetle. Today, more than thirty years later, his car still bears the advanced design he gave it then.

There was talk of this car proving that National Socialism could do what free enterprise could never do. Under Hitler, the Nazi propagandists said, every German would have his own Volkswagen within ten years. Instead, he had defeat and desolation.

Yet ideas do not easily die and the idea behind the Volkswagen was an honest one. How it originated and was finally made to prevail is the story of many men, but primarily three: Ferdinand Porsche, who had the dream; Adolf Hitler, who sought to exploit it; and Heinz Nordhoff, who turned Porsche's vision into reality.

The first of these, Ferdinand Porsche, was to spend much of his strength, genius, and almost all his years on his dream and crowning achievement; the story of his first sixty years of life is the story of how the Volkswagen got started in the first place. A brief glance at this man and his years of preparation sets the scene for the beetle.

Ferdinand Porsche was born on September 3, 1875, in Maffersdorf rechts der Neisse, a town lying in the backwoods of the sprawling Austro-Hungarian Empire. Electric power, new in the world, was unknown there until Willy Ginskey installed it to light his carpet factory, and it was there that fifteen-year-old tinsmith's apprentice Ferdinand Porsche, arriving to fix the drains, encountered it first. His interest was caught; Porsche learned fast and two years later had wired his father's home for electricity, installing incandescent lights, electric chimes, and even an intercom.

There were rapid changes in other fields as well, even though the change was hardly noticeable to the average man. The gasoline internal combustion engine had been developed; in 1890 Gottlieb Daimler formed the Daimler Motor Company to manufacture his first car, the Phoenix; Karl Benz had formed Benz & Cie; Panhard & Levassor started producing in 1891, and Louis Renault, Armand Peugeot, August Horch and Wilhelm Maybach entered the infant industry as well. In America, others started in business during these early decades: Charles E. and J. Frank Duryea, Elwood G. Haynes, Henry Ford and Ransom Eli Olds.

Ferdinand Porsche did not, of course, know of these events. Yet he was excited by the smell of the burgeoning technology, and after a while persuaded his father to send him to the trade school at Reichenberg, to test his talent. There he attended only the Werkmeisterschule, to be trained as a factory foreman. After he had finished (leaving with the lowest grades in his class), his brother Oskar took over the family tinsmith's trade and Ferdinand left for Vienna.

He left Maffersdorf on April 18, 1894, with an introduction to Bela Egger, owner of the United Electrical Company at Fernkorngasse No. 16, who put Ferdinand to work sweeping the shop and greasing machinery. Within four years Porsche had been put in charge of the experimental shop. Here he could learn and experiment, absorb technical knowledge, and devote himself to his passion, electricity. After work, he illegally attended the technical university, sneaking into the lecture galleries. He found time to court another Egger employee, Aloisia Kaes, and soon had both won the girl and produced his first industrial design. Porsche designs ultimately would total more than 380 and include the Volkswagen.

The electromobile was the rage now, however. A number of inventors had tried their best to make such a car efficient. In the 1880's a succession of cumbersome models appeared. Such battery-driven cars may seem strange to us today, as we roar along behind (or in front of) our internal combustion engines, but these motors had and still have much to recommend them. For one thing, they were noiseless and free of fumes. To Porsche, the electromobile's shortcomings seemed the big challenge in Vienna. At twenty-four, he tried to eliminate them.

He designed an electromotor to power the inside of a wheel's rim, placing the power squarely where it was needed. As Porsche told the story, this first of his designs was stolen from him at the Egger offices. Although his fiancée, Aloisia, was outraged and urged Ferdinand to press the matter, he refused to do so. "Don't bother yourself about it," he told her. "I've already got something better."

He produced it for Ludwig Lohner, owner of a court carriage factory, in Vienna-Florisdorf, who hired him as his designer in 1898. Lohner, who intended to produce automobiles, was interested in this design, which placed the electric motor right inside the hub, eliminating belts or chain drives completely. Utilizing this principle, Porsche built the Porsche-Lohner Chaise, capable of traveling fifty miles without recharging. A car which only an Imperial and Royal Court Carriagemaker like Lohner would produce, it looked like a cross between a Victoria and a surrey, and was a beautiful sight to Lohner and his young designer. They decided the village lad from Maffersdorf would take it to the great 1900 Exposition at Paris and enter it for whatever interest it might generate. This was quite a move for a former tinsmith's apprentice. At twenty-five, he was about to compete with engineers, scientists, and technicians from all over the world.

No grander fair had ever been organized than the 1900 Universal Exposition. It was attended by 51 million visitors and was described by a contemporary as seeming "as fairy-like as a stage-setting . . . creating in the heart of Paris a veritable city of dreams and illusions."

In the midst of all this, Porsche explained his car without a transmission system, powered by hubcap motors, and exhibited it in a nine-mile-per-hour run to Versailles and back. When the awards were announced, Porsche won a grand prize. It made him famous.

In Vienna, the delighted Lohner studied the future and Porsche developed a new principle. Combining a gasoline engine with an electric motor, he produced what he called a "Mixt" car. Its gasoline engine powered the generators feeding the electric motors in the wheels. They nicknamed the car "Aunt Eulalia" and in it Porche drove home to Maffersdorf to show off his technical ability, as well as his fiancée, whom he married on October 17, 1903.

This automobile did more than astound the rustics of Maffersdorf; it became the hit of the *haut monde*. Baron Nathan

Rothschild of Vienna bought one in 1905 and Archduke Franz Ferdinand drove in one during the Austrian maneuvers of 1902, chauffeured by reservist Porsche.* In the same year, a Prussian general used it at the German Imperial War Games. Bureaucrats as well as aristocrats bought it and municipal authorities used it for fire trucks and omnibuses. Now Porsche turned to plans for further cars.

Yet Ludwig Lohner was hesitant to spend more money on further advanced designs. He already had spent a million crowns on Porsche's development costs and wanted to concentrate on selling the popular "Mixt" car. It was at this time that Porsche received a tempting offer to join Austro-Daimler.

His name was already famous in 1905. Austria had awarded him its coveted Poetting Prize that year, marking him at the age of thirty as having made the greatest contribution to the nation's auto industry. It was the highest honor that Porsche could receive in his field at the time. Yet he had few ambitions for himself and little desire for the perquisites of corporate position. He was too busy with his workers in the shop. "Fundamentally," to quote Charles Lam Markmann and Mark Sherwin in *The Book of Sports Cars,* Porsche "was an engine man. Those who observed him say they could see his eyes grow brighter as he listened to the purr or the roar of one of his creations, making mental notes of what had to be adjusted, changed, or redesigned. Some have called him a martinet in his pursuit of perfection, but a listing of his accomplishments is enough to dispel any criticism of his method or manner."

In 1906, this gifted, brusque, and as-yet-unpolished man took over as technical director and board member of staid Austro-Daimler, the independent Austrian offshoot of Daimler in Germany. Porsche was to stay there until 1923, resigning eventually in an ugly argument about finances. By the time he quit, he had risen to Generaldirektor, or chief executive,

* On November 8, 1902 Franz Ferdinand wrote an archducal note to Porsche styled in the elaborate language of the court:

"His Imperial and Royal Highness, the gracious Archduke Franz Ferdinand, deigns to transmit to your honorable person a memento of this year's maneuvers in West Hungary. The performance of your automobile, as well as your sure and exact guidance of it, have satisfied His Imperial and Royal Highness in every particular."

(*"Seine Kaiserliche und Königliche Hoheit, der durchlauchtigste Herr Erzherzog Franz Ferdinand geruhen Euer Wohlgeboren beiliegend eine Erinnerung an die heurigen Manöver in West-Ungarn übersenden zu lassen. Die Leistung Ihres Automobils sowie Ihre sichere und exakte Führung desselben haben Seine Kaiserliche und Königliche Hoheit in jeder Beziehung befriedigt."*)

a position equivalent to company president. In the meantime, he did what he liked best: he produced great cars.

The staple workhorse of Austro-Daimler was the Maja, a car named after a daughter of Emil Jellinek, a financier and consular official who helped finance the Daimler Company in Germany. Another of Jellinek's daughters provided the name for German Daimler's prize car, the Mercedes.*

The Maja, in which Porsche first used the purely internal combustion engine, found a market in Austria; it had a four-cylinder engine, and an early Porsche redesign of this model generated 32 hp and included a four-speed transmission.

In order to sell the company cars by demonstrating them, Porsche entered them in races. The first major event in which he took part—and he would enter a host of races in the future —was the Prinz Heinrich race of 1909. This event, to which the auto-enthusiast brother of the German Kaiser lent his name, was less a race than a week-long endurance run throughout much of Central Europe. All three Austro-Daimler cars, one driven by Porsche himself, won top honors.

After the race ended, the rules for the 1910 run were announced. Porsche, it is said, ducked out of Prince Heinrich's banquet and into an anteroom that night, leaving his wife with the dignitaries, so as to mull over his chances of winning next year, his only food that night a hard roll.

For the 1910 event, he wanted to design a truly notable automobile; the car he entered was just that. The 80-hp Prinz-Heinrich-Wagen, achieving 90 mph, startled the other drivers and onlookers at the race. It was quickly nicknamed the *Tulpenform* (tulip shape).

It hardly looked like a blossom, but it certainly was streamlined in contrast to the boxes then sputtering down the road. Instead of a conventional square grille, it sported a moderately curved one. Its body sloped back in an unbroken line and even door handles had been eliminated. Austro-Daimler cars won twelve of the seventeen tests, three won the first three prizes in a field of over 170, and Porsche, who had driven the lead car himself, was commended by Franz Joseph. Austro-Daimler knew that now Porsche would want more money to carry the design forward.

But the designer was called to aid his country; the

---

* Markmann and Sherwin point out that "it is a nice irony of history that Adolf Hitler's favorite car was named for the granddaughter of a Hungarian rabbi."

year was 1911 and Europe had begun to arm.* Porsche had already designed airplane engines for Austro-Daimler. Although they generated more than 300 hp, they were lighter in weight than those in existence before. They helped Porsche perfect powerful yet lightweight engines for cars, and weight as well as power was becoming a prime Porsche obsession. Now, building airplanes and dirigibles, he intended to test them himself.

"Already before 1914, at Austro-Daimler, we had started to build the first aeroplane engines and also small motors for dirigibles," he recalled years later to his son Ferry. "And since I test all my children, I willy-nilly had to make at least one ascent in one of these balloons. It was rather stormy and, in order not to run into a church spire, we were forced to jettison some ballast. A little too much of it! As a result, the balloon rapidly gained height, and the pressure could not be controlled by the safety valve. I was watching the manometer intently and saw that the pressure was continuing to increase. I could calculate exactly when it would reach the point at which the fabric of the balloon would burst. We had no parachutes—we hadn't even heard of them . . . The pressure gauge had long passed the red line; but the ascent stopped just as the pressure had reached its limit. We were able to land.

"Back on firm ground, I said to the balloon crew: 'I have a nice salami sausage which my wife packed for me; that's just what we need after all this excitement.' However, how great was our disappointment, when I unpacked the parcel and found that my wife had made a mistake; there was no sausage, but instead a new corset."

In 1913, the Austro-Hungarian military developed a heavy 305-mm mortar which fired a shell weighing more than 700 pounds and Porsche designed a 100-hp vehicle to draw this monster, utilizing an adaptation of the "Mixt" car principle. After the war began, Porsche motorized an even bigger 420-mm mortar, similar to Germany's 420-mm Big Bertha. Its barrel alone weighed 26 tons and its shell another 2000 pounds. Porsche powered its tractor-like cab with a gasoline engine. This was hooked to a generator feeding hubcap motors in the

*During this period, one of Porsche's test-drivers and mechanics was Josip Broz, later Tito, president of Yugoslavia. "In 1912," he is quoted in Dedijer's *Tito* as saying, "I got a job in the Daimler factory in Wiener-Neustadt . . . The work here interested me more than in any other factory. I even became a test driver, running the big powerful cars with their heavy brasswork, rubber-bulb horns, and outside hand brakes, to put them through their paces."

eight trailer wheels. Thus, cab and trailer were both motorized.

In 1917 Porsche received an honorary doctorate in engineering from Vienna Technical University. Herr Doktor Porsche, Generaldirektor of Austro-Daimler, had achieved academic acceptance, and the proud title never left his calling cards.

Porsche's motorized trailer found other uses. As many as ten huge troop-carrying trailers were strung behind the gasoline-powered cab, each separately made mobile by means of hubcap electromotors. The entire effect was that of an undulating caterpillar, moving troop trains along the French, Italian, and Russian fronts.

The troops, however, only moved faster towards defeat. The war's end brought economic ruin and an end to the Empire. Porsche now worked in a minor republic called Austria. Maffersdorf, in the meantime, had become part of Czechoslovakia, and Porsche found himself to be a citizen of that country.

If the age of the Volkswagen were more accurately reckoned from conception, rather than from date of delivery, then today's Volkswagen would date back to the beginning of the 1920's. It was at Austro-Daimler, shortly after the end of World War I, that Ferdinand Porsche first thought of his small car for everyman, his "people's car."

In Porsche's mind, the 1920's and the social changes in Europe meant an opportunity for Austro-Daimler. They could now produce a small car for everyman, much as Henry Ford was doing with such spectacular success in the United States. Yet, despite Ford's example, Porsche's idea was a radical one not only for Austro-Daimler, but for the entire auto industry. Even in the United States and despite the impact of Ford sales, cars remained mostly for the well-to-do, and many were luxury models imported from Europe.

Porsche, in Austria, shared Ford's vision, but was scorned for it. Almost to a man, the leaders of European auto companies discounted the general public and certainly the worker as a potential customer. The worker in Germany and Austria bicycled to his job if he did not take a bus or a trolley. When he had saved some money, he bought a motorcycle perhaps, but never a car. The board of directors of Austro-Daimler reasoned that many Austrians would continue to want big, showy automobiles, a point which Porche did not dispute. Porsche merely saw that market as too limited and regarded as narrow those who could not share his vision. This time, however, he agreed to devote himself to designing large and expensive motorcars.

And so, in 1921, the company offered a select public a large six-cylinder, 60-hp touring car displacing 4.5 liters and called it the AD, for Austro-Daimler Motors. It was followed by a somewhat bewildering succession of varying models, eventually with a lower displacement, desirable in Europe because automobile taxes were rated in accordance with engine size, and also because of the high cost of gasoline.

Then, suddenly, the direction changed. An investor, movie company president Count Sascha Kolowrat, wanted a small, one-liter displacement, lightweight but high-powered racing car. Porsche built it and, of course, called it the Sascha. It was quickly entered in several European races, including the demanding Targa Florio event in Sicily, where it won both first and second place on April 2, 1922.

Porsche had proved his point: a high-performance car could be small and lightweight. After rebuilding the original Sascha, Porsche boosted displacement to two liters, transforming the tiny car into a powerhouse capable of 106 mph. The board of directors threw up their hands. They had reluctantly gone along with racing small cars but now refused further funds. Transforming Saschas into small, efficient cars for the public did not interest them. They wanted to sell aristocratic cars to rich people—"even though they may be Social Democrats."

The largest shareholder in Austro-Daimler was a bank headed by Camillo Castiglioni. Austro-Daimler's foreign income was exchanged for Austrian schillings, the foreign currencies being retained by the bank. The schilling, however, was deteriorating so rapidly in value that the entire foreign profit could be wiped out in an afternoon. At a board meeting, Porsche demanded that the hard currencies, rather than their equivalents in schillings, be credited to his company. Castiglioni refused. As Ferdinand Porsche's son Ferry today puts it, "They were, after all, primarily interested in making money for the bank." Then Castiglioni insisted Austro-Daimler economize by dismissing two thousand workers. Porsche exploded, shouted an obscenity at the board, and stormed out. In his outrage, Ferry says, he picked up a gold table lighter and hurled it onto the table in front of the directors.

Although Castiglioni has often been depicted as a villain, the fact is that Porsche and he were and remained friends, addressing each other with the familiar *"du."* When the explosive board meeting ended Porsche's career at Austro-Daimler, German Daimler called for him. Porsche's son and daughter remember that Castiglioni later visited them at German Daimler and that after World War II, Castiglioni did what he could to get Porsche out of the French prison in which he languished in 1947. The truth was that the legitimate interests of the bank and of the company it controlled came into conflict. The bank won.

From the top spot at Austro-Daimler, Porsche moved to the position of technical director and member of the board of the Daimler Motor Company in Stuttgart, Germany. (The German and Austrian Daimler companies were independent though related.) There was here a tradition of aloofness which Porsche soon shattered, to the consternation of the rather stodgy management. The front office was remote from the shop and executives kept themselves distant from those who worked in the factory. *Der Spiegel* refers to German Daimler as "arch-conservative" and as being organized like "a monastic order." Here Porsche's swearing and blunt talk often seemed out of place. The reception accorded Porsche in the shop itself was of course different. It was enthusiastic, if a little apprehensive, for Porsche had a habit of lavishing praise on bright designers while denouncing as "manure" the work of those of limited ability.

He inspired considerable loyalty among those whose talents approached his own, just as he provoked the enmity of lesser men. From Austria, Porsche brought Otto Koehler, who served Porsche as his personal technical aide in Stuttgart, Alfred Neubauer, a topflight mechanic and racing driver, and others. He felt at home with them and they, in turn, lavished devotion on their chief. Markmann and Sherwin call Porsche a man who "worked hard and faithfully at his drawing board, in the machine shop, or even in the pits to make certain that his machines performed as promised. He was a prim little man with an amiable moustache and a sharp twinkle that could become a bolt of electricity when he chose. His attire was almost a trademark. He would wear a loose-fitting tweed suit with giant patch pockets and a cloth cap pulled down to his ears. At races, a pair of binoculars would dangle from his neck and a pair of goggles would be perched on top of his cap. His demeanor was one of intense dignity and concentration . . ."

A story is told of an important car being inspected ceremoniously by a group of white-smocked front-office designers who endlessly discussed what might be wrong without once checking for themselves. Porsche climbed into coveralls, crawled under the car, found the trouble, answered his colleagues' queries with a snarling "Look for yourselves," and stalked off. This was the nature of the man. He was not easy to work with. Volatile, irrepressible, deficient in the technical theory taught at school, he designed with pure fingertip feel and sure instinct, often going directly against accepted principles of design because he knew his ideas were right. His understanding of engines was uncanny; their very sound often told him what was the matter with them or what new feature needed to be incorporated into them.

The star of the German Daimler salon was the Mercedes (known as the Mercedes-Benz only after 1926), but the 1923 Indianapolis 500-mile event, the first race the company entered after Porsche joined it, proved existing Mercedes cars were too heavy.

Porsche improved the Mercedes supercharger and engine and later designed a 100- and 140-hp, six-cylinder model better suited to competitive events. He entered this in the 1924 Targa Florio race in Sicily, averaging 41 miles an hour. Considering the terrain, the speed was remarkable, and it won for Porsche a warm endorsement from the previously reserved management as well as a new doctorate, from Stuttgart's technical university. (This was most welcome, for Porsche had found out that Germans considered Viennese honorary doctorates meaningless.)

At German Daimler, Porsche produced a number of great Mercedes cars. Six-cylinder, six-liter engines generating 140 horsepower brought the company 21 racing victories in 27 starts from 1925 to 1927. Several of these are classics of an era renowned for power, elegance, and fine coachwork; their gleaming outside exhaust pipes, together with their superchargers, became almost synonymous with the Mercedes name, for German Daimler was first in offering superchargers on its regular passenger line.*

Again, Porsche pressed for his ideal of the small car for everyman. And again he was turned down by management. The design, he was told, would be too costly and the car would

---

* Specifications of five notable Mercedes models by Porsche:

K (1927)	Horsepower: 110 (at 3000 rpm), supercharged to 160; Engine displacement: 6.2 liters (378 cu. in.); Bore: 3.70 in.; Stroke: 5.91 in.
S (1927)	Weight: 3600 lbs.; Wheelbase: 134 in.; Cylinders: 6; Horsepower: 120 (supercharged, 180); Engine displacement: 6.8 liters (414.8 cu. in.); Compression ratio: 5 to 1. Also, dual ignition and carburetors; optional 2.5, 2.76, and 3.09 axle ratios.
SS (1928)	Weight: 3630 lbs.; Wheelbase: 134 in.; Engine displace-

not be profitable. Porsche was asked to take note of the times. Germany was floundering in a depression which had wiped out all purchasing power and made the Reichsmark nearly worthless. The very man whom Porsche proposed to motorize was, in point of fact, mainly worried about whether there would be enough to eat. Germany in 1926 had one car for every 211 persons (compared with one for every 5.7 persons in the United States that year). Yet the wealthy did more than survive; many prospered, and yet they remained the heart of the automobile market.

Porsche now planned to build a modified version of the company's medium-sized Stuttgart and Mannheim models. These had solid axles, four-wheel brakes, three-speed transmissions, semi-elliptical springs, and box-type bodies. To adapt them to the demands of a truly small vehicle, Porsche developed a 1.3-liter four-cylinder engine producing 38 horsepower. Three prototypes were built, but the plans were abandoned. The question of building a small car created frictions. So did the company's 1926 merger with Benz & Cie., which created Daimler-Benz A.G. The Benz "outsiders" had better bank connections and the board was weighted in their favor. The merger doubled the managerial personnel and cost the new company a great deal. The board decided to get rid of a large number of former Daimler people, Porsche included.

The overt cause was the 38-hp Stuttgart car, which, the board claimed, failed to start in cold weather. Fifteen Stuttgarts were parked overnight in the company lot during cold weather. On the next morning Porsche was challenged to start even one of them. Fuming, Porsche went from car to car in the early morning hours and, unfortunately, not one started. A bitter argument with Generaldirektor Wilhelm Kissel ensued, and the designer flew into a rage, tore off his hat, trampled it in the snow, and marched out of the plant, never to return.

The cars apparently started during another test three weeks

	ment: 7,022 cc (428 cu. in.); Cylinders: 6; Horsepower: 170 at 3200 rpm (supercharged, 225); Compression ratio: 5 to 1; Bore: 3.94 in.; Stroke: 5.91 in.; magnesium block.
SSK (1928)	Modified SS on 116-in. wheelbase, generating 170 hp supercharged, 225).
SSKL (1931)	Modified SSK. Weight: 3960 lbs.; Horsepower (supercharged): 300. Actually produced after Porsche's departure, but retained most of his design features. "K" stands for Kurz, (short wheelbase); "L" for Leicht (light); "S" for Sport; "SS" for Super-Sport.

later at −20° centigrade, the anger abated, and the management suggested that Porsche tour the United States, studying auto design and production, and return to serve the company as a consultant. Porsche, however, declined. He felt, his son remembers, that they were trying to shunt him aside politely. An offer came from Vienna's Steyr Works, which had switched from production of arms to cars at the war's end, and Porsche accepted. On January 1, 1929, he became technical director, chief engineer, and a member of the board.

He returned to Austria at the age of fifty-three somewhat of a hero, which may have surprised him, considering the stormy way he had left the country five years earlier. Austria, however, was eager to industrialize and regarded Porsche as the man to help. Steyr did seem the right place; its prosperous past endowed it with vast holdings, including a rolling mill, a foundry, and a forge. Steyr could build a car without recourse to outside suppliers. Here, Porsche produced two which were noteworthy. The first was a modification of the "Stuttgart"; the second was the "Austria," a big five-passenger limousine. Technically a great achievement and ranking with some of the great classics of the time, it was the center of attention at the 1929 Paris Auto Show, and Porsche knew he had a winner.

A few days later, however, he picked up a newspaper in Paris to find he had no job. Steyr's finances had collapsed, and, ironically, the company fell into the hands of the very financiers who controlled Austro-Daimler. When Porsche got home he found he was unwelcome and that his "Austria" was doomed. The new bankers refused to let Steyr produce a big luxury car, since Austro-Daimler already did so. The decision outraged Porsche and eighteen months after joining Steyr, he quit. This time he stopped trying to fit himself into the auto industry. Fed up, he left the country.

Where should he go? He was fifty-five, had no taste for corporate positions and yet no wish to retire. The solution seemed to lie in a career as an independent consultant, in which his responsibility for a car would end after he designed it.

On January 1, 1931, Porsche opened up shop in Stuttgart. He chose this city because it was a center of the German auto industry, with many parts plants and machine shops. His shingle—which seemed to invite all comers—read: "Doctor, Engineer (*honoris causa*) Ferdinand Porsche G.m.b.H., Construction Bureau for the Manufacture of Motors, Motor Vehicles, Aircraft, and Ships."*

As it turned out, Porsche's venture into business for himself proved crucial to the future of the Volkswagen. From this time on, his designs for the car moved forward, if somewhat spasmodically. Events were moving rapidly to push the designer into a "socialistic partnership" with Adolf Hitler, who could provide or extort the funds needed. In the meantime, Porsche produced two "Volkswagens" for two auto manufacturers, neither of whom would benefit from them.

First to hire the Porsche Bureau at 24 Kronenstrasse in 1931 was the Wanderer Auto Company, for whom Porsche delivered the designs and prototypes of a medium-priced, six-cylinder automobile and a larger, eight-cylinder car. Again on contract to Wanderer in 1932, Porsche developed an auto suspension design which eventually proved to be a radical feature of the Volkswagen. Porsche felt that leaf and coil springs were unsatisfactory. Both types were too heavy, cumbersome, and unadaptable to a small, lightweight, yet powerful automobile. Porsche's solution was the torsion-bar suspension system. After its initial weaknesses had been worked out, it proved a major invention. Until 1950, when his patent ran out, Porsche licensed its use in many other cars, including the Volkswagen. After 1950, it became public property. As a recent Volkswagen advertisement put it, however, the number of sedans having *both* this system *and* four-wheel independent suspension "can be counted on one finger." Both VW features were part of the *original* design by Porsche.†

Two proposals were presented to the designer in 1932. One was an offer to build a small car; the second came from the U.S.S.R., inviting Porsche to become chief Soviet industrial designer. A Soviet delegation had come to Porsche's Stuttgart

* Dr. Ing. h.c. F. Porsche G.m.b.H., Konstruktionsbüro für Motoren-, Fahrzeug-, Luftfahrzeug-, und Wasserfahrzeugbau.

† The principle behind Volkswagen's torsion-bar suspension system was that a bar was held on one end and twisted from the other, where the wheel moved up and down. Such a bar, made of laminated strips of steel, will twist as it absorbs a shock. The harder the bump, the more the twist and the greater the resistance to further twisting, a principle which may be tested by twisting an ordinary piece of rubber garden hose. These laminated strips, bound together and clamped at the center to prevent them from rotating when twisted, are attached to "trailing arms" fastened onto the VW's front wheels. The rear suspension is similar, but two torsion bars, one for each wheel, are used. The outer ends of each bar are splined so that they can be adjusted to maintain correct rear suspension geometry. Each bar is a single piece of steel, pre-stressed for use on either the left or right side.

office, listened attentively, said little, and taken careful note of everything being done. It was not long afterward that Porsche received an invitation to the U.S.S.R.

He left on July 20, 1932, and after three weeks in a Moscow bed, nursing a foot he had hurt alighting from his train, he toured much of the country. His hosts were eager to impress him with their technological growth and hospitality. Once, when Porsche complained of the vodka which was endlessly served to him and expressed a wish for some beer, a case of Pilsner awaited him at the next stop. Negotiations began. Porsche was offered a luxurious Crimean villa for his family and entire staff, as well as a blank check. He would never again have to concern himself with personal or developmental expenses. The Russians were even interested in small-car designs and had shown Porsche some preliminary plans of their own. When Porsche returned home, he confessed he was tempted—and impressed. "Well, one isn't supposed to say it, but what I saw was wonderful!" he said to Ghislaine Kaes, his nephew and by then his secretary. Still, he declined the offer. It required him to break all ties with his homeland. Porsche felt too old to make the change.

He returned instead to his offices in the Ulrich Building on Stuttgart's Kronenstrasse. His hand-picked staff consisted of many who had followed him from company to company: Karl Rabe, his chief designer; Karl Fröhlich (gearboxes); Josef Kales (engines); Josef Zahradnik (axles, springing and steering) and Erwin Komenda (bodies). Among them was Ferry Porsche, the designer's twenty-one-year-old son, who was beginning his own brilliant career as an automobile designer under his father's tutelage and who today heads the Porsche company in Stuttgart. The business manager was Adolf Rosenberger, a businessman whose hobby was racing, and who owned 15 per cent of the firm. (Porsche owned 70 per cent and Dr. Anton Piëch, his son-in-law, 15 per cent.) Rosenberger, however, was Jewish and had to flee the country after 1933. He moved to Paris, where he was secretly appointed the Bureau's sales manager abroad and represented the firm until World War II, selling Porsche designs to foreign companies. At the outbreak of war, he made his way to the United States.

Fritz Neumeyer of Nuremberg's Zündapp Works, one of Germany's biggest motorcycle manufacturers, was now convinced the time was right for a small car, a *Kleinauto*. Before he visited the Porsche Bureau in November 1931, the designer had already become involved in perfecting similar designs on his own.

Such a vehicle was badly needed. All existing models were, for one reason or another, unsatisfactory. Porsche wanted to build a car which would rank as a major technical achievement. "By a 'people's car,'" as he explained on another occasion, "I do not understand a small car which . . . carries on the tradition of previous products in this field and continues to copy them exactly." He referred to the fact that most small cars were merely scaled-down big cars. Porsche considered them uneconomic and unsafe. "By a 'people's car' I understand only a completely practical vehicle which can compete with every other practical vehicle on equal terms. In my opinion, a fundamentally new approach is needed to turn 'normal vehicles' existing hitherto into 'people's cars.'"

The small car he wanted to build would have to be designed from the chassis up. It would have to be an unconventional car, built in accordance with its own demands, if it were to be the ideal small car Porsche wanted. He called it Project No. 12 and was now willing to gamble his own money on it.

He could afford little. While the Wanderer contracts had set him up in business, there was not much of it. His staff was extraordinarily devoted to the choleric little designer and many had accepted lower salaries than they could have earned elsewhere, just to work with the Master; still, there was one occasion when Porsche was driven to the extremity of borrowing on his life insurance to meet the payroll. Project 12, however, had been the hub around which his thoughts had turned so long that he launched it anyway. The fact that Neumeyer would be interested was unknown to him as he assembled his staff in September of 1931, to tell them of his plans.

He never had a drawing board of his own and so, on this as on other occasions, he simply gathered his men around any convenient board and then began to talk and sketch. Usually, he did so with lightning speed and the meetings were short; this time, he spoke and sketched from early afternoon into the evening. The room was littered with his drawings by the time he had finished.

These sketches were certainly radical and illustrated an odd-looking car. The hood dropped forward in a graceless curve to the front fender; the windshield stood upright and robbed the car of any slipstream look; the sharply sloping roof line seemed to allow little or no headroom for rear-seat passengers, and the rear window would apparently afford a view

33

only of the sky. No question about it: the designer who had built some of the most elegant automobiles known to date was planning a weird one. It hardly looked like a car. It resembled a bug—a beetle.

As the afternoon wore on, Porsche covered one detail of the construction after another. His assistants saw that he had thought out everything, in broad strokes, to be sure, but masterful ones. It was now to be their task to provide the detailed drawings, offering Porsche several solutions to each problem, until the "ideal small car" would have every nut, bolt, and cotter pin assigned. There was to be an air-cooled 26-hp engine mounted just aft of the rear axle, for this position would allow the cheaper, lower-horsepower motor to deliver torque more directly to the rear wheels. Engine weight placed over the rear wheels would also improve traction and offset the effect of the car's light weight. He planned at first a design wherein three cylinders were arranged in a radial pattern around the crankshaft, and the gearbox and differential were to be worked into a single unit just ahead of the engine. He wanted air cooling because it would also cut weight and cost by eliminating the water jacket which surrounds the cylinders of liquid-cooled engines. An air-cooled car also would need no antifreeze in winter and could cross deserts or labor endlessly up mountain roads without overheating.

Porsche insisted his car was to have a four-wheel independent suspension system utilizing the torsion bars he had just invented (but which had not yet been perfected). Any car, no matter what its size, benefits by having each of its four wheels suspended independently, but in a small car this is even more desirable. Short-wheelbase cars bang and bounce on bumps; the impacts are even worse if both rear wheels are sprung together, as they are on most cars, for then the shock travels the full width of the rear axle.

The Project 12 automobile was to be lightweight, so as to make its low-horsepower engine sufficient. Porsche, remembering his Austro-Daimler aircraft experience, cut weight sharply by eliminating the heavy steel or timbered frames of the day and using instead a principle of aircraft design. He mounted all his car's components on a large sheet-steel floor pan made stiff by shaping ripples and ridges into the metal and by forming a tunnel along the front-to-rear centerline.* When the upper portion of the body was bolted to the floor

* The principle is the same one that stiffens a sheet of paper if one folds it several times.

pan, the effect was the same as the "unit body" (or mono-coque) construction used in building aircraft; it provides the strength and stiffness of a steel pipe without involving a heavy frame.

Porsche gave his designers ninety days to finish the job. In the meantime, he sent out feelers to the auto industry, hoping to find a sponsor. No one seemed interested. Just as Porsche called a halt to the project, which had consumed all the money he could allocate, Neumeyer heard of his designs. He thought he would have a look at them, for he badly needed a new product; he had already decided a small car would enable his motorcycle customers to "trade up." Neumeyer had even gone so far as to give the car its name, before he even had a design. He decided to call it the Zündapp Volksauto, or people's car.*

When he saw the designs at the Porsche Bureau, he had only one reservation. He used air-cooled engines in his motor-cycles and felt they were too noisy for an automobile. He wanted his Volksauto to have a water-cooled five-cylinder radial engine, so as to eliminate the siren scream which an air blower, mounted in an auto chassis, makes in forcing cooling air over the cylinders. The water jacket, he further pointed out, would also help dampen much engine noise. Although Porsche never received such drastic suggestions gracefully, he acquiesced without a murmur in this case. He needed a patron badly and Dr. Neumeyer was the only one he could find. Neumeyer's factory was to make the engine and gear-boxes for three prototypes; the bodies were to be built at the Reutter coachworks in Stuttgart, under Porsche's supervision. The final Volksauto was to have an all-steel body, but the prototypes were made of aluminum stretched over a wooden frame. At the end of April 1932, the completed bodies were shipped to Nuremberg to be mated with the rest of the car, and Zündapp drivers began their tests.

Disasters happened daily. The cars had hardly sputtered the first six miles down the road when the engine oil began to boil. The great heat actually welded the pistons to the cylinder walls of two of the test cars and they screeched to a halt. Back at the factory, the cooling system was redesigned.

* The word Volksauto had already been used a great deal in the Germany of the 1920's and, indeed, a car called the Bergmann Volksauto had even appeared on the market in 1904. The impetus given the Volks-auto idea in the 1920's can above all be credited to *Motorkritik* and its editor, Ganz. Neumeyer thus was planning to give his car a name much in vogue at the time.

While mechanics struggled to make these modifications, Porsche saw that the radial engine, its five cylinders splaying out around the clock, would always prove a nightmare to mechanics.

Once the cars were back on the road, the teeth on the gears began snapping off; once more everything halted for repairs. Finally, the Volksautos were ready for high-speed long-distance tests—or at least Porsche thought they were. As the drivers raced them along the highways there was a sharp crack, like a rifle shot. Slivers of steel flew out from one of the cars; it sagged helplessly over one of its front wheels. Porsche's torsion bar had shattered under the strain. From then on the rifle reports sounded one after another as torsion bars gave out on all the cars. This problem was so basic that it could be set right only by tedious experimentation in metallurgical laboratories. These would have to produce just the right temper in the steel to make the bars more supple. Neumeyer's enthusiasm, not to speak of his funds, began to dwindle. He was also beginning to realize how costly the heavy stamping presses needed to shape the steel body parts would be. He decided to cut short his gamble on the Volksauto. Porsche was paid 85,000 marks and was allowed to keep one of the prototypes. (A company car in constant use, it was destroyed twelve years later in a 1944 air raid.) Disappointed, Porsche at this juncture received his welcomed invitation from the Soviets. By the time he returned, he had broken free of his depression.

Before the year ended, another "Volksauto" customer had presented himself at number 24 Kronenstrasse. He was Fritz von Falkenhayn, head of Germany's NSU Works in Neckarsulm, also interested in a small car. Porsche had the designs ready in his Bureau drawer. What emerged in 1933 was a car even more similar to the Volkswagen of today, although it was bulkier and contained a bulkier 1.5-liter engine (at NSU's request).

Again, the strange cars were built at Stuttgart. This time, engines were constructed at NSU's Neckarsulm factory, under Ferry Porsche's supervision. Three prototypes of this direct forerunner of the Volkswagen were rolled out of the plant, gassed up, tested, and performed successfully.*

* The three prototypes vanished until December 1950 when one of them unexpectedly reappeared in Stuttgart, driven by a crippled German war veteran who was a former NSU engineer. This ancient forerunner of the VW was parked in front of the Porsche Bureau headquarters and ogled "with curiosity and awe like a prehistoric fossil." Driven almost

36

Porsche had applied his Zündapp experience to modify the car for NSU. The body was now a bit more shapely, the headlights were recessed into the fenders, and most important, Porsche had talked Von Falkenhayn into trying an air-cooled engine. This time, however, it had four cylinders lying on their sides, opposing each other two by two; very much as in Porsche's 1912 airplane engine, which had proved most durable. There was a large blower to direct the cooling air over the cylinders.

"Sounds like a worn-out stonecrusher," the good-natured Von Falkenhayn told Porsche after his first ride in the noisy car. But he liked its performance: it whipped along at a top speed of 72 mph without ever threatening to overheat. The same old trouble with the exploding torsion bars remained, however. Deciding nevertheless that the car had real possibilities, the NSU chief arranged for its manufacture while Porsche pushed ahead with new enthusiasm to exterminate the bugs in the beetle.

Events, however, were moving fast now—and in many directions. While Von Falkenhayn and Ferdinand Porsche were poring over paper plans for their car, other forces were forming. As unlikely as it seemed, all were to play their part in Porsche's life and, even more so, in the life of the car that would outlive him. They involved many men: a new Chancellor who was a car buff, a Munich auto salesman who had become a courtier, and a lot of smart industrialists who proved in the end not to have been so smart after all.

daily before the outbreak of World War II, it survived the war and the immediate postwar years in the deserted Friedrichsruh Castle of the Hohenlohes near Öhringen. There the NSU veteran found it in 1948 and bought it for next to nothing. He installed new headlights and a new battery and tested the engine. It worked as though it were brand new.

2

Hitler and the Changed Atmosphere

IT WAS on January 30, 1933, that Adolf Hitler returned triumphant to his Nazi Party cronies in Berlin's Kaiserhof Hotel. As they recalled it, he greeted them with eyes full of tears. He had just been named Chancellor of Germany by President Paul von Hindenburg. It was shortly after noon and Adolf Hitler's sun, too, stood at the zenith.

Before three weeks had passed, he summoned Germany's top industrialists, including the heads of Krupp, I. G. Farben, and United Steel Works, to the offices of Hermann Goering, who was now President of the Reichstag. An election was scheduled for March 5, and Hitler wanted to fleece the "fat cats" for contributions to the Nazi fund. He assured them that the sacrifices "surely would be much easier for industry to bear if it realized that the election of March fifth will surely be the last one for the next ten years, probably even for the next hundred years."

As was his custom, he proceeded to cozen his listeners by appealing to their prejudices. In the presidential offices of the very Reichstag building which would be burned out within seven days, Hitler held out the promise of a chastened labor force, accompanied by a policy of governmental support for a reactionary form of capitalism.

"Private enterprise," he told them, "cannot be maintained in the age of democracy. It is conceivable only if people have a sound idea of authority." Then, in a philosophical aside, he ventured: "All the worldly goods we possess we owe to the struggle of the chosen . . . all benefits of culture must be introduced more or less with an iron fist."

His vision of a rapacious, state-protected *laissez-faire* economy was designed to please the industrialists. Krupp reportedly jumped up at the end of the meeting to express the "gratitude" of those present for his clear statement of Nazi policy towards industry. The short speech earned Hitler three million marks.

It is not surprising that industrialists hoped for a "clear picture" of intent from the new Chancellor. The economy was chaotic: more than six million workers were out of jobs and fifteen million Germans were on relief. Tight wage- and price-control measures had succeeded mainly in stifling initiative. No group of industrialists had less of this particular commodity at the time than the automobile manufacturers, whose sales had plummeted and some of whom were considering closing down their plants.

True, they had heard some good news from Chancellor Hitler at the Auto Show in Berlin. An annual event staged in the second week of February, this exhibition in 1933 was to have been a modest one, as befitted the shrinking wallets of the industrialists who were to pay for it. Yet all plans for simplicity had been forcibly cast aside a few days after Hitler came to power, for a Nazi Party official let the show's managers know that the exhibition was to be the new Chancellor's first public forum. He would address the show and the Party was to see to it that the surroundings matched the dignity of the office. The man who received the telephone call from Party headquarters was Director Allmers of the German Automobile Industry Association (the RDA, for Reichsverband der deutschen Automobilindustrie), and he was not happy about it. He was even less happy next day, when uniformed Party officers took over the exhibition hall to make sure the decorations were lavish. The conservative industry leaders who were to pay the expenses dug deep, and grumbled.

They grumbled less when they heard Hitler's speech at the Grand Opening. Dressed in black jacket and striped pants and flanked by the two other Nazis in his eleven-man cabinet (Interior Minister Wilhelm Frick and Hermann Goering, then minister without portfolio) and accompanied also by propaganda chief Goebbels. Hitler made what seemed to the industrialists an utterly amazing speech. They may not have realized it then, but it was the speech of a confirmed car buff.

A nation, the Führer said, is no longer judged by other nations by its miles of railroad track, but by its miles of paved highways. He promised to build a vast network. Nothing, he went on to say, gives a nation greater prestige in the age of the automobile than leadership in auto racing; he called upon the German auto companies to win the victories. Speaking with moderation for once, he analyzed the economy of Germany, and he did so much as the manufacturers would have done. They found his statements and his critique startling, for no other government leader they knew of had ever shown so great an understanding of the auto industry or of motorization as a whole. They were more than startled when they heard his promises; they were elated. Hitler promised to reduce the confiscatory automobile taxes, ease the stringent traffic laws, and make it easier to obtain drivers' licenses. Clearly, the new regime planned to encourage automobile ownership and to help them sell cars.

For a brief while after the show was over, Hitler's speech continued to intoxicate the auto manufacturers, but they later grew cynical and marked the promises down as pie-in-the-sky political propaganda for the March 5 elections. As for a request Hitler had made during his speech—that they develop a cheap, small car for the masses—most of them never expected to hear of that again. It sounded like another demagogic "promise" at election time.

The manufacturers were wrong on all counts. Hitler meant what he said. He built the highways, cut the taxes, eased ownership and traffic laws, encouraged automobile vacationing —and pressed for his small car. As a matter of fact, he had had that idea even before he became Chancellor. A year earlier, in 1932, he spoke about a small car with Jakob Werlin, a Munich Mercedes-Benz salesman, and had asked him to suggest to Daimler-Benz that they build one. The directors of the company turned down the idea flatly. Hitler was not Chancellor yet and a suggestion by Werlin in 1932 didn't carry the weight it would later.

Werlin had sold Adolf Hitler his first Mercedes, a 60-horsepower limousine, which the Nazi leader bought in 1923 out of Party funds, despite the impoverished state of Nazi finances at the time. He never learned to drive, but loved the sensation of being raced at top speed through Germany, and he became the first German politician to use a car extensively for political campaigns. So intrigued was he with automobiles, and especially with the powerful, large Mercedes limousines which Jakob Werlin sold, that Werlin from that time on became Hitler's crony and personal adviser on all matters automotive. Daimler-Benz, spotting an inside track once Hitler had become Chancellor, made Werlin a member of its board of directors then, hoping for advantages.

There are those who argue that Hitler most probably was captivated by the idea of a cheap car for the masses while he was imprisoned in Landsberg Fortress in November 1923. Sentenced to five years, Hitler served only nine months and used the time to write *Mein Kampf*—and to read a biography of Henry Ford. The fact that Ford was a notorious anti-Semite, as well as a production genius, prompted Hitler to call him the "greatest American" of all time; the story of Ford's automotive achievements, in any case, also impressed him, and it may have been while reading this biography that the Nazi leader became so vitally interested in the subject.

Whatever the reason, Hitler's passion for cars was real and his sense that the issue could be exploited propagandistically was realistic. Once in power after January 1933, he set about to act. The idea of a car for the masses, coming from a Chancellor, was novel—and audacious. It had appeal.

The long night of the inflation and Great Depression had cheated the German worker out of even dreaming of owning a family car, yet it was well-known that, in America as early as 1929, one out of every six Americans owned his own car, and the United States, with 23,122,000 cars, had reached the stage where an entire population could simultaneously be moved about by automobile. In Germany, however, few hoped for something comparable. It all seemed a mad fantasy.

Years later, Heinz Nordhoff discussed European small-car development and set the scene.

"During the early twenties," he said, "a wave of American cars swept over the countries of Europe which were still dazed by the aftermath of the First World War . . . They were big, powerful, quiet, and they made all European cars of similar size obsolete overnight. These magnificent machines came as a shock to our engineers and manufacturers . . ."

This invasion, Nordhoff noted, ended soon, for few Europeans could afford to buy or operate such American cars. Inadequate roads, expensive fuel, and meager repair facilities plagued Europe. Nevertheless, these cars proved, Nordhoff says, "the hopelessness of hybridizing a comparable strain in Europe. . . . The European engineer was forced to take a different approach." This, Nordhoff says, was "a new trend of thought, the revelation of a secret love, long cultivated, often in secret, among European designers, for a small car."

Nordhoff watched these developments in the 1920's and 1930's from his vantage point at Adam Opel, which also was working on small cars. But those which existed, he notes, were *ersatz* cars for those who could not afford the real thing. Most

41

were meant only for two passengers and, says Nordhoff, "while their size was reduced, their faults were doubled."

Young engineers throughout Austria, Czechoslovakia, and Germany, joined later by French and Italian designers, revolted. As they questioned all the old ideas and conceptions, debates became heated. In meetings and in the engineering press, they argued about front and rear engines, front and rear drives, water- and air-cooling systems, and the questions of weight and air resistance. The auto manufacturers resisted this debate. Their great investments, shaky finances, and innate conservatism compelled them to discourage innovations. And so, new designs came from the drawing boards of independent and consulting engineers, like Ferdinand Porsche.

"The severe depression after the crash of 1929," says Nordhoff, "aggravated the reluctance among the struggling automobile companies. At the same time, it increased the unrest among the young and enthusiastic designers. It was during this period of turmoil, uncertainty, and fear, that Hitler came to power. Demagogue that he was, he was quick to realize the propaganda value of favoring the public demand for the automobile."

The congenial atmosphere created by Nazism for his car and for auto production in general was not lost on Porsche. It was at this very time that he was working on the final paper designs for NSU. Then, in May 1933, Baron Klaus D. von Oertzen, a board member of the new Auto-Union Company, asked Porsche to accompany him to see the new Chancellor. Von Oertzen needed Porsche to help convince the Führer that Auto-Union ought to obtain a financial subsidy equal to the one Hitler gave Daimler-Benz to finance a German Grand Prix racing car.

When Adolf Hitler entered the room, he strode up to the designer with an enthusiastic "We've met before, Dr. Porsche!" Although Porsche had no idea when this might have occurred, the encounter had indeed taken place in 1924. At the time, Porsche was already famous, and Hitler was a regional politician of questionable importance. The men had met at the Solitude Race near Stuttgart, where Hitler had been introduced to Porsche by Daimler's press chief, Dr. Völter. Porsche's son Ferry recalls the event, but says his father never did remember it, and cites this fact as an example of how little interest Ferdinand Porsche had in politics or politicians.

After the auspicious beginning, however, the mood at the meeting changed. Hitler, who loved the big Mercedes cars, had become an admirer of Daimler-Benz and saw no reason why Germany needed two factory racing teams in order to win all the prizes. Daimler-Benz would do nicely. He was frank in telling Baron von Oertzen and Porsche that Auto-Union (formed in 1932 through a merger of Wanderer, Horch, Audi and D.K.W.) was a company "no one had heard of," with no record in racing even remotely comparable to that of Daimler-Benz. "What an outrageous request you make, gentlemen!" he concluded.

Now Porsche took the floor and argued for twenty-five minutes without letting Hitler interrupt him once. At first surprised, the Chancellor gradually became more and more impressed, for Porsche was pouring out a hypnotic mixture of technical language and layman's jargon, just the sort of talk that would captivate a car buff. He argued that no single German manufacturer could compete alone against all the foreign factory teams and that, furthermore, what was important was not the company, but the car. He, Porsche, had the car, and he proceeded to explain it to the Führer.

He told of the racer he was then planning for Auto-Union, with a sixteen-cylinder engine shaped in a V with eight cylinders on each side, the engine mounted just ahead of the driving wheels in the rear. It would have Porsche's new torsion-bar and trailing-arm suspension, now being perfected. The racer would have better traction because of the engine weight over the rear wheels and the suspension would make it superior in holding the road. Hitler may have understood little of the technical side, but Porsche's confidence affected him. He did a complete turnabout and promised Auto-Union the same $250,000 subsidy granted to Daimler-Benz.

Porsche's racing car did everything he said it would. It was first put on the racing circuits in 1934, at a time when Grand Prix cars had been limited to a weight of 1653 pounds as a safety precaution, the argument being that so lightweight a car could not achieve dangerously high speeds. Yet Porsche's Auto-Union racer with its 16-cylinder engine, although weighing less than the VW "beetle" does today, developed between 550 and 600 horsepower and went blazing down the tracks at 250 mph. (In comparison, an Alfa-Romeo of the same period, though 110 pounds heavier, developed only 220 hp and could go no faster than 156 mph.) Porsche had indeed given Auto-Union (and Hitler's Third Reich) a running start in the racing business.

He was far ahead of the rest of the world with his rear-engine racer design. In 1963 a group of European Grand Prix drivers invaded the Indianapolis 500 race, and all were driving rear-engined cars made by different companies. A Scot, Jimmy Clark, amazed American auto racing experts by driving to an easy second. In 1966, despite a first-lap accident which eliminated eleven cars and kept racers under the yellow "no passing" flag for forty-one minutes, Graham Hill of England led a massive rear-engined assault on Indy and took first place with an average speed of 144.317 mph. The only cars that went the full 500 miles were rear-engined. Writing for *Life* just before the 1963 race, Britain's great racing driver Stirling Moss had this to say about rear engines:

The battle [at the Indianapolis Speedway] will be easy to follow. All your regular Indy drivers will be in front-engine cars—all of them except one or two powered by old reliable Offenhauser engines. All our Grand Prix boys will be in cars with engines in the rear. In Europe the front-engine racing car is regarded as hopelessly out of fashion. We have learned that engines in the rear give better traction, eliminate the driveshaft beside the driver and cut down on frontal area, which means less wind resistance. I can tell you, too, that it's usually cooler for the driver with the engine in the rear—even inside the car I used to drive, the temperature got up to 160 degrees. It's a bloody sauna bath.

All that Moss said is true and Porsche recognized it well before most others did. So much was he convinced of the merits of the rear-engine cars he was working on in 1933 that he prepared a lengthy memorandum to the German Government's Transport Ministry, spelling out the specifications of just the small car for the masses which Hitler had called for in February, at the Auto Show. He sent it off on January 17, 1934, just after the 1934 Berlin Auto Show.

While he was still planning it, two different events occurred. The time was late 1933. Porsche got word that NSU had now decided to abandon preparations to build automobiles. For one thing, the investment required would be too high and, for another, it had an agreement with Fiat in Italy never to build a four-wheeled vehicle under the NSU name. As Von Falkenhayn himself explained a few years ago, it was hard at the time to obtain credits for the investment required (he estimated it would be between 15 and 20 million marks); further, bicycle and motorcycle sales were picking up so satisfactorily after 1934 that he could hardly meet the demand and decided to concentrate on doing so. Yet Porsche was nevertheless to construct three prototypes of the NSU cars he was designing, for that was part of their contractual agreement.

The news from NSU came as a severe shock to Porsche and his staff. It seemed to them that their small car would never be built. Just then, and entirely coincidentally, Jakob Werlin showed up at the Porsche Bureau headquarters. He had come down from Berlin that very day and had some time to kill before his first important appointment. Not having seen Ferdinand Porsche for five years, since the designer had left Daimler-Benz, Werlin thought he would find out what he was up to.

Porsche greeted him with reserve, for he thought Werlin might be trying to find out as much as he could about the Auto-Union racer then being designed, which would be competing against racers of the company the Mercedes dealer represented. And so, rather than talk too much about his rear-engined racing car, Porsche told Werlin about his rear-engined small car for the average driver. Chafing at the news of Von Falkenhayn's withdrawal, he spoke passionately. Knowing the interest Hitler had in an inexpensive small car, Jakob Werlin listened more and more attentively. This talk of Porsche's, he well knew, would interest the Chancellor, and Werlin, more and more the courtier, no doubt also realized that the Führer would be grateful to the man who brought him news of it.

By the time Hitler addressed the 1934 Berlin Auto Show in January it was clear that he did know already that Ferdinand Porsche was working on a car more or less of the kind he himself wanted. Some of this he must have gained from his May 1933 meeting with Porsche and Von Oertzen, some he learned from Werlin after the latter's autumn 1933 visit to Stuttgart.

Firmly in power by 1934, Hitler appeared in his Nazi Party uniform, instead of conservative dress, and his far less temperate speech underlined the tougher posture. "So long as the automobile remains only a means of transportation for especially privileged circles," he said, "it is with bitter feelings that we see millions of honest, hardworking, and capable fellowmen whose opportunities in life are already limited, cut off from the use of a vehicle which would be a special source of yet-unknown happiness to them, particularly on Sundays and holidays. One must have the courage to grasp this problem in a decided and comprehensive manner. What

45

will not be possible in one year will, perhaps, prove to be a commonplace fact ten years hence."

This message had an impact on the auto industry. Hitler in 1934 was already Der Führer, and *"Der Führer wünscht"* —"the leader wishes"—already had assumed the nature of a command.

"To placate this dangerous man, the automobile manufacturers decided to give at least lip-service to his fantastic scheme," said Heinz Nordhoff. The extent of even their lip-service was minimal and their foot-dragging, which was monumental, would cause them plenty of verbal abuse—and more —at the hands of Hitler. They would learn in no uncertain terms that it was not the age of democracy which made free enterprise impossible, but the *Führerprinzip*—the "leadership principle"—on which the German state was now organized.

In May 1934 Porsche was summoned from his offices in Stuttgart to Berlin. His document urging the construction of a *Kleinauto* had come to Hitler's personal attention. He wanted to meet the designer again and spell out some of his own requirements. Accompanied by Werlin, Hitler met with Porsche at the Kaiserhof Hotel.

The two men saw eye-to-eye for several reasons. Both came from small towns in the old Austro-Hungarian Empire and, in a very real way, spoke each other's language; both were always to feel more comfortable among backwoods Austrians than among the polished members of Germany's industrial society. Both mistrusted the wealthy industrialists: Porsche because they had always frustrated his plans, Hitler for less clear-cut reasons rooted in his arsenal of hatreds. They were linked on that day in the Kaiserhof Hotel by a common boyhood, by a sense of jousting against the giants of capitalism, and by their love of cars. They got along well. The politically disinterested Porsche saw the new Chancellor simply as someone in a position of power who shared his enthusiasm about automobiles and his vision of the small car. For the first time, the possibility of a Volkswagen dawned for the general run of the people. Porsche was delighted with the events as they were unfolding themselves.

He outlined his ideas for a small car. In its essentials, he proposed a 26-horsepower (at 3500 rpm) car weighing 1430 pounds with four-wheel independent suspension, capable of achieving 100 kilometers (62.2 miles) per hour, and with a one-liter (61 cu. in.) engine displacement.

Hitler liked what he heard, then added a few of his own ideas. Such a car, he insisted, should use up no more than

46

seven liters of gasoline per 100 kilometers (approximately 40 miles per gallon, and one liter less than Porsche proposed); must be a four-seater to accommodate the family; should be air-cooled to protect the car in cold weather (because private garages were few); and should maintain, not just reach, 100 kilometers per hour.

A few more details were ironed out before the two men parted company. Porsche asked to be paid for all expenses and a royalty per car built. Then came the matter of price; Porsche had calculated this carefully and suggested 1550 marks, or $620 at the 1934 exchange rate. This sum, he believed, would just cover the costs.

Shortly, word was passed on to the auto manufacturers' trade association, the RDA, that the Führer had decided to move ahead, as he had warned, with the development of a *Kleinauto*. It was to be placed under the wing of the RDA. The RDA contract with Porsche was "to further the motorization of the German people on the basis of cooperative action and by enlisting the best talents of German auto manufacture."

There was nothing for the RDA to do but cooperate. Adolf Hitler had made up his mind, and the industry had learned that the dictatorship which was "to keep the workers in line" was keeping them in line as well. Wilhelm Vorwig, then head of the RDA's technical department (and today director of its postwar successor organization), says, "We knew we had to do something, because this was not a government to fool around with."

Nordhoff, discussing these events later, said, "It soon became apparent that the jealousy between the automobile companies was far too deep-rooted to make a concerted effort possible . . . Porsche was chosen . . . How and where such a car would be manufactured after a satisfactory design had been achieved, remained completely open, and there might have been a hidden hope that the whole very unwelcome plan would go on the rocks when this decision had to be faced." A suggestion by the RDA that this "people's car" be a three-wheeled vehicle was rejected out of hand by Hitler, for he had already seen Porsche's plans for a four-wheeler. Vorwig says the three-wheeled car was proposed because it was unheard of in Germany that "the common man would be driving a car and we were thinking more of a sort of covered-up motorcycle." Yet, once the contract was drawn up, Vorwig claims, the RDA "honestly intended to build a car." None of the members, he says, "were keen on it," but they were willing to give it a try."

The contract between the RDA and the designer contained two clauses which shocked Porsche: he was not given a full year, as he had requested, but only ten months, and worst of all, his price of 1550 marks had been shaved to 900 ($360). The new price was a serious blow threatening the whole design concept and Porsche at first considered it "idiotic."

The price had been arrived at for several reasons. For one thing, it was good politics. The average German's savings in 1934 fell below 1000 marks; thus the 900-mark price had great appeal. For another, the Opel entry into the small-car field, the P–4 then being developed, was to sell for around 1550 marks—and out of this had to come a 20 or 25 per cent dealer commission. Because even the early Volkswagen plans counted on no dealers who would require commissions, it was felt the car could be realistically priced below 1000 marks. Ferdinand Porsche's son Ferry says that his father let himself be convinced by this argument; he thought at least "it might be possible."

The contract negotiations had begun in May (with Heinz Nordhoff representing the Opel company); the signatures were affixed on June 22, 1934. Liaison man between the Porsche Bureau in Stuttgart and the RDA was to be Wilhelm Vorwig. As for money, Porsche was to submit monthly statements and time-sheets, covering staff hours, overhead, and a salary for himself. These, says Vorwig, "always were very correct." They began by running about 20,000 marks a month, later climbed slowly to 50,000 as more staff was required, then leveled off at about 40,000. Porsche, returning home to Stuttgart in June 1934, was to build three prototype automobiles. But no one volunteered to help him.*

Despite the conditions, Porsche and his team began work in earnest. "They meant business, not lip-service," Heinz Nordhoff remarked later. "This outstanding man was engineer and designer not by profession, but at heart. Short-tempered and energetic . . . he was not regarded as being successful in the normal sense of the word, but he was a fanatic and an unusually gifted engineer. He had his own very clear ideas about a small car, and he gripped with all ten fingers this

* According to Herbert Quint, one German manufacturer said to Porsche, after the RDA contract had been signed, "Right, Herr Porsche? You'll design what they demand and then, when the budget is exhausted, you'll tell them it won't work." He quotes another as claiming Volkswagens weren't necessary: "One should build omnibuses; the worker can ride those into the countryside, if he absolutely must go. But not everybody needs a car!" According to Ferry Porsche, this latter remark was made by the head of BMW (Bayerische Motoren-Werke).

opportunity to materialize his dreams. He had the rare gift of surrounding himself with a team of devoted followers who loved him and were dedicated to his ideas. Among them there was a unity and a determination to accomplish the outstanding and an unbounded willingness to follow their leader and idol."

Idol and idolators started building their small cars. Since they did not have a factory or a machine shop at their disposal they built the cars in the garage of Porsche's home on Stuttgart's Killesberg. They brought to the garage a couple of lathes, a drill press, a milling machine, a grinder, and some other equipment, made room for a dozen workers, and proceeded to hand-tool the cars. Ten months later, when the contract came due, they were still trying.

Another auto show was held in Berlin. Even with the prototypes uncompleted, Hitler sounded optimistic in 1935.

"I am happy," he said, "that due to the abilities of the superb designer Porsche and his staff, we have succeeded in completing preliminary designs for a German people's car, so that the first models will finally be tested by the middle of this year. It *must* be possible to make the German people a gift of a motor vehicle which will not cost them more than they have heretofore been accustomed to paying for a medium-priced motorcycle and whose gas consumption will be low!"

Much of this was stalling for time, and Hitler knew it. He was well aware of how slowly the little garage in Stuttgart was forced to operate and knew the car could not reach the test stage by mid-1935.

Nevertheless, Hitler took great pride in his designer. In 1934 he had learned to his apparent dismay that Ferdinand Porsche was a Czech citizen and had taken immediate steps to "Germanize" him. On December 17, 1934, Ferdinand Porsche received a letter from the man in charge of sports activities under the Nazis, Reichssportführer von Tschammer und Osten, which stated: "The Führer wishes that the greatest German automobile designer become a German citizen. I urge you to use this letter as the basis for your application for naturalization." The matter of citizenship meant little to Porsche. Ghislaine Kaes remembers the morning when he showed the designer the letter. Porsche cast his eyes over it and handed it back with the remark, "Well, I guess we can't do anything about it. Take care of the matter today."

In 1936 Hitler continued to sound optimistic at the Berlin Auto Show. To make certain that his message regarding a small car was not lost on those most important to its fulfillment, the Ministry for Propaganda and People's Enlighten-

49

ment broadcast the Führer's address into every motor-vehicle and auto-accessories plant in Germany. Hitler's February 15 speech held out "no doubt" that the day was dawning on which three to four million Germans would be driving their own cars.*

Hitler said the purchase price and upkeep costs of the car must be "brought into conformity with the owner's income." He sought to dispose of the argument (no doubt raised by the auto manufacturers) that a small car would elbow big ones off the market. The opposite was true, he said, for "it has been conclusively demonstrated that the low-priced car had not only popularized the motoring habit, but had gradually stimulated the demand for more expensive makes."

"I have no doubt," he concluded in his address to the still-ambulatory worker, "that the costs of this car will be brought into a tolerable relationship with the income of the broadest masses of our German people, as we have seen this done so brilliantly in America."

The problem in Germany, however, was not one of lowering a car's costs artificially, by fiat as it were, in order to meet the generally low wages of 1936, but of raising personal income to a level where a car might be a reasonable investment. Even at the low 900-mark price, Hitler's *Kleinauto* would cost the German worker more than three times as much in man-hours as one of the low-priced three Detroit cars cost an American worker of that day.

To many at the time, the entire scheme seemed crazy, just an idea being insisted upon by the Chancellor who already was declared absolute ruler over all phases of German life. Little except the design being produced in Stuttgart made sense.

And while the ideas were Porsche's, the designs also owed much to Karl Rabe, who made them work. This brilliant engineer, a first-rate automotive designer in his own right, with several cars to his personal credit, had served with Porsche ever since 1913, when he met him first at Austro-Daimler. Rabe stayed at Austro-Daimler during Porsche's stormy sessions with German Daimler and with Steyr, but when Porsche

* The U.S.A. in 1936 contained 24 times as many cars as did Germany, despite the fact that its population was only twice as large; 70 per cent of the world's 40,287,000 motor vehicles were in the U.S. (Actual figures: U.S.A.—24,219,000 passenger cars; Germany—1,061,000). In relation to population, there was one car per 4.5 Americans, versus one per 49 Germans. (Other nations in 1936: Italy—103 persons per car; Belgium —41; Denmark—27; Great Britain—21; France—19; Canada—9; and New Zealand—7.)

set himself up in business as a consultant, Karl Rabe could not resist his call. He rejoined Porsche in 1931; today, more than thirty-five years later, and more than a half century after first meeting Porsche, Rabe continues serving the Porsche company as a consultant near Stuttgart. Until a few years ago, he continued on in his capacity as Chefkonstrukteur (chief designer) for Ferry Porsche as he had for Ferry's father before. Says Vorwig, "Rabe is actually the man responsible for the finished design. Porsche had the grand idea and the concepts, but it was Rabe who designed a mechanism that worked. Porsche could not have performed without Karl Rabe." From 1934 to 1938, says Heinz Nordhoff, Porsche and this team fought against great odds. "Without question," he says, "Porsche led a fight against the entire German auto industry . . . a secret, underground fight of course and one which ended to his and the Volkswagen's benefit only because Hitler stood behind the entire plan." Even Nordhoff was involved, as the Opel man on RDA. Vorwig remembers him saying at an RDA meeting which discussed Porsche's initial engine design, "This is an airplane engine. We can't produce that at this price." "He was completely disdainful," says Vorwig. "He never dreamed he'd one day be the man who'd build this car."

Porsche now decided to visit the United States to see at first hand how cars were mass-produced. No comparable facilities existed in Europe and Porsche was, as always, concerned only with using the most advanced methods. On September 19, 1936, he told his secretary, Ghislaine Kaes, to prepare to accompany him, and on October 1 they left for Paris by train. Kaes would be indispensable, not only as Porsche's traveling companion and secretary, but also as an interpreter, for English was his native tongue. He was a British subject, born in London, where his father, Otto Kaes, had represented Ferdinand Porsche as far back as the end of World War I, when Porsche was with Austro-Daimler. Otto Kaes was the brother of Ferdinand Porsche's wife Aloisia and his son Ghislaine was, therefore, the designer's nephew by marriage.

The two men boarded the North German Lloyd liner *Bremen* at Cherbourg on October 3 (after spending a day at the Paris Auto Show) and arrived in New York City on the eighth. There they checked into the Hotel Commodore and gaped at the city like tourists. Kaes's notebooks began to fill with the specifications of Radio City Music Hall, the Empire State Building, and New York highways. Everything interested the designer—and everything was noted down for future reference. On October 12, they drove to Roosevelt Raceway at Westbury, Long Island, where they saw Tazio Nuvolari win the Vanderbilt Cup. Racing drivers and team managers recognized the famed designer instantly and deplored the fact that no Porsche racer was running at Roosevelt that year. Porsche studied the track carefully and, no doubt, began formulating his plans for the 1937 event. In that year, a Porsche-designed car would sweep the field at Westbury.

From New York, they took a train to Detroit on October 13, where they remained until October 22, touring the Ford Motor Company's River Rouge plant, the Lincoln factory, Packard, General Motors, Fisher Body, and other plants. Then they took a train to Chicago and on October 27 visited Bendix Aviation Corporation in South Bend, Indiana, as well as Notre Dame University. From there they traveled to Cincinnati, Ohio, and on October 29 returned to Detroit. Porsche had hoped to buy a new model Ford, but the car he wanted was not ready yet and instead he bought a six-cylinder Packard for $1000. With it, he drove to Niagara Falls, to Albany, and back to New York City. On November 4, after observing the U.S. elections, he and Kaes boarded the *Queen Mary* for Europe and sorted out their impressions.

A few months later, on January 29, 1937, Ghislaine Kaes spoke in Germany about his tour of the United States. He gave largely a technical lecture, detailing facts and figures of every factory they visited. He did, however, include some observations of American life, of facets which had particularly impressed the designer and his aide. In making the transcript of this lecture available, Kaes explained to me, "Sentences in it appear which were not written by me. When I finished drafting it, I had to present it to a German censor who added a few sentences to please himself and those he served. Mainly these disparaged the French. Well, I don't have to tell you about the thousand-year Reich we have somehow survived. . . ."

One of their first New York impressions was of the "courtly" behavior of American motorists. Kaes said they obediently drove for hours, one behind the other, without impatience or attempting to force their way ahead. The courtesy American men showed towards women was also a surprise. In Detroit, Porsche and some top executives were kept waiting (Porsche very impatiently) while a receptionist finished speaking to her friends. The prosperity of American workers impressed them and they noted down exact pay scales, working conditions, vacation schedules, and the means by which workers bought homes, automobiles, and appliances on the installment plan. Time and again, they compared conditions with those then prevailing in European industry. "One's heart leaps with joy to see how spotlessly clean American factories are," Kaes reported. At Bendix Aviation and "in all the factories we visited," he said, they were impressed by the "relaxed and polite manner in which even high executives address the lowliest workers." (At Bendix, however, they noted a sign which read, "No one here has to belong to a union to keep his job!") In general, they found the trip exhilarating, if sometimes puzzling. At the Cincinnati Milling Machine Company, for example, where they ate in the workers' cafeteria and carried their trays about by themselves, Kaes wrote, "I had to laugh heartily at the sight of Herr Dr. Porsche managing his own plates. Well, other lands, other customs!"

From Cherbourg, where the *Queen Mary* docked, they traveled to Great Britain, to see a British automobile factory. On November 10, they toured Austin Motors in Longbridge, near Birmingham, where they were greeted by Lord Austin. After a day there, they left, singularly unimpressed. "Compared with the manufacturing facilities of U.S. factories, Austin is a poor, old, small plant," Kaes noted. On November 14, they returned to Stuttgart, Porsche by train, and Kaes by Packard.

The official RDA road-test of three prototype *Volksautos* (as the German and U.S. press were calling them) had already begun, on October 12, 1936. Two had earlier been tested by the Porsche Bureau, in Alpine conditions, one for 500, the other for 3000 miles. The third was not ready until the last minute and joined the RDA test on October 13, a day late. As a matter of fact, all three were almost eighteen months late, for the June 1934 RDA contract demanded that Porsche deliver his car by April 1935, evidence again that the auto manufacturers hoped to kill the project with impossible conditions. Hitler had, however, insisted they extend the contract to give Porsche more time. Whereupon Wilhelm von Opel said to the designer, "You'll give up in a year or so. You'll have earned enough money by then and that should satisfy you."

Opel obviously was a poor judge of character. Money interested Porsche very little; all he ever was interested in was seeing his ideas actualized. As a matter of fact, it was his personality as much as anything that caused delays. Vorwig, watching everything as RDA's "project manager," grew increasingly concerned as month after month went by. "Porsche kept rushing in while they were building his cars," Vorwig says. "He'd always have another change to make in the design, more or less like a woman building a house. There was just no arguing with him. If objections ran counter to his ideas, he'd just pooh-pooh them." Just as it was at Austro-Daimler, where Porsche turned out a bewildering series of changed designs, so it was in Stuttgart in 1935 and 1936. The cars were at first to be powered by a variation of Porsche's 1912 Austro-Daimler airplane engine; it was this idea that prompted an exasperated protest from Opel's Heinz Nordhoff at the time. Later, Porsche installed a two-cylinder, two-cycle, water-cooled engine in one of the three prototypes being built; this was an improvement over the principle used in the Puch motorcycle engine, but it proved unfit for long distances. Then he tried an air-cooled, four-cycle, two-cylinder engine, but this turned out to have too little power in the low ranges. Ultimately, he settled on an air-cooled flat-four engine similar to the one designed for NSU, and it was this that was installed in all three test cars. The bodies of two of these cars were of wood and thin metal; only one had an all-steel body.

The test conditions were grueling, for both cars and drivers. Each car was to cover a total of 30,000 miles, the drivers logging 200 miles of rough or hilly country roads each morning and another 300 miles along the Stuttgart–Bad Nauheim Autobahn each afternoon. Although there was to be no night driving, the cars were to be kept running six days a week. At night, they were to be kept outside, under canvas, so as to subject them to cold starts in the mornings.

"Because the production had been improvised and specifications were not always adhered to," Vorwig later stated, "errors had to be expected from the start." The Porsche Bureau did not have the necessary equipment, and was therefore unable to test all the materials going into the prototypes for reliability; Porsche's men had, in Vorwig's words, virtually "knitted" the car together, and didn't have enough spare parts. All this of course was the result of the lack of cooperation of the auto companies; no doubt they hoped that their man Vorwig would test the cars to death.

Vorwig, however, turned out to be a pro, interested in checking the cars out, not in burying them. He may have expected errors to crop up, but their number began to amaze even him over the months. "Once we started testing," he says, "I found out just how much could go wrong with a car." On car No. 1, the headlights turned out to be too weak, the gearshift broke, the front wheels began to wobble after 5000 miles, the valves needed to be reground at 10,000 miles, the brakes gave out at 13,000 and again at 16,000, and a rear shock absorber broke at 27,000.

The other two cars had even more problems; one which plagued all three was broken crankshafts. "The sound a crankshaft makes as it breaks," says Vorwig, "is enough to turn you pale." After a while, they were breaking with monotonous regularity and soon the entire reserve stock had been used up. Daimler-Benz produced a new supply in two days' time. But these, like the original shafts, were cast, and the breaks did not stop until forged crankshafts were used. (Although some manufacturers even today employ cast crankshafts, VW has never gone back to using them after that experience.)

A Bureau service vehicle followed the cars around—and towed them in as they became disabled. Back in Stuttgart, a workshop was set up to repair the cars throughout the nights. Bad luck plagued the test drivers even when the cars were performing well. One car ran into a truck, another into a motorcyclist, and once a car hit a large deer at full speed going down the Autobahn. The collision knocked out a headlight and demolished the front-end bodywork. "In this case," Vorwig remembers, "the results weren't entirely negative. The crew of the vehicle tossed the stag into the rear seat, its four legs sticking out a window, and raced back home at full speed, to get it there before it began to stink. We had a feast of venison and the accident further proved that a rear-engine vehicle can drive away from a collision."

Vorwig and his drivers maintained their optimism, and of course Ferdinand Porsche maintained his confidence. As Vorwig noted later, only developmental mishaps were occurring, not basic ones. Nevertheless, these—and the fact that they were short of drivers—were causing delays. To counter this, tests were now being run on Sundays and at night as well, and even Vorwig took to the road. "We were pushing hard to get through before Christmas," he explains. "None of us wanted to be driving cars on Christmas Eve." They just barely made it. On December 23, each of the three cars had covered 30,000 miles. The drivers, exhausted, went home for the holidays; Vorwig prepared his report. If the manufacturers whose narrow interests he was supposed to serve thought Vorwig was now about to issue a death sentence, they were disappointed. They were not alone, for if Hitler expected the wildly enthusiastic judgment which a more sycophantic official might have given him, knowing his wishes, then he too must have been disappointed. Vorwig's report, in the light of the Führer's interests, seemed coldly impertinent in its dispassionate tone. He stuck to the facts and did not offer a value judgment. The furthest he went was to say that a further development of the designs could be recommended and that most of the shortcomings could be overcome without great difficulty. Vorwig himself today regards his report as positive and says it did not place undue emphasis on the difficulties. "I liked the vehicle," he says. "I thought it was a good and unique design. I felt the concept was good and hoped the difficulties could be surmounted." He did not, however, let this note of enthusiasm creep into his RDA report. Its ruthlessly factual tone is still interpreted by the Porsche family as an expression of the RDA's negative attitude; there are those who feel that Vorwig's positive attitude today may reflect the beetle's postwar successes rather than mirror the expression of his own views while he served the RDA. Referring to it in 1949, Vorwig pointed out, "It is clear that a privately owned industry had no interest whatever in a Volkswagen with which it would be in competition." Yet his report, filed in January 1937, urged further testing and on a larger scale. This time thirty *Volksautos* should be used, these to be manufactured under better conditions, in the factories of RDA member companies.

Necessary or not, the further tests now being recommended would further delay the project. Hitler, never known for patience, began losing his temper. It was now four years since he first broached the subject of a "people's car" at the 1933 Auto Show. He felt, with justification, that a good deal of foot-dragging was going on. He read the riot act to the manufacturers on Sunday, February 28, 1937. The occasion was his opening speech at the Berlin Auto Show that year. The previous day, the government announced a price reduction on automobile spare parts and "the production of a small car to be called a *Volksauto*, a people's car." Hitler hailed this latter announcement, and then in loud and angry tones shouted:

"It is my irrevocable decision to make the German automobile industry, one of our greatest industries, independent of the security of international importations and place it on a solid and sure basis. *And let there be no doubt: so-called private business is either capable of solving this problem or it is not capable of continuing as private business. The National Socialist state will under no circumstances capitulate*

56

before either the convenience, the limitations, or the ill-will of individual Germans."

These were the words of a ruler who would brook no opposition. Germany had already been converted into a Roman state with the panoply of the Imperium. When Hitler drove to the 1937 Auto Show, he was paced to the exhibition hall from the Chancellery by Germany's top racing drivers and driven through streets lined by 12,000 motorized storm troopers, black helmets gleaming over their brown shirts. Once in the hall, he was angered by an exhibit of Opel's own small-car entry and in his speech also warned the German auto industry that only one model of *Kleinauto* would be permitted.

Heinz Nordhoff stood beside the aging Herr Geheimrat von Opel as Adolf Hitler passed the Opel exhibit. Opel showed the Führer his new small car, with its sign, "Opel's latest achievement, P–4, the automobile of the little man: 1450 marks." With paternal pride, he said to Hitler, "And that, my Führer, is *our* Volkswagen!" Whereupon Hitler whirled around, his face red, and marched off without a word in reply. To demonstrate that he would not brook any last-ditch attempts by private companies to enter the small-car field on a competitive basis, Hitler made it difficult for the company to obtain materials necessary for the car. Later, when Opel offered to shave the P–4's price by 200 marks, the company was told unofficially that such price cuts would not be permitted, because no German car would be allowed to approach the price set for the Volkswagen.

In the spring, progress remained questionable. The New York *Times'* Associated Press report from Berlin on April 23 read:

HITLER'S CAR REMAINS A MYSTERY

Chancellor Adolf Hitler's cheap people's car, which he promised Germans for three years and with which the Führer dreams of conquering the European Market, will remain a myth for at least two years.

Three models of the mysterious "Volkswagen" were secretly put on test runs before Hitler proudly exclaimed on opening the 1935 Berlin Auto Show: "We will solve the problem of the cheap car. Production of this newly-designed car, which will be as inexpensive as a middle-priced motorcycle, will be started this year."

But Hitler's midget car failed to make the grade and will

have to continue trials "at least until 1938," it was learned from the Federation of the German Automobile Industry.

Finally, inaugurating the 1937 Auto Exhibition, Hitler banged his fist on the speaker's table as he burst out: "Either automobile makers produce the cheap car or they go out of business. I will not tolerate the plea, 'It can't be done!'"

In the spring, the Nazi brass discussed the overwhelming question of how actually to produce the car. The auto manufacturers schemed in every way possible to frustrate these plans. They suggested that each company might supply a portion of the parts for the car, or that each manufacturer could produce a set number of Volkswagens alongside regular production. Both suggestions, Nordhoff believes, were stalling tactics. Finally, says Ferry Porsche, the manufacturers told Hitler that they could produce a Volkswagen themselves if the government would subsidize them to the extent of 200 marks per automobile. Hitler figured that this would come to 200 million marks for the one million cars a year he wanted to produce, and decided that it would be money down the drain. He would have nothing to show for it. The 200 million marks could instead be used to build a factory. It was in this way, Ferry Porsche believes, that the decision was reached that the State itself would produce the Volkswagen in its own plant.

"The auto manufacturers were foolish," says Dr. Volkmar Köhler, the archivist of today's Volkswagen company. "Had they been smart, they would have produced a cheap 'people's car' for Hitler just as the radio manufacturers produced a 'people's radio' (*Volksempfänger*) when he asked for it. It might have been enough to satisfy Hitler. Instead, because they thought they could out-stall and out-fox Hitler, they ended up having the Volkswagen as competition."

3

The Nazis Lay Their Plans

FOR THE first time in his life, Ferdinand Porsche was not beset by money worries. For the first time, too, he was free of the dictates of auto manufacturers. The State, with its unlimited power and apparently endless funds, had decided it would build the small car of which Porsche had dreamt for years.

In late May 1937 the Nazi brass formed a new firm, the Volkswagen Development Company (Gesellschaft zur Vorbereitung des Volkswagens*), capitalized with 480,000 marks. Its management consisted of Ferdinand Porsche, Hitler's confidant Jakob Werlin, and Dr. Bodo Lafferentz, aide to German Labor Front chief Robert Ley, whose organization was to supply the necessary funds. Now the sizable capital of the German Labor Front was at Porsche's disposal and he could move forward energetically. Concern over budgets—which he so despised—plagued Porsche no longer; Ley's organization, by extension, had at its disposal the funds of the Nazi Party and, by further extension, those of the German Reich. (On July 1, 1939, the company's capital was increased to 150 million marks.)

The decision was made to go ahead with the RDA plan and test thirty more prototypes; later, another thirty prototypes were built for propaganda purposes, making a total of sixty. Porsche set up a large factory-like shop in Zuffenhausen, an industrial suburb of Stuttgart. The first thirty prototypes took shape there and at the Daimler-Benz plant in Stuttgart-Untertürkheim, the very one in which Porsche had worked years earlier. All of the first and second series of thirty which followed had 60.7-cubic-inch engine displacements, a

* Promptly nicknamed Gezuvor ("After you!") for its initial syllables.

fraction smaller than the 61 cubic inches originally envisaged.

All sorts of facilities became available. A command from Berlin was all that was needed for the Porsche-Gezuvor group to borrow the large-scale motor pool, garages, and service facilities of the German Army's Kornwestheim barracks near Stuttgart, and it was there that test headquarters were established. The RDA was now out of the picture. "I was not even called upon for advice when the tests started," says Vorwig, "even though I knew more about the car than many others." As for personnel, Werlin came up with two hundred SS men who were experienced drivers drawn from all over Germany. The tests were continuous and demanding. As soon as a driver brought his car back to the Kornwestheim barracks, it was inspected, refueled, and taken out again. When the tests were over, the Volkswagen prototypes had been driven *more than 1,242,000 miles!* Says Ferry Porsche, "This was the first time in Europe that as many as thirty test cars had been used by a manufacturer." The cost of production-plus-testing of the prototypes alone rose astronomically to an estimated thirty million marks, resulting in a car which, as events have proved, was far ahead of its time. What was being perfected was a highly efficient, serviceable, yet low-cost vehicle. Not one feature of Ferdinand Porsche's *Kleinauto* of the mid-1930's was for show; each served a distinct purpose. The now familiar sloping hood of the car's beetle shape, for example, was designed to minimize the power needed in high-speed driving, for a car with a blunt hood requires far more power to push air forward at high speeds than does the VW.

By the early summer of 1937 Hitler actually had his Volkswagen, at least in prototype, as he had promised the Germans for years. Now what he had said earlier in the year at the 1937 Auto Show really had come true: all that remained was to go into production. But that was to pose its own problems.

Porsche, still impressed by his last pilgrimage to the mass-production mecca of America, Detroit, was determined that his cars would be produced along American lines. Yet there were not enough German engineers and production men familiar with these methods. The answer to the problem suddenly seemed clear: recruit them from America.

And so another trip to Detroit took place and a meeting was planned with Henry Ford, whom the German government decorated in 1938 with the Grand Cross of the German Eagle for his pioneer work in "giving autos to the masses." On his previous visit, Porsche had arrived with just his secretary; this

60

time, he had an entourage and a new rank.* With him went Bodo Lafferentz; Jakob Werlin; Ghislaine Kaes; Ferry, his son; Dr. Anton Piëch, his son-in-law; and Otto Dyckhoff, a production and design expert.

Arriving in New York City aboard the *Bremen,* they immediately went to Roosevelt Raceway in Long Island to prepare for the Vanderbilt Cup Race in which one of Ferdinand Porsche's Auto-Union cars was entered. From there, they went to Detroit, where they met Henry Ford. Porsche regarded this meeting as the high point of his visit. He idolized Ford as a genius who had materialized Porsche's own personal dream in another country. They conversed through interpreters and Porsche poured out all his plans for the Volkswagen. Did they worry the elder Ford? Not in the least. "If anyone can build a car better or cheaper than I can, that serves me right," he said.

Ferry Porsche, in his mid-twenties, was present at this meeting and Henry Ford asked him to talk about the car of the future, not necessarily the Volkswagen, but the ideal European car of the next decade. "Let *him* tell me," Ford said. "The young are the ones who will build that car."

Ferry spoke of independent suspension, streamlining, low gas consumption—actually enumerating the VW's specifications. Would Ford care to visit Germany, asked Ferdinand Porsche? Would he like to see what they were building? That would be impossible, said Henry Ford, because there would be a war in the near future.

Porsche was astounded. He and his colleagues looked at each other with the naïveté of those who read only the technical press."No!" said Porsche. "We cannot believe that! We live in an era of economic improvement, in which many problems exist which take time to solve. Why should there be war?" Ford murmured that he hoped they were right, but he had his doubts. Then he excused himself. Four hundred orphans were waiting to see him.

After the meeting with Henry Ford, they revisited New York City for the July 5, 1937, race, returning directly afterwards to Detroit to recruit German-Americans for the Volkswagen plant. They bought a Ford V-8 and drove through Canada to Niagara Falls, to Albany, New York City, and Philadelphia. En route, they stopped at various manufacturers to buy machinery for the factory in Germany. From the U.S., Porsche

---

* Hitler had designated Porsche Reich Auto Designer (Reichs-Auto-konstrukteur), a laureate-like title which apparently only amused the designer.

also shot back a cablegram ordering a further change in the design of his car. All the Volksautos so far had doors which opened from the front (as had many other German cars); Porsche ordered these changed, to open from the rear. In the U.S., he had learned that this was the trend now, and also safer.

The recruiting of U.S.-trained personnel continued through 1938, carried on by German consuls in various cities. Altogether, about twenty signed up. Most of them were German nationals working in the United States; a few were American citizens of German descent. All of the latter returned home from Germany after World War II started in 1939.

"My wife received a telephone call one day in spring 1937, asking me to see a Dr. Porsche in the Book-Cadillac Hotel," says Joseph Werner, then a special machine designer at Ford's River Rouge plant. "I assume he got my name through the German consul. My wife warned me to be careful—that she didn't know what they were after. I went anyway and met Porsche, Dyckhoff, and Lafferentz. They told me they were going to build a Volkswagen and needed American-trained designers and production men. I remember asking them if they had any idea how much just the machines for such a project would cost. They answered that they had plenty of money. Then they mentioned that they were also going to build their own factory. When I heard that, I knew it was one of those dreams of Hitler's, but I never thought he'd actually carry it out." Werner, who had been away from his home in Germany for ten years, finally agreed to go, "because my parents were still there and I'd always intended to come back. Still, I didn't think it was very sound for them to try to start a company when they didn't even have a factory." They offered him a salary of 1250 marks a month ("about what I'd been earning at Ford," he said) and agreed to pay all moving expenses, including the cost of transporting his car and furniture to Germany. He and several others who had been recruited from Ford and General Motors —all of them designers—sailed together and started working for Porsche in Stuttgart on September 1, 1937. Werner has remained with the company ever since and is today head of Volkswagen's huge factory in Hanover.

Another of today's Volkswagen executives who was recruited in the U.S.A. at the time is Otto Hoehne, now production chief of the Volkswagenwerk and a member of its *Vorstand,* or management board. He had lived in Chicago from 1926 to 1939 and was thirty-three years old when he first read an offer of a job with Porsche in a U.S. German-language newspaper. Hoehne had spent some years on the assembly line at International Harvester and moved from there to the National Tea Company, where he was in charge of night truck maintenance, working twelve hours a night, six days a week. This was an unpleasant and dirty job and Hoehne disliked being away from home each night (he even had to work the night of Christmas Eve). He submitted a résumé to the German consul in Chicago and was hired. They offered him free transportation, an apartment, and at least one mark per hour. "What attracted me," he says, "was that they promised me a chance at advancement." He started as a tool and die maker at the Volkswagen factory on June 1, 1939. A third member of this group is Kurt Hocke, today a motor pool driver at the Volkswagenwerk in Wolfsburg (his calling card reads, "Call me 'Mike' if you like"). Hocke was a thirty-year-old unemployed cabinetmaker in Chicago when he was recruited by the German consul in that city. Times had been tough for Hocke. He and the German-American girl he had married in 1934 lived in a tiny flat near Wrigley Field with their daughter and his adopted son. "We had to steal coal during the depression," he says. He was dissatisfied and wanted to better their lot. Then the offer came from the German consul, who had addressed a pro-Nazi German-American club in Chicago called "Friends of the New Germany," of which Hocke was a member. For workers like Hocke, the New Germany was not too generous. No moving expenses were paid, although Hocke spent only four hundred dollars for ship's tickets for himself, his wife, and two children. "When I reported to Berlin," he says, "I told them I'd rather stay there than work at the Volkswagen plant, but they raised quite a fuss. So I reported to work at VW in February 1939."

The vast enterprise, however, still seemed illusory to many in 1937, when Ferdinand Porsche visited the United States. A German Embassy press attaché in Washington was quoted at the time as saying, "The Volkswagen really ought to be called 'Christ,' because everyone talks about Him without ever having seen Him." The skeptical and blasphemous aide was promptly recalled by an embarrassed German Foreign Office. The time for jokes was over.

On both his 1936 and 1937 trips, Ferdinand Porsche had visited Roosevelt Raceway in Westbury, Long Island. On October 12, 1936, he saw Tazio Nuvolari win the race; now, on July 5, 1937, the victory went to Germany's Bernd Rosemeyer, who drove his rear-engined Auto-Union car at an average speed of 82.56 mph, covering the 90 laps in a fraction over 3 hours, 38 minutes, beating Nuvolari by 17 miles per hour. Rosemeyer won the cheers of 75,000 fans—and $22,100 in prize money. The 1937 race has been called "probably the most spectacular automobile marathon ever witnessed in this country" and was an important milestone in Porsche's continuing racing career. His reputation in the field was soaring throughout the 1930's, for even as he was perfecting his small car, he designed and developed some of the greatest competitive automobiles Europe has ever seen. After decades of French and Italian dominance, Porsche's cars brought Germany unquestioned supremacy and launched a battle between the two German giants which continued until World War II broke out. Porsche was the Auto-Union "general"; his rear-engined "P-car" created a sensation. Alfa-Romeo dropped to the background. The final success was attained in 1937 when the Germans produced two cars, each of which could reach over 200 miles per hour: the 650-hp Mercedes W125 and the 545-hp Porsche-designed Auto-Union C-type Grand Prix cars.*

Germany, like Alfa-Romeo and Bugatti, also developed great drivers, among them Rudolf Caracciola, Hans Stuck and Bernd Rosemeyer. The latter, a favorite of Porsche, was killed on the Autobahn at the age of twenty-seven while straining to set a new record in his Auto-Union car on January 28, 1938. He was determined to better both his own record of 223.9 mph and Caracciola's 268.3 mph. "Some said there was a sudden boisterous gust of wind," write Markmann and Sherwin. "Others swore a front tire was wrenched from Rosemeyer's Auto-Union. Most said it was both. Travelling at tremendous speed [over 266 mph] the car skidded 80 yards, somersaulted twice and was thrown 200 yards through the air. Rosemeyer

* Four great Porsche Auto-Union racers:
1934 P-car (Type "A"): 295 bhp, 16-cylinder V engine (4500, later 6000, rpm): 265.96 cu. in. engine displacement; 7-to-1 compression ratio; front and rear independent torsion bar suspension; 1628 lb. weight.
1935 P-car (Type "B"): engine displacement increased to 301.95 cu. in.; bhp boosted to 375 at 4800 rpm; compression ratio raised to 8.95-to-1.
1936 P-car (Type "C"): engine displacement raised to 366.61 cu. in.; bhp boosted to 520 at 5000 rpm; compression ratio increased to 9.2-to-1.
1937 P-car (Type "C," modified): engine displacement raised again to 386.13 cu. in., and bhp boosted once more, to 545 at 5000 rpm.

was hurled out in midflight and landed in an embankment. He died instantly."

The tremendous horsepower built into these small cars is significant; the racing seasons of the mid-1930's were tailor-made for Porsche. As was noted before, the rules for Formula 1 races had been changed, specifically to reduce the dangerous speeds at Grand Prix races. Yet it was precisely the high-powered, lightweight racing car which had fascinated Porsche ever since he had initially grappled with the problem in the Sascha car a decade earlier. Heading the Auto-Union team, he realized its fullest potential.

After his return to Germany, Porsche and others of the Volkswagen Development Company devoted themselves to completing their plans for the actual manufacture of the people's car.*

A factory had to be built and fully equipped and a suitable site had to be found for such an enterprise. It was also a problem to find workers to construct the factory (much less build cars), for the Third Reich's labor force was busily building for war. Other problems existed, even financial ones. While the German Labor Front had vast funds at its disposal, these of course could not be given over completely to this car. The solution was ingenious. It involved the KdF, a subsidiary organization of the German Labor Front.

The German Labor Front (DAF), established by Hitler to maintain industrial peace and indoctrinate the workers, had in fact turned into a repressive, pro-management organization without the slightest resemblance to a labor union. It was responsible only to the State and the Party and prohibited strikes or other "unruly" demonstrations. Its leader was Dr. Robert Ley, an alcoholic chemist, who had become Gauleiter of the party organization in Cologne.

Upon accepting the job of DAF boss, Ley promised "to restore absolute leadership to the natural leader of a factory—

* One man at the Porsche Bureau who had an artistic streak was at this time making plans for something which was to last as long as the Volkswagen—and a lot longer than any of the Nazi plans then being concocted. He was engine designer Francis Xavier Reimspiess, who in 1937-1938 produced the famous "VW" emblem (letters one above the other, enclosed in a circle) without ever being asked to do so. Reimspiess showed his design to Ferdinand Porsche and Porsche was impressed; he even gave Reimspiess a 100-mark bonus for it on the next payday. In subsequent years, Reimspiess's original design was embroidered with gear-teeth and other decorative elements, but after the war, it was again used as originally designed.

65

that is, the employer . . . Only the employer can decide. Many employers have for years had to call for the 'master in the house.' Now they are once again to be the 'master in the house.' "

This was in full accord with the Nazi law governing labor-management relations, the so-called Charter of Labor of January 20, 1934, which proclaimed the employer as "leader of the enterprise" and his workers as the "following" (*Gefolgschaft*). "The leader of the enterprise makes the decisions for the employees and laborers in all matters concerning the enterprise," the Charter stated, and he was charged with caring for their "well-being," without of course any backtalk from them.

For the benefactions from the German Labor Front the worker paid dues which enriched Robert Ley's coffers by 160 to 200 million dollars a year. Of this, 10 per cent was allocated to a DAF organization called Strength-Through-Joy (Kraft durch Freude, or KdF), which organized all recreation, travel, sport, and leisure-time activities. It offered workers bargain cruises and packaged holidays, inexpensive tickets to concerts, theater and opera, and worked into many of these activities heavy doses of Nazi indoctrination.*

KdF, then, had an income ranging between 16 and 20 million dollars a year. Furthermore, accounting was secret and the funds could be spent as the Party liked; it amounted, in short, to a slush fund.† Now, was not Hitler's *Volksauto* a car meant for the German workers and was it not logically a matter of concern to the German Labor Front? Furthermore, Hitler had said at the 1934 Auto Show that it was to be "the source of yet-unknown happiness to them on Sundays and holidays"— and this made the car clearly a matter of concern to the Strength-Through-Joy organization.

The matter was decided: KdF would sponsor the people's car. An ingenious 5-mark-weekly layaway plan was devised and on August 1, 1938, Ley announced the scheme to the German worker in a speech at Cologne.

This small car, Ley said, is "the greatest social work of all time and all countries. The *Volksauto* is the Führer's very own work. The Führer lives and works with this as his pet idea." As for the plant, he said it would become the "materialization

---

* KdF holidays, Germans used to say, were occasions during which girls daily lost strength through joy.

† In November, 1934, Admiral Raeder was told by Adolf Hitler not to worry about the costs of the new program to build up the German Navy. In case of need, Hitler said, he would get Ley to put 120 to 150 million marks at the Navy's disposal from the funds of the German Labor Front.

in stone and iron of the idea of class education, settlement work, national health, and the beauty of work." From a start of 150,000 cars a year, the plant was to boost production to 1,500,000 annually.

Moreover, Ley said, "It is the Führer's will that within a few years no less than 6,000,000 Volkswagens will be on German roads. In ten years' time there will be no working person in Germany who does not own a 'people's car.'"

The price of the Volkswagen had by this time been boosted from Hitler's originally stipulated 900 marks to 990 ($396). But was even 990 marks the true price? This remained in doubt. Ley had claimed at one time that the 990-mark price included insurance and even garage and maintenance costs;* at another time he referred vaguely to the fact that "of course, we shall attempt to find rational solutions to the problems of garaging, repair shops, and replacement parts." In point of fact, the Volkswagen contract, as we shall see, did not commit the state to any specific price for the car; it also specified that the cost of insurance for the first two years would be charged to the purchaser. The *Frankfurter Zeitung,* then the only paper to mention this contradiction, estimated insurance to add up to a total of 200 marks for the two-year period. In actuality, it appeared that the Volkswagen would cost the purchaser a total of 1190 marks, not 990.

The New York *Times* commented on this on October 16, 1938:

> . . . it appears that every successive announcement raises the effective prices of the *Volksauto* just a notch above the previous announcement. The original statement was that the price of 990 marks included insurance for two years, garage charges and the cost of periodic overhauling, so that the net price of the car would come to only about 574.20 marks, or $230. But according to the latest calculations, the effective price of the limousine is as follows:

> | | |
> |---|---|
> | Basic price at factory | 990 marks |
> | Two years' insurance | 200 marks |
> | Delivery cost, average | 50 marks |
> | Total | 1,240 marks |

> These prices are valid only for members of the Labor

* If this were true, the New York *Times* noted on August 2, 1938, then "the actual part payment on the car figures out to only 2.90 marks weekly [of the 5 marks paid in] . . . On that basis, the real cost of the *Volksauto* will amount to only 574.20 marks—or $230 . . ."

Front; others must pay in addition to the regulation price the Labor Front dues fitting their income. The delivery charges may be saved by driving the car home from the factory, to which special buses will transport purchasers, but the insurance premium has become an extra charge and there is no further talk of free garage or overhauling. Nor is there any guarantee: the buyer buys on trust.

How much would it cost the average German to run? A German emigré, Joachim Haniel, in 1938 estimated the total at between 75 and 125 marks a month. Writing in *Neues Tagebuch,* a Paris weekly put out by liberal German emigrés, Haniel calculates this as follows: At 27 miles per gallon, he writes, the average owner might consume 25 gallons a month, at a cost of 40 marks. In addition, he would have to pay approximately 10 marks a month insurance once the first two years had passed; 20 to 30 marks garage rental in large cities, and the unavoidable expense of oil, tires, repairs, parts, etc. Few Germans, Haniel says, could afford this 75 to 125 marks and certainly "not the Germans whom Ley likes to address, those earning from 160 to 500 marks a month." While Haniel's figures seem high (few VW owners would garage their cars), the breakdown of costs indicates some expenses which had to be faced. Still, as the New York *Times* of October 16, 1938, pointed out, several million workers earned about 2000 marks a year and a good proportion could, therefore, afford the *Volksauto* at 990 marks, "especially when it can be paid for under the special installment plan announced by the Labor Front."

The installment plan was in actuality a gigantic layaway scheme. William Shirer refers to it as "Dr. Ley's ingenious plan [whereby] the workers themselves should furnish the capital by means of what came to be known as a 'pay-before-you-get-it' installment plan—five marks a week, or if a worker thought he could afford it, ten or fifteen marks a week."

Under this gigantic layaway plan, 336,668 Germans actually put aside 280 million marks ($67,000,000). In postwar years, these "savers" came to haunt Volkswagen management.

Subscription offices were opened in all Labor Front headquarters, while specially appointed agents received subscriptions from workers in large industrial plants. A hard-sell campaign was immediately inaugurated. Germans who earned from 200 to 300 marks a months ($80 to $120) were to take up individual subscriptions; those earning less were asked to join with friends in group subscriptions.

Opening such a "layaway" account was tantamount to placing an order for a Volkswagen. The extraordinary contract was weighted heavily in favor of the State. It neither mentioned price nor even obligated the State to deliver a Volkswagen once the last payment had been made. The regulations are worth quoting here in full. (Italics are mine.)

RULES GOVERNING APPLICATION FOR A VOLKSWAGEN SAVINGS BOOK

1. The original Volkswagen savings book will be issued by the agent in the applicant's place of residence or work against payment of a fee of 1 mark. The book is made out in the name of the applicant and *neither it nor the rights it confers are transferable*. Acceptance of the savings book is equivalent to placement of an order for delivery of a Volkswagen, subject to the rules herein set forth.
2. Current installment dues are payable at offices of Labor Front or the Strength-Through-Joy organization which carry Volkswagen savings stamps. No liability is assumed for payments unless they are made against the immediate exchange of savings stamps in the amount of the payment. At least one stamp in the value of 5 marks is to be pasted in the book each week, such stamp to be canceled by the holder by writing the date of purchase thereon. A special premium must be paid in the case of open cars and cabrio-limousines [i.e., convertibles and sunroof models].
3. Each car carries limited insurance against collision and public liability for a period of two years from the time the car leaves the plant, *the cost of such insurance to be charged against the purchaser*.
4. Payments must be made at the designated places of payment by the purchaser, though collectors may be employed.
5. When all the spaces in the savings book have been filled with stamps, the book is to be promptly turned in at the regional Strength-Through-Joy office in exchange for a new book. After the start of production an order number will be issued through the nearest Gau office. The final savings book is to be turned in at the Strength-Through-Joy office *in exchange for a certificate of ownership*. Lost or misplaced savings books cannot be replaced.

6. For reasons of technical improvement and consequent lowering in the price of the Volkswagen, *no interest will be paid on paid-in savings.*
7. Until further notice, the Volkswagen will be produced in a deep blue-gray finish.
8. *Volkswagen contracts are non-cancelable.* In exceptional cases the Strength-Through-Joy Gau office may authorize cancellation. *In such cases a fee amounting to 20 per cent of the payments made will be retained.*
9. Inquiries should be directed to the nearest office in this leaflet.
10. In case of change of residence the savings book must be submitted for correction to the agent who originally issued it.
11. Tampering with the savings book is punishable by law.
12. Applications for issuance of a savings book may be denied without reason.
13. No supplementary agreements not embodied in these rules shall be binding.
14. In case of legal disputes the courts of the city of Berlin shall have the jurisdiction.

The fact that paid-in savings accumulated no interest is less surprising today than when Haniel noted it in 1938 as being especially outrageous; the "layaway" Christmas Clubs of U.S. banks operate similarly today. The nastiest part of the contract was its non-cancelable and non-transferable nature. Workers who missed an obligatory weekly payment or who decided they could no longer afford to make any payments risked losing every single mark they had put into the scheme. The state might in exceptional cases permit cancellation, but it was under no obligation to do so and would in any event confiscate 20 per cent of the paid-in sum. Because contracts were non-transferable, they could not be used as collateral; in effect the payment books had no intrinsic value whatever, except for the purchase of a Volkswagen. The state was not even committed to coming up with a Volkswagen once all payments had been made, it was merely obligated to deliver "a certificate of ownership." This certificate included an order number, entitling the purchaser to a car—once a car had been produced.

At the rate of 5 marks a week, it would take a "saver" four years and seven months to pay in the required 1190 marks. And then he would only become *eligible* for the car. It is not too farfetched to suppose that he might have to wait another

70

four or five years before delivery could be made if he were assigned a high number.

There naturally arose the suspicion that the Volkswagen scheme was a plan to defraud the German people. Writing shortly after the Volkswagen plant was dedicated, the emigré Haniel concluded that "the 500-750 million marks annually to be collected is the true meaning of the Volkswagen plant . . . The production of automobiles, which it conceivably may undertake some time in the future, is merely a sideline. With its halls, machines and warehouses, it is in essence the gigantic backdrop for the world's biggest installment swindle." Shirer also refers to it as a "swindle" and notes, "Tens of millions of marks were paid in by the German wage earners, not a pfennig of which was ever to be refunded."

It seems, however, that in this case at least, the Nazis were *not* out to defraud. The idea that Hitler—who dealt in billions —would construct so elaborate a plan to cheat workers out of 67 million dollars is nonsense. We have seen how the auto-enthusiast dictator was interested in the VW and in motorization. As for the cash paid in by the workers, that was deposited by the Strength-Through-Joy organization in the Bank of German Labor in Berlin and was intact when Berlin was conquered. The $67,000,000 in marks was seized by the invading Russians.

That Hitler was dead serious about building his car could be seen also from other data. After the war, a U.S. Strategic Bombing Survey team pointed out that "the start of the war found the plant's management as well as the authorities in Berlin unprepared for utilization of the plant in the war effort. The German government expected a short war and accordingly decided to keep the plant intact for postwar production of automobiles. This is supported by the fact that the plant remained virtually idle, its 1941 production representing only 20-25% of the plant's capabilities. During the entire course of the war the plant never produced more than 50 per cent of its capacity."

Of course the Nazi regime *did* intend to build Volkswagens. What has led many persons to conclude that the plan was fraudulent is a lack of knowledge of its history, as well as a belief that all Nazi schemes were suspect. Further, the plan appeared bizarre and grandiose and the idea that "every German worker" would own a car in ten years seemed absurd. Nevertheless, Hitler had now committed himself for four years to a Volkswagen. He would brook no opposition to

71

any of his plans, however inflated. The Volkswagen scheme had gained momentum. No one could call a halt to it. Hesitation was tantamount to economic sabotage. It was heresy to doubt the Führer's will. Also, who could doubt the plan's eventual success, if Hitler was prepared to underwrite the costs, subsidize the company, and make up all losses?

Dr. Bodo Lafferentz, an economist turned administrator and Ley's aide in KdF's Travel, Excursions, and Vacation Bureau, meanwhile hunted for a suitable location for the plant. The site was to be about twenty square miles in size, near transportation facilities, close to sources of raw materials and yet not too close to Germany's western boundaries. Under consideration were several possible locations: the Weser River Valley, the Mannheim industrial area, the Fürstenwalde region near Berlin, a site near Regensburg, and another near Stendal on the Elbe River. All were rejected for reasons of congestion or distance from raw materials.

Lafferentz commandeered a light plane so that he could fly over the other proposed regions and find a place with *Lebensraum* for the factory; in congested Germany, that would be quite a trick.

Lafferentz's interest increasingly centered on the Lüneburger Heide, a heath which stretches from north of Hanover and Brunswick to the moor and marsh country beyond the Autobahn from Bremen to Hamburg. It is a lonely region, thinly populated, with ancient villages which still retain the qualities of another world, full of the rustic homeliness of simpler days.

Lafferentz, however, was less interested in the peaceful villages than in the open spaces. From the plane, it seemed perfect for the purpose he had in mind; perhaps he was not aware that below lay a mosquito-infested swamp. Below also lay Schloss Wolfsburg, the fourteenth-century castle belonging to Count Werner von der Schulenburg, built on lands granted his ancestor Ritter (Knight) von Bartensleben by Emperor Lothair II in 1135. The grant rewarded his defense of the area against the Slavs, and the lands had in succeeding generations been held successfully against all comers.

Of these landlords, it was written in 1584, "In particular the von Schulenburgs and the von Bartenslebens were the true captains of men . . . the noble lord Otho took the field against the proud Junkers . . . nor was any of them strong enough to confront the proud young lion. But he routed them again and again . . ." Ironically, his lands were fated to fall before the assaults of such a one as Robert Ley.*

On the morning of September 15, 1937, a number of events puzzled Count Werner von der Schulenburg. His gamekeeper came across a stranger wandering around his lands and the man explained that he had recently flown over the area and was now examining its beauty on foot. Then the Fallersleben village schoolteacher came bicycling to the castle to tell the count that he had just encountered a caravan of official cars parked on a nearby bridge. People were peering at the countryside and discussing it among themselves. Within a short while, this mysterious caravan was seen near the castle. No sooner had the cars disappeared than the count received an agitated telephone call from the mistress of the neighboring Mörse estate. She had been out riding that morning and encountered a Maybach limousine in the forests belonging to Herr von der Wense, another neighbor. She approached the man seated beside the chauffeur and told him that no one was permitted to enter these lands without express authorization, whereupon she was smilingly told, "My dear lady, *I* am allowed to drive anywhere my car is able to carry me!" She was outraged.

The mystery was cleared up after lunch. An innkeeper in Fallersleben who had served lunch to some of the official delegation made it his business to overhear their conversation and conveyed his findings to Count von der Schulenburg. These men, he said, were not here in connection with the planned Autobahn, as had been suspected, but in connection

* The von der Schulenburgs, forced to surrender to the Nazis in 1937, were to prove themselves "proud lions" in later years. Count Friederich Werner v.d.S., whom Shirer terms "an honest, decent German of the old school," served as ambassador to Russia from 1934 to 1941. He had worked honestly to improve Russo-German relations, was respected in Moscow, and was never informed of German plans to invade the U.S.S.R., an event which caught him completely by surprise. He later joined the July 20, 1944, plot to kill Adolf Hitler. Count Friederich Dietloff v.d.S. joined the Nazis in 1932 and became deputy police president of Berlin in 1937. However, he soon became an active anti-Nazi and joined General Halder's stillborn plot to overthrow Hitler in September 1938. He resigned from the Nazi Party in 1940, and also became involved in the 1944 conspiracy to assassinate Hitler. Both men—the former sixty-nine and the latter forty-two years of age—were murdered by the Gestapo in late 1944. The wife of Count Werner v.d.S., who was resident in the castle in 1937, met an ironic end: driving a Volkswagen near the VW plant in 1951, she died after crashing into a gas station on the very land her family had surrendered in 1937. Her castle is today being restored and transformed into a municipal art center. Count Werner, still living, no longer occupies it. His son Rudolf spent five months employed by Volkswagen of America before taking up studies for a doctorate at Harvard.

with a *new city,* one which threatened not only the existing lands, but their very homes, perhaps the entire nearby village of Hesslingen.

Official confirmation soon came. Dr. Bodo Lafferentz—the very man who could drive "anywhere" his car could take him—informed the count that two-thirds of his ancient lands were to be surrendered "for an important national project." Compensation was offered.

The count fumed and was not interested in assurances of payment. He decided to resist. He knew that private reasons would never prevail and so he decided to undermine the effort through official agencies. The count and his countess moved to Berlin's Eden Hotel to direct their offensive more effectively.

The Minister for Church Affairs, Hanns Kerrl, had grown up in Fallersleben and was a boyhood friend of Count von der Schulenburg. In addition to his main duties, Kerrl was also head of the Bureau for Regional Planning, an office responsible directly to Adolf Hitler himself. The count reached Kerrl immediately, but Kerrl was unable or unwilling to help his old friend. He tried to comfort him by saying that he was being asked to surrender only 7600 morgen (approximately 5000 acres) of the required 15,000 morgen. The rest would be commandeered from Herr Gebhard von der Wense, who would give up 2500 morgen, and from twenty-six other smaller landowners, who would make up the balance.*

Whatever the reasons for the basic decision, the count continued to resist. His family, after all, had owned these properties for over five hundred years, and he was not to be put off his lands so easily.

His arguments convinced the Ministry of Transport. It reported to the government that the site would overload existing railway facilities and would prove too much of a burden for the important Mittelland Canal which flowed through the area. The count convinced the Forestry Department that the ancient oaks on the property were worth preserving. He even convinced the Luftwaffe that the planned site would prove a ridiculously easy target for enemy planes and that the open countryside, the industrial complex to be erected, the railway lines, and the canal would prove irresistible to bombers. Finally, he rallied the aid of the mosquitoes and made it known that

* Von der Wense was ruined by these and subsequent events. He bought land in Mecklenburg with the money received for his land in the Fallersleben area, but this was lost to the Russians at the end of the war. Back home, the only land he owned was the family graveyard. He took a job with the postwar Volkswagenwerk as a guide, touring visitors around the plant. His younger son works for VW's service department.

the proposed location was an insect paradise, unfit for human habitation. (Joseph Werner recalls his first sight of the proposed factory area, towards the end of 1937, a few months after he had arrived from the U.S. to work with Porsche in Stuttgart. "It was a sandy field and didn't look like it would support a factory," he recalls. "No private company would have wasted money building there.")

Despite the importunities of Transport, Forestry, Air Force, and insect specialists, the party leadership was adamant. Lafferentz and Ley won out.* As for the mosquitoes, an appropriate specialist was sent to Fallersleben from the Reich Institute for Soil, Water, and Air Pollution to inspect the area and offer recommendations. The man examined the region carefully, then reported, "Under no circumstances must you drain the water meadows of the stream valleys, because this would destroy the breeding grounds. A unique opportunity to study about 70 of the most interesting gnat species would be lost!" This scholarly gentleman's misplaced scientific curiosity was throttled. He was permitted to select and mount the more interesting species, and then the Third Reich moved exterminators into the insect paradise.

Finally, in January 1938, all opposition ceased. Papers transferring the land to the state were drawn up and signed. Albert Speer, the talented and outspoken thirty-three-year-old Minister for Armament and War Production, was charged with the construction of the plant. Speer himself was busy with grandiose plans for rebuilding Berlin into a city called Germania, a magnificent center of the expanding Nazi empire. He looked around for an architect to whom he could entrust the job of planning not only the factory near Fallersleben, but also an *Autostadt* (auto city) to house the 90,000 people who would be brought (from where no one knew) to the site.† Speer recalled a young Austrian architect, Peter Koller, an international prizewinner whom he had met lecturing in Berlin. He found him working in obscurity in the Augsburg regional planning office and offered him at thirty a chance to be top man at Fallersleben.

* There reportedly was a meeting in Berlin to argue all positions. After heated discussion, which took some time, Kerrl produced a paper containing the news that Hitler himself had decided in favor of Fallersleben. After that there was no point in pursuing the matter further. The delegation from the Forestry Administration, which objected to the destruction of centuries-old oaks, left the room muttering, "You could have notified us of *that* on a postcard!"

† Plans called for 12,000 workers in each of two shifts. The families of these 24,000 would bring the population to 90,000.

Koller threw himself into the task enthusiastically, evolving elaborate plans. The mile-long factory and a tall administration building would lie along one bank of the Mittelland Canal, while the city itself would reach out from the other shore. Vast blocks of apartments and two-family houses would shelter the *Kleinauto* workers and their families; parks, hotels, market places, and broad boulevards to rival Berlin's would beautify the site. At the center would be a cultural core, the site of theaters, public halls, palaces of culture, government and Nazi Party buildings. It was to be, as Ley put it, "a materialization in stone and iron" of Hitler's grandiose visions, "proof" of what National Socialism could produce.

These plans were worked out "bombastically, of course, as was the custom in those days," Heinz Nordhoff noted in his 1963 address to the city council. They were "singular in that the emphasis lay in the subordination of the town to the factory, the latter being planned as the center of all life. Such symbolic overestimation of the value of work was in line with the German Labor Front."

The public got its first glimpse at the plans for the city at the 1938 Berlin Auto Show, where a model of Peter Koller's town was put on display. Hitler, as usual, opened the show. The New York *Times* correspondent referred to him as seeming somewhat pale, but vigorous enough to thump the rostrum for twenty minutes. The Führer emphatically announced that "we soon will build the cheapest car in the world." He was followed by Propaganda Minister Goebbels, who reviewed the gains made by motorists under Nazism. In 1932, he said, Germany had 548,700 passenger cars; by 1937 there were 1,108,500. Before Hitler, there had been only one car per 40 inhabitants; after Hitler, one for every 24.* The atmosphere was generally optimistic. Construction of the plant, it was announced, would begin immediately.

A month later, Hitler invaded Austria and annexed that nation. Even in Vienna, he could not resist throwing out the lure of the *Volksauto*. This German car, he told the Viennese, "will also make a wish come true, a wish harbored by so many hard-working underpaid Austrian people."

In Germany there was a good deal of activity at Fallersleben. The town planners filed their preliminary drawings and government inspectors came to the site to review them on the spot. Some of these bureaucrats were apparently unaware of what had been decided and they took a strictly

* Goebbels was, as always, exaggerating. As late as 1939, there was only one automobile for every 49 Germans.

official view of the project. "The regulation relating to building in the open countryside applies here," they snapped. "It doesn't permit houses with more than three stories." With this they dismissed Koller's plans. The Koller crowd insisted that the government had decided to build a major city on this open field, but were told that the officials had no information about this in their files in Berlin. "Very well," said the planners. "We withdraw our applications to build a town." The bureaucrats triumphantly went on their way. The next day construction started behind their backs.

Elsewhere, others were just as confused. Two of Koller's engineers went to the Reich Transport Ministry in February 1938, and asked casually for a railroad station for "a city of 100,000 people which we're building near Fallersleben." The functionary who heard their request nodded gravely to humor them and later dismissed them from his mind as two lunatics, the kind of cranks that hardworking officials must occasionally put up with.

The dedication of the cornerstone was scheduled for May 26, 1938. It was a busy week in May for Adolf Hitler, seven days which had given Europe its worst war scare in twenty years. It became clear that Hitler, who had just annexed Austria without a shot being fired, was planning boldly to seize Czechoslovakia as well. His troops were stationed all along that nation's frontiers and Nazi propagandists launched a hysterical barrage of accusations against the Czechs, who allegedly were persecuting Sudeten Germans within their borders. On May 20, the Czechs became alarmed enough to mobilize their reserves. The French, treaty-bound to aid them, sent a stiff warning to Hitler not to attack. The British followed with a limp reminder to the Führer that they in turn were treaty-bound to France, and the Soviets declared they would assist the Czechs if Hitler invaded.

Events were moving rapidly and presumably the last thing pressing on Adolf Hitler's mind was the cornerstone ceremony to which his aides had committed him some time before. On May 22, the Führer was forced to stall for time, to reassure the Czechs of his "peaceful intent." In actuality, he had, on April 21, ordered the High Command of the Armed Forces (OKW) to prepare plans for a Czech campaign; these had been submitted to him in mid-May and Hitler was now furious that information about their existence had apparently leaked out and he was meeting unaccustomed opposition.*

And it was in the very midst of this turbulent May crisis, with the Führer's blood aboil and armor rolling all over Europe, that he was scheduled to attend a cornerstone-laying ceremony for reasons of public relations. All the grandiose plans for the car must have sounded uninteresting to him, for now there was conquest on his mind, not a little car for the German worker to enjoy on holidays. Those who saw him at the ceremony thought he seemed strangely silent and distracted.

---

* By May 30, his anger over having to give such humiliating assurances to the Czechs, whom he called "subhumans," would reach such a point that he was to order the OKW to plan for an even speedier invasion, by October 1. In the intemperate covering letter, he stated, "It is my unalterable decision to smash Czechoslovakia by military action in the near future."

4

The War Years

O N Ascension Thursday, May 26, 1938, Adolf Hitler laid
the cornerstone of the Volkswagen factory near Fallersleben, Lower Saxony. He had arrived by special express train
from Munich, accompanied by Reichsleiter Alfred Rosenberg,
the Nazi Party ideologist, Sepp Dietrich, an SS Obergruppen-
führer, and Jakob Werlin. At the Fallersleben railroad station,
he was greeted by Robert Ley; Bodo Lafferentz; Heinrich
Himmler; Viktor Lutze, head of the SA (storm troops); Minister Hanns Kerrl; and Ferdinand Porsche. The party left the
station in a column of cars and drove to the construction site
along streets garlanded with Party flags and banners. They
drove to the top of the Klieversberg, a hill which commanded
a view of the countryside. It was 1 P.M. and the day was a
gloriously sunny one.

An elaborate structure with 60-foot-high swastika banners
had been erected at the Klieversberg, overlooking a brick
court. At 12:40 P.M., as Adolf Hitler and his entourage made
their way to the site from the railroad station, trumpet blasts
called the celebrants to attention. Three hundred standards of the SA, the NSKK (National Socialist Motorists
Corps), Hitler Youth, Labor Front, and SS were marched up
to the tribunal and placed in position. Honor guards from the
army, air force, and the SS Junker School at Brunswick came
to attention. The 600 guests of honor and 150 reporters who
occupied the tribunal became hushed as the column of cars
approached. Altogether, 70,000 people had been assembled.
They came by car, by bus, and by 28 special trains. Two
chartered buses from Stuttgart had brought the employees of
the Porsche Bureau to the site. A special section had been set
aside for them. Karl Rabe, Porsche chief designer, spotted

the RDA's Wilhelm Vorwig in the crowd and invited him to join the Porsche group.

At 1:15 P.M., Adolf Hitler pulled up in his big Mercedes-Benz limousine. "Drummers and trumpeters of the Hitler Youth, stationed on the tribunal, raise their instruments," wrote the *Braunschweiger Tageszeitung* on the next day. "A wave of 'Heils' breaks over the tightly packed mass of people. Commands are shouted, a march is sounded, and the Führer's standard is raised beside the cornerstone. Fanfares and the roll of drums are heard." Hitler stepped from his car, reviewed the honor guards and received a bouquet of flowers from a little girl. On the podium, he acknowledged the greetings of other dignitaries, including Artillery General Wilhelm Keitel, the Army chief of staff, and NSKK-leader Hühnlein. "70,000 people raise their hands in greeting, for the Führer is here!" the Brunswick reporter said. The construction of the plant, he wrote, "is an act of such gigantic proportions as to be without parallel in the entire history of mankind."

Certainly the ceremonies were impressive. The scene glittered with uniforms and with the traditional costumes of the 3000 construction workers who had been given the day off to attend the festivities—bricklayers in white with black top hats, carpenters in black velvet and corduroy. Those from the Porsche Bureau felt conspicuous in civilian clothes, reports Ferry Porsche, who was there with his father. Count and Countess Werner von der Schulenburg, who had been invited along with the twenty-seven other dispossessed landowners, mingled among the guests and later left outraged because Hitler failed to mention the patriotic sacrifices of the property owners on whose land the factory and its city were to be built.

Robert Ley opened the ceremonies. "My Führer!" he said, "what has been started here—this factory and everything which will come of it—is fundamentally and singularly your work, my Führer! Your great idea and your great faith taught us that man develops himself only through work and that deeds, rather than words and phrases, represent socialism, and that man benefits only from that which he has won through work . . . This Volkswagen factory is one of your own dearest works. We know how you thought of giving the German people a good but inexpensive motor vehicle even before you came to power and how you have ever since imbued with new strength all the designers and others who labored on this car!"

Ley was referring to a little legend about Hitler which was

being propagated with energy. Jakob Werlin, writing in the May 26 issue of Berlin's *Völkischer Beobachter*, the organ of the Nazi Party, had mentioned it again. He claims he once drove with Hitler on a cold rainy night long before Hitler came to power, and says they encountered a motorcyclist on the highway. The man was huddled over his handlebars, wet, trembling with cold, and pitiable. According to the story, Hitler turned to Werlin and said, "If I were in a position to do so, I'd like more than anything to give every one of these people a car as a present."

Bodo Lafferentz stepped to the podium. An extraordinarily tall man, he towered over the others on the rostrum as he reported to his leader. The KdF, he said, had decided to allocate an immediate 50,000,000 marks for the construction of the factory and was meeting "every conceivable requirement" set by Dr. Porsche, despite "enormous difficulties." The car, FOB the plant, would be a "pricing miracle" at 990 marks, he added. (The New York *Times* on May 27 agreed, noting that "the cheapest German car now costs almost twice as much.") Lafferentz mentioned the customers which his organization planned to sign up. "The guaranteed demand for the gigantic production insures that the price of the car need not be raised; it posed a unique and heavy challenge which only the German Labor Front could meet."

Then Lafferentz pointed to the surrounding countryside. "Over there," he said, "we shall build our beautiful city which, when completed, will house ninety thousand inhabitants. The lovely wooded green landscape offers an opportunity for a superb urban development, so that the city which will be built here will rank among the most beautiful in the entire world."

There was of course nothing "over there" for Hitler to see except scenery. A day or so earlier, there had been great excitement over the possibility that Hitler might visit the non-existent city after laying his cornerstone at the factory across the Mittelland Canal. Working overtime, the planners marked out the proposed main streets with white lines, so that the Führer might at least visualize the skeleton of the town. At the last moment, however, one of the officials had second thoughts about the markings and ordered them all removed. "The entire landscape is ruined!" he raged. By May 26, the plans again existed only on paper.

Then Adolf Hitler delivered his speech. He grasped the rostrum with both hands and reminisced:

"When I came to power in 1933, I saw one problem that

had to be tackled at once—the problem of motorization. In this sphere, Germany was behind everyone else. The output of private cars in Germany had reached the laughable figure of forty-six thousand a year.* And the first step towards putting an end to this was to do away with the idea that a motor car is an article of luxury . . .

"The factors which compel persons to seek out cheaper products are simple and sober ones. Those who find it possible to buy expensive items will do so in any case! The broad masses, however, cannot do so. It is for these broad masses that this car has been built. It is to meet the transportation requirements of these masses and it is to bring them joy! . . ."

Hitler was trying to reassure the German auto industry, with which the VW seemed likely to compete unfairly. He had always insisted that the car would *not* steal customers from established manufacturers, but would reach those who could not become buyers of the more expensive cars. It would also, he claimed, stimulate an interest in motoring and ultimately prompt those who later could afford it to buy bigger cars. His prediction proved accurate after the war.

"This car," Hitler concluded, "shall carry the name of the organization which works hardest to provide the broadest masses of our people with joy and, therefore, with strength. It shall be called the 'KdF-Wagen'! I undertake the laying of the cornerstone in the name of the German people! This factory shall arise out of the strength of the entire German people and it shall serve the happiness of the German people!"

And so the automobile was named "Strength-Through-Joy Car." Ferry Porsche says the name was a complete surprise to both his father and himself. "We were horrified," he says. "My father commented that we'd never be able to sell the car abroad with such a name." Joseph Werner had the same reaction. "What American would buy a car called 'Strength-Through-Joy-Wagen'?" he asked himself. Of course no one, except obdurate Nazis, ever called it that. The general public continued to call it "Volkswagen," as did the regulations governing the layaway plan; the factory, then as now, was called the Volkswagenwerk, although advertising brochures and such

* After Hitler eliminated the unpopular automobile tax in 1933 to spur motorization, passenger car production rose sharply. Figures for 1934–1939—*including, however, deliveries to the growing armed forces—1934:* 144,542; *1935:* 205,233; *1936:* 240,530; *1937:* 267,910; *1938:* 289,108; *1939:* 250,788. Of thirty-five automobile manufacturers, four dominated the industry and accounted for 64 per cent of total sales. These were Adam Opel, owned by General Motors (30% of total sales); Auto-Union (14.5%); Ford (10.7%); and Daimler-Benz (9.2%).

other printed materials as the savings-stamp book called it "KdF-Wagen."*

When the ceremonies ended, Hitler seated himself in one of the three "KdF-Wagens" which Ferry Porsche and two others had driven from Stuttgart for the ceremony, then had Ferry drive him back to the Fallersleben railway station in the car, eschewing for once his Mercedes.

On the next day, the New York *Times* reported that the car would serve another purpose besides bringing joy to Germans: "Hitler declared that if the German people spent all their money on foodstuffs, some of which Germany does not have, the result would be a 'catastrophe.' Therefore, he said, the nation's purchases of cheap new motor cars will do much to check over-development of the demand for foodstuffs." It was, in other words, to drain off at least 20 marks a month in disposable income and thus contribute to economic self-sufficiency for the nation. As matters developed, Hitler almost did achieve self-sufficiency in food production; Shirer says the Nazis reached 83 per cent of this goal.

The local press also reported the speech of a certain Dr. Glehn, representing the workers' city about to be built. He felt called upon to issue lofty sentiments to the effect that "here labor's noble ethic, the primal source of life-affirmative emotions, shall find convincing expression." It was phraseology typical of what VW's postwar head, Heinz Nordhoff, has called the Nazis' "symbolic overestimation of the value of work."

The correspondent of the Hanover *Anzeiger,* equally enraptured, wrote:

"A world is being built. The fist of a cyclops has seized the clear Lower Saxon landscape. But it is a modern cyclops, one who understands the concept of the beauty of work . . . One looks from the ceremonial square out over the canal at the softly swaying forested heights. It is there that the German Reich shall bed down the most modern and beautiful workers' city . . . Happy people, who will find their homes here!"

The first to move in were not to be Germans, however, but Italians. Mussolini sent Hitler three thousand of his unemployed construction workers, accompanied by Tullio Cianetti, Robert Ley's Italian counterpart. They were quartered in wooden barracks clustered about an A-frame community building called Cianetti Hall. "Chianti bottle and dagger

* Today, Volkswagen of America, Inc., the U.S. importer, is understandably interested in making the point that "Volkswagen" was *not* Hitler's name for the car. It became the official name only after the war.

ruled," *Der Spiegel* wrote years later. "And the crocodile whip in the wooden watch tower of the SS guards . . . the first girls pregnant with the babies of Mussolini's unemployed began to appear . . ."

German companies in the construction, metals, machine tool, and automobile industries were now ordered to free some of their work force for the plant and for the construction of the workers' city. These also found themselves in wooden barracks. In requisitioning them, the Nazi Party demonstrated just how ruthlessly it was prepared to operate in furthering this plan to which the Führer had committed himself for so many years.[*]

It seemed as though Hitler's experiment in true national socialism might succeed. The layaway plan eliminated middlemen, dealers, distributors, and others usually necessary to automobile marketing. Customers were even to pick up their cars at the plant, where a gallery was to be built from which they might watch their KdF-Wagen roll off the assembly line. The entire resources of Joseph Goebbels's Ministry of Propaganda and Public Enlightenment, which controlled all media of communication, were at the car's disposal. This amounted to an unlimited advertising budget. One of the first promotional efforts made by the Nazis on behalf of the automobile—an almost *Life*-size, multi-page, illustrated handout entitled *Your KdF-Wagen*—is interesting as an example of advertising techniques employed at the time. Neither color photography nor slick paper was utilized, although the same cannot be said of the language employed by the Nazi copywriter, whose breathless prose was plenty slick and colorful.

"The baggage space of the car," the brochure promised, "is especially roomy. It is completely sufficient for four to five people even on long trips. Behind the back seat, there is room enough for many large handbags or grips, together with smaller pieces of luggage such as typewriters, gramophones, bathing clothes, and so on. Under the front hood, blankets or a medium-size suitcase may be accommodated along with rucksacks . . .

"All windows are very large, including the rear window, which is also made of glass . . ."

---

[*] Postwar Germany's news magazine *Der Spiegel* comments that such plants tended to keep their best workers and sent only expendables to the Volkswagenwerk. This Nazi levy is an example of the regime's arbitrary actions towards German private enterprise. Another curious example appears in the Nazi sales brochure for the KdF-Wagen. After citing the fringe benefits enjoyed by workers at the KdF auto plant, it urged other German workers to demand comparable benefits of their employers.

The copy then goes on to compare the KdF-Wagen with Porsche's Auto-Union racing cars. Stating that Porsche "drew largely on his experience in building racing cars" when he designed the KdF-Wagen, the copywriter says that a comparison between the two may seem "peculiar" but that "the technical man finds many parallels." The brochure points out that the suspension and weight distribution of both the KdF-Wagen and the Auto-Union racers were similar, as were the axles. Not only would an owner have the satisfaction of driving a 23.5-bhp relation of Porsche's 545-hp P-car, but of being the envy of everyone. Becoming positively rhapsodic beneath a headline reading "Enthusiasm wherever it shows itself," the KdF-writer said, "It makes no difference where the cars go: wherever they are recognized, one sees beaming faces and, when they come to a halt, they are immediately surrounded by a great mass of people. Everyone is amazed at the miracle car. All are enthusiastic about the pleasing, smart lines, and the solid construction."

Soon the 1350-meter (1476-yard) front of the factory began to rise to half its finished height. Hitler promised it would be bigger than the Ford plant in Michigan and would outproduce it as well.* A New York *Times* editorial clucked that "Adolf Hitler's KdF-Wagen . . . will leave much to be desired" in the way of American-style comfort, but added that Porsche "is an engineer of such high standing in Germany that its practicability can hardly be doubted." A later article (July 3, 1938) said that the car was already nicknamed "the Baby Hitler." It also referred to the fact that Germany's shortage of raw materials was "so bad that sardine cans may no longer have steel openers attached," and claimed that the first 200,000 KdF-Wagens would have bodies requiring "only 10,000 tons of inexpensive plastic material and so little iron and steel as not to matter at all," as well as Buna (German synthetic rubber) tires.

Construction of Germany's vast "Westwall" fortifications, which faced France's Maginot Line, was launched as a crash program in July 1938. Virtually overnight, most of the construction crews building the workers' city vanished, shunted over to this priority task. Peter Koller's blueprint for "one of the most beautiful cities in the entire world" was rolled up at least until September.

When that month came, there again did not seem much point in starting up energetically. Now construction materials

* Today's postwar VW plant, vastly enlarged, is indeed the world's largest automobile factory.

were rationed. Work moved slowly; a year after the dedication hoopla only one building, a home for unmarried workers, had been completed. Then in September 1939 came war. Construction slowed still further. By December 1941, when all new civilian housing units were halted by decree, only 2358 apartments (less than 10 per cent of those projected) had been completed, and for the remainder of the war, wooden barracks had to serve as substitutes. The workers' city, which the Nazis referred to as the Stadt des KdF-Wagens, bore no resemblance then to the city of Wolfsburg as it exists today. As for its name, some people called it "die Autostadt" ("the automobile city"), while others made do with the clumsy Nazi name for it. Not until June 1945, when its city administration renamed it, would it bear the name of the Schulenburg castle, Schloss Wolfsburg. As a matter of fact, it was not certain before the war that the castle would survive Peter Koller's urban development. As it turned out in postwar years, it did, and in the changed atmosphere, Count Werner was even to proclaim that "the Volkswagen plant and the Volkswagen city will carry the name Wolfsburg forward into the future."

In the late summer of 1938 Porsche was asked to open the Great German Mountain Prize auto race (Grosser Bergpreis von Deutschland) in a Volkswagen. The scene was the Hochalpenstrasse (high Alpine road) on Austria's highest mountain, the Grossglockner. Tens of thousands of onlookers had their first look at the car on this occasion and Bodo Lafferentz hoped that the nationwide publicity would excite their interest in his layaway plan. Porsche, accompanied by his son Ferry, drove the steep, tortuous 13-kilometer (approximately 8-mile) mountain road, which rose 1240 meters (4068 feet), in just 21 minutes, 44 seconds. A technical journalist evaluated the performance: cars with far more powerful engines, he said, "require an average of 25 minutes for the run, if indeed they do not boil over and come to a complete halt. The KdF-Wagen took this climb as though it were child's play . . ."

On August 3, 1938, the New York *Times* reported the Nazis "jubilant" as queues formed early in front of KdF offices a day after Robert Ley had publicly announced his five-mark-a-week layaway scheme in his speech at Cologne. A little more than three months later, the *Times* reported that payments of five marks *monthly* would now be accepted to stimulate Volkswagen sales, especially among young people. At that rate, the paper noted, it would take sixteen years to complete a purchase! The KdF promotional brochure makes mention of the monthly payment scheme, adding that the company "reserves the right" to increase the rate of savings to five marks weekly if the young people involved made more money later. So far, a somewhat disappointing 150,000 applications had been received. The *Times* said that "the international crisis was blamed for lack of interest as savers feel insecure." By the war's end, the "KdF-savers," as they came to be called, never totaled more than 336,668, most of whom had opened their accounts before 1940.* The number may seem large, but it represents a seven-year (1938-1945) total and raises the question of what Hitler would do with the remainder of the 1,500,000 "KdF-Wagens" he planned to produce each year.

At the Berlin Auto Show in February 1939, Adolf Hitler lent himself once more to the task of publicizing his car. *Time* magazine on February 27 of that year commented on the car's birth tremors: ". . . for the second time in a year, Adolf Hitler posed alongside a gleaming sample of his $396 Strength Through Joy flivver. Well did he know, but nothing did he say about the wretchedly slow progress in production of the *Volkswagen,* which was conceived more than five years ago, but will not be on the market until 1940 . . ."

Porsche commuted between his Bureau in Stuttgart and his job in Wolfsburg, overseeing the construction of his plant. He settled down in "a wooden, four-room bungalow built in the middle of the forest where the Volkswagen factory was to be erected," his son Ferry reminisced later. "My father did not wish to direct its construction from afar; he wanted to be there while the plant was growing."

Despite the pressure, there remained time for relaxation. He loved movies and sometimes, on Saturdays and Sundays, saw several each day. In summer Porsche liked to fish or sail and he owned his own boat. These were days of personal triumph, best shared with those who contributed to it. At the height of his career, Porsche celebrated in the simple, backwoods manner of a man from Maffersdorf, Bohemia.

"Around the hut there was excellent hunting," Ferry says, "and from time to time my father came along. Carrying the

---

* Hitler's analysis of the VW market and his claim that the car would not steal away customers of companies producing other cars proved accurate: questionnaires filled out by KdF-savers showed that 70 per cent had never owned a car; of the remainder, 40,000 were motorcyclists (90 per cent of whom did not own a heavy motorcycle comparable in price to the VW). More than half, says the KdF-Wagen brochure, earned less than 300 marks monthly.

gun on his shoulder, he tried to find mushrooms. 'I am somehow sorry for the deer,' he said.

"He often took . . . his collaborators . . . along to the 'hut.' And in the evening, dinner—preferably goulash, a highly spiced Hungarian goulash—was served to a large number of people. My father liked strongly flavored dishes. And his engineers, who were not very partial to them, had to put up with it and resorted to drinking large quantities of beer. Evenings of this kind were always very pleasant and people were apt to start telling stories. However, whatever subject was touched on initially, it was always merely a question of time until the talk finally turned to technical matters. Technical matters appeared to us a kind of focal point of the whole world."

Nazi Germany honored its leading designer in 1938 with its own equivalent of the Nobel Prize. Hitler refused to have anything to do with the Swedish awards ever since the 1935 Nobel Peace Prize was awarded to Carl von Ossietzky, a pacifist editor who died in a Nazi concentration camp on May 4, 1938. In 1937, he established his own National Culture Prize. On September 6, 1938, Porsche won it for his work on the Volkswagen. Other 1938 winners were Ernst Heinkel, for his bombers; Willy Messerschmitt, for his fighters; and Dr. Fritz Todt for his Autobahnen.* Dr. Goebbels announced the prizes and Adolf Hitler delivered an anti-Semitic harangue.

From November 9 to December 21, 1938, Karl Rabe, Joseph Werner, and Otto Dyckhoff toured the United States again, to buy additional American machines for the factory. "The atmosphere in America had changed," Werner remembers. "The night we left was the *Kristallnacht,* when the Nazis began to accelerate the persecution of the Jews. I remember that German offices in New York were picketed when we arrived." They were able nevertheless to do business with American manufacturers and their expedition proved successful.

"At the beginning of the war," Heinz Nordhoff reminisced in his speech marking the plant's twenty-fifth anniversary, "when construction of both city and factory was halted, the plant had been only partially completed. . . . [It] never passed

---

* Todt—who also built the Westwall—was killed mysteriously in an accident after a February 1942 conference with Hitler, during which differences were aired. He was an engineer with whom Porsche worked smoothly during World War II, and was succeeded as war production chief by the boy wonder Speer, an architect who, Porsche felt, knew little about technical matters and with whom Porsche feuded bitterly.

the improvisation stage during its first years . . ." By the time it shifted over to war production, only 210 KdF-Wagens had been built; these had not even been constructed at the factory, but elsewhere, and all went to Nazi bureaus or officials. Not one was sold to a KdF-saver or any other "little German."

Discouraged and exhausted, Koller, the builder of Wolfsburg, gave up and joined the Wehrmacht. He was sent to Russia, fought, was captured in 1944, and landed in a Soviet prison camp for the remainder of the war. He could not have imagined it then, but he would eventually complete his city.

Despite—or due to—the totalitarian nature of the Third Reich, confusion and lack of standardization characterized its war production. Virtually every German auto manufacturer produced his own model of car for the armed forces and it was not until 1944 that even an attempt at standardization was made. The models selected were two motorcycles, one passenger car, and nine trucks. The only car manufacturer chosen was the Volkswagenwerk. This plant was singled out because the vehicle it produced was one of the finest to be manufactured during World War II.

Porsche had been asked to adapt the Volkswagen for military use. He boosted horsepower to 25 and engine displacement to 1.13 liters, redesigned its body, increased its road clearance, but kept it light and maneuverable. It was a strange-looking automobile, meriting its name of Kübelwagen ("bucket car"): an open, almost square automobile, with the familiar VW slanting front, on which a spare tire was mounted. First produced in 1940, its air-cooled engine proved impervious to both African heat and Russian cold and its good traction kept it moving where other cars stuck, spinning their wheels in the snow, sand or mud.

The Reich Government, each year more and more enthusiastic about Ferdinand Porsche's designs, in 1940 saw to it that an honorary professorship was added to his doctorates. At the suggestion of the Nazi minister of education, Stuttgart University promoted Dr. h. c. Porsche to Professor Dr. h. c.

Elsewhere, however, the professor's designs were less popular. One of the reasons it took so long for the Kübelwagen to be approved by the German Army as its basic vehicle was the pressure exerted by the auto manufacturers, each having his own stake in continuing production for the Army. None wanted the state-run VW plant to become exclusive producer of military passenger cars. Carl Borgward, head of the automobile manufacturing company which bore his name, was, for example, head of war production in northern Germany, and in charge of all military-vehicle manufacture in Lower Saxony. Standardization in favor of the Kübelwagen might have put him out of business.

Another wartime version of the VW was the amphibious Schwimmwagen or Schwimmkübel. Its sealed body, equipped with a retractable propeller, was completely waterproof. So seaworthy was it that a committee of the Weapons Bureau (Heereswaffenamt) seriously tried to get Porsche to equip it with a green light to starboard and a red one to port, to conform with international navigation rules. Displacing 1131 cubic centimeters, this model generated 30 brake horsepower.

The square Kübelwagen bodies were manufactured in Berlin; the chassis were built in one section of the Volkswagen plant, while other parts of the plant produced a number of other war implements, such as mines and parts of the Ju–88 bomber. Toward the end of the war, the plant was briefly engaged in assembling V-1 flying bombs as well. One of its more prosaic tasks during the war years was to build 1,500,000 primitive stoves with which the freezing German troops on the Russian front could warm themselves.

Then came the Allied raids. The factory was completely unprepared for them. It had never been built for war. Lying uncamouflaged in the open countryside, it was a beacon alongside the Mittelland Canal, its massive rectangular buildings seeming to invite bombers. Allied pilots had only to look for the colossus beside the silvery ribbon of water and they could not miss. It was just as the German Air Force warned in 1937, when Count von der Schulenburg attempted to use this argument to save his land.

The factory was not even equipped with subterranean air-raid shelters. It had no basement in which the workers might seek refuge because it was built on a swamp. When the alarm came, the only place to go was into bunkers built on the ground floor. Just before the war started, an air defense general had protested the plant's construction as inadequate for war requirements. The general wanted to scatter the plant through neighboring forests, to hide its buildings from view. Porsche argued that this would be impossible. The general had held things up and Porsche, exasperated, had hurried to see Adolf Hitler on the Obersalzberg, to settle the matter.

"Am I mistaken?" he reportedly asked Hitler. "Am I to build a Volkswagen or an armored car? A car for peace or a car for war?"

"I believe," Hitler answered huffily, "we spoke exclusively of the Volkswagen."

"And may I assume that the plant at Fallersleben is being built for that KdF-Wagen?"

"I gave you the assignment for the Volkswagen!" Hitler answered. "I think it is clear that everything else follows from that."

Porsche returned to the plant site and told those who warned of war and bombing raids, "Please, you go to the Obersalzberg."

No one went, of course, and in time the bombers came.

Otto Hoehne and Joseph Werner had been expecting them all along. "Most of us who had come over from America felt the war was lost for Germany the moment the United States entered it," Hoehne says. "We tried to explain to those who had not worked in America that it might take U.S. mass-production a while to get mobilized but, once it did, it would inundate us. We were resented for our gloomy predictions."

Joseph Werner says the factory air raid warden kept insisting for a long while that bombers would never come. "The factory is not strategically important," the warden assured everybody. Then, as Werner recalls it, he changed his mind one day at the very beginning of April 1944. He said he thought "something would happen very soon." His premonition proved correct; the factory underwent its first air raid on April 8.* Other raids followed over the next five months and did considerable damage. The raids were part of a concerted Allied attempt to knock out the entire German automobile industry.

It is interesting to note that one particular bomb, which landed between the power plant's two turbines, could have had very far-reaching effects. It was a dud and was deactivated

* That day, between 40 and 50 aircraft approached from the southeast and dropped approximately 500 high-explosive, 1000 twenty-pound, and 400 to 500 incendiary bombs. The raid lasted only four minutes, from 2:15 to 2:19 P.M. There was little damage, although 13 workers were killed and 40 were wounded. On April 29, at 11:19 A.M. a pilotless British bomber crashed into Hall 1, destroying various roofs and the floor of the hall. Three heavier raids followed. On June 20, 1944, 90 bombers, accompanied by 30 fighters, attacked the plant from 9:04 to 9:14 A.M., dropping 500 high-explosive bombs, 180 of which found their target, as well as 130 incendiaries, 32 of which hit buildings. Result: 27 workers killed, 93 wounded, and some damage to all buildings. On June 29, 65 aircraft attacked from 9:39 A.M. to 9:41 A.M., with approximately 350 high-explosive and incendiary bombs, killing 14 persons, and considerably damaging the plant, town buildings, and the prisoner of war camp. The last raid occurred between 1:30 and 1:40 P.M. on August 5, with 80 aircraft dropping 300 high-explosive and incendiary bombs, killing 7 and wounding 27, as well as doing a good deal of damage to the assembly plant, kitchens, streets, and barracks.

and removed by British troops after the end of the war. Had it exploded, however, it would have destroyed those turbines and, with them, Volkswagen's entire postwar future. The plant depended on power generated by the turbines and replacements for those were impossible to obtain in Germany shortly after the war. Detonation of that single bomb would have meant that there would be no further work possible in the plant at all and probably no effort would have been made to start the Volkswagenwerk up again.

After the war, the bomb damage throughout Germany was examined by a United States Strategic Bombing Survey team, whose members included George W. Ball and Paul H. Nitze, later respectively Under Secretary of State and Secretary of the Navy in John F. Kennedy's and Lyndon B. Johnson's administrations. A total of 2,700,000 tons of bombs was dropped against Germany, 72 per cent of this number after July 1, 1944. Recorded civilian casualties totaled 300,000 dead and 780,000 seriously wounded from raids alone. Despite this, Germany actually increased production during the months of the heaviest Allied air attacks.

Surveying the damage which bombings had caused the Volkswagenwerk, the team found that 20.2 per cent of the total floor area was completely destroyed, 13.6 per cent was heavily damaged, and 20.9 per cent was superficially damaged. Floor area rendered unusable due to total or heavy damage amounted to 33.8 per cent, or 1,859,417 square feet. As for the 2476 machines which the plant contained, more than 20 per cent were damaged in the raids, about half this number totally destroyed.

The company claims that at least 60 per cent of the plant was destroyed and Heinz Nordhoff personally says that destruction was, in effect, total. Mere measurement of damaged floor area proves nothing, he says, for the destruction of one area often puts ten others out of business. In a sense, the factory after the bombings was like a decapitated man who, because his torso and limbs are intact, is regarded as only partially disabled.

The Volkswagenwerk, as noted, never produced even nearly at capacity during the entire war. Production of military vehicles was, on the whole, remarkably small. Most sources claim the plant produced 55,000 Kübelwagens and 15,000 Schwimmwagens from 1940 to 1945; the U.S. Strategic Bombing Survey says production never came to more than 48,548.

After the raids, production dropped to about 25 per cent of the previous average. In October 1944 it rose again to 1380 units and by January 1945 it had climbed to 2030. In February 1945 all raw material allocations were stopped because of the critical war situation and output plummeted to its lowest level.

Why was production so very low? The capacity of just the first unit of the factory was originally to be 150,000 cars per year; to achieve that, the Reich had invested more than 50 million dollars (215 million marks) from 1938 on. For all those millions, *Hitler received in five years as many vehicles as the postwar plant turns out in less than two weeks!*

The Strategic Bombing Survey claims that "no experienced or qualified men of the caliber required were put in charge of all operations. It was chiefly a political plant." But this does not completely stand up under examination. Ferdinand Porsche himself was in full charge both at the factory and at Stuttgart throughout the war; while he was away, his son-in-law, Dr. Anton Piëch, represented him at Wolfsburg, while Ferry Porsche was deputized in Stuttgart. Other experienced members of the Porsche Bureau team were active at the factory during these years. There were plenty of qualified men. The answer is more complex.

Plant management and even the authorities in Berlin were unprepared at the onset of the war to use the factory for the war effort. Expecting a quick victory, authorities hesitated to shift the plant over to war production, preferring to wait until peace-time KdF-Wagens could be produced. The plant, says the USSBS, "remained virtually idle, its 1941 production representing only 20-25 per cent of its capabilities."

There were other reasons. What was to have been the "most modern automobile factory in the world" had in actuality become an Oriental bazaar of war materiel manufacture and the plant which had been conceived of and built as one enormous unit had been broken up into a host of small factories lodged under one roof. Most halls worked on different projects. Lack of intelligent planning and much disorganization in Berlin, together with that confusion which is always generated by totalitarian bureaucracies, never allowed the plant to be operated as a modern mass-production facility. Otto Hoehne remembers it as "chaos."

"It was amazing how few concrete plans there were," he says. "And when it came to aircraft manufacture, there had been a great deal of planning—too much of it, as a matter of fact, with too many planners on the payroll, for this was regarded as a glamour industry at the time and every engineer seemed to want to work in it. But as for utilizing those sections of the factory which were not engaged in working for the aircraft industry, there seemed to be no plans at all, nor did anyone seem to have any clear idea as to how the factory facilities might be used to full advantage."

Yet another factor may have been a human one. Today, the factory is manned by free men; in World War II, two-thirds of its workers were slaves. The labor force increased more than 600 per cent, from 2732 in 1939 to 17,365 in 1944; the vast majority were foreign prisoners. Some were Russian and Polish prisoners of war, most were forced laborers from France, Belgium, and Holland, and others were court-martialed German soldiers sentenced to work at the plant. While treatment of the prisoners at Wolfsburg appears to have been better than elsewhere in Nazi Germany, it is a fact that many of those who arrived there were half-starved. When one contingent of emaciated Russians arrived, Ferdinand Porsche was outraged at their condition. He had them photographed and then took the picture to the Führer's headquarters, the Wolfsschanze at Rastenburg, East Prussia. He protested to Hitler that he could not get such men to work effectively. Hitler, wishing as always to keep his favorite designer happy and productive, ordered improvements. Eventually, prisoners were fed by the factory's own farms and food became decent enough, notes Ferry Porsche, for the Nazi officials to complain that prisoners were being "pampered."

Ferdinand Porsche could not always keep an eye on things at the factory. Ferry Porsche remembers his father as being almost constantly on the road throughout the war, traveling between Stuttgart, Berlin, the "KdF-Wagen City," Paris and points east. He always tried to spend at least two days a week at the Porsche Bureau in Stuttgart, where his staff had by 1940 increased to 291 (from 23 in 1933). There and in the Nibelungen Works south of Linz, Austria, Porsche designed a succession of tanks and other military vehicles, for which he was lavishly honored by the Third Reich. At the height of its activity, in 1943, the Bureau had a staff of 600.

Throughout this period, Porsche dealt with Armaments Minister Albert Speer. Animosity developed between the two men, and Speer finally had Porsche kicked upstairs by naming him Reich Armaments Councilor (Reichsrüstungsrat), head of a council which never met. In the autumn of 1944, upon Speer's insistence, Porsche moved his Bureau to Austria. As his new headquarters, Porsche chose a small woodworking factory in Gmünd, near his summer home in Zell am See.

The Hitlerian *Götterdämmerung* was begininng. Production had virtually ceased at Wolfsburg. Now Hitler ordered that

94

nothing was to survive him. On March 18, 1945, an alarmed Albert Speer pleaded with the increasingly irrational Führer, "We must do everything to maintain, even if only in a most primitive manner, a basis for the existence of the nation . . . We have no right at this stage of the war to carry out demolitions which might affect the life of the people. We have the duty of leaving to the nation every possibility to insure its reconstruction in the distant future . . ."

Hitler replied, "If the war is lost, the nation will also perish . . . because this nation will have proved to be the weaker one and the future will belong solely to the stronger eastern nation [Russia]. Besides, those who will remain after the battle are only the inferior ones . . ."

As the end hastened, Berlin ordered the transfer of all machinery from the Volkswagenwerk to mines in Longwy to protect it from future air raids which never came. Longwy lies in an iron-mining and metallurgical district near the Belgian and Luxembourg borders; the mine shafts were enlarged to house the equipment. A train took the first two hundred machines to the new location, and they were installed just in time to be captured by advancing American soldiers.

After the transport left the Volkswagenwerk, Porsche listened to the passionate arguments of the plant's chief inspector. This official railed against the decision to move the machines into "damp caves," pleading with Porsche to stop the transfer. The machinery, he said, should be scattered throughout the surrounding countryside: engines into a potato-dehydration plant at Neindorf, motor parts into a barracks in the forests at Soltau, front ends and steering mechanisms into a barn at Fallersleben, and light machinery into Lüneberg. The heavy presses could remain where they were. Assembly might continue at the plant as well. Such a move, he stressed, would insure the postwar future of the VW. "We will save the machines which we need if we are *ever* to build your car," he told Porsche.

It was already too late to halt the first transport to Longwy but Porsche decided to save the rest. His decision—although he could not have suspected it—did indeed prove crucial to the car and the company. Had the factory lacked machines in the immediate postwar years, it is certain that there would not now be a Volkswagen or a Volkswagen company.

As American armor rolled within ten miles of the plant, another precaution was taken for the future. Vital parts were removed from those machines still in the plant, packed into crates, and hidden in the conduits carrying electric cables underneath the factory.

At 8:45 P.M. on April 10, 1945, the sirens in Wolfsburg sounded a warning that tanks were approaching the city. At 9 P.M., the sirens warned of an air raid. Neither materialized. American armor had indeed reached nearby Fallersleben, but the Americans did not come to the factory. They could not conquer Wolfsburg, because Wolfsburg did not appear on their maps. The town was too new.

Polish, Russian, French, Belgian, and Dutch forced laborers waited in their barracks. Their SS guards had fled;* German soldiers and Nazi city officials burned or buried their uniforms and records, or drowned them in the Mittelland Canal. By 11 P.M., the decision was reached not to defend the town. The Volkssturm—that "army" of old men and young boys whom the Nazis had assembled into a rabble of "home guards"—disbanded.

When it became apparent that their jailers were gone and their liberators were not about to appear to establish order, some of the prisoners broke loose. They sacked the executives' homes in the town and turned on the factory. Chaos reigned in the unguarded halls and offices of the administration building, although the machines in the plant itself, many of which remained manned by German workers, were left untouched. "Every telephone had been torn from the walls," *Time* later reported, "every typewriter had been sledgehammered to junk, every file and record had been scattered and burned." Even the dental office was reduced to dust.

At the railroad station, the prisoners swarmed over a freight train, tore apart its contents, and captured, along with guns, sugar, and flour, several crates of costumes belonging to a troupe of actors. Powdered, painted, and costumed, the exhilarated looters marched on. Soon they liberated a cache of schnapps and, roaring drunk, threatened to burn the town. They were joined by Germans anxious to get in on the pillage.

Most of the prisoners, however, remained in their barracks for the time being, somewhat dazed by their freedom. It nevertheless became clear that large-scale disorders would result if the town remained without authorities for much longer. Late that night, the factory's chief inspector, Rudolf Brörmann, accompanied by a colleague, drove to Fallersleben to urge the

* Mönnich (in his book, *Die Autostadt*) says that the Germans derisively referred to a "National Socialist Escape Organization" (NS-Fluchtorganisation).

Americans to occupy Wolfsburg before rioting broke out in full force. They returned without success.

On the next morning, April 11, Pastor Antonius Holling, then Roman Catholic chaplain of the German Army's punitive battalion attached to the plant, determined to try where Brörmann had failed. "Because I do not speak English," he told me, "I went to the forced laborers' camp and asked the French priest there, who did speak English, to accompany me. Although he himself had been a prisoner, he was just as afraid as I was of what might happen if another night went by without law and order. He agreed to go and we drove off in an abandoned German Army ambulance. When we arrived, we found that the U.S. occupation 'army' consisted of eleven men and one young lieutenant. We explained our situation and the lieutenant was impressed by the fact that we corroborated what Brörmann had said the night before, by the fact that we were both priests, and by the testimony of the Frenchman. Then I told him that he should hurry, because there were about 20 American children in Wolfsburg who needed protection. He looked incredulous, so I explained that these were the U.S.-born children of German-American engineers whom Dr. Porsche had brought to Germany before the war." The lieutenant cranked at his field telephone. That same day, twenty Sherman tanks and two hundred U.S. soldiers arrived. The Americans posted signs saying that looters would be executed on the spot.

5

Years of Improvisation

HITLER'S Germany was dead, and so, it would seem, was the Volkswagen. For six years, Hitler had prepared for war; for six more years, Germans had fought that war, and now their nation lay prostrate and torn apart. The war had cost that country 11,800,000 casualties and 282 billion dollars; little was left. Germany had been crushed by enemies restored by men and machines from across the Atlantic. The limits of Nazi Germany's human and material capacity were reached in 1941–1942, at a time when her foes were just beginning to mobilize their own strength. The very American factories whose productivity and efficiency Porsche so much admired poured out a torrent of war materiel which engulfed the overtaxed, comparatively antiquated, and large inefficient war machine of this totalitarian state.

"When elephants clash, the grass gets trampled," says an ancient proverb, and World War II not only crushed Ferdinand Porsche's honorable and long-fought-for vision of a car for Everyman, it crushed Porsche himself. It smashed his factory and what there was of his small town, much of it now a sea of mud and wooden barracks in which thousands lived wretchedly, often ten to a room. Along the canal his colossus of a factory stood crippled, its roof gone, its halls shattered, its interior battered behind windowless walls, its machines idle and corroding in six inches of water.

The fate of the various participants in the drama of Porsche's shattered dream differed. Hitler had killed himself; Albert Speer, who claims to have tried unsuccessfully to do that job for his Führer (by introducing poison gas into the ventilation system of Hitler's Chancellery), was captured. For his part in the war, Speer drew a twenty-year sentence which ended, finally, on October 1, 1966. Robert Ley, whose German Labor Front played so prominent a role in the development of the KdF-Wagen, escaped trial at Nuremberg by hanging himself in his cell, from rags tied to a toilet pipe. He had earlier presented his American captors with a memorandum urging that Germany become part of the U.S.A., that the U.S. should adopt a "non-anti-Semitic" form of National Socialism, and that Ley himself should be put in charge of the scheme, directing it from Nuremberg Prison. After that, he wrote to Henry Ford, reminding him of his connections with the Volkswagen factory, and applying for a job with Ford Motor Company on the basis of his "extensive automotive experience." A short while later, he lost his nerve completely, stuffed his mouth with his underwear so as to silence his death-rattle, jammed cloth into his ears and nostrils, and hanged himself. When Hermann Goering (who was later to commit suicide himself) heard of it, he said, "Thank God! He would only have been a disgrace to us!"

The fate of Dr. Bodo Lafferentz, Ley's aide, is another matter and provides an interesting insight into Nazi society. He was, according to Dr. Volkmar Köhler, "an extraordinarily intelligent manager, and expert at the adroit use of official connections, less a Nazi than a man who used the Nazi era to his own advantage." Lafferentz married into the family of Richard Wagner, had many artistic and musical friends and, in his capacity with the KdF, organized popular German Army tours of Bayreuth, home of the Wagner festivals. As nominal *Hauptgeschäftsleiter* (general manager) of the Volkswagenwerk throughout the war years, Lafferentz not only represented management, but also the workers and the government itself, by virtue of the post he held in the government's German Labor Front. He was, Köhler remarks, "the very embodiment of the *Führerprinzip* (leadership principle), for he needed only to meet with himself and make decisions from whatever point of view he wished: labor, management, or regime." During the war, Lafferentz found the factory too confining for his entrepreneurial nature. He formed another company, also with DAF funds, called the Research and Development Company (Gesellschaft für Forschung und Entwicklung). Like many others of its kind, it created a great many draft-exempt jobs, presumably benefitting Lafferentz's very large circle of friends and acquaintances. The company engaged in Utopian research of a most visionary nature. One major if ill-starred project, for example, was the development of a small wind-powered electric generator, named a *Volkswindkraftwerk* ("people's wind power plant"), which was to electrify the Russian farms which the Nazis hoped to settle with German farmers west of the Ural Mountains. These farms, which of course never materialized, were to be protected from "the barbarous Asiatic hordes" by Ural Mountain forts manned by SS men, who were supposed to be aided in case of attack by the armed pioneer-farmers themselves. Another project was to bombard U.S. coastal cities with rockets, fired from cigar-shaped containers which Lafferentz's company was designing. These were to be towed to America by German submarines. When all these plans ended with the end of the war Lafferentz fled south and settled near Lake Constance.

Up north, near Fallersleben in Lower Saxony, lay a town unmarked on the conquerors' maps. In spring of 1945, it did not even have a name, for the use of "City of the Strength-Through-Joy Car" had become, to say the least, unfashionable, and no one had named the city Wolfsburg yet. In it, an epidemic of despair, fear, hunger and violence raged. Former slave laborers, freed prisoners of war, displaced persons, and escapees from the Russian Zone of Occupation, which lay five miles east, jammed the town. The Volkswagenwerk, or what was left of it, was now a "prize of war" and lay idle, awaiting the pleasure of its conquerors. These changed and Americans were replaced by Englishmen in the early summer of 1945. A unit of the Royal Electrical and Mechanical Engineers (REME) arrived and set up a repair shop for British Army vehicles within the factory; in August, Major Ivan Hirst was placed in charge of this facility. The plant itself had been marked down for dismantling and was under the authority of Colonel C. R. Radclyffe, C.B.E., D.S.O., who was in charge of all motor vehicle production in the British Zone, and under Major John P. C. Macgregor, his deputy for Lower Saxony. Victors and vanquished concerned themselves only with maintaining health and safety in the area. No one spoke of the future; indeed few could conceive of one. It was a time when the Morgenthau Plan, which intended to turn industrial Germany into a pasture, was seriously considered.

The few German workers in the factory sloshed through the shin-deep water, trying their best to clean up the debris with their hands. They brought back to the plant the machines which had been dispersed and hidden before the surrender, and began to put them into working order. Before the British were aware of it, they had made two complete cars with one surviving heavy press. It was, however, not one of these which triggered off the postwar VW production start. Major Hirst says that the car which launched the boom in beetles had been a Nazi KdF-Wagen.

"One of the few VW's that had been built at the beginning of the war was sprayed Khaki green and driven to H.Q. 21 Army Group as a demonstration model," Hirst reports in the April 1962 *REME Journal*. "The resulting order for the first batch of saloons [i.e., passenger cars] was taken as the signal to go ahead." And so, as Heinz Nordhoff was to remark later, "by one of the ironic jokes history is sometimes tempted to produce, it was the Occupation Powers who, after unconditional surrender, brought Hitler's dream into reality."

The English were delighted with the VWs, especially with the Kübelwagens which the workers began to hand-tool for them. They had come to know these vehicles in Africa where they had outperformed the easily overheated and heavier British and U.S. cars; there the going rate for one Kübelwagen reportedly was two Jeeps. They were especially welcome to the British occupation troops, for the United Kingdom was not supplying its soldiers with enough cars, using its output instead to try and build up its peacetime market.

The Americans had placed Rudolf Brörmann in charge of the plant; he was the former chief engineer who had approached them on April 10, pleading for help for Wolfsburg. The British confirmed him in his post.

One of the first production Volkswagens was then sent to England with the suggestion that it might be well for the British to take over the plant and produce this remarkable little car themselves. In Britain, however, the enthusiasm of the military was not shared by the automotive "experts." They reported it as too ugly, bizarre, noisy, and flimsy, a mere toy not to be taken seriously, and something which even the Germans would not want once present shortages were overcome. A British commission visited Wolfsburg to inspect the ruins. Its members were displeased by the sight of the workers tramping through the debris, and recommended that the plant be dismantled and razed. Headed by Lord Rootes, then Sir William, the commission predicted that the factory would collapse of its own inertia within two years. Certainly, they said, it was nothing in which the British auto industry was interested, even as gratis war booty.

Said the commission: "The vehicle does not meet the fundamental technical requirements of a motorcar. As regards performance and design it is quite unattractive to the average motorcar buyer. It is too ugly and too noisy . . . a type of car like this will remain popular for two or three years, if that. To build the car commercially would be a completely uneconomic enterprise . . ." The commission predicted that—if Germans produced the VW—"it would mean no undue economic competition on the world market against British products."

Refugees from East Germany and from the territories handed over to Poland poured into the area, into nearby camps, and gravitated toward the Volkswagenwerk. The British soon found themselves with a mile-long white elephant on their hands and with thousands of people who expected help from them. The plant was the only source of work; something had to be done. They decided to start the plant operating again, at least temporarily.

British Army trucks now started bringing in Ruhr coal for the plant and, by the end of 1945, its six thousand workers had produced 1785 Volkswagens. Half of these workers, said *Time*, "were cleaning up rubble; the others were virtually handtooling [the cars] . . . Falling bricks were a constant menace; live wires lay tangled in the mess." Just getting raw materials for the cars and the basic necessities for the workers proved an enormous problem. It was solved in part at least by means of barter.

"We traded cars for steel in the Ruhr, for food, shoes, and clothing," says Joseph Werner. "We even traded with the British Army to get tires. Sometimes we exchanged new cars for these commodities, sometimes overhauled ones, sometimes a wartime Kübelwagen or two. As time went by we even got food from Switzerland by sending a car down with a driver. We'd pay the driver five bananas and a few oranges to make the trip and he'd come back with packages of food and other necessities in exchange for the car." Barter was necessary at the time, for the average wage of one mark per hour the workers were being paid bought next to nothing in 1945, except on ration cards (and these, for example, provided a family with an eighth of a pound of cheese per month). Werner remembers eating little but bread and potatoes in Wolfsburg at the time. "I'd travel to my relatives all the way to Munich on weekends," he says, "just to get a decent meal."

Wing Commander Richard H. Berryman, O.B.E., had been put in charge of production at the factory, as Technical Liaison Officer. "The supply of material got so bad," he says in Britain's *Safer Motoring* magazine, that we had a fleet of small vans and trucks going to all sources of supply, picking up twenty, thirty, or fifty of whatever we needed and bringing it back just to keep the place going. At times we'd have as many as a hundred cars on the floor with no wheels or tires or glass, waiting for further supplies."

Not only were the British officers at the VW factory plagued by shortages, but their customers faced the same problem. Fritz Fricke, then in charge of maintenance at a British motor pool in nearby Celle, remembers that he needed spare parts desperately for his fleet of forty British Army Volkswagens. "I happened to have heard that the British in Wolfsburg wanted one hundred 100-watt light bulbs at the time, so I approached my own major and asked him for a supply. I told him they were extremely valuable then and that they'd command a good price on the black market. When I finally convinced him we badly needed the spares for our VW's, he let me have the 100 bulbs. I took them to the British at the VW factory. 'Here they are,' I said. 'They're worth a lot on the black market.' But the British officer said, 'Oh, we do not want them for the black market! We have a recreation room and we want to hang them above our billiards table.' I pulled out my list of automobile parts, the officer filled the order, and I gave him his bulbs."

Much barter had to be done secretly, for while many of the officers in Wolfsburg saw the need for this illegal business, others in headquarters far distant were very disturbed at talk of such trade. Many vehicles, therefore, were simply "lost in delivery" and never turned up again. What turned up instead was steel for the factory and food for its workers.

In August 1946, the British reorganized management and replaced Rudolf Brörmann, with whom they had difficulty working, with Dr. Hermann Münch, a tractable Berlin industrial lawyer selected largely because he was postwar custodian of all German Labor Front properties. Eventually, Otto Hoehne was made production chief. "He got his first paycheck from me," says Berryman. "He did a wonderful job." Julius Paulsen, then purchasing agent, was another of the German executives Berryman singles out for special credit. "It is due to his efforts in getting materials that the factory was able to keep going." Somehow, the factory seemed actually to be moving ahead. Its employees grew in number. In April 1945, the month the war ended for Wolfsburg, the factory had 450 workers; a month later, it had 1105; by December 1945, there were 6033, and by August 1946, the number had risen to 7951. In 1946, these workers produced 10,200 cars.

These, and the 1785 produced in 1945, were the first true "civilian" Volkswagens, although all had gone to the British military and other occupation forces. "Up until the end of the war, not a single Volkswagen, in today's sense of the term, had been produced in the Wolfsburg factory," says Nordhoff. "The few sedans that had been made were custom-built at Daimler-Benz for the cream of the Nazi hierarchy at a cost per unit similar to that of a Rolls-Royce."

As the ten thousandth VW was turned out in October 1946, it was the focal point of what one writer called a "pathetic celebration." Across its windshield, the workers had placed signs reading: "Better and tastier food, or there will be many things we won't forget!" and "10,000 cars and nothing in the stomach—who can stand that?" (*Mehr und schmackhafteres Essen, sonst können wir vieles nicht vergessen! 10,000 Wagen, nichts im Magen, wer kann das vertragen?*)

Now things were getting worse. Production in 1947 fell to 8987. "The vultures," reminisced Nordhoff later on, "began to circle over the town and factory. Everything seemed hopeless." The mark was worthless; the index of industrial production in Germany had crashed to 40.* It was hardly a sensible time to build a car; it was a time, Konrad Adenauer said, when "every German would have been lucky to get a new suit every 40 years, a new shirt every 10 years, and a pair of socks every four years."

That year, Wing Commander Berryman, on leave in London, telephoned Sir William Rootes at the latter's Devonshire House office in Piccadilly and asked for an appointment, reminding him of the days before 1942 when they had met, working at the Ministry of Supply.

"I went over to see him and his brother Reginald," Berryman says in one of his articles in *Safer Motoring*. "I told them all about the VW's construction and the production problems that had been overcome. I said that I had tried to break up the VW on numerous occasions in 'destruction tests' over the most atrocious roads, and that I had failed to destroy the car, and had proved to my own satisfaction that it was exceptionally durable and practical. I told the Rootes brothers that I thought the Volkswagenwerk was a gold mine waiting to be exploited, and I suggested that the whole place could be bought for reparations at a comparatively low figure—a few million pounds maybe.

"They listened to what I had to say, then Sir William told me that he had had one of the Volkswagen cars tested by his

* 1936 = 100.

own staff and that it did not come up to expectations and was considered to have not much future . . . " Years later, at a London Motor Show, Berryman happened to encounter Rootes again. "I wish I had listened to you a bit more the time we last met," Sir William said.

There was one more occasion on which Berryman tried to interest the British in the VW, showing it to an old RAF acquaintance then running a British factory. Berryman reports, "They were interested in the body construction, but after a careful examination they decided they could not learn anything from it."

This remarkable inability to learn anything from Porsche's remarkable design repeatedly saved the Volkswagen for the Germans. Even the Australians, Berryman says, turned it down. In February 1947, he met members of the Australian Reparations Commission in Antwerp, but the meeting proved fruitless. Berryman regrets it, for he says he had been "promised the job of Production Manager if the Australian VW plan had come off."

While all these conversations went on, more practical matters had to be settled at the plant. Entire trainloads of coal were sidetracked to the factory to keep its heart—the power plant—alive, and more bartered Volkswagens found their way into the hands of cooperative railroad officers. Major Hirst, by now a great enthusiast for the car and its factory, protected it ferociously, even against interfering British authorities. At one time, a British company demanded the return of two British machines and Hirst wrote them back: "I know the machines are needed in Britain, but we need them even more badly here!" According to his driver, Mike Hocke, Major Hirst once told him, "This factory belongs to the German people and I'm here to see they get it." Hocke, who returned to Wolfsburg as a discharged POW after wartime military service in Italy, says Major Hirst was so fond of his Volkswagen that for three months after Hocke arrived, he would not let himself be chauffeured. "He wanted to be behind the wheel himself," says Hocke.

Hirst's fondness seems to have been shared by the other British officers, all of whom were especially enthusiastic about the amphibious VW "jeep," the Schwimmwagen. They would hold games in which they would run it off wharves into the Mittelland Canal at 40 miles per hour, hitting the water with a great splash and then driving the cars up and down the canal. The amphibian, as a matter of fact, has been credited by Major Macgregor as saving the factory at one time in its turbulent early years.

As he tells the story, there was no sheet metal large enough at the time to make the roof and doors of the VW of one piece. Smaller sheets were used and a seam ran across the roof and the doors to join them. (Macgregor says they tested these cars by rolling them over, and every fiftieth car or so would be dropped upside down, to see if the seam held.)

To make this seam, they needed a butt welder, which they finally found down in the Ruhr industrial area of Germany. This was a machine the Germans had seized in France during the war, and teams of French officers were then running around conquered Germany trying to locate valuable machinery of this kind for repatriation. "They were crawling all over the place," Macgregor says. Knowing the French must be after this butt welder, which was hard to replace at the time, the British quickly grabbed it, along with those Germans who knew where it had come from, and brought both machinery and men to Wolfsburg, to set them to work and keep the machine from the French.

Early one morning, two French officers showed up in Wolfsburg. They had heard of the machine and wanted to inspect it. The razzle-dazzle treatment they received at the hands of the resourceful British shows with what ferocity the latter protected their plant and just how determined they were to see it in effective operation.

Major Macgregor says he and Berryman greeted the two Frenchmen cordially and invited them to the REME officers' mess, located in the building which was later to become the Volkswagenwerk's first Guest House. So cordial was this inter-Allied discussion that the French were half-drunk by noon, having been liberally provided with brandy by the two British officers. After several hours' drinking, Macgregor and Berryman put their guests into one of the Schwimmwagens and, chauffeuring them, charged along the bank of the Mittelland Canal. "Then we suddenly swerved off the embankment and into the water, flying out over the surface at top speed before we landed smack in the canal," Macgregor says. "We gave the Frenchmen quite a wild ride in the water too, and then the bilge tank plug just happened to come out and our vehicle just happened to sink. Those two Frenchmen were getting a good ducking, what with Berryman and I thrashing about a bit and shoving them under every now and then. We prudently had a rescue vehicle standing nearby and hauled them out after a while, dried them off, and got them into dry British uniforms."

They warmed the two visitors with more brandy but noticed that they were getting "a little nasty now." Berryman offered to show them the factory. "He gave them quite a tour in one of the regular Volkswagens," Macgregor says, "skidding about corners and even tearing through the building at 40 mph. By this time, the Frenchmen were insisting even more strongly that they must see their machine, but of course they were quite drunk and dizzy, which is what we wanted, and we had gained some valuable time."

A machine was finally presented for their inspection. It was a mockup, designed to look like a butt welder, but clearly not theirs. Disappointed, the Frenchmen left town. Had they been soberer, they might have been curious about the tarpaulin-covered object standing next to the mockup they were shown. There, a few feet away from them and hidden under canvas, was their butt welder. If they had seen and confiscated it, the factory would have had to shut down production.

The years 1945, 1946, and 1947 were years of improvisation and ingenuity for the British in Wolfsburg, years of sacrifice and hard work for the Germans at the plant, and fateful ones for the "Wolfsburg Motor Works," as the Volkswagenwerk was then also called. Had this handful of British officers not engaged themselves so daringly for the factory and its workers, there could never have been a VW today. Inevitably, the factory would have decayed or been dismantled. Despite their dedication, hard work, and self-sacrifice, the German Volkswagen executives there at the time would have been powerless to save the plant in those years, had they stood alone. Fortunately, they did not, nor were they in the hands of victors seeking to exploit them.

Porsche knew little of all these events at Wolfsburg. When the war ended he was far away, at Gmünd, Austria. There he was briefly and politely questioned by a British technical commission and a guard placed in front of his house, less to watch him than to protect him against marauders.

In July 1945 he was ordered to Frankfurt in the American Zone, to be interrogated further along with others prominent in the Third Reich. Because of his advanced age (he was now seventy), Porsche was allowed to drive to Frankfurt in his own car, accompanied by his chauffeur, Josef Goldinger, who had served him since 1908. He spent three months in the "Dustbin," a castle outside the city. Another prisoner in the

Dustbin was Albert Speer, who, despite his wartime differences with Porsche, defended the old man energetically and said it was ridiculous to interrogate Porsche about political matters of which he knew nothing.

Porsche was well treated and upon release was permitted to return a free man to Zell am See, Austria, where he had his home near his workshop in Gmünd. On his drive back, he stopped by Stuttgart to visit the former offices of the Porsche Bureau, quarters which were now occupied by Americans. He was rebuffed sharply and the U.S. commander was not willing to let him enter the building. Porsche left deeply hurt, politically naïve as always.

In Gmünd and in Zell am See, Porsche and his colleagues set up shop, repairing cars used by occupation troops. They even designed and manufactured wheelbarrows and small wagons. Karl Rabe, his chief designer, worked in Gmünd in the British Zone, while Porsche worked in Zell am See in the American Zone; neither could visit the other because interzonal passes were not issued to Germans in mid-1945.

In November an event of far-reaching importance to Porsche occurred. A French officer, accomapnied by a former Porsche engineer, approached the designer with an invitation to visit French headquarters in Baden-Baden, where a French technical commission waited to offer him an "interesting assignment."

Porsche, extremely cautious, finally agreed to go to Germany if Ferry could precede him to conduct preliminary negotiations and then report back. In Baden-Baden, a Colonel Meffre, in charge of French Zone industry, explained to Ferry that France's Minister of Industry, Marcel Paul, wanted to invite his father to built a true "people's car" for the French Government. The chassis was to be identical to the Volkswagen's, since the French were satisfied with its technical excellence, but the body was to be redesigned to give the car "a typical French look."

Ferry hurried back to Austria to report. The offer seemed bona fide and the terms acceptable. Exhilarated that his talents were once more in demand, Ferdinand Porsche went to the spa in the German French Zone on November 16, 1945, looking forward to the exciting new turn his life was taking. He was, of course, aware that some Volkswagens were being produced, but undoubtedly he believed that the Wolfsburg plant was doomed and about to be dismantled. He had been given to understand that the British were offering the factory to France and that the French wanted to have a French version of the car built and tested before they accepted the plant. He had been told that preparations to dismantle and ship the plant to France were already underway in Wolfsburg and that the French also wanted Porsche's help in assembling it again. It was understandable that he should have believed this, for the factory did indeed stand on the dismantling lists in 1945, having been classified as a munitions plant because of its wartime production of bombs and V–1 flying bombs. After so many years of heartbreaking work on the car and seeing his 25-year dream shattered by war, Porsche must have been doubly convinced that only governmental sponsorship would ever get his car built.

In Baden-Baden, the negotiations with the French commission went smoothly. The officer who had invited Porsche, a Monsieur Lecomte, headed the French delegation. Ferry Porsche assisted his father, for he spoke French. Porsche's son-in-law, Dr. Anton Piëch, was also there. Finally, an agreement was reached over a champagne breakfast. Then Porsche was asked to wait two days while Paris was consulted.

The Germans waited in comfort over the weekend, well supplied with food and drink in the beautiful resort. On Saturday, December 15, 1945, while they were still awaiting word of Paris's reaction to the terms, some French officers whom they had never seen before entered Lecomte's quarters, the villa Bella Vista, in which they were living—and summarily arrested them. The officers were from the Sûreté. Porsche, Ferry, and Piëch were placed in a crowded cell block in Baden-Baden's former SS prison. Lecomte, completely surprised at this new development, later drove to Gmünd to assure Porsche's daughter, Louise Piëch, that he had nothing to do with the arrest of her father, husband, or brother. He said he would do what he could to free the three men.

When Porsche was finally informed of the charges which had been brought against him, he learned that his enemies were again executives of big automobile companies, this time French ones.

The "French VW" scheme had apparently been concocted by left-wing French politicians, including Marcel Paul. French auto manufacturers, however, were determined to kill any such idea in its cradle, despite the dangers involved. Louis Renault had been arrested by the French government on charges of collaborating with the Germans during the war, and his company had been seized and nationalized. There are many who believe Renault was innocent and that he was arrested only to permit the left-wing government of the day to grab his company. Renault died in prison and has still not been exonerated, although several Germans who knew of his activities during the German occupation of France assured me that Renault never cooperated willingly, but resisted the Germans as best he could. The example of Renault was a constant reminder to the French auto makers. The French VW plan was a comparable threat. They wanted to save their companies and would not countenance a competing, government-backed car. The fact that the designer of this car was a German supplied them with the ammunition to sabotage the scheme. And so, Jean Pierre Peugeot charged Porsche with war crimes.

It was not difficult to make such an allegation in 1945-1946, and it was likely to be believed, no matter which German stood accused. It was an atmosphere which encouraged mischief; arrest immediately followed the charge, and trial could be postponed indefinitely.

Specifically, Porsche was charged with violation of the Hague Convention governing the treatment of war prisoners, with being guilty of disciplinary reprisals against French workers at the Peugeot plant during World War II, and with responsibility for or complicity in deportations from France. The Peugeot plant was under the direction of the Wolfsburg VW factory during World War II, and it is true that Porsche regularly consulted with Peugeot's engineers and technicians in France. He had of course nothing to do with repressions or deportations. He had been there purely in a technical capacity, and so it would be proven two years later. Ferry Porsche recalls three specific instances in which his father had actually aided the Frenchmen from Peugeot. Once, when the Nazis proposed to deport Peugeot workers to Wolfsburg, Ferdinand Porsche effectively resisted this move, arguing that people work better when they are close to their own homes. Another time, Porsche stopped the Nazis from arresting Peugeot directors after an act of sabotage had occurred in the plant. Jean Pierre Peugeot himself visited Wolfsburg during the war and on that occasion Porsche saved him from arrest by the Gestapo. He intervened and arranged for Peugeot's safe return to Paris.

It now seemed as though the French Volkswagen scheme had been effectively defeated. Porsche sat in prison along with his son and his son-in-law, and Lecomte fretted helplessly. It was at this point that Ghislaine Kaes, Porsche's loyal secretary, turned up.

Kaes had always been a British subject and this finally got him in trouble with the Nazis. Ferdinand Porsche could not have cared less about Kaes's citizenship; in fact, Kaes remembers, Porsche never once mentioned it during all the years of their association. (After the war started, Porsche did, however, know that Kaes listened illegally to the 9 P.M. BBC newscast from London, and he would occasionally ask him what had been said.) Throughout these war years in Germany, Kaes said, "I felt as if I was on the wrong boat and couldn't get the captain to change his course." On February 9, 1944, the Nazis finally arrested him and sent him to the eastern front in a German Army punishment battalion. He was wounded in East Prussia, fighting the advancing Red Army, and was shipped to a hospital in Denmark, then still under German occupation. "On May 5, 1945," Kaes says, "I saw the British flag flying over Copenhagen." Enthusiastically, if naïvely, he rushed to British headquarters, "to report," as he put it, but they refused to help him or to believe that he was a British subject. Instead, they turned him over to Danish resistance fighters who first took him to Hellerup where they pressed a pistol against the back of his neck and told him to prepare for death. At the last moment, a Danish officer stopped the execution and Kaes was shipped off to prison. He was released after a short while and began working for a British unit. Because of his wartime presence in Germany, Kaes was tried for treason. The court acquitted him, and he was freed. Then he rushed to Gmünd "to find the Herr Professor," and from there to Baden-Baden, where finally he found him in prison.

"I was able to get meals in to him," Kaes says. "He'd ask me for some soup or a Schnitzel and I'd get it to him the next day. A woman in town cooked for me. Each day I had to bribe the guard 20 marks to get into the prison and another 20 to get out again." After a while, Porsche asked Kaes to get him better quarters by claiming that his eyes needed treatment. The ruse succeeded and the designer was transferred to a hospital, Kaes meeting him at the prison and carrying his suitcases for him to his new quarters.

Throughout this period Ghislaine Kaes lived with Lecomte at the Bella Vista. Lecomte, still obsessed with the desire to build a French Volkswagen, told Kaes to go to the British Zone of Austria and get the blueprints of the car so that Lecomte could get them to Paris. He warned him that Porsche would be killed unless he agreed to do so. "It was a bluff," Kaes told me, "but I had no choice. I went to the professor to ask him what I should do. He suggested I notify the British liaison officer in Baden-Baden and so I sneaked over there one night under cover of darkness and talked to a British captain.

There was a brigadier in the room as well, who listened attentively and said nothing. The captain wanted to know all about the Frenchmen involved in this plan, what they had told us, where their offices were, even what their telephone numbers were. I had all this in my notebook of course. Then they told me to cooperate fully with Lecomte for the time being. They thanked me for informing them of the plan and assured me that nothing would happen to me as a result."

While Porsche still lay in his Baden-Baden hospital bed, his son Ferry was transferred in March 1946 to the Hotel Sonnenberg in Rippoldsau, a Black Forest spa. There he was well treated, for the French also wanted Ferry, who already had a reputation as a brilliant designer, to work for them. Ferry refused, saying he could not design anything while he was still a prisoner. Besides, he emphasized, his only thoughts were with his father and his family. Then the French insisted they wanted the VW blueprints, and Ferry supplied Kaes with a car in which to drive to Gmünd. This was a special four-wheel-drive Kübelwagen, with a regular VW passenger body, which went under the special name of Kommandeurswagen. Lecomte supplied the gasoline and funds and joined Kaes in the car. They drove off on March 17, 1946, and, after picking up necessary papers in Innsbruck, arrived at Gmünd in the British Zone late on the evening of the nineteenth.

"After Lecomte had gone to bed," Kaes told me, "I sat down with Mrs. Piëch and Karl Rabe to try and find a solution to this problem. Rabe insisted that he was responsible to the British and did not feel free to hand over any blueprints to the French. They told me to report the matter to the officers at British headquarters in Klagenfurth, 60 kilometers away. I drove there the next day without Lecomte and spoke with a British major in the Field Security Service. He listened to me for a long while and then ordered me not to turn anything over to the French—and to tell Lecomte that this was the decision of British headquarters. I was worried about what Lecomte would do, either to me or to the professor, when he found out, so when I returned I told him that the British had discovered his plans by themselves."

Lecomte did not believe this and suspected that Kaes had informed. He ordered Kaes to take the blueprints into the French Zone of Austria, carrying them over the Alpine mountain passes on foot. He also wanted machinery from the workshop and said he would arrange to have that transported out of the British Zone.

Lecomte was now prepared to move rapidly and the situation was becoming critical. Once again, Kaes consulted with Rabe and Mrs. Piëch and on Thursday, March 23, again drove to British headquarters in Klagenfurth. As a result, the British sent a soldier to Gmünd by motorcycle that very night, to order Lecomte to report to Klagenfurth at 10 A.M. the next day. Lecomte accused Kaes of treachery, then ordered him to come along on this trip.

"Lecomte wanted to arrive in Klagenfurth ahead of time, so as to meet with the French liaison officer there before we reported to British headquarters," Kaes says, "but this was one time the Volkswagen failed to make it. I was determined to arrive at ten sharp and I made sure I had to stop several times to get the 'failing' engine running again."

They arrived in Klagenfurth just in time for their appointment with the British. Lecomte reported to them while Kaes waited on a bench near the French headquarters, which Lecomte now wanted to visit after he was finished with the British. After a while, Kaes saw two officers emerge from British headquarters and march over to the French offices. He did not know it, but they were looking for him. Not finding him there, they returned to British headquarters and after another fifteen minutes, emerged once more, this time with Lecomte between them. Lecomte led them to Kaes, seated on the park bench. Suddenly he broke away from his companions and dashed toward Kaes. "Quick, give me your notebook!" he said. He referred to the diary which contained the particulars of the French authorities at Baden-Baden. Kaes refused to obey. In a moment, the two British officers reached the bench and ordered Kaes to accompany them. "I gave Lecomte the car keys so he could go wherever he wanted," Kaes says. "I found out later he had been ordered out of the British Zone within twenty-four hours."

British M.I.5 intelligence officers now began interrogating Kaes for a week, six hours a day, and then put him in the state prison at Langenfurth. "I was in there without charges," Kaes says bitterly. "The British told me it was for my own protection—apparently they meant from the French. If you ask me, there was no sense in it at all. Besides, they broke the promises they made to me in Baden-Baden." After four weeks, Kaes was transferred to the Federaun Internment Camp outside Villach, twenty miles west of Klagenfurth, where he was kept another sixty days. Then he was released without explanation. By that time, Ferdinand Porsche and Dr. Piëch had been taken to Paris. "Lecomte was behind that,"

Ferry Porsche says. "He probably thought that, if he could get my father to Paris, he might still be able to salvage his French VW scheme. Besides, having my father in France as a prisoner represented cheap labor."

The two men were placed in attic rooms in Louis Renault's villa, where they stayed until the spring of 1947. Periodically, they met French engineers and were consulted on various problems. "My father made no basic alterations in the Renault 4CV car," Ferry says, referring to the many reports that this automobile was redesigned by Porsche while he was in France. "The car existed before he arrived there. My father made some suggestions regarding its faulty weight distribution, but made no important changes." Ferry says that the design of the Renault 4CV had been suggested by a Daimler-Benz engineer during the war, while Renault worked for Daimler-Benz.

In the spring of 1947, Porsche and Piëch were handcuffed and transported to an ancient, unheated dungeon at Dijon. There they remained until the end of July, under circumstances so wretched that they broke the aged Dr. Porsche's health. Their only friend was a German Benedictine priest who visited them in their cells.

Then the French decided the two men could be released on 500,000 francs bail each. Although it was almost impossible for a German to raise that sum before the 1948 currency reform, Ferry Porsche managed it. Freed from Rippoldsau at the end of July 1946, Ferry designed a racing car for Italy's Cisitalia firm to raise the bail money. For this piece of work and others, he received about $62,000, more than enough to cover the bail. Two Frenchmen, Raymond Sommer, the Grand Prix driver, and Charles Faroux, an automotive writer, gave him valuable assistance. While Faroux got food packages to Porsche, Sommer served as middleman between Cisitalia and the French, for Ferry himself could not transfer funds directly. On August 1, 1947, Porsche and Piëch were released. Thus the designer had paid with almost two years of his life for his close association with Adolf Hitler and the National Socialist regime.

It is obvious that Porsche had benefited by the Nazi regime and that his racing cars and Volkswagen brought prestige to the Reich. Yet he had not been a Nazi, perhaps mainly because he was totally absorbed in his work and politically uninterested. Also, he faced the world of politics with great naïveté. He has been criticized for not being "political" enough and for bolstering Nazi prestige indirectly by his continued activity. As Herbert Quint sees it, "Simply because Ferdinand Porsche worked in the Third Reich . . . he gave [it] the opportunity of saying: See here, this man works whole-heartedly for us, with all his strength, this man stands on our side; how can anyone, therefore, have doubts about our state, if such outstanding men like Ferdinand Porsche obviously support it?"

Porsche seemed oblivious to such considerations. Under Hitler, as before, he gathered in honors and medals, always hurrying from the tedious ceremonies back to the drawing board. He worked under Germany's post–World War I Weimar Republic, oblivious to the forces fighting to destroy or preserve it. He turned down Stalin's offer largely because he dreaded homesickness; he did not seem to give a thought to the aggressive and totalitarian nature of the Soviet regime. To Porsche, a state was only a place in which to work and politics concerned him only insofar as they impinged upon that work. While he served the Nazi state, the facts are that Porsche was *not* guilty of war crimes or of involvement in deportations. His record was more than just scrupulously correct; it was humane. He judged a man only by whether he was talented and a hard worker, or whether he produced "manure" and was therefore to be ignored. Porsche seemed temperamentally incapable of accepting Nazi notions about racially superior or racially inferior persons. Despite the fact that it was dangerous for him to do so, he retained Alfred Rosenberger, a Jew, as his foreign sales representative until World War II ended all foreign business. His protection of Kaes during the war and his aid to Peugeot, his directors, and his staff also showed his humanity and courage.

Porsche's tragedy lay in the fact that the world had changed. "Could he, the unpolitical one, grasp what is meant by . . . 'totalitarian state'?" Herbert Quint asks. "Could he grasp the fact that it is impossible to be apolitical in a totalitarian state?" Apparently not. It is perhaps unfortunate that in today's increasingly political world, it is not enough for a man to have lived a good life. Our times demand a political morality as well as a personal one, particularly of the highly placed.

For those who feel he should have been punished, there is the fact of his harsh imprisonment. Baden-Baden, Paris, and Dijon deprived him not only of his freedom but of his health as well. After returning to Austria, Porsche was finally permitted to reenter Germany in 1949. At the end of September 1950, Ferry drove him to the Volkswagenwerk in Wolfsburg, where he spent a day talking with Heinz Nordhoff and technicians about the future development of the car. On the road to Wolfsburg and back, Ferdinand Porsche saw his dream fulfilled: the Autobahnen seemed filled with Volkswagens. Ferry remembers that his father was very much moved. "He had to pull himself together not to start crying," Ferry says. It had, after all, been a long time. There had been so many disappointments, so many short-lived successes.

Shortly after he returned from Wolfsburg, his health collapsed. Circulatory troubles plagued him and he began to sink. Before he died, there were two more occasions to delight him. Although the French never returned Porsche's half-million francs bail, a French court acquitted him of all war-crimes charges. Then, on September 5, 1950, he was honored at a seventy-fifth birthday party given by old friends and acquaintances. Drivers who had played an important role in his racing days attended. The parking lot outside the hall was filled with Volkswagens and Porsches. The old man was elated and his friends joyful. They did not realize that he had so little time to live.

He died on January 30, 1951. His son and daughter called for the Benedictine friar who had tended him at Dijon and it was this priest who read the burial service.

6

Nordhoff and the New Beginning

IN 1948 it would have been hard for anyone to believe that Volkswagen would within a few years become one of the world's largest car manufacturers, after General Motors, Ford, and Chrysler. Before the currency reform launched German recovery, what little life there was in Wolfsburg centered upon the plant's piddling production. Even then, its future remained very much in doubt, for it was still classified as war booty. The car itself seemed a sorry reminder of Nazism to almost everyone. To foreigners and most Germans, it was a shabby product out of a noxious past; to others, it was a galling reminder of Hitler's failure, here as elsewhere.

The two protagonists in the Volkswagen story were both out of the picture. Hitler, who had seized upon Porsche's dreams and designs for his own reasons, was dead. The designer, who had struggled since the early 1920's to see the car born, was an old, sick man in 1948. Who was there now to pick up the pieces of his vision? At that time, there was no one.

Dr. Hermann Münch, the industrial lawyer whom the British had placed in charge of the plant, was not much interested in the car or its future. He did not understand the auto business and presumably cared little for it. His might be called a "caretaker administration" devoted to maintaining jobs; Münch himself was grateful that he had a good job at a time when any work was welcome.

As for the workers at the Volkswagenwerk, only the few who had been there before the war remembered Porsche's dream. The majority were homeless, drifting refugees, living

117

in a ramshackle town and working in a plant which might shut down for good any day. All were waiting, less for someone to take charge than for the economic situation to change.

In 1947 it was the end of an era for the Volkswagen. All connection with the past had been broken and no fresh start seemed likely. The car might still be encumbered with the Nazi image, had it not been for the fact that the KdF-Wagen was such a monumental flop. Though it is hard to conceive, the Volkswagenwerk at Wolfsburg never built a VW production model until after Germany's defeat. The first prototypes and the ones which followed were hand-tooled in Stuttgart. A very few Volkswagens were put together at the Wolfsburg plant during the war for the personal use of Ley, Lafferentz, and other Nazi Party and government officials. But these were made by hand, as it were, outside the course of regular production. The Kübelwagens and Schwimmwagens produced during the war, while modifications of the VW, were not models of the car Porsche had planned for the civilian population and cannot be considered Volkswagens. Hitler at any rate might never have made a success of this car, even if history had given him the chance. Only 336,668 Germans signed up to buy the car from 1938 to 1945, despite the hoopla and pressure which assailed the ears of millions. Most of the sober populace chose to be prudent, for wages were low in Nazi Germany. Hitler would never have put 10 million Germans in KdF-Wagens, as he boasted, nor would he ever have found a market for the 1,500,000 cars his plant was supposed to produce each year.

His arbitrary price of 990 marks could not allow the company to buy new machinery or to expand. The Nazis had plans to obtain such funds by selling the car abroad at a higher price, but these were vague. The factory could have "succeeded" only as part of a socialized economy, and there is reason to believe that many National Socialists considered it a pilot effort of this kind. German free enterprise survived because of the brief life of Hitler's regime; had it lasted longer the State would almost certainly have taken over more and more. Manipulating prices and costs, it might have produced a Volkswagen under socialistic conditions, subsidizing the company for political reasons. Still, there were other basic flaws in the Nazi plan. They expected, for example, to produce 1.5 million VW's with 30,000 workers, yet today's modern, highly automated plant has only recently reached that production figure and has needed more than three times the workers to do so. The fact is, of course, that there is little use in speculating about what

118

might have happened, nor would the car's fate matter any more than the fate of Porsche's Austria model or, for that matter, Ford's Edsel. The Volkswagen is a phenomenon not only because of what it is technically, but also because of what it has become commercially. It is simply not enough to design a great car. That car must be produced in enough numbers to matter and to affect events. It must then be placed in the hands of an organization energetic and imaginative enough to build a worldwide market against enormous odds, and must eventually be entrusted to a global network of salesmen capable of turning it into a success. The man under whom all this was accomplished is Heinz Nordhoff.

He was, in some ways, a most unlikely man to do all this. What previous association he had had with the VW caused him to dislike it. He had been inside one only once before he took the job of building it; after the war, a friend once drove him to a railroad station in a beetle. Yet he had never driven the Volkswagen itself and had never seen the inside of the factory. He was no visionary like Porsche, nor is he likely to be remembered for his technical achievements, though they are many. He is, instead, an American-style industrial manager, placed in charge of a product he at first despised. Today, the press calls him "the master magician of the Volkswagen miracle," yet there is little of the theatrical in Nordhoff's technique. Like sawing a woman in half: once explained, it seems easy.

The success Nordhoff achieved is, of course, apparent to any American used to turnpikes bristling with beetles or to suburban shopping centers aswarm with bugs. It is apparent to any who visit Wolfsburg, a teeming, uncompleted, and heavily damaged village at the war's end, which Nordhoff helped transform into a city exceeding even the youthful dreams of Peter Koller. It is apparent at the sight of the company's other huge German plants in Kassel, Hanover, Brunswick, and Emden, which have, along with the main factory in Wolfsburg, produced 12,000,000 VWs and more, have helped make the beetle the largest-selling single automobile model in the world. There are VW factories in Melbourne, Australia; São Bernardo do Campo, Brazil; and in Uitenhage, South Africa. There is a VW-owned assembly plant in Xalostoc, Mexico, and importer-owned assembly plants are located in Brussels, Belgium; Dublin, Ireland; Manila, Philippines; Caracas, Venezuela; Montevideo, Uruguay; Asunción, Paraguay; and Wellington, New Zealand.

It has been estimated that at least a quarter of a million persons the world over earn their living by building, transport-

119

ing, distributing, selling, servicing, and—yes, also—repairing Volkswagens, and that these 250,000 support as many as 1,000,000 family members. When one adds to this figure of 1,250,000 all the personnel of service and supply organizations who derive at least part of their incomes from orders placed by Volkswagen, and all those whom Volkswagen employees themselves help support through purchases of their own, the figures become impossible to compile—and even impossible to imagine. The economic and social benefits poured forth from a huge undertaking like this are staggering. They not only accrue to company shareholders (and VW today has more of these than any corporation except AT&T), but to entire cities (such as Wolfsburg), for as a company like this spends money to earn money, its contribution to economies the world over is immeasurable and by no means abstract. What an auto industry can mean to a country like Brazil which never had one; what an inexpensive car can mean to a man setting up in a business of his own; what a well-paid job can mean in places where jobs are scarce and well-paid jobs are scarcer—all this is considerable, and its impact is human. The homeowner in Wolfsburg who today enjoys prosperity and security after living in this city when there was hope for neither can perhaps best be understood in the United States by those Americans who suffered through the unemployment of the Great Depression before they ever met the Affluent Society.

The achievement, it has been said, is Nordhoff's, and many who know the company claim it is a "one-man show." Yet this claim of course bears only a limited relation to the truth. What this one man, Heinz Nordhoff, did in fact show was that he knew how to judge other men and attract them to his team. He also had a few tricks up his sleeve, the kind not every industrialist is willing to use. One key trick was integrity, another was a policy of being honest about his car. In an age when many another manufacturer regards potential customers as knuckleheads, those are pretty sneaky weapons. Especially since they worked.

The new era for Volkswagen started at the beginning of 1948 and was launched with an argument. On January 2, Dr. Hermann Münch admitted Heinz Nordhoff to his office, believing that he had come to head production. "No," Nordhoff told him, "I've been put in charge. I'm replacing you."

Münch could not believe his ears and refused to budge. Nordhoff suggested they telephone Colonel Radclyffe, who had given Nordhoff his assignment. Because Münch hesitated, Nordhoff made the call himself. "I told Radclyffe I'd be obliged if he straightened Dr. Münch out, so I could get to work," Nordhoff recalls. Münch then talked to Radclyffe also. After hanging up, he said he still wasn't sure he'd been replaced, because Radclyffe had told him to "iron things out between yourselves." When Nordhoff heard that, he once more called the colonel. "I can't work under these conditions," he said. "Either make a clear-cut decision or count me out!" This time, Radclyffe agreed to tell Münch he was through and Münch left, quite shattered. "It was one of the most painful episodes in my life," Nordhoff told me, "but it was necessary."

Münch was not the only one who did not welcome Nordhoff's arrival; Major Hirst reportedly had his own reservations. Many who knew him believe he may have wished to become head of the Volkswagenwerk himself, as much for love of the car as for reasons of personal advancement, but that Colonel Radclyffe was determined to choose "a good production man." The one he chose was Nordhoff and Hirst may well have resented his authority, though he had played a part in selecting him. Hirst knew a man like Nordhoff was badly needed, for the factory at the end of 1947 had reached a low point, despite the fact that it had produced almost 20,000 Volkswagens since the end of the war. As Hirst points out in his *REME Journal* account, almost every single one of these cars had gone to the Occupation Forces or to individual members of these forces. There could be little future in this, nor was the factory in any way producing at even the capacity it might have attained then, had an experienced automobile executive headed it. Radclyffe, realizing this, searched for one. Nordhoff's name was suggested to him by the Association of Automobile Manufacturers, successor organization of the RDA, which Radclyffe had helped form.

Who was this Nordhoff, whom *Time* described as a "compact (5 ft. 10½ in., 165 lb.) man with the steady eyes of a production whiz and the courtly manners of a diplomat"? The war's end in 1945 found Heinz Nordhoff just another homeless, jobless refugee, one among millions dispossessed by the advance of Communism, scraping along on starvation rations. At forty-six, he was no longer a young man and it seemed to him that his most productive years had passed, for the future looked empty of promise.

He was born on January 6, 1899, the second of three sons of an employee of a small bank in Hildesheim. He was christened Heinrich (later also using its variant, Heinz). In 1910-1911, the bank failed. Johannes Nordhoff and Heinz's mother, Ottilie Lauenstein-Nordhoff, lost every cent they owned. Penniless, they moved to Berlin, where Heinz's father found employment at a small insurance firm and where he worked his way up to become one of the firm's two directors, "through unbelievably hard work," as his son recalls with pride. Heinz was enrolled in a technical high school, for by this time he had already decided on a career in mechanical engineering. At first his interest was in ships, but this shifted later on (though his taste for the sea is still lively and is attested to by ship models in his suite of offices today). Then came World War I. Despite his youth, he served in the Army as a private and was wounded in both knees. On his discharge he went back to school and later to a university. In 1927 he graduated as a certified mechanical engineer from the Berlin-Charlottenburg Technische Hochschule, or technical university.

Upon graduation, Nordhoff worked on airplane designs at BMW, the Bavarian Motor Works (Bayerische Motoren-Werke) and soon developed an even greater interest in automobiles and in the possibility of a future in the growing automobile industry. Looking around, he became increasingly aware of the fact that "there existed an overabundance of technical ideas and construction designs in the automotive field," as one writer puts it. He saw that management seemed to offer the best opportunity for growth and he decided to enter automotive production and sales.

He wrote to the Nash company in the United States and, for a while, it looked as though he might get a job there. Then came the 1929 crash and his hopes were dashed. He was told that there was not even enough work for Americans. Nordhoff looked elsewhere, still convinced that an American company would be the place in which to learn the automobile business. In Germany, the obvious choice was Adam Opel, which had just been acquired by General Motors.

"He was soon confronted—and impressed—by American casualness and fast action," says *Time*. "Appearing for an interview, Nordhoff found his prospective boss in bed with a hangover. When could Nordhoff start work? In a couple of months, said Nordhoff. Said the American: 'Come next week.'"

At the Opel plant in Ruesselsheim, Nordhoff was given the uninspiring job of writing service manuals, but a year later was put in charge of the company's customer service organization, a stepping-off point for management jobs. It is typical of the man that he almost always worked seven days a week and that he spent his vacations on Opel's production line.

The company, spotting him as a comer, sent him to the United States to soak up Detroit marketing and production techniques. "Work was not a duty at Opel," Nordhoff recalls. "It was a sporting event to show what you could do." In this atmosphere, his abilities developed and he was soon "forged into an efficient successful automaker by General Motors," as one reporter put it. In 1936, he became a member of the Opel board of directors and, from this position, took a hard look at Hitler's plans for a Volkswagen. He didn't like what he saw.

Those were not happy days for Adam Opel and his men. The company itself intended to produce a *Kleinauto,* but Hitler was trying to frustrate these plans. The dictator's snub of the venerable Geheimrat von Opel at the Berlin Auto Show was an insult to the boss and a rebuff to the company which Opel management men could not easily overlook. It festered in many of them until it produced, as it did in Heinz Nordhoff, a strong dislike of "that car of Hitler's."

In 1939 Nordhoff was sent to Berlin, and in 1942 he took charge of the company's nearby Brandenburg truck factory, the largest in Europe, which produced four thousand units per month. By that time, of course, the Opel factories had been seized by the Nazi authorities. "Despite bombings, shortages, and personal privation, he produced heavy trucks," wrote Charles Barnard in *True* magazine. "Whatever was going on down at the people's car ranch at Schulenburg's swampy acres, was no concern to him in those days—except as it might be the butt of an automaker's private joke . . ."

Nordhoff took his family with him to the new job in Berlin. In 1930, he had married his childhood sweetheart, Charlotte Fassunge, and in the course of time they had two daughters. (Both are today involved with Volkswagen, each after her own fashion. The elder, Barbara, has worked for VW for several years, now lives in New York City and works in the public relations department of Volkswagen of America, Inc. Her sister, Elisabeth, founded a Porsche-VW-Nordhoff dynasty in 1959, by marrying Ernst Piëch, eldest son of Ferdinand Porsche's daughter Louise Piëch.) Nordhoff worked at Brandenburg until almost the very end of the war.

Nordhoff's wife and daughters had been evacuated from Berlin in 1944 to escape the heavy bombings and were now living in one room of a large hilltop house in the Harz Mountains. As the end of the war drew near, Nordhoff contracted pneumonia and the cellar life which the day-and-night air raids demanded made it worse. He was ordered out of the city to recuperate and joined his family in the Harz.

The last days of the war were approaching when Nordhoff had fully recovered and he was now anxious to return to Berlin. "He didn't want his workers to face the end of the war alone," Barbara Nordhoff says. "He knew there would be chaos there, so he made plans to get back and help as best he could. Mother pleaded with him not to go and he promised to sleep on it. The next morning, he and Mother went for a long walk along the ridge of the mountain. Because he had always hunted, he customarily carried binoculars with him, and did so that day too. While he and Mother were debating his return to Berlin, they saw clouds of dust rising in the distance. Father trained his binoculars on the dust and saw that these were American troops, advancing on the area. Thank God they came, for it meant he couldn't go back to Berlin. They had cut him off. If the troops hadn't come and he had decided to go, he would have had to drive by night with no lights on his car and that would have been very dangerous. He might also have never come back. He probably would have suffered the fate of the other Opel executives who were still in Berlin. They were deported to Russia and have never been heard of since."

From their mountaintop, they watched the battle raging below, as the American troops advanced through the valley and met the German defenders in the hills. "We knew the war was over and thought it was foolish for them to continue fighting," Barbara says, "but it was terrible to see anyway. They were our countrymen, after all, and we were watching them being killed." A short while later, an American unit pulled up in front of the house and a U.S. Army command post was set up in the living room. "Because Father knew American-style English from his years with GM," Barbara recalls, "the American commander invited him down to the living room, where he could watch the progress of the battle on a map spread across a card table. I was twelve years old then and I can remember hearing them talk in a language I didn't understand at all. I was ill at the time, and an American Army doctor looked after me."

Once the battles were over, Heinz Nordhoff made plans to get back to work again. Because his own plant was now in the Soviet Zone of Occupation, he felt he should report for duty at Opel headquarters in Ruesselsheim, near Frankfurt/Main, in the U.S. Zone. He was able to locate a charcoal-powered truck and he and Barbara made the trip west together with a driver. There, he deposited her with friends and returned to the Harz to fetch his wife and other daughter. By the time he reached them, the American troops had left and no one knew to whom the mountain area would fall. (As it turned out, most of the region ended up being assigned to the Soviets.) The trip back to Ruesselsheim was frightening, because they could not be sure which troops were occupying the area. They drove fast and used only back roads so as to avoid a possible encounter with the Soviets. They knew what all of them would face at the hands of Red Army soldiers.

Reunited in Ruesselsheim, all four Nordhoffs lived together in one hotel room, until they were given a small flat and Nordhoff was set to work at Opel. "It was obvious, however, that they were just keeping him busy," Barbara says, "and he was very unhappy. He doesn't like being a fifth wheel." Shortly thereafter, the American occupation authorities charged everyone in their Zone who had served in a supervisory capacity with being a Nazi and Nordhoff was out of a job. Then came an offer from Hamburg and, leaving his family behind so that they would at least be certain of a place in which to live, he traveled north into the British Zone. There the widow of an old friend who owned an Opel dealership had asked him to manage what was left of the business. And so it was that the former general manager of Europe's largest truck factory and the future head of Germany's largest industrial enterprise began work running a small repair shop. He was grateful for the job at that, because just staying alive and providing for a family was a job in itself at the time.

In late 1947, Colonel Radclyffe contacted him and offered him the job of running the Volkswagenwerk. Nordhoff met the colonel in Minden and told him he felt loyal to GM and still expected that he would be called back; he was therefore not interested. Radclyffe, however, insisted he think it over and return for another talk and Nordhoff urged the colonel to cable a friend of Nordhoff's at GM in Detroit, to find out what the chances were of his getting back again.

The day before he returned to meet Radclyffe a second time, Nordhoff received a letter from U.S. Military Government, declaring that persons in Nordhoff's category (former executives) would never be able to work again in the American Zone except as manual laborers. "It was probably a routine announcement," Nordhoff said, "but the coincidence of its arriving the day before I was to meet Radclyffe helped decide my fate."

When Nordhoff arrived at the colonel's office, Radclyffe handed him a letter from Detroit. It was evasive and Nordhoff felt certain he could never go back to GM. When he got through reading it, he tossed over the letter he had received from U.S. Military Government and he and Radclyffe had a good laugh. "Well, I'm ready," Nordhoff said. Radclyffe asked him whether there were any conditions he wanted to set.

"I have only one," Heinz Nordhoff answered. "I want no interference from any side."

"Does that mean the British as well?" Radclyffe asked.

"It means the British first of all!" Nordhoff answered.

"All right," Colonel Radclyffe replied. "You have a free hand."

During Christmas week, 1947, Frank Novotny of the Press Department at the "Wolfsburg Motor Works" received a telephone call at his home from Dr. Münch. "Herr Nordhoff is in my office," Münch said. "Would you please come down and tell him some things about the factory?" Münch sent over his car and Novotny was driven to his first encounter with Nordhoff. They talked about an hour and Nordhoff asked countless questions about the people at the plant and about the factory itself. "All this time, Münch said nothing," Novotny reports. "But I don't think he was worried about being thrown out, because he was not only general manager but also the German trustee for the plant and he expected to continue at least in the latter capacity." (Aside from Münch, the trustees were all British. At Nordhoff's later insistence, trustees lost their authority and, eventually, the trustee system was abolished entirely.)

The bushy-browed, portly and short executive whom Heinz Nordhoff was meeting for the first time that day was one of several of those there already who would later play key roles in the development of the company. Julius Paulsen, who has headed purchasing at the factory ever since 1943, was then desperately, ingeniously, and ultimately successfully, searching for materials to buy for the plant. Hans Hiemenz, who had joined VW in 1940 and who had been in charge of finances since 1942, was also there at the time, playing another vital part in the company's lean "British years." It was his task to reestablish the company's credit and financial standing at a time when no one knew who owned the plant or even how long it might remain functioning. Otto Hoehne and Joseph Werner of the "German-American contingent" were there also, of course. Two others who played major roles in the immediate postwar years and who were to play even larger roles under Heinz Nordhoff's management were the late Dr. Karl Feuereissen, who headed Volkswagen sales and service until he died (at work) in June 1955, and Wilhelm Steinmeier, now retired, who in those years was Otto Hoehne's boss, in charge of production at the Wolfsburg plant. It was in 1946 that Steinmeier received a letter from the British, asking him whether he might be interested in heading production at the Volkswagenwerk; he thought it over for a month and then accepted, "never thinking I'd remain so long with VW," he later said. "The conditions under which we worked were unbelievable," he reports. "The worst thing of course was this shortage of materials. We could get them only through barter and Julius Paulsen even had it figured out that one car was worth a four weeks' supply of steel." Steinmeier later rose to deputy general manager (*stellvertretenden Geschäftsleiter*) of the company and retired at the start of 1962, when he reached the age of seventy. By that time, Otto Hoehne had already succeeded him as production chief.

The achievement of Dr. Karl Feuereissen defies a brief description, for the "Volkswagen miracle" that took place in the Nordhoff era resulted in large part from the efforts of this singular and dedicated man. He provided the "missing link" in the corporation, for while the car and a factory which could be repaired and modernized did exist at the war's end, the Volkswagenwerk had not a single dealer anywhere. It had no sales or service organization, within Germany or outside it; no parts depots or policies; no shipping or transportation facilities. The factory could manufacture cars, but there was no one to get these to customers, nor anyone to sell, service, or repair the cars once they had been bought. Setting up a worldwide network from absolute scratch was Feuereissen's job. He brought to it a passionate and lifelong interest in motor vehicles, derived from an association with the industry which dated to 1924, when he took charge of sporting activities for the German motorcycle drivers' association of the time. This led to a post with the German Automobile Club, the ADAC, and in time brought him to the attention of Baron K. D. von Oertzen of Auto-Union, who had met him at races throughout Europe. In 1935, von Oertzen offered Feuereissen, then thirty-eight years old, the job of running an Auto-Union racing team—a job which led to Feuereissen's close and abiding friendship with the top aces of the era, as well as with the designer of Auto-Union's racing cars, Ferdinand Porsche. Feuereissen, who had been a flight lieutenant in World War I, served a hitch as a major with the Luftwaffe during World War II, but in 1944 he was released, at Porsche's request, to serve VW at its offices in Berlin. It was there that the end of the war caught him and, after a time as a farm laborer in East Germany, Feuereissen joined the millions of refugees streaming west. It was only natural that he head for Wolfsburg and, once there, go immediately to work. It did not bother him that there seemed to be no future here; Feuereissen had been reared to believe that work for its own sake was enough. He set himself up in a tiny office made of cardboard walls, in the large hall which is now the lunchroom of the factory's Sector I, and began to plan marketing strategy. What ultimately came out of this workshop was an incredible worldwide organization which today encompasses more than 2000 VW service facilities within West Germany and about 6000 outside it, and which today has made the Volkswagenwerk the largest exporter of motor vehicles anywhere in the world. It was also Feuereissen's task to begin VW advertising, sales promotion, product publicity, and merchandising; it was he who helped give VW the distinct "style" for which it has since become known. When he was laid to rest in Wolfsburg's Forest Cemetery, his funeral was attended by thousands from near and far away who had either known him for a decade in Wolfsburg or for twenty or more years in the industry. The loss to the company was severe. Expressing his own shock and dismay at the sudden, unexpected death of the fifty-eight-year-old executive, Nordhoff said, "It will be a long time before I know for certain that I can't any longer find my way out of a difficult situation by saying, 'I'll have to talk this one over with Feuereissen . . .' "

Of these early veterans, some deceased, some retired, many still very much on the job at VW, Hiemenz, Hoehne, Novotny, and Paulsen are today members of the company Vorstand. All of them and, indeed, all of the others who lived through those early years have sagas of frustration and achievement of their own to tell, for World War II and the immediate postwar years shaped turbulent destinies even for those who might have preferred tranquillity. It is impossible here to tell even a representative sampling of such stories, but one brief personal account in any case requires recounting, for in its own way it mirrors the chaos of the 1945–1948 period, as well as helping to introduce the new era about to begin. It concerns Frank Novotny, the man who met with Heinz Nordhoff at Christmastime, 1947, in Dr. Münch's office. Novotny is today in charge of a host of activities at the company, running not only public relations but community, governmental, and industrial relations as well. "He is the kind of a man who always lands on his feet," one reporter remarked, and what must have attracted Heinz Nordhoff early to this executive is a

128

certain "American style" he has about him, a way of doing business with which Nordhoff had become familiar at GM's Opel. One VW executive explains it this way: "When Nordhoff took over, he met a lot of people at the plant who were completely dispirited. The ones to whom he gravitated were, naturally, those who had not let the times destroy them. Novotny was one of these. He got things done."

Just how enterprising he proved himself may be seen from events in his life immediately after the war's end. 1945 found him and his wife in their home town of Prague; there and in Vienna, Novotny had a prospering export-import business of his own. As the Russians approached the city, Novotny sent his wife west, to the very Harz Mountains where Nordhoff and his own family were waiting out the end of the war. Mrs. Novotny arrived at nearby Fallersleben an hour before the American Army rolled in and never did get to the mountain retreat. Instead, she settled in Wolfsburg.

Frank Novotny stayed on in Czechoslovakia for two months after the Soviets entered Prague and then set out for Blankenburg in the Harz Mountains, where he expected to find his wife. There a friend told him she had heard his wife had gone to Wolfsburg, and Novotny set out in his car once more. He reached a narrow river and found the Russians on his side of the bridge, letting no one cross, and American soldiers on the far end. Novotny thought fast and reached into his wallet, pulling out a wrinkled honorary press card he had been given on a 1933 visit to Chicago and which he had kept more or less as a souvenir ever since. He called out to the Americans that he was a war correspondent whom the Russians were trying to detain and one of the GI's responded by crossing the river to look at Novotny's card. "Oh, you're from Chicago," the soldier said. "You're a gangster!"

"I certainly am!" Novotny answered in English. The reply seemed to satisfy the soldier that Novotny really did come from Chicago and he persuaded the Russians to let him pass and cross the river.

The wrinkled old press credentials saved the day for Novotny several more times before he reached Wolfsburg and on one occasion provided him with fuel for his car. Novotny had flashed his card to some British soldiers and told them he was an American correspondent trying to do a story about a nearby Nazi concentration camp. The British unit gassed up his car and the soldiers waved him on. Finally, Novotny arrived in Wolfsburg. It was summmer of 1945 and Novotny surveyed the scene to determine how an enterprising man could make a living there.

As it turned out, his knowledge of English proved invaluable. On one occasion, he saved a farmer from being executed by the British for possessing two guns, and out of gratitude the farmer allowed Novotny unlimited amounts of foodstuffs. After a while, Novotny had established himself with the British as a sort of counsel and negotiator for farmers throughout the area who needed to deal with the Occupation Forces.

Strolling in the woods or walking the streets of Wolfsburg, he used to encounter Dr. Münch frequently, and before long the two men began to pass the time of day. "Münch often complained that newspapers were attacking the VW," Novotny reports, "and when he brought the subject up again one day in 1946, I asked whether he didn't have someone who provided the newspapers with information and in general handled press relations." Münch remarked that he didn't have such a person on the staff, and after a while, he asked if Novotny might like to take the job.

Four weeks after this conversation, Novotny wrote the words "Press Bureau" on a piece of paper and put it up outside his new office door in the VW factory. About an hour later, Major Hirst came by and said that he had noticed the sign. "You ought to change the wording to read 'Public Relations,' " Hirst suggested. The paper was removed, reworded, and put up again. It is a safe bet that this scrap of paper made the Volkswagenwerk the first postwar German factory to have a public relations department of its own. It is today also the only German enterprise of major consequence to have a public relations executive on its Vorstand.

Novotny, who had been prosperous in Czechoslovakia, now told Münch that he wanted 2000 marks a month in pay, which caused some consternation, as the highest salary in the plant at the time was 1000 marks. Novotny thereupon agreed to work for nothing until they could agree on what his work would be. "I'd been doing all right and didn't need the money," he explains. "I worked from June to December 1946 for nothing, but after everyone there insisted I had to be paid, we finally settled on 850 marks a month, retroactive to the time I started."

The times are mirrored also in the experiences of Joseph Werner, who until the war's end headed chassis, motor, and transmission production at the VW factory. He had left Wolfsburg by 1948—for good, he thought. At the end of the war, he had gone to Austria to work with Ferdinand Porsche and had returned to Wolfsburg's chaotic conditions some time later. But the nearby Russians constantly harassed the town and the atmosphere was charged with tension and fear. Wing Commander Berryman reports that all the British officers in 1945 and 1946 kept cars constantly gassed up and waiting outside whatever building they might be at, ready to jump in and get out if the Russians decided to take over the city. Werner, like the British, also had a car at the ready. Finally, he and his wife had enough of the uncertain atmosphere and left, hoping to get to the United States, but an American consul in Munich told them they had no chance at all. The outer office was jammed with displaced persons and Jewish refugees. "They come first," the consul said. Then, one day in 1947, while Werner was sitting on a bench in Munich, passing time, two British officers pulled up in a Volkswagen and asked him to return. After thinking it over for a while, he decided to go back after all. He and his wife had been living off CARE packages sent by friends in America; these contained cigarettes which, at the time, could buy almost anything. But he was anxious to find work again. Since 1959, he has headed the company's transporter and engine works in Hanover.

"I had never even heard of Nordhoff before he started on the job," Werner says, "but I remember being impressed with him during those first days, watching him as he walked around the plant and talked to the workers. He was encouraging them —one might say appealing to them—to stay on the job. I don't know whether he really believed in the Volkswagen's future at the time, but he sounded convincing."

Nordhoff did more than come to work: he moved in, bag and baggage. For six months, he lived inside the factory, separated from his family. He slept on a cot in a room near his office. At night, he says, he "was kept awake by the sound of rats racing through the empty plant searching for scraps of food." He was not living in the factory because of dedication, he says, but simply because no suitable quarters were available in town. Still, his night-and-day presence at the plant had a psychological effect on the largely demoralized work force.

"I had to start from scratch in the real sense of the word," Nordhoff has said. "Seven thousand workers were painfully producing at the rate of a mere 6000 cars a year—provided it did not rain too much. Most of the roof and all the windows of the factory had been destroyed. Pools of stagnant water were under foot . . .

"When I came to Wolfsburg, I was as poor as a church-mouse . . . I was hungry too, and about 60 pounds under my present weight. All the people I met in the factory were not only as poor and hungry as myself, they were desperate and without hope. Nobody belonged to Wolfsburg . . . and what remained was only a torso, abandoned after its founder had proved to be the greatest flop in our history and a criminal in every sense of the word . . .

"It was really an overwhelming undertaking to make these people believe in their future at a time when one Chesterfield cigarette had three times the value in buying power of one hour of hard work. They had to be convinced that there was a future which could be won only by themselves. It could be won only by the hard work of creating something of value."

The size of the job Nordhoff faced in reassuring the workers can be seen from the way today's production chief, Otto Hoehne, describes the times. "There were many days on which I came to work with shaky knees and an empty stomach," he says. "And at the end of the day, my knees would be even shakier and my stomach emptier. That winter the assembly line workers stood in water up over their ankles when it rained. Some of them had to work outside and were protected only by a makeshift sheet-metal 'roof.' We had to keep fires burning near the machines so the hydraulic fluid wouldn't freeze."

On one of his very first days on the job, Heinz Nordhoff showed Frank Novotny a speech he wanted to deliver over the plant's public address system. It was largely political and fiercely anti-Nazi; clearly Nordhoff wanted to get a lot of sentiments off his chest. Novotny, however, talked him out of it. No matter how much he agreed with Nordhoff, he was convinced that a pep talk would be better because, after all, some of the workers might well resent a political talk like that. Nordhoff acquiesced. He admitted he was more interested in winning over the workers than in lecturing them about the past.

"His arrival had a tremendous impact," recalls Guenter Hellman, later Volkswagen parts manager for Canada, who started out in Wolfsburg in 1945. "Everybody was in a rut before Nordhoff came. We had no food or materials to speak of and no one had any real idea where we were heading. When Nordhoff came and took charge, he just quietly got everything moving. It wasn't anything specific that he did which changed the atmosphere. You just felt his presence, felt he was there and had taken firm command."

"One of the first things Nordhoff did," says Otto Hoehne,

"was to survey world markets and plan a global service organization. No one had even thought that way before!"

Not only was a service organization being built, but a sales organization was being developed as well. Nordhoff—"a great organizer," as Novotny describes him—set up a table of organization and assigned duties all around. The production department, the finance department and the personnel department were formalized and the latter was charged as much with finding food for the workers as with finding the workers themselves. A purchasing department was represented on the board and Nordhoff insisted immediately upon an inspection department as well, showing that he meant business about quality production even then.

Despite all the activity, Nordhoff himself felt too little was being done. "After two months, I knew things could not continue this way," he says. "There was an air of desperation and confusion. No one even knew how many hours it took to build a car, but it must have been 300 or 400."

He decided to be brutally frank to the workers and had them all assemble in one of the large halls of the plant.

"He spoke," says *Der Spiegel*, "in a dry, even, effortless tone. But his sentences were honed to a sharp, ironic point. He did not rely on gestures or grimaces. Even as his eyes swept round the hall, they seemed to rest on an imaginary point. A self-confident, somewhat malicious smile tugged down the corners of his mouth whenever he paused."

Nordhoff addressed the workers as partners in the enterprise. The approach was realistic and not patronizing, for Nordhoff and his workers *were* in fact "partners." Nordhoff represented neither stockholders nor a board of directors, for the company's status had not been clarified at the time and it literally belonged to no one. The only interest to be served, therefore, was that of the work force. Nordhoff felt himself part of that. He had no contract, no assured future. In every way, he and his workers were in the same position. And so, he felt, he could afford to be frank and tough.

"For the first time in its history," he told them, "the Volkswagenwerk will this year have to face the necessity of standing on its own feet. It is up to us to make this largest of all German automobile factories a decisive factor for Germany's peacetime economy."

He then discussed how he proposed to go about doing this. He pointed out that it now took the workers as much as four hundred hours of labor to produce a car. "If we continue in

133

this manner, we shall not continue for long," he said. "We must reach one hundred hours per car!"

A muffled groan swept through the ranks of workers, followed by laughter. "They all thought I was crazy," Nordhoff says, "but they began working harder."

That speech helped change the climate. The workers could see that they finally had a boss who knew the auto business. "Somehow," said one who remembers the period, "you could feel Nordhoff's presence almost at once. There was a new spirit that was contagious. I had worked here under Dr. Münch. Whenever one of the British officers wanted to talk with Münch, he would say, 'Go tell Münch I want to see him in my office.' And I would deliver the message and Münch would hurry over to get his orders. In those days, any young British lieutenant was more important around here than Münch. There was a picture of the King of England in every office. Then, when Nordhoff came, it changed. I remember the day when Major Hirst said to me, 'Go tell Nordhoff I want to see him . . . no, never mind, I'll go to his office myself . . .'"

There was other evidence of the newly independent spirit. Nordhoff had two signs removed: one on a parking lot which said, "For British Officers Only," and another, outside the plant, which said, in English, "Wolfsburg Motor Works." He replaced the latter with a German sign: VOLKSWAGENWERK. The significance of this act was not lost on his workers.

Nordhoff recalls that he changed those signs on his very first day in the job or immediately afterwards. "A friend had driven me to the Volkswagen factory on my first day," Nordhoff says, "but he refused to drive me further than the canal. The factory grounds were in such bad shape that he was afraid his car would never survive if he tried to drive me all the way to the headquarters building. I remember thinking when I first saw the factory that it looked just as it must have looked after the last bomb had exploded in it; then, on the way in, I saw those British signs and made a mental note to have them taken down. Later, when I asked my secretary to have that done, several people were afraid I would bring down the wrath of the British on us, but as it turned out, they let it pass without comment."

It might be noted in this connection that signs reading "Volkswagenwerk" were unlikely to outrage the British, for they themselves employed the designation "Volkswagenwerk GmbH" in official correspondence, using it either interchangeably with or in addition to their own "Wolfsburg Motor

Works." Volkswagenwerk GmbH, incidentally, was the name of the company which had been set up to manufacture the KdF-Wagen before the war, and it continued on as the name of the postwar company until public ownership transformed that into a corporation with the name of Volkswagenwerk AG.* Nordhoff himself provides the background for the story regarding Major Hirst's summons to the new company general manager. On the day he took command, he says, Nordhoff received a telephone call from Major Hirst. "He asked me to come to his office," Nordhoff recalls, "and I knew then that this was the crucial moment for me to show I was in charge and was not to be marched about. So I told Major Hirst that I was busy just then, but that he could come to see me in *my* office at eleven o'clock. When he agreed, I knew I was truly in command here."

Now Nordhoff also was beginning to have some hope. Soon after he came to the plant, he test-drove the VW for the first time. "The 'repulsive Porsche-Invention' . . . was not just another small car," he discovered. "It had definite features which were greatly desirable and not found in cars of comparable size." The Volkswagen he had despised now seemed to him "an extraordinarily amazing automobile with a special personality [and] unlimited possibilities." With this realization came a new enthusiasm for the job. By the end of 1950, he would be able to say with less braggadocio than

* A word about German corporate terminology may be helpful. The initials *GmbH* stand for *Gesellschaft mit beschränkter Haftung* or "limited liability company," while *AG* stands for *Aktiengesellschaft* (literally "stock company"), or a corporation owned by shareholders. Two other German terms, employed in all "AG" corporations such as today's Volkswagenwerk, require explanation. One is *Aufsichtsrat* and the other *Vorstand*. The former corresponds to a board of directors more or less as it is known in the U.S.; it is two-thirds composed of shareholder representatives (including in VW's case the Federal Republic of Germany and the *Land*, or state, of Lower Saxony) and one-third of labor. The Vorstand, with whose members we are here more concerned, is referred to often as a "board of management," but perhaps may better be compared to a corporate "executive committee." The head of the corporation serves as the Vorstand chairman and the various Vorstand members are either in charge of departments or divisions of the enterprise, or have sundry other responsibilities. Membership in this executive committee introduces an executive into a corporation's top ranks and the title he has is that of *Vorstandsmitglied*, or Vorstand member, German corporations having neither "presidents" nor "vice presidents." (The title *Prokurist* is the nearest comparable one to a vice presidency in an American corporation, for it signifies an officer who can act in the name of the corporation. A member of the Vorstand, while he is of course an officer also, abandons use of any Prokurist title he may have had, once he reaches executive committee rank.)

confidence, "It is my life's aim to make this plant into the greatest car factory in Europe!"

With pride, he reminisces: "This was a time of political extremists and gangsters, but it was also a time when faith, and willingness, through hard work, to build rather than destroy, made possible the miracle that is Wolfsburg. In this respect, the job of reinstalling hope and confidence in the hearts of a desperate people was a much more difficult task than getting a line of presses back in operation. But somebody had to show them the way, and that I did."

Yet there was—in addition to the countless other difficulties —one more factor beyond his control which he had to face. In 1948, a little more than two months after Nordhoff took charge, the British decided to make one last attempt to give the plant away, this time to Henry Ford II.

The meeting with Ford and his executives, still keenly remembered by Nordhoff, took place in an "Allies-only" hotel in Cologne in March 1948, and he recalls needing special authorization to attend. Breech's evaluation of the plant as "not worth a damn" saved the day.

One other incident is worth recording in connection with attempts to give the Volkswagenwerk away. In mid-1948, the Soviets expressed their "willingness" to take the Volkswagenwerk off the hands of the British authorities. By this time, however, the British were planning to turn the company over to the West German authorities, who were forming a central government for British, French, and American Zones of Occupation. (The formal transfer occurred on October 8, 1949.) Relations between the Western powers and the Soviets had already cooled drastically, and the Berlin Blockade had begun in June. Despite this, the Soviets offered a plan whereby they could take the factory over "conveniently." Since Wolfsburg lies just five miles west of the Soviet Zone border, the Russians suggested that the boundary be shifted just this small distance so as to place both plant and town inside East Germany. The offer was firmly declined. Town and factory would remain in the Free World. Now Nordhoff could really get to work.

7

The Years of Fulfillment

GERMANY was beginning to stir again. The changed climate of the Cold War forced the Western Allies to reassess their policies toward the vanquished foe. Military government retreated into the background or changed to mufti. Germans began to rule themselves again. The nation's industry, flattened more by defeat than by wartime bombings, once more was set into motion.

"The year 1948," says the Bonn government, "will be recorded in German history as the pivotal point in the postwar economy of the present Federal Republic. Two almost simultaneous developments served to lift the economy out of the morass . . . the currency report of June 20 and the advent of American Marshall Plan aid." Eventually, this aid was to total 3.5 billion dollars.

Overnight, 170 billion Reichsmarks in banks and in circulation shriveled to about 10 billion new Deutsche marks (or "D-marks"). Combined with the U.S. aid, the new hard currency stabilized the economy and provided it with a basis for growth. A free-enterprise economy was established, and Heinz Nordhoff believes it was this lifting of restrictions on industry that was even more responsible for the subsequent growth of the West German economy than was the currency reform itself. "We never asked for Marshall Plan aid," he says, "because we felt we didn't need it. We were, however, indirect beneficiaries of the aid, for many of our suppliers received it and were thereby able to raise the quality of the products they sold us."

The psychological boost which the lifting of restrictions provided started business of all kinds moving again. Germans with things to sell—farmers at first, manufacturers later—did so, sure of the value of the new paper money, which was pegged at 4.20 to the dollar.* Shops which had remained empty for years now began to fill up again. The cigarette-economy was snuffed out. It finally made sense again to manufacture. For the Volkswagenwerk, the times meant than an attempt could now be made to sell to Germans and not just to produce for the occupation forces. For Nordhoff, it meant that he might actually have a business to run, not just a factory.

Ultimately, Major Hirst left Wolfsburg altogether and the remaining British moved out slowly thereafter, unit by unit. "After a few months," says Heinz Nordhoff, "I had the place to myself."

And what a place it was! The factory buildings were a shambles; the turnover of workers was almost as great as in 1946 (and it was 100 per cent then); the makeshift town would have to be built if Nordhoff were ever to attract—and hold—competent help; the company had no dealers, no salesmen, no sales organization—virtually nothing. Worst of all, there was no cash.

Amazingly, there was also no cost-accounting system. Under Dr. Münch, the plant had no accurate idea of what it cost to produce a Volkswagen—and, indeed, the cost of one sedan often had little relation to the cost of the next. Nordhoff quickly corrected this basic flaw in the system.

He needed money to do the rest. He had no one to turn to and no foreign country helped him. The German government, as he remarked later, didn't even notice the Volkswagenwerk until it found to its surprise that VW had become the biggest taxpayer in the state of Lower Saxony. Bankers remained as horrified of the VW as they had been whenever Ferdinand Porsche talked to them of a "people's car."

Nordhoff tried to introduce the VW in the United States in order to raise hard currency. An emissary came to the States in 1948; Nordhoff himself followed in 1949. When both attempts failed, he realized that "we would have to make our own way in the world without a source of American dollars."†

The week of the currency reform proved critical for the company. The change had cut Volkswagenwerk's cash on hand to 62,000 of the new marks. "Our 7000 workers needed between 300,000 and 500,000 DM to be paid," Nordhoff says, "and we had only five days in which to raise that sum." He

* As of September 1949; it stands today at just about 4 to the dollar.
† For this visit and the story of VW's growth in the U.S.A., see Chapters 8–10.

did not want to ask his workers to wait two weeks until sales supplied the new funds; he felt it was essential they be paid on time, or they might lose what faith they had in the new currency. He telephoned some of the dealers and distributors who had already been appointed by Dr. Feuereissen and asked them for a short-term loan, to be repaid in two weeks. The day before payday, they arrived, cash in hand. One of them, company historians recall, showed up with a suitcase full of money, which popped open upon arrival. "Notes to the value of 175,000 D-mark [about $43,000] were blown merrily over the place—an enormous fortune, a rare sight indeed," reported *VW Informationen,* a company magazine. "Even Croesus would not have caused more excitement . . ."

By late 1948 the Volkswagenwerk had established the beginnings of a good distributor-and-dealer organization. It was the only German automobile manufacturing company to be functioning this soon after the end of the war; its "head start" enabled it to sign up many automobile dealers who earlier had handled other makes. Some, like those who had handled the now-defunct Adler, were looking for another car to sell; others, such as BMW and Auto-Union dealers, were also ready then to sign up with VW. Now that people had hard currency with which to buy, they began to sell.

Gradually, cash reserves grew. This was quickly followed by a demand for higher wages. Faced with this demand—which he feared would jeopardize the company's growing financial strength—Nordhoff in 1949 decided again to talk tough and be frank with his workers.

"If we kill the cow on whose milk we want to live later, just because it has fattened up a little—as we are advised to do by those who want to make the people happy—then we shall have no future, we shall go to the dogs, the whole lot of us, and our grandchildren will curse us because we did not think of them."

He instituted a policy—which continues—of reporting completely and regularly to his entire work-force. It was, and remains, an unusual policy for Germany—and, indeed, for industry in general. It seemed to Nordhoff an essential one, however, if he were to obtain his workers' full cooperation, even to the extent of having them voluntarily defer requests for wage increases. He addresses his "fellow workers" (as he calls them) every three months and circulates bulletins to them as well. Orally and on paper, he spells out the company's financial position and its prospects in plain language and blunt words. The news has happily been good ever since he started his quarterly meetings, but the honesty of the approach also tided the company over the first difficult years of extreme hardship.

Despite the austerity and the poor living conditions many of the workers had to endure in those years, morale at the plant was high, for pride in workmanship had begun. The atmosphere is recalled today by Guenther Kittel, VW parts manager in the U.S.A., who then worked in Wolfsburg as a packer in the parts department. "The workers took a real pride in the idea of helping the words 'Made in Germany' stand for top craftsmanship once again," he says, "and the strict and rigid inspection procedure initiated in those years helped give them this feeling. There was also pride in working in this plant, because Volkswagenwerk paid higher wages than anyone else in manufacturing in West Germany, and jobs in Wolfsburg were at a premium at the time." A freeze had been put on employment in order to keep costs down, because money was needed for reinvestment purposes. Heinz Nordhoff notes with pride that, prior to the stock issue of 1960, Volkswagen earned every pfennig of its own money through reinvestments and sales. The same policy of reinvesting earnings, it should be noted, was followed in other segments of German industry and contributed in great part to the German "economic miracle."

In the ten years following 1948, the country's gross national product and level of industrial production rose sharply, surpassing 1936 levels; by 1958, West Germany's aggregate G.N.P. stood 77 per cent higher than in 1936 and manufactured goods 116 per cent higher. This was achieved by a nationwide practice of each year reinvesting 23 to 25 per cent of the G.N.P. into maintenance and expansion of plant and equipment.

The future which Nordhoff saw in those early years seemed implausible to many at the plant. The immediate present loomed large; the problem of providing food for the workers and of setting the plant in order seemed the biggest immediate concern to the average worker. Cash, now available through the modest start in sales, made an effort in both directions possible. Nordhoff opened up kitchens and provided his workers with one meal a day, a meal that may well have been the most nourishing one of the day for them. Factory farms, beside the plant buildings, cash purchases, and cars bartered for food, helped make this possible. Hungry men, Nordhoff knew, could not do much of anything.

As money trickled in, the factory was repaired and enlarged. More than three million square feet of plants and offices were rebuilt; another four hundred thousand square feet of factory space were created after Nordhoff reshuffled machinery and placed the huge assembly line under one roof, where it belonged from the very start. He was beginning to reconstruct the plant along the "American" lines envisioned by Ferdinand Porsche, for he, like the designer, had been on pilgrimages to Detroit.

At the end of 1948, so much was still destroyed in West Germany that a German magazine felt called upon to cheer its readers with the unexpected news emerging from Wolfsburg.

"So much now lies in ruins and ashes," the *Stern* said, "but the Volkswagen factory is still standing. What is more important, however, about 8000 men are working again. On the average, a new Volkswagen leaves the conveyor belt once every three and a half minutes."*

The editors pointed out that "skeptics" regard the VW as the private property of the "Occupying Powers"; but said that "readers will be astonished to hear that [their] current requirements . . . are comparatively small." During the three months from September to November 1948, only 300 VW's went to the occupation authorities, while 2154 Volkswagens were produced in October alone. Of these, 1270 were sold to Germans and the rest were exported. "At the moment," *Stern* added, "there is a waiting list of 15,000 for Volkswagens in Germany. And about 7000 export orders are outstanding."

Publications issued by the Volkswagenwerk reflect the company's attitude toward its past. While they refer to these days as a time "of almost forgotten sorrows," those times, nevertheless, lent a romance to the company's resurgence which today's prosperity cannot supply. There is in these almost nostalgic references the same note so often struck in histories of American towns and industrial enterprises: the note of pride in the early and then-hated hardships, the wistful backward glance at a pioneering atmosphere, the blushing acknowledgment of an early, embarrassing poverty. Indeed, many newsmen referred to Wolfsburg in those days as having a "gold rush" atmosphere. The company says they did so unkindly, to denigrate the town and its factory, but it is clear in retrospect that they may have been right. There was in Wolfsburg in those years, along with the makeshift buildings and mud

* Contrasted with one every eight seconds today (calculated at actual working time, that is, two shifts during a five-day week).

141

streets, a sense of great things about to happen, an awareness that any day now the town might hit pay dirt.

Writing about the city in 1961, the company (a real town booster) contrasted its 300 lampposts with 1948, when "there were only 20 along the concrete road which terminated abruptly and became meadows and fields." In those days, a Wolfsburg bus passenger was wise to take along an umbrella, "since the cardboard roof could not stand up to the continuous rain." Then, too, there were only two and a half miles of "tenth-rate" road.

"The huge pot-holes made every trip an endurance test for drivers . . . the workshop proprietors would rub their hands in glee at the number of cars that would turn up damaged. From 1952 onwards, drivers were spared these horrors, for the Braunschweiger Strasse was completed." (To mark that occasion, the town bought the road gang and the guests of honor each a cigar and a glass of beer.)

Across the Mittelland Canal, the factory recovered slowly. It was "about as efficient at producing cars as a starving man would be at his job," the company notes. Cars were being manufactured at the miserable rate of 78 a day. They were transported out of the plant by "two old wheezy low-powered diesel locomotives built long before the war," together with "second-hand track of rather doubtful quality." Signals wouldn't work, and whatever did had to be worked by hand.

Nevertheless, production chief Steinmeier managed to coax 19,244 Volkswagens out of the plant by the end of 1948. It wasn't much, but it was ten thousand more than the previous year and clearly the beginning of an uphill climb. When the year-end figures were announced, workers began to realize that the plant might after all have a real future with this new man Nordhoff around.

"Gradually, painfully," Charles Barnard writes, "like a man with no credit rating and nobody to borrow from, Nordhoff earned his own working capital by selling cars; he bought the machinery he needed—and even set aside a little money . . . as a sort of 'pretend dividend.' In this period, Nordhoff ruled Volkswagen with such an iron hand that he was often called autocratic and dictatorial; money men were critical that Nordhoff made all his decisions in 'splendid isolation' and that even his *opinions* represented final authority in Wolfsburg. To the bankers and other critics Nordhoff snapped a reply: 'When we began, without any capital, to build the first cars here, and we needed help urgently, no one—no country or bank—as much as lifted a finger.' "

If Nordhoff was an autocrat then, it seems today that an autocrat was just what this sick auto company needed. "When I assumed the responsibility of putting this wrecked factory into high volume production," Nordhoff says, "the car itself was still 'full of bugs.' It was really what you call an 'ugly duckling.' As usual, I had the dubious benefit of a great many well-intentioned advisers."

The Volkswagen of those days, he says, was noisy and badly sprung; its upholstery and paint job left much to be desired, and the life of its engine was short. The pressure Nordhoff underwent to abandon the design was terrific, as he and several of his executives recall. It came from everywhere and continued for years; it originated from within the Volkswagenwerk's own ranks and from outside them. One Swiss dealer, for example, warned Nordhoff in the early 1950's that he would not be able to keep on selling this same model, year after year, in a country as sophisticated about cars as Switzerland, and he placed great pressure on Nordhoff to redesign the car.

In most cases, those demanding changes demanded only "sheet-metal changes," not fundamental improvements within the car itself. Yet tests had shown that the slightest sheet-metal change affected the fundamental design radically and raised costs sharply. In one such test, for example, the hood was reshaped slightly to allow for more luggage room; the result was that the redesigned VW now needed more horsepower to maintain a given cruising speed. It became ever more apparent that Porsche's bug-shape design had been carefully worked out to call for the very minimum of sheet metal, thus guaranteeing low cost. It further became apparent that changing the outside would have made the car appear grotesque on its present chassis.

Nordhoff resisted all the pressure and rejected all the "advice." He, too, wanted to improve the car—but only "organically," from the inside out, without touching the basically sound Porsche design. "First of all," he recalls, "I wanted to obtain better-quality materials to put inside the car, specifically for the engine, so as to keep it from breaking down so early." At the time, Nordhoff was offering a gold watch and sending a personal letter of congratulations to any VW owner who had driven his car 100,000 kilometers (62,000 miles) with no more than routine maintenance. This policy has had to be discontinued, because that number of miles is no longer an achievement of note for a VW, thanks largely to the fact

143

that Nordhoff in those early years had stood firm against the crowd which wanted outer changes first.

"Perhaps I was too busy to listen," he says, "and in any case, I myself knew exactly what to do. . . . I brushed away all temptation to change model and design. In any sound design there are almost unlimited possibilities—and this certainly was a sound one. I see no sense in starting anew every few years with the same teething troubles, making obsolete almost all the past . . . Offering people an honest value, a product of the highest quality, with low original cost and incomparable resale value, appealed more to me than being driven around by a bunch of hysterical stylists trying to sell people something they really do not want to have . . ."

In 1951, Nordhoff hired a new chief engineer, Dr. Alfred Haesner, another former Opel man, to introduce improvements. Ultimately, a platoon of engineers and designers were employed full-time to knock every kink out of the car, as the company bettered it year after year. *Der Spiegel* cites the fact that the 1953 and 1954 models, which resulted from the basic redesign, contained not a single screw which exactly corresponded to its Porsche-designed forerunner. Seen in this light, today's Volkswagen is the product of Nordhoff's redesign. But this "redesign" was *organic*, not superficial.

Nordhoff did not just want to keep the plant above water in order to provide jobs for needy Wolfsburgers; he wanted to plan on a larger scale and think much more in terms of the future than did the British authorities who had given him his job. His mind surveyed the Europe of the first postwar years. It was clear to him that there was indeed "fire in the ashes." He did not question the future of Europe, including Germany. He sensed, at a time when some thought him a dizzy optimist, that this reborn Europe would be prosperous as it had never been. Such a Europe would need cars, but certainly not luxury cars which devour enormous quantities of gasoline and groan under their loads of chrome.* Nordhoff saw that Europe required *transport*—and transport in numbers never before conceived of on that continent.

He began to prod output. His tactic, *Time* noted in 1954, was one of "pressure-vacuum production." Materials poured into the plant, while produced cars vanished from it immediately. "The combination of large stocks of materials on the

* Inevitably, though, prosperity brought a cry for luxury cars as well. The extremity in ostentation today is the "Grosser Mercedes" at $15,000, the longest car in the world, 200 of which were ordered in 1963 by the nabobs of Düsseldorf before the model was even in production.

144

inside and no reserve of cars on the outside . . . exerts a psychological pressure on workers to produce faster," Nordhoff explains. "In six months," *Time* added, "production almost tripled, to 1,800 cars a month; by mid-1949, Nordhoff had so much faith in his product that he arbitrarily ordered production doubled." The reaction in the plant was one of incredulity, even among some executives who could hardly be numbered among the congenital doubters. "I remember a meeting back in 1949," says Otto Hoehne, "when Nordhoff ordered us to change over from one hundred cars a day to four hundred. Nobody said a word, but afterwards, as we were walking out of the meeting, Wilhelm Steinmeier poked me in the ribs with his elbow and said, 'Where does he think he's going to sell those cars? He'll never do it, I tell you, never!' "

In May 1949, the plant produced the 50,000th postwar Volkswagen. To celebrate, Nordhoff asked the kitchen personnel to make a special effort. The account of the festivities has a somewhat poignant air, as well as an earthy ending.

"The cooks," according to *VW Informationen*, "worried themselves stiff about what to put on the menu—then a gift of food from Switzerland came quite out of the blue: real coffee and flour. We had noodles (which were actually white in color), goulash and coffee and cakes to follow . . . We had to drink the coffee out of paper cups as no china ones were available, but that didn't lessen the enjoyment, at least not at first. But there was nevertheless a sting in the tail (and how!) when countless members of the staff had to go to see the company doctor—all suffering from stomachache, colic, and diarrhoea. Reason for the trouble—the paper cups had been impregnated with paraffin . . ."

By July, the magazine reports, the kitchen still had problems. "July 1st, 1949, and in the Hall 3 dining room the umbrellas were up—so that the ladies serving did not get wet, or the food watered down. It was raining like hell. The building had never entirely recovered from what the heavens had had to offer on a previous occasion and the makeshift repairs just could not stand up to the heavy downpour of rain. The bomb damage to the southern part of the factory had been too great."

At the end of Nordhoff's second year, the factory produced its first eight trucks. Overall production in 1949 totaled 46,154 VWs and the plant was now turning out 185 vehicles a day.

Other German auto companies were starting up as well. In 1946, Volkswagen's 9878 sedans represented 99.7 per cent of all cars manufactured in West Germany that year; by the end of 1948, VWs represented 64.6 per cent of the total, and by the end of 1949, VW's 46,154 vehicles comprised 50 per cent of all cars made in West Germany. Still, no company was moving as rapidly as was the Volkswagenwerk, nor was any company thinking on as large a scale. The company's export program had begun, at a time when other German automobile manufacturers concentrated almost exclusively on their domestic market.*

The VW dealer organization, which Nordhoff vowed would "provide the best service in the world," was beginning to take shape. By this time more than 200 dealers were scattered throughout West Germany; almost 8000 mechanics worked in more than 200 service stations and repair shops.

The eight commercial vehicles produced at the end of 1949 were delivery vans, as were all the ones exhibited in March 1950, when Volkswagen officially introduced its "Transporters." As far as the company was concerned, these vehicles were to "revolutionize the truck industry," but it admits that "the reception that greeted these 30 vehicles was slightly less than spectacular. In fact, the truck world viewed the project with skepticism, and for good reason. Here was a truck designed with no preconceived ideas, no outmoded traditions to follow, no existing tools and dies."

Just as Ferdinand Porsche had discarded all preconceptions about what a small car should be like (merely a scaled-down big car), so Nordhoff and his postwar designers insisted on producing a commercial vehicle from scratch, with an eye only on quality and service and not on what might be expected. Nordhoff blazed a trail, one which would eventually be followed by other manufacturers, including several in America, after it was apparent how successful VW's strange-looking, box-shaped "trucks" could be.

Ferdinand Porsche had actually designed a VW truck before the war, and prototypes had been built for testing. This delivery van did not in any way resemble today's VW Transporters; it was simply an adaptation of the familiar VW sedan. It never saw production.

To call Volkswagen's commercial vehicles "trucks" is somewhat misleading. Officially, the company refers to them as "Type II" vehicles, and they include not just commercial vehicles of all types and styles, but also what America has come

* For a glance at VW exports to countries other than the U.S.A., see Chapter 12; exports to the U.S. are covered in Chapters 8–10.

to know as the Volkswagen station wagon. This latter is called the Microbus in Europe, a far better name for it, but one which, it was felt, would not have endeared it to the U.S. public.

The Microbus station wagon is really just the familiar VW truck dressed in its Sunday best—a Transporter to which have been added 21 windows, a sunroof, chrome, and a comfortable, passenger-style interior. It is a remarkable vehicle, hardly bigger than the little sedan, but holding nine passengers and/or as much paraphernalia as imaginative stowing can provide. (One Brazilian rancher regularly gets more than twenty calves into his.) This Microbus and other Type II vehicles rapidly followed the original delivery van into regular production. In October 1951, for example, a VW ambulance was produced and a year later a fire truck; while few of these are built, they provide interesting evidence of the versatility of the basic design.

The 100,000th vehicle in this series left the Wolfsburg plant in October 1954; by the end of that year, Wolfsburg had reached an annual total of 202,174 passenger cars and 40,000 Transporters. Capacity had not yet been reached even within the existing facilities; the factory could readily produce more than a quarter of a million units annually (and was shortly to do so), but Nordhoff was once more planning a bigger future and preparing for it in advance, despite the cautionary advice of many.

Already, the "mother plant" in Wolfsburg had available to it a small factory in nearby Brunswick, built in 1938 as a "Vorwerk" to the Wolfsburg installation and meant then to supply the main plant with parts and training facilities. Running this for nine months during the war had provided Otto Hoehne with his "first big break," as he recalls it, for it allowed him to show management then what he was capable of doing when handed enlarged responsibilities.

Now Nordhoff decided to put up an entirely new factory along modern postwar lines—and the job of building it and getting it started fell again to Otto Hoehne. After a review of "presentations" by three hundred German mayors, the community of Stöcken, a suburb of nearby Hanover, 47 miles from Wolfsburg, was decided upon. Hanover would allow for easy communication, but in addition it had twenty thousand unemployed workers and the new factory there would prove a shot in the arm for the entire Lower Saxon region, in which both Wolfsburg and Hanover lie.

Dr. Carl Horst Hahn, who joined the company in 1954 as Heinz Nordhoff's personal assistant, recalls that there was in that year no rigid plan concerning the construction of the Hanover plant.* We didn't even have a detailed budget for it," he reports. "Nordhoff farmed Otto Hoehne out to build the factory and get it going. Hoehne added whatever was needed to it as he went along and soon, of course, had it running as smoothly as a Swiss watch."

The first commercial vehicles rolled off the Hanover assembly line in March 1956, only fourteen months after the decision to build had been reached. Under Joseph Werner's direction since 1959, production has climbed from an initial 247 trucks and station wagons to about 14,300 monthly. Today the Hanover installation also manufactures all VW engines. It employs 23,000 workers, covers 273 acres, and contains 100 acres covered with buildings.†

Nordhoff has sold more than 1,700,000 VW commercial vehicles since he produced the first eight in 1949; currently, Type II's account for 11.8 per cent of Volkswagen's overall production and include, of course, also those which have been sold as passenger station wagons and "Campers." Despite the initial skepticism, the VW commercial vehicles proved so dependable and so versatile that within less than a year, the Transporter had become the best-selling commercial vehicle in its class in Germany. Sales rose year after year, as new customers were found for a design which adapted itself to a surprising variety of needs.

On January 5, 1960, Nordhoff addressed his truck salesmen after they had sold 121,453 Transporters the previous year. His talk provides an insight into the earliest period of Transporter manufacture, as well as an example of Nordhoff-style prodding.

"There simply does not exist any reason," he said, "why truck sales should be good in one country and poor in a neighboring country. I know this isn't an easy business to get, but I repeat what I said two years ago—that the really big period for the Transporter hasn't even arrived yet. He who is smart will take his chances now, to prepare himself. I've asked our sales

* Hahn, today the Volkswagenwerk Vorstand member in charge of worldwide sales and service, headed VW in the U.S.A. from 1959 to 1965. His career is covered in greater detail in Chapter 9.

† The Brunswick plant's 5600 workers today produce front axle units for the Wolfsburg, Emden, and Ingolstadt assembly lines. The smallest of the VW complex of factories, it contains 18.3 acres of buildings on a 50.4-acre site.

department for years whether we shouldn't enlarge Hanover's capacity. I know that I've been tiresome about this, but I now ask again with increasing urgency, for it takes us at least two years to implement such a decision . . ."

He drew attention to Europe's industrial growth, which by now was in full swing, and to the fact that it could not continue without trucks. He urged his salesmen to draw the necessary conclusions from this. As for other companies' trucks in the same price and weight range, he said, "the VW Transporter still has no real competition."

Then he looked back at the early days to remind his listeners how easy it is to miscalculate. He told them that when he decided years ago to boost Transporter production from 40 to 60 a day, he was urged to reconsider, because no market allegedly existed for so many trucks. "Today," he said, "we produce 530 a day and I'm certain that even this isn't enough! . . . We must move ahead," he concluded, "not in a wild kind of optimism . . . but with the courage to do what has never been tried before, to take what the Americans call a calculated risk . . ." Transporter sales spurted up from about 120,000 that year to more than 180,000 in 1962.

Heinz Nordhoff did not only talk of calculated risks, he took them as well. The introduction of the VW Karmann Ghia coupé was one example. Volkswagen's relationship with the Wilhelm Karmann company at 49 Neulandstrasse in Osnabrück, Germany, dates back to 1949, when Karmann, an accomplished coachbuilder, began to produce a limited quantity of Volkswagen convertibles. In 1955, Nordhoff assigned that company the task of producing bodies for the "Volkswagen in an Italian sports jacket," as a VW advertisement describes the Karmann Ghia. The KG bodies were designed by Ghia of Turin, Italy, and Ghia's styling, in accordance with VW policy, has remained constant since introduced.

All Volkswagen convertible bodies are assembled and all Karmann Ghia body parts are today produced at the Osnabrück factory, while VW's Wolfsburg plant delivers to it all the required chassis, including engines and transmissions. Hand-welded, hand-sanded, hand-padded and hand-sewn, the KG receives the kind of personalized attention which the automated VW plant at Wolfsburg is not equipped to provide. The car immediately became popular and in its first four years sales rose from 500 to 6000 a year. By September 1961, sales were so good and production was so efficient that, after studying his lower costs, Nordhoff passed the savings on to his customers by lowering the Karmann Ghia's price.*

Shortly after he opened the Hanover plant, Nordhoff added another factory to the VW network, this one in Kassel, an industrial center in Hesse, along the Munich-Hanover Autobahn. There, another 13,000 workers today manufacture transmissions, truck front ends, and VW replacement parts, and also recondition Volkswagen engines and components. The factory extends over 573 acres and has more than 125 acres of roofed production area. The original Kassel plant was not built by the company; it existed before the war and was almost completely destroyed in the heavy air raids which Kassel endured during World War II. Nordhoff had it repaired, expanded, and modernized. In 1958 he sent 25 workers there from Wolfsburg to start production. By the end of two years, the new set of factory buildings had been built and there were 9000 workers reconditioning 10,000 engines and 3000 axles a month.

As fast as the company grew—and as hard as Nordhoff pushed—it could not grow fast enough to suit him. By the mid-1950's, it had spawned two huge offspring in Hanover and Kassel and the parent plant at Wolfsburg as well as the small Brunswick factory had both grown and been modernized as well. Daily output rose from 312 in 1950 to more than 1000 in 1955 and, as production and sales grew, so did the cash position. Nordhoff now was able to buy more machinery.

Today, 40 per cent of the body presses used in Wolfsburg are U.S.-built, as is all the ring- and pinion-gear-cutting machinery. For many years, the company bought large quantities of American steel, magnesium, and aluminum as well. In recent years, U.S. steel prices became prohibitive and VW reduced its purchases sharply. Europe today produces steel which meets VW's high standards at prices lower than United States manufacturers'. On the other hand, VW purchases of American tires have recently become significant; under a new contract, it buys 500,000 tires a year from the Goodyear Tire

---

* In addition to VW convertibles and KGs, the Karmann company today also produces all hardtop Porsches. This car, which Ferry Porsche and his staff designed just after the end of the war, is not connected in any way with the Volkswagenwerk. The Porsche company, now headed by Ferry, still operates out of the Porschestrasse in the Stuttgart suburb of Zuffenthausen. Income from sales of the VW helped put this company in business because Nordhoff chose to continue paying Porsche and his heirs a royalty. Relations are close all around and the Porsche Bureau continues to serve Volkswagen as consulting engineers.

and Rubber Company. The Volkswagenwerk today is also the world's largest consumer of magnesium; its foundry uses about 35,000 tons a year, one-fifth of the Free World's production.

Three months after the dawn of the "Soaring Sixties," in March 1960, Heinz Nordhoff reviewed the company's situation. Sales had jumped from 90,000 to 697,000 vehicles a year during the ten years that had passed and plans for 1960 called for 817,000.* Speaking in Switzerland on March 9, 1960, Nordhoff referred to the nagging disparity between the supply and demand of VWs. To that date, the company had never been able to meet the astounding demand for its vehicles, despite all the measures it took.

"We decided two years ago," Nordhoff said, "to do something decisive to normalize the relationship. In 1959, we invested 500 million D-marks [approximately $125,000,000] and boosted production by 1000 Volkswagens per day, to 3000 per day. In 1960, we once again invested 500 million D-marks and in January boosted production by 100 VWs per day. In February, by another 100 per day, and in March, once again by 100 per day. By the end of 1960, we shall produce 4000 Volkswagens daily. Then we believe we shall have reached a balance between supply and demand, so that we can finally deliver Volkswagens to customers without a waiting period . . ." The company, he noted, employed 54,000 workers. It had an income *per worker* of 62,000 D-marks (approximately $15,000). More than a third of all cars in West Germany were Volkswagens by 1960.

The vast investment program of the late 1950's to which Nordhoff referred was, says Carl Hahn, " a turning point" for the Volkswagenwerk. "No one thought it possible to sell so many automobiles," Hahn recalls, "but when the big U.S. market for imported small cars developed in 1959, Volkswagen was ready for it and best able to supply it." The size of VW's investments in those years astounded almost everyone, Hahn remembers. "One of Nordhoff's best friends even said to him, after a board meeting called to discuss them, 'This is nonsense! You'll just get yourself in trouble!' and one of West Germany's most prominent automakers made speeches warning against manufacturers who were 'overinvesting.' There was no doubt whom he meant. But Nordhoff has a sure instinct about just how far he can go. He never butts his head against a wall; he just manages to walk through a door in the wall which no one else sees."

* Sales proved again to exceed predictions. VW produced 865,858 vehicles in 1960.

A year later, on December 5, 1961, Volkswagen production had reached the 5,000,000 mark. It had been fourteen years since Nordhoff accepted Colonel Radclyffe's offer to head the shattered and demoralized plant; as this occasion rolled around, Nordhoff took a moment to recollect the past. He presented the flower-bedecked 5,000,000th beetle to the International Red Cross, and noted the achievements over the past fourteen years. It was, he remarked, just fourteen days after he had joined the company in 1948 that the 20,000th Volkswagen had rolled off the assembly line.* "We have good reason to be proud," Nordhoff continued, for the Volkswagen is "a symbol of one of the biggest industrial successes ever reached . . . the result of hard, unremitting work and of diligent attention to a correctly set goal."

Nordhoff defined that goal and, in doing so, summarized VW's philosophy:

". . . to develop one model of car to its highest technical excellence;

". . . to dedicate ourselves to the attainment of the highest quality;

". . . to destroy the notion that such high quality can only be attained at high prices;

". . . to subordinate technological considerations to human ones;

". . . to give the car the highest value and to build it so that it retains that value; and

". . . to build up an enterprise which belongs to its workers more than any other industrial concern in the world."

In honor of the 5,000,000th VW, the Bavarian State Mint issued gold and silver coins commemorating the occasion; they bore a profile of the car on one side and of Nordhoff on the other. The Volkswagenwerk had already become West Germany's leading industrial enterprise, with sales totaling more than 1.4 billion dollars. That year, it was also the world's *third* largest automaker, after GM and Ford, a position it held until 1963, when Chrysler recovered and also acquired sales of the Simca. ("Since then," as a VW executive puts it, "we're in fourth place, unless Chrysler has a bad year. Then we move back up to the number three position.")

Six months after the 5,000,000th VW was produced, Nordhoff warned that profits must keep pace with production, for

* Intervening anniversaries: the 500,000th VW was produced on July 3, 1953; the 1,000,000th on August 5, 1955; the 2,000,000th on December 28, 1957; the 3,000,000th on August 25, 1959; the 4,000,000th on November 9, 1960.

the postwar boom "stemming essentially from postwar needs cannot continue to go up and up . . . without reacting sharply." Nordhoff well knew that Volkswagen was riding the crest of that boom and was troubled by one result of the continuing disparity between supply and demand. The urgent necessity of closing that gap had forced the company into ever-increasing investments. By 1961, the amount laid out for automated and other late-model equipment was, he said, "enormous."

Two years earlier at Geneva he expressed the belief that the 1,000,000,000 D-marks invested between 1958 and 1960 would push the plant over the hump. This did not happen. "Despite a present daily production of 4600 vehicles, the demand still cannot be met, making further large expenditures necessary," Nordhoff said. He was in the unusual position of bemoaning the staggering demand for his product, but with good reason. A shortage of trained workers plagued management and importing foreign workers did not prove a total solution. Furthermore, it was harder to keep costs down everywhere. "This situation," Nordhoff said, "subjects us to the utmost strain, forces us to keep our organization tight, efficient, and highly effective."

The Wolfsburg plant by the early 1960's was enormous. It housed 10,000 production machines and covered 10.8 million square feet in roofed area alone—more space (about 270 acres) than all the houses of Wolfsburg combined. Daily production had skyrocketed to 5091 and the plant employed 43,578 workers, about seven times as many as in 1948, when Nordhoff took over. The two "wheezy old locomotives" of that earlier day had long since been replaced; today, the VW grounds include 31.2 miles of railroad track, with 25 tracks side-by-side at one point, plus 21.9 miles of paved roads. Its continuous-flow conveyor lines now total about 110 miles, enough to reach from Wolfsburg, right through the Russian Zone, all the way to Berlin. By 1962, Heinz Nordhoff had spent 675 million dollars on factory expansion alone, had brought sales to 1.6 billion dollars and had seen VW's share of the ever-growing West German auto market reach 34.5 per cent of the total number of passenger cars and 42.3 per cent of all commercial vehicles below 2750 pounds capacity.

His constant prodding had paid off. Over and over again, he had pressed his people to work harder, cut costs, avoid complacency and the accumulation of corporate fat. The man whom "General Motors had forged into an efficient automaker" proved also to be a steely-eyed administrator and a fiery sales manager.

"We shall some day speak of the Golden Fifties," he warned his salesmen in January 1960. "We are now moving away from them and we must recognize that fact and use the time given us. The wheel of history never turns back! Whatever opportunities you miss today will never return! The new year will have 366 days this time; every day, we will cross one off —and soon there will be only four left. No power of heaven or earth will bring those days back. Let us use this time, as long as we are free to do so, as we are now, and as we shall still be for a few years . . ." He was speaking of the fact that markets were still unusually receptive, Volkswagen sales, by and large, were easy, and the company's growth was constant and rapid. Yet he knew that there were specific traps into which a highly successful enterprise can fall—the psychological dangers of complacency and smugness.

He never stopped trying to intensify the enthusiasm and sense of urgency of his men, to make them feel a dread of a lost opportunity. He tried to keep watch over everything: the plant itself, its offices, the offices of dealers and distributors, and the repair shops. His questions were incessant and his demands those of a perfectionist. During a January 1960 staff meeting, he warned of "bureaucratic departmental thinking," of "indecisiveness and hesitancy." He urged his executives and dealers to make certain their organizations were "lean, wiry, and productive."

"We must never become lazy or sink into deadly patterns of thought," he said. "We must never become bureaucrats or administrators—that would be the end of our success!" On this occasion, he pressed his executives to read *Parkinson's Law*, which describes the growth of unproductive bureaucracies. ("That unique book," he said, "will open your eyes.") "We want to remain salesmen and engineers," he said. "Every one of us must prove daily, through initiative, action, and hard work, that he is the right man in the right job."

Volkswagen was growing older, he warned, and young people had to be brought up fast to positions of authority. He still worries about this problem and about those who in turn worry about being replaced by younger men. "I know how afraid people are and I also know the noise they make claiming there aren't young people available," he told his men, "There is a contradiction here which should stimulate you to some reflection." Blisteringly, he contrasted the modern, automated factory with its administrative offices. "Antiquated thinking is big here and missed opportunities are legion!"

In his impatience with incompetence, Nordhoff resembles Ferdinand Porsche; neither could countenance mediocrity and each drove himself hard to set an example. Nordhoff remembered his first six months at the rat-infested plant, when he lived in his office and worked seven days a week; he was determined that what he had built up would not be choked to death in a wrangle of memoranda and a proliferation of offices. This spirit has largely proved infectious and the continuing VW boom seems due in large measure to this psychological momentum which Nordhoff has created, as well as to his ability to recognize, employ, and promote men who approximate his own flexibility.

As the annual rate of production has climbed over the years, Volkswagen anniversaries keep moving closer together. It took five and a half years to build the first million Volkswagens; it took a total of fourteen years to build the first five million, but the second five million were produced in only three and a half. The ten millionth Volkswagen rolled off the Wolfsburg assembly line in September 1965, while the Frankfurt Auto Show was taking place in Frankfurt/Main, West Germany, and closed-circuit television brought the event to a room in Frankfurt where several hundred Auto Show reporters and editors from the world over had assembled. I myself was there and watched these journalists spontaneously burst into prolonged applause as the ten millionth came down the line in Hall No. 1 of the Wolfsburg plant. The accolade, however deserved, struck me as unusual, for such journalists are generally cynical about the companies whose affairs they report to the world and one does not often see them cheering corporate achievements. Yet there was no doubt about it on this day: they shared the feeling of pride and understood the sense of fulfillment which must have filled Heinz Nordhoff as he stood among them in that room, watching the distant ceremonies projected onto the huge TV screen there. "It's an incredible achievement," one of them said later. "I think everyone here feels it, because there's something about the VW that captures the imagination. There isn't another automobile that's got as much romance to it, except maybe the old Model T."

The romance today is apparent only to those who know the full history, for as the decade of the 1960's comes slowly to a close, the Volkswagenwerk seems to the casual observer a coldly efficient corporate enterprise, rather than a place of personal triumph and fulfillment. Highly automated equipment throbs in halls wherein workers once labored ankle-deep in rainwater; management consultant firms today advise where once seat-of-the-pants decisions were enough; a small army of market statisticians plot graphs and sales projections, and computers issue forth their chilly pronunciamentos. Behind the tall office building at the northeast corner of the Wolfsburg factory sprawls an ever-growing complex of buildings, housing the earsplitting production plant and the hushed spaces of support services such as technical development and marketing. The Volkswagenwerk factory area in Wolfsburg today continues to be concentrated in the same position along the canal, but this and its frontage is all that remains today to remind one of the prewar factory; behind that mile-long façade there now sprawls a colossus *three times* as large as the plant which Ferdinand Porsche saw on his last visit to Wolfsburg before his death.

Everything at VW has of course over the years grown bigger, more grandiose, more expansive, more complex, and far more organized and structured than it was earlier. Today, the company has even entered into a relationship with Mercedes-Benz wherein both work cooperatively in many areas, including research, and VW has also bought control of Auto-Union GmbH, adding this company's Audi to its own expanding line of cars. Another large VW factory, at Emden, today helps supply the demand for the new model VWs which Heinz Nordhoff launched in the 1960's, to broaden the product line his company can offer its customers, and still more factories elsewhere in the world manufacture and assemble Volkswagens as well. VW's total production today exceeds 1,600,000 per year (and 6800 per day); in 1965, Volkswagen produced 48.6 per cent of all cars made in West Germany that year, a rise of 3.3 per cent over 1964. If the Audis produced at Ingolstadt under VW's direction are added to this total, then cars built by Volkswagenwerk and its Auto-Union company account for the majority (50.4 per cent) of all West German cars produced that year.

This achievement tends to overawe a visitor coming for the first time to the home of Heinz Nordhoff. One tends to encounter the leading industrialist of any country filled with certain preconceptions and expecting a certain stereotype, no matter what one may have heard of the man in advance. Writers who are acquainted with businessmen and industry executives in the United States and elsewhere learn from the experience of many encounters with such men that the business world molds them into a handful of well-defined types. One expects perhaps the executive who is a chilly corporate machine which has successfully slaughtered its individuality in the struggle with faceless organization men, or perhaps expects the frequently encountered "self-made man" who blusteringly boasts of having majored in Sharp Dealings in some sleazy "school of hard knocks." Certainly one has learned to expect that the top industrialist's world begins and ends in the executive suite, and one has encountered a host who are filled either with contempt or condescension for the world of art and intellect, or who patronizingly act their "patron," at the prompting of public relations counselors. And so it was with considerably more than curiosity that I discussed Heinz Nordhoff with those who have known him long and well, and formed my own impressions during many hours in Heinz Nordhoff's home and office over the past several years. These are now difficult to sort out, for while it is a simple matter to describe a lesser man, it is a larger task to describe a man whose giant size seems to derive from an inner simplicity.

As for the preconceptions, Nordhoff tends to destroy them gently on one's first visit to his home. Walking there, one passes along a winding, tree-lined street of modest, two-story "executive-row" homes, until one comes to where the road curves back again towards the Steimkerberg guest house (the very building which once served as the British REME mess). At this curve of the road stands Nordhoff's home, a somewhat larger, but quite unpretentious, L-shaped house; one is struck by the fact that it might belong in the United States to a middle-echelon executive, and it bears not the slightest resemblance to the huge homes, mansions, and estates which American manufacturers inhabit in Westchester County or Fairfield County, Grosse Point or Bloomfield Hills, or in the North Shore suburbs of Chicago. Either Heinz Nordhoff or his wife usually answers the doorbell here, takes the visitor's coat and ushers him into the living room. Immediately one is struck by the scent and sight of flowers; by paintings, sculpture, and other objets d'art, and by a profusion of books—a great many in English—which litter a table beside the chair in which Nordhoff seats himself. A visitor's glance at one of these books, or his indication that he is familiar with a title here, is enough to start this automobile executive talking at length about any of a variety of subjects, whether it be the politics of medieval France or of today's Germany, Eastern philosophy or the sociology of the West, a recent *New Yorker* short story or the current Munich theater. Nordhoff speaks quietly, in an almost hushed voice; one recognizes it as the tone of a man who does not need to raise his voice for attention. As the conversation continues, one notes that Nordhoff has an easy familiarity with a surprising array of subjects and that a visitor with preconceptions soon finds himself quickly put in his cultural place. Wine is poured and Nordhoff now earnestly discusses the character of the vintage, expressing satisfaction with it or disappointment with another; he flatters his visitor by disarmingly assuming that, of course, his guest has an equal understanding of the merits of these wines. As one begins to hunt for a term capturing a first impression of this man, there comes to mind a word which one uses seldom in today's age of sound and fury: one is struck by Nordhoff's *graciousness*. He does *not* offer compliments, nor does he say or do anything which might be calculated to put a visitor at ease, but he flatters his visitors nevertheless by placing them completely on his own level. There is in this nothing that seems affected, nor have I noted the slightest suggestion of condescension or superiority in the man, though I was alert for it, for Nordhoff has been criticized as "arrogant." He simply puts his visitors at ease by paying them the irresistible compliment of assuming they are honorable, intelligent, and cultivated men; he flatters them further by being utterly and disarmingly frank with them. No matter the subject, Nordhoff offers his observations in a way that makes clear he does not have advisers who suggest what views he "ought to" express. One asks Nordhoff, for example, to explain a recent reshuffle of management in a competitive company; he replies at length and offers a detailed, informed, and dispassionate appraisal of the strengths and weaknesses in the men and forces involved. As the evening progresses, one adds another word to one's lexicon regarding Nordhoff, and it is *detachment*. Now one begins to understand whence his reputation for "arrogance" derives; dispassionate and detached men are often mistakenly thought to have a superior air. One senses Nordhoff has learned from life to be surprised at very little which events and men may offer and that looking back on his career he sees not only the highs of achievements, but regards with detached equanimity the frustrations and difficulties through which he has had to pass. He may be—and is—impatient in details, but has won a reputation for regarding important and far-reaching matters with detachment and objectivity; one notes from his conversation that he has the natural tolerance of a man who either was born, or grew to be, philosophically inclined, and one is reminded again of

Carl Hahn's statement that Nordhoff never butts his head against walls.

"He always has time for important things," says Carl Hahn. "When you sit down with him, he never ends the conversation after fifteen minutes, nor does he set any arbitrary time limits at all. He'll give you as much as two or three hours. And throughout that time, you have his undivided attention. Everything is quiet and there are never any phone calls interrupting, and at the end of your talk he gives you the feeling that it's wonderful of you to have helped him spend the afternoon— as though he had been worried about how it would have gone, if you hadn't arrived."

Reporters have also noted in Heinz Nordhoff a slight mischievous instinct and the ability to be cynically realistic about himself and others. He has seen more than his share of human weakness and knows that people can be motivated by a man who knows these weaknesses. His detachment extends to himself; in his darkest days, he loathed looking back in anger or self-pity. "The future begins when you cut every tie with the lost past," he said when he took over the factory.

Just as he demands the right to a private life for himself, he eschews paternalism towards his workers. "We have a rule here," he says, "that when a man crosses the bridge over the canal [which separates the factory from the town], then his life is his own." He adds, with characteristic cynicism, "Why shouldn't they be free to be fools if they wish? All I want to do for these people is to create the conditions for a decent life —but not to interfere with that life. The minute the factory becomes a landlord as well as employer, then the worker is no longer a free man—he is a slave."

One man who knew Heinz Nordhoff almost forty years ago is John Eschenlohr, now a member of the board of directors of VW Canada Ltd. and for years general service manager of that company. He worked with Nordhoff in the Opel service department in 1929, and it is interesting to note his recollections of Germany's greatest industrialist when he was starting his career. "Nordhoff was a very detached fellow even then," Eschenlohr says. "He sometimes threw delightful parties and he knew all the good jokes, but he never liked to just go out and drink with the boys. He was very ambitious and much addicted to the fine arts and that sort of thing."

"I have never seen another German industrialist," says Carl Hahn, "or any industrialist for that matter, who is as diversified in his interests as Nordhoff is. His mind ranges from roses to hunting to painting to orchids and from there on almost

159

infinitely. Part of this can be attributed, of course, to his wide and constant reading, which keeps his mind active and open to many ideas."

If one asks him about these interests, one learns that flowers, art, and literature are neither Nordhoff "hobbies" nor the cultural affectations a successful industrialist might cultivate in his later years, but that they are the important avocations of a cultivated man. Nordhoff proves knowledgeable in a host of fields and he puts his knowledge to practical use. He cultivates his own orchids and tends his own flower gardens; he collects paintings and has tried his own hand at the art, and he is an insatiable reader who seems as well-informed about the Napoleonic Code as he is about his car or the Common Market. He reads widely in English and receives *Time,* the *New Yorker,* and the *Wall Street Journal* regularly. He learned English, which he speaks fluently with a soft German accent, while with Opel, "reading *Automotive Industries,*" he says. He knows classical Greek as well as Latin, his company's publicists proclaim proudly. (They go so far as to claim he "reads ancient manuscripts with the ease of an American reading a detective story.") "I find there are more books which interest me published in English than in German," Nordhoff says, "and I go through more of them today than I ever did, reading late into the night." On a 1963 visit to the United States, he bought a handful of historical books, among them Alan Moorehead's *The White Nile* and *The Blue Nile* and *Eichmann in Jerusalem* by Hannah Arendt. He had of course read the news reports of Eichmann's trial, but wanted to study the record once more in a comprehensive book. Unlike many Germans one meets, he does not hesitate to face the past and to keep it alive. "You cannot make the past go away," he has said, "by turning your back on it or refusing to look at it." Characteristically, he decided, upon reading the history of the Eichmann trial in Jerusalem, that he would buy a dozen copies of the book and mail them to German acquaintances who even today will not or cannot believe that all this horror was wrought by their fellow Germans during the Nazi era. "I think all Germans should know about this and that they must face these facts," he says. "The horror of it is overwhelming and reading this record of Nazi atrocities will make them understand why there are people who are not only anti-Nazi, but anti-German."

His "missionary zeal" in sending out books to "educate" others is characteristic of the way all his interests express themselves. His interest in fine arts, for example, extends from

The late Heinz Nordhoff, president of Volkswagenwerk AG 1948–1968. *Bachrach*

Dr. Kurt Lotz, president of Volkswagenwerk AG since 1968. *Atelier Sandau*

Professor Nordhoff and Dr. Lotz at the opening of the new Volkswagen generating plant in Wolfsburg in 1962. Dr. Lotz was then head of the company which sold Volkswagenwerk the steam turbine and generator for the plant.

Bomb damage at the factory in 1944. Note wrecked aircraft wings, produced at the plant in World War II, at lower right.

British officers and Volkswagenwerk workers celebrate a milestone. At far right are Major Hirst and Rudolf Brörmann.

The first VW to be brought into the United States by the company is unloaded in January 1949. At left is Ben Pon.

In chronological order, the three men who created the VW success in America: Will van de Kamp, lower left, who came here in 1955 and by persuasion and energy convinced Americans to become "pioneers" in the VW organization; Carl H. Hahn, upper left, who replaced van de Kamp in 1959 and set the basic pattern and tone of the American marketing program; and J. Stuart Perkins, upper right, who since 1962 has led the organization in becoming the envy of many major U.S. companies. (The photo of van de Kamp, taken in 1957, shows a young man, Stuart Perkins, hurrying to catch up with his boss.)

The "body drop" on one of the eight final assembly lines at Wolfsburg mates completed body shells to platform chassis. The Wolfsburg factory turns out about five cars per minute and employs 55,000 workers. Virtually all of the new cars leave the factory on double-deck trains, each carrying 250 vehicles.

Stretching nearly a mile from one end to the other, Volkswagen's "home" plant in Wolfsburg rates as one of the world's largest factories. There are five other VW plants in Germany.

home to office to the community in which he lives. Visits to the Far East have resulted in a collection of Japanese brush paintings and statues of the Buddha, now set in his home among German baroque wood carvings and an original Renoir. Persian carpets and statues from the Far East also add a note of dignified opulence to his offices. He has been the guiding light behind Wolfsburg's artistic life, originating the company's sponsorship of major art exhibits, one of which drew 500,000 visitors. Another popular show covered 120 years of French art and included 237 works on loan from 60 collections throughout the world.

His interest in the performing arts also express itself in the same way. Once a year, he brings the Berlin Philharmonic to Wolfsburg, and his daughter Barbara remembers the first such concert, conducted by the famed Wilhelm Furtwängler. A large hall, originally constructed as a factory kitchen, but later used as a testing and experimental facility, was set aside for the purpose. It has tiled walls and ordinarily poor acoustics; the moment, however, it is filled with three thousand persons, its acoustics are excellent. When Furtwängler encountered it for the first time he could not have known this and it is therefore understandable that he balked at conducting there. Not only would the acoustics be terrible, he said, but the workers probably wouldn't appreciate the music. Finally, he was persuaded to conduct anyway, but did so with many reservations, as Barbara Nordhoff remembers it. "I think Furtwängler thought the workers would probably applaud in the middle of the concert," she says, "but you could hear a pin drop when there was a pause and, at the end, there was so much applause that Furtwängler claimed he had never heard the like." "I wish I could play for your workers every day," he told Nordhoff afterwards. As it turned out, he was able to come only once more before he died. Since then, a number of other halls in Wolfsburg have been looked into as possible replacements for the hall now housing testing equipment, but none has been found with the same excellent acoustics. Today's conductor of the Berlin Philharmonic, Herbert von Karajan, refuses to conduct anywhere in Wolfsburg except in that "tiled kitchen."

Nordhoff also has arranged for theatrical companies to come to the Volkswagen city. "Nowadays all the leading plays are performed in Wolfsburg," Barbara says, "and I think we have one of the most sophisticated and critical theater audiences in Germany. In the beginning, we used to go and see whatever

161

was being offered in town, but so many companies come here nowadays that we are much more selective."

Heinz Nordhoff's interest in gardening is also not only a hobby but part of his orientation toward nature, part of a view of life which shows itself in the spacious green areas which are scattered throughout Wolfsburg. It is also reflected in other hobbies such as big game hunting, which he pursues each year in Africa, but with camera as much as with gun. These are not the big safaris which are usually arranged for executives of comparable stature: motorized caravans with all the luxuries and amenities of life in New York City. Nordhoff ventures out alone, accompanied only by a native guide, and they carry little, living off what they can find or hunt locally. "We know the general area in which he is traveling," Barbara Nordhoff says, "but we have no idea of his exact whereabouts until he emerges a month later. He usually comes home with a wretched stomach—the result of unbelievable food—but well rested." He has also come back from many of these trips with film footage of professional caliber. "He could get a job with any film company in Germany if he wanted to," Barbara claims. So far, his films are only for close friends and business associates. He filmed, for instance, Angkor Wat, the ancient jungle temple of Cambodia, near Angkor Thom, the old capital of the Khmers, and prepared a narration, using ancient Eastern texts. Heinz Nordhoff's interest in motion pictures has prompted him over the years to commission a series of award-winning documentaries for the Volkswagenwerk. Produced by Konstantin Kalser's Marathon International Productions, New York City, these have won prizes at international film festivals such as those held at Venice and Edinburgh. Kalser, who has won an "Oscar" for documentaries, told me that at first he had no idea Nordhoff was an amateur film-maker. "I saw that movie of his on Angkor Wat after we started working for Volkswagenwerk," Kalser told me, "and I can assure you that I'd never have signed a contract to produce a film for this company if I'd seen that movie earlier. It's absolutely first-rate and I would have been worried about getting too much professional criticism from him." As it turned out, it was precisely Nordhoff's professionally amateur interest in cinematography which led him *not* to interfere with the Kalser camera crews. His only stipulation has been that the films must be entirely noncommercial in nature, with no "product publicity" worked into them. To be sure, the documentaries deal with matters of vital concern to Volkswagenwerk, but they are of broader significance as well. Automation, foreign trade, and international communications are subjects which have been chosen and a recent film entitled *The Way of a Ship* reminded audiences that the bulk of the world's international cargo, even in the jet age, is carried by freighter. The low-key script was written by the author of *The Cruel Sea,* Nicholas Montserrat, and what public relations benefit the company may derive directly from the film stems from the fact that many of the ships shown are part of Volkswagenwerk's fleet of time-charter vessels.

Heinz Nordhoff's wife and daughters share a fierce sort of pride in his accomplishments and catholicity of tastes. "We have a game we used to play called 'trying to corner Daddy,'" says Barbara Nordhoff. "We tried to stump him, but rarely succeeded." When she and her sister Elisabeth lived at home they would look up various subjects in reference books and challenge their father with them. "It seems he's always able to offer some information about almost anything," she reports, "whether it's Telstar or the latest Paris fashion. He even has wonderful taste in clothes. He bought me my first evening dress, selecting it by himself, and it was exactly the style and color that proved perfect for me."

It is clear from her comments that family life is close. Nordhoff's wife and daughters have shared with him not only the executive life in Berlin during the war, when he headed the Brandenburg Opel plant, but also the years of poverty, joblessness, and crowded rooms after the end of World War II. These years of adversity had their effect. Barbara Nordhoff recalls the time in 1948 when the mother and daughters came to Wolfsburg for the first time. Their father had moved out of the factory after having camped in his office for six months and had sent for them. "When we arrived after a drive of about seven hours," she remembers, "the driver took us into a very nice quiet street with one-family houses along it and I remember thinking that maybe we would have a home like one of these someday. Then the driver stopped in front of one of them and said, 'This is your home,' and out came Daddy. He had somehow managed to get some furnishings and when Mother saw the house, she just broke into tears. She had so geared herself for a life of poverty that it was too much for her."

His wife is a slender, elegant lady who has devoted herself to her husband's interests exclusively, now that her children are no longer at home. She has an unostentatious way, drives a standard Volkswagen sedan, and can be seen walking home alone from market. The Nordhoffs' lack of ostentation may be natural, but it also proves to be good employee relations, and Nordhoff has won his workers' admiration by buying a beetle on the same terms as do the rest of them. (This is his wife's car; Nordhoff, like other VW executives, has a company car.)

The life of poverty has, of course ended, and the man whom the American occupation authorities had promised a life only as an unskilled laborer has since risen to high position and achieved considerable honors. The Brunswick Institute of Technology awarded him an honorary professorship and doctorate in engineering and he lectures there periodically on industrial relations. As a result, he is addressed as Professor Nordhoff in Germany. Berlin Technical University conferred upon him the unusual rank of honorary senator and the West German government awarded him its highest civilian medal, the Great Federal Cross of Merit with Stars (Grosses Bundes-Verdienstkreuz mit Sternen). The Vatican, which takes pride in him as an outstanding Roman Catholic layman, has also given him awards, first making him a Knight of the Order of the Holy Sepulchre in Jerusalem and, more recently, presenting him with the Medal of St. Gregory (Gregorius Orden).

"I have to be careful what I think sometimes," Nordhoff admits. "Some other man might not have done what I have done—it's true. Volkswagen could have failed. Even I must admit that. And, had another man failed, people would have said: 'Well, naturally it wouldn't work. No one could make it work. Nothing Hitler ever started ever came to a good end. The VW was just a mad scheme. No wonder it failed.'"

The fact that he has succeeded has made him somewhat of a legend in West Germany. Charles Barnard wrote in *True* that Nordhoff's fellow countrymen regard him sometimes as "a new Nordic superman" and Nordhoff admits there have been friends who have urged him to enter public life. "Some people told me they thought it would be a good thing if I got into politics," he says, "but I'm too busy to give any thought to it." Further, he reminded me that industrialists do not always prove to be well suited for political life. "Remember what happened to Charlie Wilson," he said, referring to the General Motors president who was appointed Defense Secretary in Dwight D. Eisenhower's first cabinet. He knows that his own industrial eminence would make him, as it has already done, the target of much sniping and criticism.

Yet Nordhoff's political views remain significant even if not given practical scope, for they are after all those of the man who heads the largest corporation in Europe's mightiest industrial nation, West Germany, and become by extension the views of Germany's most powerful industrialist. These views were given partial expression in an Alexander Graham Bell lecture on communications he delivered at the Boston University School of Business Administration in October 1962. Here Nordhoff spoke of his deep-felt belief in closer Free World ties. "We must be ready to think about uniting the western world of the Atlantic Community," he said. "Otherwise, time will begin to work against us. Time is not on our side. It is on the side of the enemy. The man on the street is ready for unity. He is ready in France, and he is ready in Germany, where the problems of national self-interest are worsened by one thousand years of history. We in Europe know that you are equally ready here in America, where with the flexibility and eagerness of youth, concepts of international thinking come more readily." He spoke of the Marshall Plan as "the first important step toward unification of Europe" and called it "history's greatest act of community unselfishness, a massive example of democratic generosity." He again expressed concern over the "protectionist thinking of certain high-tariff groups" in the European Common Market and denounced the idea that the Common Market might form a "Third Force" in the world today. Its members, he said, must "share everything—not only with its members, but also with those outside its ranks."

He made his own commitment clear. "In this area," he said, "the liberal thinking of the United States is an outstanding example to the world. Tariffs here are low. The policies of your government during the Eisenhower and Kennedy Administrations show clearly that the majority of Americans favor this attitude. *So do I.* And so do *many* others in Europe." * Nordhoff shows himself to be a liberal committed to free trade, international cooperation, and even Atlantic union. His views are important in Germany, for they are heard attentively.

Although Nordhoff disavows any interest in participating actively in German politics, he is outspoken in his views. He is disappointed in Germany's politicians. Neither the Socialist Party nor the Christian Democratic Union tell the German people the truth about their situation, Nordhoff says. "The truth is that we and all Europe are utterly dependent on the United States," he maintains. "But no one will tell the public that." While he is hopeful about the future of German democracy, there is a note of pessimism as well. He quoted

---

* Italics are Nordhoff's, as provided in a reprint of his address published in 1962 by Boston University Press.

Heinrich Heine to me—*Denk' ich an Deutschland in der Nacht, dann bin ich um den Schlaf gebracht* (If I think of Germany during the night, then my sleep is ruined). He feels that Germany may have recovered too fast after the war, that prosperity may have come too easily to the German people. "They all think that it should always be a boom period," he says, "and I do not know what they will do if it ever stops. Perhaps they will think there is something basically wrong with the system."

In the meantime, Nordhoff is content to go on building cars. Although past sixty-five, he has no immediate plans to retire, for, as he says, he continues to feel strong and healthy. He expects to see Volkswagen's boom continue and is full of plans which he would like to see through to maturity. "We still have many arrows in our quiver," he once said. "We are prepared. We cannot build as many cars as mankind needs. And if the worst comes to the worst, the last car to be bought will be a Volkswagen."

8

Coals To Newcastle

VOLKSWAGEN'S extraordinary success in the United States —that home of the chrome and bastion of big cars—was somewhat unexpected, even by Heinz Nordhoff. Today, the U.S.A. represents the Volkswagenwerk's second biggest market (after Germany) and its biggest overseas customer, with more than two million VWs on U.S. roads and the number growing at the rate of more than four hundred thousand a year. Yet VW had no preferential position when it first entered the American market and, indeed, made its bid for U.S. sales late in the game. Britain's Rootes Motors was the first European car manufacturer to export seriously to the U.S.A. after World War II and a variety of other British, French and German manufacturers sent cars over well before VW got going. Yet Volkswagen is today so far ahead of all foreign car competition that it has even skipped ahead of all U.S. compact cars as well, and it shows no signs of slipping. Its sales may represent less than five per cent of total U.S. auto sales, but the car is far from lost in the crowd. It is recognized instantly by Americans who can't tell a Fiat from an MG, a Saab from a Volvo, or even a Plymouth from a Ford.

The "familiar line" handed out by Wolfsburg has become so very familiar indeed that few Americans are aware that virtually every one of the two million-plus VWs on their roads was bought in the comparatively few years which have elapsed since 1954. In the first nine years after the end of World War II, VWs were virtually unknown in the United States, except as weird-looking souvenirs which a handful of veterans of the U.S. Army of Occupation had brought home from Germany. That the VW organization which has been built up since then was built so quickly and effectively is amazing.

167

The enormous achievement of constructing a network of distributors and dealers throughout fifty states has all the earmarks of a brilliantly conceived plan, of carefully charted strategy, and of a high-powered organization ready to push it to fruition. Yet nothing, in actuality, could be further from the truth.

It all started without much of a plan at all, with very little strategy, and with no organization to speak of. The success story of the VW in the United States was written in the beginning by less than a score of men, some Americans, some Germans. Of the Americans, several became VW distributors; if they seemed reckless at first in joining up, their recklessness has since rewarded them by making them rich men. Of the Germans, a number cruised around the country in VW trucks, preaching the gospel of service at a time when there were virtually no VWs for mechanics to look after. The man responsible for sending these men round was one of the most colorful and remarkable individuals to appear in the history of Volkswagen, a super-salesman possessed of both demonic drive and courtly charm as well as a sure and personal vision of what would someday come to pass. His name was Will van de Kamp. He and a few others built everything up in a few years, starting from scratch. This is their story.

Before van de Kamp got started, however, the climate in the United States was radically different. It was back in 1948 that Heinz Nordhoff decided to make his first stab at selling VWs in the U.S.A. It was not so much that he needed the sales, for in that year (and all succeeding years) he actually had more orders to fill than the factory could meet, but what he did need was American machinery for Wolfsburg. The way to buy it was with dollars and the way to get these was to sell Volkswagens to persons owning the precious hard currency.

The man he chose to make the first foray into the Land of the Big Cars was big Ben Pon, a colorful Dutchman who had successfully sold the German beetle to his fellow countrymen at a time when anti-German sentiment ran high in Holland. If Pon could do that, Nordhoff reasoned, he ought to be able to sell it to Americans.

Ben Pon brought to America the first VW "officially" exported to that country, traveling with it aboard the Holland-America Line's M/S *Westerdam* and arriving in New York on January 17, 1949. No sooner had the ship docked than Pon ran into trouble.

"An American friend of mine helped me stage a press

conference aboard the freighter," Pon says. "We got a lot of publicity—all of it bad. I even tried calling the VW the 'Victory Wagon' to take the curse off it, but the press referred to it only as 'Hitler's car.' "

Problems ashore were different, but no less maddening. Everyone whom Pon tried to enlist as a VW dealer turned it down. "I drove the car to Massachusetts to see a Packard dealer," Pon says, providing one example of the American reaction. "I raced through a heavy snowstorm to get to him by 9 A.M. When I arrived at his home, he wouldn't even open the door. He just took one look at the car through the window and turned away in disgust!"

After three weeks in New York, Pon had begun to run out of money, for his government allowed him to spend only ten dollars a day. "I had a big bill at the Roosevelt Hotel," he says, "and I couldn't meet it. So, in desperation, I sold the car and all the spare parts I had brought with me to a New York imported-car dealer for eight hundred dollars, just to pay that hotel bill."

Pon reported the disappointing news to Nordhoff and also warned him that many European automakers were sending cars into the U.S. without establishing adequate service facilities. "I felt we would kill the VW if we did the same," he says. "I felt we should not even try to sell the VW in the U.S. before we could do a good job."

Nordhoff was also disappointed, for U.S. sales were needed to bring in dollars for the purchase of machinery. In late 1949, he flew across the ocean to check things out for himself.

Armed with a stack of photographs of his car, he arrived in New York City and took his place at U.S. Customs. The Customs inspector opened his suitcase, picked up the bundle of pictures, and asked Nordhoff what these were. Told they were photographs of a German car Nordhoff hoped to sell, the inspector proved skeptical.

"No, this is no automobile," Nordhoff quotes him as saying. "I've never seen one like this; these must be drawings or promotional artwork." As such, he explained, they were subject to duty. Nordhoff tried in vain to convince the inspector that what he held in his hands were actual photographs. "But it was all no use," he remembers. The inspector refused to believe him and insisted that he pay ten or twelve dollars duty for them as advertising sketches. "That hurt badly," Nordhoff says, "because I was allowed only fifteen dollars a day for my expenses."

The trip, Nordhoff reports, proved "an utter failure." The

Volkswagen again failed to impress a single American automobile dealer. Not one believed the car could ever be sold in the United States. Newspapermen to whom Nordhoff took his case felt the same way. The VW, they said, was hopeless as a marketable commodity in the U.S.A. Nordhoff returned home discouraged. "I realized then that we would have to make our own way in the world without a source of American dollars," he says.

It was not surprising that the American dealers hesitated to handle the Volkswagen. This was a time when the American public, which had been starved for new cars during the war, clamored for other kinds of automobiles. Detroit saw the trend coming: what the public seemed to want were heavy, wide, long, low cars; cars whose bumpers were festooned with the protuberances the trade came to call "Dagmars"; cars with flaglike fins and chrome hugging each seam; cars with ever more powerful engines. Not only did the Volkswagen's design seem as out of date as that of the Tin Lizzie, but the press kept emphasizing that the car's history was suspect as well. Wasn't its name a Nazi name? How could Nordhoff expect to sell "Hitler's pet" to Americans four years after the war?

As it turned out, the Volkswagen did not prove to be out of date; it proved to be ahead of its time. Americans weren't ready for it yet. American interest in imported cars began to climb in the mid-1950's and by then the car did not seem nearly so bizarre or objectionable. By the time Nordhoff made another try at the U.S. market, the country was almost ready.

The first Volkswagen officially exported to the U.S., apart from Pon's "display model," arrived there in 1950. To be sure, a few had come in before, brought home privately by American servicemen returning from duty in West Germany. Two were sold in 1949. In 1950, however, the company decided to make another formal try at the U.S. market and appointed a New York foreign-car dealer named Max Hoffman exclusive VW importer and agent for the United States east of the Mississippi. Few people noticed the 330 Volkswagens he sold in 1950; they were lost among the 6,660,000 other cars Americans bought that year as well.

Max Hoffman, however, did not just sell Volkswagens; the beetle was more of a sideline to his main and more profitable business, that of selling a wide range of better-known foreign cars, many of these high-powered and high-priced ones such as Porsches and Jaguars. Hoffman's status as exclusive importer of many European makes meant that many Americans then entering the growing foreign-car field found themselves buying from Hoffman—and many of them also found themselves stuck with a funny little German car called the VW.

Typical were Carl and Oliver Schmidt of Chicago, two unrelated namesakes who had then joined forces to form Import Motors of Chicago, selling a line of foreign makes. When the Schmidts went to Hoffman to buy a Porsche, they found they got one more easily if they also bought a Volkswagen. "Funny thing was," Oliver Schmidt remembers, "we sold that first VW right away. Then, when we went back to buy more Porsches, and ended up again with more Volkswagens as well, we sold those beetles right off too. One day I came around to Hoffman for more cars. I was asked if I'd come to buy Porsches. 'No,' I said. 'I just want you to sell me some VWs.'" Hoffman's Chicago warehouse was filled with quite a few; the Schmidts began selling them faster than they or Hoffman expected.

Other car dealers were buying from Max Hoffman too and having much the same experience. One was Howard Sluyter of Grand Rapids, Michigan, who visited the Hoffman showroom in New York City in 1948, intent on buying a Jaguar for himself. Sluyter was in the furniture business at the time, but he fell so much in love with his Jag that he decided to branch out into the foreign-car field as well. Sluyter formed Import Motors Limited of Grand Rapids and in 1949 asked one of the men from Sluyter's furniture business, Peter C. Cook, to run the new company. Nothing could have delighted the auto buff Cook more; he quickly sold the company's first six Jaguars and eventually also acquired the MG and Morris franchises for the new firm. Another Grand Rapids businessman, Edsko Hekman, joined him at Import Motors in 1953, and when Hoffman began offering VWs for sale, Cook and Hekman began selling these too.

Thousands of miles away from the United States, another man who was to figure prominently in the history of VW in America was selling Volkswagens—to the Moroccans. This was Arthur Stanton, today the largest-volume VW distributor (for Connecticut, New Jersey, and New York), not only in the U.S.A., but also throughout the entire world. In the late 1940's, Navy veteran Stanton found editorial life at Crown Publishers too restrictive for his entrepreneurial instincts and, together with his brother Frank and another friend, set up an export-import firm in Morocco. In 1948, their firm was appointed to distribute Chrysler products in that country and also developed into a large importer of virtually anything that showed promise. (Stanton at the time even bought an abandoned U.S. Army camp in Italy, then rented a local arena for eighteen months to sell off its equipment, item by item.)

In 1949, just as Ben Pon was heading for the United States, Stanton and his colleagues decided they wanted a small car to sell to the North Africans. Two wartime VW Kübelwagens had been parked in one of their garages, and on the basis of the cars' performance, they decided to try to get the VW franchise for the area. Stanton went to see Heinz Nordhoff in Wolfsburg. He must have impressed the new head of VW, for he got his VW franchise and started to produce sales. "Twelve months after we began handling Volkswagens in North Africa," Stanton reports, "we were selling fifteen hundred a year."

That buyers for this odd-looking car could actually be found in the United States was becoming apparent to a few others. One was a racing enthusiast by the name of John von Neumann; impressed by the Porsche VW concept, he early sensed the potential in the beetle and with his wife shuttled from Los Angeles by bus to Hoffman's New York headquarters, to return West in two VWs, which they promptly sold to two more West Coast foreign-car enthusiasts.

In Columbus, Ohio, a young World War II Air Force officer named Robert Fergus was another man who was buying cars from Max Hoffman. Fergus's Columbus Sports Car Company, formed in 1951, sold Morris, Austin and Jaguar cars— and soon VWs as well. Again the beetles were at first taken on reluctantly, to get the popular Jags. Two years later in Overland, Missouri, John Barry, a sports car enthusiast, and Fred Vincel opened a small auto dealership and got into the VW picture with a total starting inventory of six imported cars, two of them beetles.

Here and there, then, people *were* selling Volkswagens— one by one and in small quantities. Often they had bought them for resale with considerable reluctance, so as to expedite delivery of Porsches and Jaguars; although they frequently found that the low-priced VWs were outselling the high-priced sports cars, the business in beetles remained erratic and unorganized. Projected over the nation as a whole, sales by the end of 1953 (2173 VWs since 1950) totaled fewer than the number of counties in the United States; VW, in short, was not making even the slightest inroads on the roads of America.

Back in Wolfsburg, where this was being studied, the realization grew that the patchwork Hoffman "network" had to be dropped. Because John von Neumann's Competition Motors was by 1953 selling enthusiastically and successfully along the

Pacific Coast, VW that year appointed him Hoffman's counterpart west of the Mississippi, and as the end of that year approached, the Hoffman contract was not renewed.

"Hoffman was in general a very perceptive man," says Stuart Perkins, today head of Volkswagen in the United States, "but somehow he just couldn't see the future in the VW." Manuel Hinke, expert chief of the Volkswagenwerk, agrees. "We felt there was a potential that Hoffman would not recognize," he says.

In point of fact, this seems hardly surprising, for few Americans looked upon the car as one which might truly become popular. Hoffman had then (and has now) a prosperous imported-car business; he was less "Volkswagen's U.S. importer" than an independent importer of a wide line of cars. Also, his responsibility ended at the "wholesale level," once he had sold his beetles to dealers for resale elsewhere. He did not have to concern himself with what happened to them later; neither did he have to have the long-range interests of the VW company at heart. He was, after all, in business for himself, not for the Volkswagenwerk.

That this, however, should prove intolerable for Wolfsburg is clear if one recalls that, by 1953, Nordhoff had been on the job for five years already and that, while the VW business in the U.S.A. was tiny, it was elsewhere growing large indeed and very highly organized. VW's annual payroll in Wolfsburg had by the end of 1953 reached almost thirty million dollars; total worldwide exports that year had reached almost 70,000, and production had climbed close to 180,000 cars. Yet the number of VWs bought in the U.S., the biggest auto market in the world, was so tiny that year that Wolfsburg's production line could even then fill the entire U.S. demand in less than a day and a half.

Throughout much of the world, in short, VW was an efficiently functioning and rapidly growing company, whose policies and distribution pattern had not only been set, but had already proved themselves. It had established its networks of importers, distributors, and dealers, most of them devoting their efforts to selling VWs exclusively; it had developed service and sales standards; had worked up uniform service and repair facilities and procedures; had determined methods of training mechanics and sales personnel; had created a uniform appearance for VW showrooms and service centers, and it had tested its policies in markets in Germany and elsewhere, finding they worked. It also found that the United States in 1953 was a glaring contradiction of all that the company believed in.

173

A disorganized, superficial, and slipshod network had evolved from among dealers who sold VWs along with a host of other cars; while some of these men were doing a fine job under the circumstances and could be retained in a later and better organization, the fact remained that all of them had to be re-evaluated by the company. Those who might be reappointed had to be made familiar with VW policies, aided in following them, and had to be provided with direction and guidance, rather than just with cars. Already a VW policy of moving into new territories by means of establishing "service first, sales second" had been developed throughout existing markets and had proved essential to the car's success; people were clearly buying Volkswagens not just because they were good cars, but because they were assured adequate service and parts facilities. It was clear in 1953 that the continent-size U.S. market needed such policies—and lacked them.

Once the decision to cancel Hoffman's contract had been made, Nordhoff asked Arthur Stanton to size up the U.S. situation for him. Stanton left North Africa, returned home, and made his independent judgment. It seemed clear to him that everything needed to be rebuilt from scratch.

Back in the field and well before the end of 1953, those who were selling the Hoffman-imported Volkswagens sensed that a major shake-up was due to come. Trade rumors and industry journals hinted that Hoffman's contract with VW was about to end. Several of his dealers decided not to wait, but to protect their interests by contacting Wolfsburg. Because they had until then dealt solely through Hoffman, they did not know whom to address in Germany.

Don Marsh, then manager of Fergus's Columbus Sports Car Company, was one of several who wrote to the "sales department" in Wolfsburg; boldly, he asked not just for "some territorial rights" but for everything east of the Mississippi. Oliver and Carl Schmidt, in Chicago, were two others who wrote the factory, also asking for a franchise to distribute VWs. Marsh got a letter in reply, advising him that a "factory representative" would visit Columbus "presently" to discuss the matter; other dealers, like the Schmidts, were left in suspense until the factory man actually showed up out of the blue. This suspense must have been keen among those who had successfully been selling beetles, for they were beginning to see the potential in the car, yet did not know what was brewing.

Certain plans were indeed being formulated. These had to be flexible, for the United States was virgin territory for VW

174

and, aside from a few Americans such as Stanton and von Neumann, almost no one with VW had firsthand experience of the demands this huge market might make. "We didn't know too much about the United States," Heinz Nordhoff has admitted. "We just looked at a map and saw that the Mississippi River seemed a good dividing line, so we split the market at that point." In doing so, VW continued the previous pattern and decided to send two factory representatives to the U.S.A., give them equal authority, and have them open up headquarters in New York and San Francisco respectively.

First to arrive was Gottfried H. Lange, formerly an Opel man, whom the Californians rechristened "Geoffrey" soon after he assumed his West Coast "beat." To some extent, his territory was an easier one to tackle than the East Coast; for one thing (and for unknown reasons), sports cars and European cars in general had caught on earlier along the Pacific. For another, John von Neumann's enthusiasm for the Volkswagen had brought results. Manuel Hinke explains, "Johnny is a sports-car-loving fellow, a former racing driver with a real love for the VW, who had never made a botch of selling it." Translating and extending some of this native enthusiasm into organization terms was the job Lange now faced. Of course he immediately confirmed von Neumann as a distributor; then, with von Neumann's help, went out to find others.

Lange, apparently, liked to match up partners carefully, selecting one for expertise in automotive matters and picking the other for shrewd business know-how. One man who seemed to combine both qualities in himself was an old automotive pro, Reynold C. Johnson.

Johnson's automobile career began in 1924 when August Johnson, his father, hired him as a used-car salesman for a truck distributorship he owned. By 1927, Reynold Johnson managed a small branch of the business and, nine years later, had earned a partnership in the corporation. By the 1940's, both Reynold Johnson and his brother Luther (today a VW dealer in Oakland, California) were industry men with experience; Reynold Johnson had his own Packard dealership in 1941 and, after the end of the war, set up Willys branches throughout the state of California.

At about this time, a Navy air veteran named Kjell Qvale whom Johnson knew well said he too wanted to get into the auto business. "He had eight thousand dollars and a lot of guts," is the way Johnson remembers it. With Johnson's help, Kjell Qvale, son of a retired Norwegian sea captain, had become a Willys Jeep dealer in Alameda; in the ensuing years, he handled several British makes as well and, by 1953, was offering Volkswagens also. He and Johnson had spotted the "bugs" for the first time while on a 1950 trip to Europe; they had even driven in a VW then, say they were impressed with it, but at the time made no move towards representing Volkswagen. As interest in foreign cars peaked upwards, however, this changed.

Then came Lange and, with him, some further changes. He suggested that Qvale give more emphasis and attention to Volkswagens and, also, that he get himself a partner who could devote the time necessary towards realizing the beetle's potential out West. Kjell Qvale immediately thought of the man who had gotten him into the auto business in the first place: Reynold Johnson, who had gone into retirement in 1952. He approached Johnson, who liked the idea of returning to a distribution activity; Lange, recognizing the prestige and help Johnson's name would give, as well as the value of his experience, gave the partnership his blessing. After three months of operating under the name of Riviera Motors (Qvale's old company), the distributorship was renamed Reynold C. Johnson Co. Both men were equal partners and, while Qvale concentrated on his British makes, Johnson started building up his Volkswagen organization.

Lange, meanwhile, appointed other distributors. One of these distributorships was VW Washington, whose partners were aircraft industry scion William Boeing, Jr., Dr. Dean Johnson, a car enthusiast, Jerry Barker, an aeronautical engineer, and Jim Cleland, an experienced used-car operator. VW Washington sold Volkswagens in northern Idaho, Washington and Alaska. Subsequently, this distributorship was combined with Riviera Motors (see below), the Portland-based distributor for the Northwest.

As Oregon, Montana and southern Idaho were still "open," Lange invited Reynold C. Johnson to set up a distributorship there as well. He did so in partnership with Kjell Qvale, naming Kjell's brother Knute Qvale as president, a post Knute Qvale still holds today. The company assumed the old Riviera Motors name. As time went on, ownerships changed. The two Qvale brothers bought out Reynold Johnson's interest in this new distributorship and Johnson, in turn, bought out Kjell Qvale's interest in the company bearing his name. Johnson retained the presidency of Reynold C. Johnson Co. until 1964, then turned it over to Robert W. Hansen, who had joined as wholesale manager in the mid-1950's, and became chairman of the board.

Lange not only appointed distributors on the West Coast,

but also in San Antonio, New Orleans, and Hawaii. The island distributorship was set up under the leadership of Donald McKay who had been, in effect, a sub-importer from the U.S. "mainland." After McKay's death, the Hawaiian Islands territory was transferred to the Los Angeles distributorship.

Sales on the West Coast were climbing and, for some years, were even disproportionately high. In 1954, VW distributors in just four West Coast cities (Los Angeles, San Francisco, Seattle, and Portland) sold slightly more than half (50.2 per cent) of all VWs sold in the U.S. A year later, that percentage climbed eight points, and even in 1956, West Coast sales amounted to 40.1 per cent of all U.S. beetles. By 1957, the percentages had dropped to 32.8, but even that was an amazing figure, for by that time, East Coast distributors as well as those in other parts of the country were picking up steam fast.

The pioneering effort in the West had been von Neumann's; distributors like Johnson and the Qvales had then helped to give the beetle a fast and early push in a part of the country most of us tend to associate more with high-powered sports cars and gadgeted gas-guzzlers. Gottfried Lange's contribution was to take a loose organization in hand and to organize it in a way the factory at Wolfsburg liked. He was, says R. W. Hansen, "a fine gentleman who represented Wolfsburg astutely." Hansen recalls how hard Lange worked at his job; he was a business-oriented man who launched the VW entrepreneurs into such needed practices as uniform financial statements. He communicated effectively, having learned almost perfect "British" English in the 1920's, while working for a U.S. bank. A confirmed anglophile, he seems to have been by nature reserved, and there were those on the often-flamboyant West Coast who regarded him as too conservative in his attitudes. In any case, those with whom he worked seem today split down the middle in their evaluation of the man. He and the representative whom the factory had sent over to tackle the eastern portion of the United States seem to have been opposites in personality and methods; it was inevitable that a rivalry would develop between the two regions (and men). Ultimately the New York office, by virtue of its relative nearness to Germany and the exuberant drive of its chief, would become the VW headquarters in the U.S. In 1960, Lange transferred to the Volkswagen organization in Australia and has since joined Auto-Union in Europe; the man to replace him on the West Coast was Alfred Kalmbach, who headed San Francisco operations until April 1962, when activities were consolidated in the East, and Kalmbach became vice president in charge of dealer relations. Since then, Kalmbach has moved to VW-Brazil, where he is general sales manager.

An initially more complex situation prevailed east of the Mississippi, for sales had proved tougher there and the number of states and territories to be assigned was larger. To handle the job, VW sent to New York a man who not only measured up to it, but who towered above it, Will van de Kamp.

Van de Kamp was in his early forties when he arrived in the United States; tall and handsome, with hair graying at the temples, he struck Americans as having the formal, courtly manners of a European aristocrat and something of the dash of a fighter pilot. He appeared impeccable in British Savile Row suits, a homburg, and a tightly furled umbrella and no one was ever to see him sloppily or even casually dressed; one person who once saw him on a weekend, working on his lawn, swears that even then he was dressed to the nines and wore pigskin "work gloves." As may be inferred, van de Kamp was formal, somewhat unbending, unfailingly "correct"—but also overwhelmingly charming, whenever he wanted to be.

He arrived in New York towards the end of January 1954 and immediately started on a tour of his territory, intent on setting up the nucleus of his distributor and dealer network as quickly as possible. He was armed with a sheaf of letters which had been written to Wolfsburg by interested automotive dealers, several of them members of the earlier Hoffman group. Among these letters were Marsh's letter from Columbus and the Schmidts' from Chicago.

He must have seemed very strange indeed, stepping out of airplanes in the towns of America's wheat and corn country, or traveling through New England and the South, much like a diplomat from the Court of St. James's who is visiting a land of Levi's and galluses, of shirt-sleeve conferences and just plain talk. Yet the first impression he made was not the last, for there was underneath his mixture of correct formality and charm something else again. And it was this that did much to put VW on the map in the United States.

Will van de Kamp was an evangelist, possessed of a near-fanatic missionary zeal. He believed passionately in the Volkswagen and in the truth, beauty, and justice of his company's policies; he never doubted for a second that Volkswagen would become a tremendous success in the United States; he regarded it as heresy for a dealer to believe in (much less sell) any other car but VW, and he considered it his personal mission in life to infect others with his faith. With that confidence—and following his instructions, admonitions, or suggestions to the letter—the men he would appoint could not help but succeed, and make VW succeed as well. Those who argued policies with him, those who questioned the methods he insisted upon, those who balked at the "VW way of doing things" were regarded by him as the not-yet-saved, the benighted whom it was his duty to convert. He did so mainly with the sheer force of his personality, his conviction, and his expert knowledge; often he did so with his charm, sometimes with exasperated anger. "Why do you make it so hard for me to like you?" he was soon to groan repeatedly at one stubborn distributor. "If you will only stop arguing and do *exactly* as I say, I assure you, you will become a millionaire!"

"If ever a man ought to appear in the *Reader's Digest* as 'My Most Unforgettable Character,' " says Carl Schmidt, "that man is Will van de Kamp. He was one of those rare individuals one can never overlook, never ignore; he commanded every situation and everyone's attention, from the moment he entered a room. We met for the first time in February; he had come to Chicago to choose a distributor from among about three applicants for the franchise. We had asked him for the states of Iowa, Indiana and Illinois; when he finally appointed us, he gave us only the latter two at first. He never told us *why* he picked us over the other applicants. I think he went on instinct largely."

The experience of the Fergus brothers in Columbus, as well as of others, confirms the belief that van de Kamp operated less on any notion of "market research" than on what the Germans call *Fingerspitzengefühl*—sheer sensitive intuition. "Van de Kamp met with us very briefly in Columbus at the end of January 1954," says Robert Fergus. "He'd received Don's letter to Wolfsburg and looked us over. Then, in mid-February, he asked us to meet him in Cleveland."

Robert Fergus, his older brother John (an attorney), and Don Marsh drove to Cleveland on February 19 and used the trip to set up the three-way partnership they meant to offer van de Kamp as his local distributorship. "He'd already met with some pretty substantial and established businessmen who applied for the franchise," John Fergus recalls, "and we were up against some tough competition. We were young fellows, thirty-three, twenty-nine and twenty-one years old. He never really did tell us that day that he had chosen us; he just asked us to place our order, so we knew we were in business and we ordered seventeen beetles and three trucks." At a later date, when they asked him just why he had picked them to be distributors for Ohio and Kentucky, van de Kamp answered in deadly earnest and in his heavy German accent, "I liked the sparkle in your eyes."

If that sounds arch or questionable, it was nevertheless largely what van de Kamp was looking for. He was searching out Americans who, by and large, were young, energetic, capable of flexibility and growth, able to devote enthusiasm and energy to the job, and who, he hoped, would trust his judgment completely. As he traveled throughout his territory, he tried to imbue each with his unshakable faith in the future of the Volkswagen.

He had that rare combination of vision and shortsightedness that achieves success through sheer determination. "He had blinders on," one distributor says. "Van de Kamp simply could not see that what he was trying to do was just impossible! If you raised the possibility that the VW might fail in the U.S., van de Kamp just scoffed at you. 'It's succeeding in Germany, isn't it?' he'd say. 'So it will succeed in America!' If you argued with him that conditions in the States were different, that there was 'Detroit' to consider, he just stopped listening. He was completely uninterested in what Detroit was doing or how it was doing it. To him there was only *one* car—the Volkswagen—and only *one* way of doing things: the VW way!"

During that first year in the United States, van de Kamp appointed eight of the ten VW distributors operating in his territory; Geoffrey Lange's own West Coast distributor organization was also virtually complete by the end of that year. Although some states have been reassigned among distributors in the years since then, the pattern of distribution that was largely developed by van de Kamp continues in force today.* Appointed by the end of 1954, in addition to Arthur Stanton and John von Neumann, were the following distributors:

Hubert L. Brundage, of Miami, Florida, had written VW, hoping to be assigned Dade County or some small area around Miami. Brundage was a friend of sports-car enthusiast Glenn Curtiss, scion of the famed Curtiss aircraft family, and Curtiss had suggested they try for a foreign franchise so they might

---

* The following paragraphs show territories of each distributor today, which differ in only a few cases from the states originally assigned in 1954. To detail all changes in the distribution pattern would serve no purpose unless corporate and marketing reasons for each shift were discussed in detail as well, which might prove of only minor interest to readers not immediately involved.

get cars for themselves at wholesale prices. Their letter to VW resulted in a visit from van de Kamp, who took an order for fifty cars and immediately handed them all of Florida and Georgia (South Carolina was added later). Brundage rented a small shop in Miami Springs and, using a list of foreign-car dealers which van de Kamp had given him, drove out to each in a VW and talked them into a consignment, usually selling his beetle and returning by bus. By the end of the year, Brundage had sold 102 new Volkswagens to seven dealers. Subsequently, he located his distributorship, Brundage Motors, Inc. (later changed to Volkswagen Southeastern Distributor, Inc.), in Jacksonville, Florida.

John MacPhee and Tage Hansen, of Hansen-MacPhee Engineering Company, Inc., Waltham, Massachusetts, were appointed distributors in Maine, Massachusetts, New Hampshire, Rhode Island, and Vermont. "Van de Kamp came to us and asked us for an order for five hundred cars," Hansen recalls. "I explained that we did not have that kind of money, but he looked me straight in the eyes and said in that German accent of his, 'I assure you, Mr. Hansen, that if you will only listen to me, you will become a very rich man!' I believed him; he had this way about him, insisting he knew better than you did. So we somehow managed to order three hundred cars and that proved the turning point in our careers, because now we had to concentrate on selling them.*

Carl and Oliver Schmidt's Import Motors of Chicago, Inc., today distributors in Illinois, Iowa, Minnesota, the Dakotas and Wisconsin, was operating out of a headquarters near Wrigley Field. The site was close by the Chicago & North Western Railroad tracks, and the Schmidts used these as a rugged demonstration ground for prospective dealers. Going over them at full speed was a bone-jangling experience for the dealers, but an effective way of demonstrating the advantages of a four-wheel independent torsion-bar suspension system; as Oliver Schmidt says, "Those tracks made more money for us than they did for the railroad." Skeptical prospects were told to try for themselves. One, who questioned the Schmidts' enthusiasm by calling them "damn liars," was challenged to take the beetle out for a drive alone, to see if it lived up to the advance billing. The Schmidts reported that the prospect drove the VW around for several minutes, raced it back, jumped out, slammed the door, and shouted, "The car's a

---

* As will be reported in somewhat greater detail later, both the Brundage and Hansen-MacPhee distributorships have since been acquired by the Volkswagen company itself.

damn liar too!" Gradually, however, the scoffers were won over even in the Midwest, never very hospitable to foreign products.

Cook, Hekman and Sluyter's Import Motors Ltd. of Grand Rapids, Michigan, had been assigned the state of Michigan in which to distribute their little German car, later adding Indiana as well. The prevailing climate in which they sold was summed up by an officer of a prominent Detroit bank in 1954, who turned down their business with a sneer. "Gentlemen," he said, "you may be able to bring coals to Newcastle, but I assure you that you will never bring foreign cars to Detroit!" (Not much later, this same officer pleaded that his institution be considered as the bank for one of Import's Michigan dealers.) Today Sluyter is chairman of the board, Cook is president, and Hekman is vice president of this distributorship.

Charles F. Urschel, Jr., of Inter-Continental Motors Corporation, San Antonio, Texas, was another west-of-the-Mississippi distributor appointed by VW's San Francisco office. Today, run by Urschel's partner, vice president, and general manager, William J. Dick, Jr., this distributorship covers the largest territory in the VW network, running north-to-south along the entire Rocky Mountain area from Wyoming to the Gulf of Mexico. Urschel and Dick, as befits Texans, have interests in oil as well as in other enterprises.

A New Hampshire Yankee who came to Louisiana in his thirties and who has since become a major political force in the state is Willard E. Robertson, whose New Orleans–based International Auto Sales and Service Inc. was appointed VW distributor for Louisiana, Alabama, Mississippi, and western Tennessee.

Robertson arrived in New Orleans in 1948 to operate a sales office for a Connecticut boat company. His customers were diverse, including Standard Oil, which used the boats to transport crews to offshore drilling rigs, and the Mexican government. A year later, the company foundered and Robertson looked for a new opportunity in his adopted city. He heard of 360 Renaults which were being stored in a warehouse in New Orleans, formed his company, International Auto Sales and Service, and began to sell the French import. He sent out cars on consignment to dealers in four states, the same states his company now serves for VW. Before taking on VW exclusively, his company was handling twenty-seven different makes of imported cars.

In the early 1950's, a Belgian student arrived at his New Orleans dealership with a VW that needed repairs. The youth had been traveling through Mexico and the U.S. when the engine gave out. Robertson's mechanic, who had never worked on a VW before, telephoned Hoffman for an air shipment of parts. When these arrived, he rebuilt the engine and urged Robertson to get the VW franchise, adding, "I'll buy the first car you get."

Robertson recalls that when he approached Hoffman about a VW franchise it was suggested he would find more profit selling Rolls-Royces, Jaguars, and Porsches. Undaunted, Robertson wrote to the factory about distribution rights. He received no answer and assumed the request had been ignored until one day Lange, unannounced, visited him and named him distributor. He continued to handle other makes, including Renault. His first VWs, he remembers, were five dull brown beetles which he repainted to be able to sell. That was in 1954; by 1956, International was distributing VWs exclusively.

By 1961, Barry's small auto dealership in Overland, Missouri, already mentioned, had developed into a distributorship in St. Louis, serving Arkansas, Kansas, Missouri, and Nebraska. In that year it was purchased by George H. Capps and Frank Pipe, and the name was changed to Mid-America Cars, Inc. Capps, an attorney and former FBI special agent, is president and controlling owner. Like many other VW distributors, he is active in other businesses as well and jets about from one of his global interests to another.

As has been noted earlier, one of the first to be appointed by van de Kamp was Midwestern VW Corporation, the partnership of the Fergus brothers and Don Marsh, covering Ohio and Kentucky.

A year after he had arrived in the United States, van de Kamp could, therefore, look on the beginnings of a national network which to a very large extent he alone had created. This was certainly true, at least, for the vast majority of newly appointed distributors; aside from von Neumann and Stanton, both of whom had been on the job before Lange and van de Kamp arrived, nine distributorships had been set up within a year, eight of them by van de Kamp. Doing so, while at the same time periodically returning to Wolfsburg for discussions, was a tremendous achievement possible only for a man of boundless energy and determination.

"In the first year or so," one distributor says, "we'd see him every two or three weeks, sometimes more often than that. He'd come flying into town, lunch with us, and fly on to the next city. He was a gadfly, encouraging, pushing, checking, admonishing—and always infecting us with his complete and utter faith in this small car."

He also tried to help them convey that faith to others. The distributors, after all, were responsible for appointing the "sub-network" of dealers, for motivating and enthusing them, as well as for getting them to work in that special "Volkswagen way" van de Kamp insisted upon. Doing so was quite a job, for inculcating faith in the VW at that time was not easy.

Americans who drove Volkswagens in those early days had to have thick skins. The somewhat more than two thousand VWs sold before 1954 had been joined by another 6614 sold during that year; sales may have "soared" in just twelve months, but it still remained a fact that fewer than 9000 VWs were on U.S. roads by 1955. American owners therefore looked queer indeed. "A lot of people thought they resembled nuts," writes Huston Horn in *Sports Illustrated*, "and they were rewarded for their courage by the sneers of other drivers who regarded them with envy mixed with contempt." The car itself was regarded at best as a passing and minuscule fad and the VW owner sloughed off as a faddist. Not only was this the attitude of most American automobile drivers, but also of a small army of dealers. Any number of VW distributors and dealers, reflecting today on the brilliant stroke of genius (and sometimes luck) which led them to throw in their lot with Volkswagen, have pointed out to me that they each know several men in their towns who kick themselves each morning for having said "Thanks, but no!" to Will van de Kamp in the early 1950's. Paul Lee, a onetime Chevrolet dealer who later served for some years as a VW advertising man, was so convinced in the early 1950's that VW was a crazy passing fad that when a friend came to him and urged him to invest five thousand dollars and open a Volkswagen agency with him, he talked his friend out of the whole idea. "There was just no reason to believe the car would last," Lee admits. He has since avoided his friend, who regards himself as "a thwarted millionaire."

Simple mathematics shows how big the job was, how many skeptical Americans had somehow to be convinced that this car had a future in America and a future too for a VW dealer. Today, the Volkswagen organization in the United States consists of about one thousand dealers and annual sales are now at such a level that each of these, on the national average, sells about three cars every two days, yet Volkswagen has yet to make significant inroads into the overall U.S. car market, even if it *has* captured its price class. There are, in short, still plenty of people to convert, even today. In 1954–1955, however, the number of potential U.S. converts defied analysis and reaching them demanded as rapid a buildup of Volkswagen dealerships as could be managed.

Doing so while maintaining high dealer standards was of course an absurdly disproportionate job for one man, even if he now had distributors covering the field for him. Van de Kamp needed an organization to help, yet almost everything in his psychological makeup resisted building one. He finally surrendered to the need, but he was never happy unless he did everything himself.

The first man he hired was a twenty-five-year-old Englishman named J. Stuart Perkins, who is today president of the entire Volkswagen operation in the United States. Perkins arrived in New York from VW in Toronto, Ontario, on February 14, 1955. "We didn't have much," he says. "There were just the three of us—van de Kamp, a secretary, and myself—operating out of a suite in the St. Moritz Hotel on Central Park South. We had to build everything from there."

Next, van de Kamp sent for three men from Germany— and their arrival underlined one of the company policies he was trying to drive home. Not one of the three was a salesman; all were service representatives. Three more arrived after some months, and in 1956, Wolfsburg sent over another twenty-six, to tour the country in specially built Volkswagen panel trucks, chock-full of tools, and to train mechanics in those dealerships that had already been appointed. At about the same time as the twenty-six arrived, two parts representatives came over, bringing the total service and parts contingent to thirty-four. Each had undergone a year's training in Wolfsburg, including instruction in the language and customs of the United States.

"We believed sales would come if we started with service," Perkins says. "There is nothing odd in the fact that we had thirty-four service and parts people touring the country while hardly any Volkswagens were being sold. When I was assistant service manager with VW in Canada, we didn't have a single sale. We didn't even have a single Volkswagen to show customers. We actually had to borrow one from a private owner in New York City for an exhibit in Canada. But we had more than thirty thousand dollars' worth of spare parts stocked ready for the day when sales would come along!"

On April 19, 1955, van de Kamp, Perkins, and the gradually growing staff moved out of their hotel suite into sixth-floor offices at 720 Fifth Avenue in New York City. In June

1955, a company called Volkswagen United States was formed, only to go out of business at the end of that same year (and finally to be dissolved in 1958). A new corporation, Volkswagen of America, Inc. (VWoA) a wholly-owned subsidiary of the Volkswagenwerk in Wolfsburg, was established and appointed sole VW importer for the United States.

Making Volkswagen of America sole importer immediately presented nightmares for the small staff. Until then, each distributor had, in effect, acted as his own importer, arranging for the arrival of the cars he needed. Now, all this fell on the new corporation. With what seems justifiable pride, Perkins remembers that the tiny company set up the kind of network of ports of entry in three weeks that usually takes much longer to establish. "I confess I had no idea how to go about it at the time," Perkins says. "I simply called ships' brokers in a dozen ports, let them advise us, and soon we were in business. Wolfsburg helped us as best they could at long distance, but most of it was handled over the telephone from New York."

Two more distributorships were appointed in 1955. In January, Knute Qvale's Riviera Motors Inc., of Beaverton, Oregon, was named; it now distributes throughout Alaska, Idaho, Montana, Oregon, and Washington. In July, Capitol Car Distributors Inc., today in Lanham, Maryland, was appointed and now represents Volkswagen in Maryland, North Carolina, eastern Tennessee, Virginia, West Virginia, and the District of Columbia. Behind the latter organization lies the story of a story.

The story in question was written by Blake Clark, a *Reader's Digest* roving editor, and it appeared in the February 1954 issue of that magazine. Entitled "The Car That Built a City," it dealt with the VW and the town of Wolfsburg, and it reached the eyes of Will van de Kamp just after he set foot in the United States. Van de Kamp was delighted with the valuable unsolicited publicity and, after appointing a Washington foreign-car dealer named Jack Pry as his distributor in and around the nation's capital, he suggested to Pry that he take Clark in as a partner with a token percentage of the Capitol Car stock as a gesture of appreciation for the nice article. Pry didn't mind doing so, for this concession was so small then as to be meaningless; he didn't even mind when Blake Clark, sniffing the winds of change faster than Pry did, later purchased enough stock to own half of the company. Then the beetle's sales began to soar and Pry found that he had cut himself out of fifty per cent of a business moving into the millions of dollars. Eventually,

VWoA had to move into the picture to correct an impossible situation created because the two equal owners could not agree on policy. Pry's half-share in Capitol Car Distributors, Inc., was bought out by Schroeder-Rockefeller and Co., Inc., a New York investment company, whose president, James E. Madden, serves as chairman of the board of the distributorship. President and operating head is Alan M. Dix, an able, enthusiastic veteran of VW operations all the way from South Africa and Oregon to Wolfsburg itself. As for Blake Clark, he continues as a roving editor and is relatively inactive in the firm which has since made him very rich indeed; he serves it as chairman of the executive committee and vice chairman of the board and exemplifies in his own life the upbeat ending of a *Digest* "Life in These United States" anecdote.

In 1955, plans were formulated to manufacture the Volkswagen in the U.S. as well, and a Studebaker assembly plant in New Brunswick, New Jersey, was purchased. Six months and one day later, it was sold again and the plans were abandoned. Preliminary estimates had proved to be too low and it now became clear that the venture would cause the Volkswagenwerk to lose money. "You don't have seats in your cars," said one U.S. supplier who boosted his estimates after a close look at the beetle. "You have chairs."

"The decision to sell," says Dr. Carl H. Hahn, then a rising young man in the Wolfsburg export department who would soon be slated for even greater things, "was taken one afternoon in Germany by Professor Nordhoff himself. He never asked who obtained the inaccurate estimates, nor did he blame anyone. 'Well,' he said, 'I made a mistake. Let's sell.' "

Van de Kamp and his men continued to race all over their part of the country, interviewing prospective dealers and helping to appoint and train those who impressed them and their distributors. They had their problems with many. "One of the first things we had to do," remembers one veteran of these visits, "was to get in there and have them clean up the dirt in their workshops. We wanted these to be neat and uniform— we had to convince them to get rid of pink and green shops— so that Volkswagen facilities could have the same single and recognizable image in the country that the car had. We wanted our workshops to be attractive and tidy, even to have flowers placed out front if possible, so as to make them really stand out from other dealerships." A lot of American dealers thought they were crazy.

One Virginia dealer, who dated back to the Hoffman network, worked out of a dilapidated wooden building. "The filth was indescribable," says E. W. Valentin, today VWoA's personnel chief. "We found this man sitting behind a cluttered rolltop desk and repairing everything from motorcycles right on up and down the line. We finally straightened both him and his place out. Another whose ways we finally changed was a New Hampshire dealer who used to dress like a beatnik and thought the whole VW idea a big joke. He'd talk with customers while sitting cross-legged on the floor, as though he were in an artists' colony."

VWoA's general service manager, Hans-Dieter Deiss,* recalls another encounter, typical of many of the day. Deiss, then a young service manager with Capitol Car, had driven to the address given for a "VW dealership" near Washington, D.C., only to find a men's clothing store at the site. "Sure we sell Volkswagens, Mister," the haberdasher said. "Out back behind the store." It turned out that the store owner found his "dealership" an easy way to get cars cheaply for his friends. When he learned Deiss's identity and was threatened with cancellation, he pleaded for another week's time. "You come back next week," he said, "and you'll see that everything will be the way you people want it."

A week later, Deiss arrived to find a storefront with a VW sign above it close beside the haberdashery. A Volkswagen sedan was actually to be seen in the otherwise bare shop. Deiss wandered in and found a man standing in the empty rear "store room," neatly dressed in a starched white coat. "Who are you?" Deiss asked without identifying himself. The fellow turned around and smiled. "Oh, heck," he said. "I don't really work here. I work across the street in that plant over there. Fellow just hired me for the day to stand around here because he's expecting some big shots from Germany to come in."

Dealerships such as this were canceled rapidly. Van de Kamp himself toured with a baleful eye. He walked into one Washington dealership and saw three salesmen in the showroom, one reading a newspaper in his shirt-sleeves. "This is out!" the impeccable van de Kamp announced to the dealer. "You either straighten out that man or you fire him!"

There was no stopping this determined German. He could neither take "no" for an answer nor regard anything as impossible. Stuart Perkins describes the harrowing way in which van de Kamp would get himself airline tickets after his secretary had failed to get him on the particular flight

* As of January 1, 1967, Deiss left VWoA to join the management of Volkswagenwerk at Wolfsburg.

which he insisted on using. "Van de Kamp would just call the president of the airline and start in on the man in his heavy accent until he gave in," Perkins says. "Then afterwards, van de Kamp would write him a charming letter, thanking him for his trouble, but also explaining that he did, after all, expect service, since he flew thousands of miles on that airline. The next time van de Kamp wanted to fly, he'd just telephone the president directly and say, 'Remember? You promised to help me next time I needed a ticket and I'm holding you to your word!' Of course the airline president had never made such a promise. He had never even answered van de Kamp's letter. But van de Kamp always got his tickets."

Generally speaking, van de Kamp got results by overwhelming the Americans he met. He did so, apparently, without artifice and completely naturally. With his commanding appearance, accent, and suave manners he dominated every situation. No one ever forgot him.

"He would, for example, go into an elegant restaurant for the first time," Stuart Perkins recalls with fascination, "and the headwaiter, not recognizing him, might say all the tables had been reserved. Van de Kamp would ignore the remark or just proceed to enlighten the man. 'I am Mr. van de Kamp!' he would tell the headwaiter, spelling his name out carefully: 'van de Kamp—*from Volkswagen!*' Half the time, the headwaiters would not have understood him, but they did understand *one* thing: that one did not refuse this man. Van de Kamp always got his table—and they always remembered his name, even when he returned months later. There are restaurants I frequent today who still ask about him by name."

"We were out to the theater in New York City with Will van de Kamp one evening," John Fergus says, supplying another anecdote illustrative of this man's stubborn will to win. "There were about four of us, with our wives. Van de Kamp wanted a taxi afterwards and it was no use arguing with him that we could walk the six or eight blocks to our restaurant, that he would never get a taxi in Manhattan when the theaters let out, and that he might as well join us. '*I* will get a taxi!' he said. Last thing we saw of him, as the rest of us started walking crosstown, he was standing in the middle of Eighth Avenue, with the cars streaming by on either side of him, waving his furled umbrella and occasionally even banging on the sides of passing cabs. Then, just as we got to our destination about ten or fiften minutes later, a taxi pulled up, with Will van de Kamp inside. His umbrella was upright between his knees and his hands rested, folded, across its handle. He half-bowed to us through the window. 'I *told* you I would get a taxi,' he said."

Van de Kamp's determination absolutely overwhelmed, sometimes appalled, but always impressed. It was clear he was used to issuing orders and the combination of his often peremptory commands and his equally enormous charm usually was enough to get them obeyed. After one early distributor meeting, for example, van de Kamp said, "Gentlemen, we will all now go to our rooms and clean up and then you will be my guests for cocktails and dinner!" One of the distributors objected that he had a train reservation for early that evening. Van de Kamp asked him if he couldn't get another reservation, but the man answered that nothing else was available. Whereupon van de Kamp looked him straight in the eye and said, "Your train leaves tomorrow morning!" The flabbergasted, but awed, distributor stayed for the evening.

"Never in my life," says Perkins, whose task it often was to make van de Kamp's directives more palatable to others, "have I met a man like him! He could antagonize you and in the next moment charm you to the point where you forgot the slight you had received earlier. You could switch from hating to loving him in thirty seconds.

"His broken English and his heavy German accent insulated him from all criticism or objections. He simply never recognized them. The word 'no' was never allowed. As for the market, he was such a fanatic believer in the Volkswagen that he paid no attention whatsoever to U.S. car manufacturers or their methods. He never even discussed them. The issue was very simple: the Volkswagen had been a success elsewhere, so why shouldn't it be a success in the United States? The fact that the U.S.A. was the country of big cars didn't bother him. He would simply answer that point by saying, 'Yes, but you don't understand. *This* is the Volkswagen!' He was absolutely blind and deaf to whatever criticism he might hear and he had this enormous personal horsepower and terrific force of personality with which to overcome it."

Eventually, however, these characteristics of his did him in. As the end of 1958 approached, van de Kamp was told by Wolfsburg that he should find himself an opportunity elsewhere. For four years, Will van de Kamp had poured out his energies and his enthusiasm into the job of laying the groundwork for the U.S. Volkswagen network that exists today; why, then, the need for a change?

The answer lies less in any mysterious "company politics"

190

than in the changing situation VWoA and its parent company were now facing. Van de Kamp had been a freewheeling, intuitive operator, the typical "one-man show," satisfied only when he knew personally everything that was going on and could do every job himself. The only "management systems" he knew were his own and, instinctively, he distrusted those of others. His small staff had learned to live with both him and his methods and had even developed ways of getting around him, so as to establish some procedures and a semblance of a corporate organization, but the fact remained that Will van de Kamp was getting in the way of the very network he had built up. He considered this network *his* baby and he continued personally to mother (and, some say, smother) it after it had grown too big for that. Van de Kamp's time had passed him by, thanks to his own success.

It had been possible in 1954 for van de Kamp to know almost everything about VW in the U.S.A. and to handle it all by himself; four years later, when sales had passed 100,000 a year, when "his" distributors and their dealers were operating efficiently and growing rapidly, this was no longer the case. Van de Kamp found himself often in the dark and making mistakes; like an army platoon leader who suddenly finds himself a general, he was unhappy with staffwork and planning and still insisted on being in the front lines, personally leading the attack, rather than dealing through subordinates and building a team.

To be sure, his insistence on being in these front lines had its charming and amusing sides too. Once, when driving a VW along a turnpike, at a time when very few Volkswagens were to be seen on American roads, van de Kamp spotted a disabled beetle parked on the turnpike's shoulder. Without hesitating a moment, he zoomed in front of it, stopped, and leaped out to confront the distressed lady driver. "How may I be of help?" he asked gallantly and, when the lady pointed to her car's flat tire, van de Kamp and the other VW executive with him immediately whipped off their jackets and changed it for her. After they were finished and van de Kamp once more stood before her in his homburg hat and immaculately tailored British suit, she thanked him and asked if she might pay him something for the trouble they had gone to. In reply, van de Kamp snapped his heels together, bowed, and presented her with his business card as head of VWoA. "A pleasure, madam!" he said, "Just typical Volkswagen service, nothing more!"

It was this kind of personal contact that he enjoyed and

that the pressing need for a relatively impersonal organization would deny him. It may have been a shortcoming of his that he apparently could not grow with his growing job, but surely it was a virtue and much to his credit that he had honorably worked himself out of that job. There is a time when his kind of pioneering enterprise no longer serves a need and managers have to take over. That time had come.

Van de Kamp now looked around the distributor network for some opportunity that might exist. A financial settlement had been worked out between him and Volkswagenwerk, but he wanted to continue to be associated with the American end of the business. To some distributors, however, van de Kamp's dominating personality was perhaps a fault; while all the distributors appear to have liked and admired him, working with him full-time or having him as a partner was another matter again.

Two who were not apprehensive about this were Oliver and Carl Schmidt of Import Motors of Chicago. Indeed, both profess to have been anxious to get van de Kamp into their organization.

"I couldn't think of a better man for us," Carl Schmidt says today. "We both liked him a great deal and respected him enormously. We were growing so fast then that we badly needed a man of his caliber."

Van de Kamp wanted twenty per cent of the business in return and, while Carl Schmidt says he was willing to part with ten per cent of his own share, Oliver Schmidt admits he was not ready to do the same. (A tragic accident in his family, requiring the most costly type of long-term care, he felt, required that he place the financial security of his family first.) A settlement was reached: van de Kamp was willing to join the Schmidts as executive vice president and general manager of their VW distributorship, in return for salary and bonus, plus an agreed-upon sum, to be paid out over five years. In addition, the Schmidts let him buy a share in a Porsche dealership they also owned.

Van de Kamp's relationship with VWoA had ended before 1958 was up and he formally joined Import Motors of Chicago in the early spring of 1959. That he apparently harbored few (if any) resentments was evidenced at the first "post-van de Kamp" VW distributor meeting, at which his successor was introduced to men van de Kamp himself had largely appointed.

"To my amazement," says Stuart Perkins, who was there, "Will van de Kamp attended this meeting, seated among the distributors, between Carl and Oliver Schmidt, and looking perfectly calm and comfortable. Another man might have waited a year before showing up in public 'at the other side of the table,' but not he! He was too big to be in any way embarrassed by the turn of events."

If he looked cool and comfortable, that seemed to be how he felt. He and his wife, a charming and attractive German lady with whom he enjoyed a very close and devoted life, had moved into a handsome house in Illinois and could devote more of their energies than ever before to leisure and the cultivation of their own cultural interests.

Then, just six months after he had moved to Chicago, van de Kamp was killed, in the early autumn of 1959, at the age of fifty. It happened while he was away in Germany, on business; he was driving a Porsche at night, and speeding over a rise on the Autobahn, he slammed into the rear end of a truck he had apparently failed to see in time. He died instantly. He may have had some premonition of his death, for it was during that trip to Germany that he reportedly had for the first time in many years resumed contact with his family there. According to all reports, Will van de Kamp actively avoided any contact with or discussion of his family members in Germany while he was at VWoA. The van de Kamps had no children and it seemed as though his entire private world centered only on his wife. But just before he was killed, he reportedly had taken up that broken link again.

Stuart Perkins, his close associate for four years, happened to be in Wolfsburg when the accident occurred and he attended the funeral. Afterward, Perkins noticed a German whom he had never before met and he introduced himself. The stranger told Perkins that he had come to the funeral because he had been van de Kamp's Luftwaffe squadron leader on the Russian front during World War II. "You know," the former fighter pilot said, "van de Kamp used to fly on my wing during the war. I came to rely on him. He was quite a man."

9

Detroit Meets the Beetle

BACK in the summer of 1954, a twenty-seven-year-old German economist attached to the Office of European Economic Cooperation in Paris had an idea regarding the "Europeanization" of the Continental auto industry. At the suggestion of his father, a member of the Auto-Union board, he outlined the idea in a letter to Heinz Nordhoff, whom he had never met. Nordhoff's answer was disappointing.

The plan, Nordhoff wrote, wouldn't work, and he sketched out his reasons for thinking so, remarking as an aside that "there are already a lot of international organizations like this and the one thing most of them seem to have in common is that they want their headquarters to be in Paris." But Nordhoff had liked the young economist's thinking and invited him to stop by when he found himself in Wolfsburg.

This is just what Carl Hahn did, and sometime after stopping by, he decided to stay. Nordhoff had invited Hahn to become his personal assistant. "I was assigned a big office," Hahn says, "but there was no real work for me to do, because Nordhoff is so used to doing everything himself. I complained about this once or twice and, when nothing happened, I finally threatened to resign." This provided the shock Hahn had wanted to administer and he was reassigned to the export department's sales promotion operation. In what free time he had left, he helped Professor Nordhoff prepare his Brunswick University lectures. Hahn himself had been educated in Germany, Switzerland, France, Italy, and England, and had received his doctorate from the University of Berne in 1952, his thesis being on European economic unification. The Nordhoff lectures were more practical—they tried to teach the students the hard facts of industrial life, to prepare them for business—and while this work and that in the export department interested Hahn, he felt he wanted still more scope.

There were actually plans afoot that Hahn should manage VW's Canadian operation and that the man who had built up this market, Werner Jansen, would take over in the United States now that van de Kamp needed to be replaced. It was during this period that Heinz Nordhoff underwent an operation for ulcers at the Mayo Clinic, and using his visit to North America also to talk with Jansen, he found that this executive, now growing older, did not like the idea of being given the huge U.S. assignment at his age.

On January 5, 1959, Carl Hahn returned from a skiing trip in Switzerland to find that he had immediate instructions to proceed to New York City with his boss, VW export chief Manuel Hinke. Nordhoff was waiting for them at the St. Regis Hotel, having been released from the Mayo Clinic. He told Hahn that he and Hinke would like him to take over the U.S. operation; ever since van de Kamp had left, VWoA had been without an official head man.

"Hahn was very uncertain about whether he could do a good job," Nordhoff remembers.

"I was overawed," Hahn admits.

The two men spent the entire day in the hotel. "I wanted to give him some confidence and also explain what I wanted done here," Nordhoff says. "For decades, no one had believed that European cars could ever be a success in the United States. Then, after the war, the British showed that it could be done. I knew that we could do the same." The talks were intense and strenuous for Heinz Nordhoff. "I was so weak from my operation that we could only talk for an hour at a time before I'd have to rest for a bit," he says.

"That day in the St. Regis," Nordhoff reports, "I told Hahn I wanted VW to have more dealers in the U.S.A., I wanted fresh dealers, and dealers who would want to sell Volkswagens exclusively. I suggested to him that he go after people who had no automobile franchises at all, because so many of the best dealers had been taken on by Detroit."

Nordhoff urged Hahn to place even more emphasis on service. "I had already been told by many to look at the British operation in the U.S.A.," Nordhoff says. "Many of their early successes had dissolved because they couldn't adequately service the cars they had sold. When we planned entering the U.S. market, people kept telling us, 'Be careful! Look at the British!' Well, I looked—and I learned a lesson!"

After Carl Hahn had been appointed head of the U.S. operation, he and Manuel Hinke took a tour of the country to see for themselves. It was during this trip that they decided that the United States VW operation should no longer be "split down the middle" at the Mississippi River, but that the country should be regarded as a unit. Gradually, they began to de-emphasize the West Coast operation and in 1962 it was dissolved completely.

"After van de Kamp had left and before Carl Hahn took over, we had gone through a period of considerable worry," says Stuart Perkins, who was to serve as Hahn's sales manager and, later, as his assistant general manager. "There were rumors that the factory was going to close down the whole U.S. operation and work directly through dealers, so it was a relief to see that this had not come about. The first thing one noticed about Hahn was a completely refreshing approach. He could make a decision and have it followed through, because he had Nordhoff's complete confidence, which van de Kamp never really enjoyed. Hahn immediately took to modern techniques. We got computers in and we got consultants to develop a training program and to do essential research jobs for us. Hahn proved to be a slide-rule man, which is what we needed. He also proved fast in adapting to American ways and that contributed to his success in the United States."

In a very real way, Carl H. Hahn was the right man for the U.S. market at that moment. The organization was expanding; it had enthusiasm and drive, but it needed someone to direct its vigor. And just such a man was (and is) Carl Hahn. Just as van de Kamp's evangelism had been an essential ingredient earlier, so was Hahn's vision, with its emphasis on modern techniques, essential now if the Volkswagen curve was to continue upward.

The creating of a national VWoA organization, expansion of the dealer network, standardization of service facilities, and modernization of the entire network into an efficient and well-managed one occupied Hahn's tenure in office. Under him, also, marketing became a science for Volkswagen, advertising began, and standards of service and sales were raised.

"Our customers buy service along with the car as part of a single sales package," says Hermann Bruns,* VWoA's vice president for service and parts and for long one of the most influential men in the organization. Another VW service specialist once put it this way: "At Volkswagen, we feel that sales without service is a little like kissing your sister. It's very nice, but there's no future in it." Far from permitting sales

* As of January 1, 1967, Bruns left VWoA to join the management of Volkswagenwerk at Wolfsburg.

to grow in an ungoverned and uncontrollable manner, the company refuses, says Bruns, to "let sales outpace the service facilities of a single dealer. His sales potential (the number of cars given him to sell) is increased only as his service potential grows. We also insist that each dealer maintain enough service facilities to care for *all* Volkswagens in his area for which service is demanded. Market studies show us just how large his facilities must be. We tell him, if you want to get something out of this business, you've got to put something into it."

Distributors select dealer locations and, once approved by VWoA, choose a suitable applicant for the dealership. Again VWoA joins in the final say on each man. "We set high standards as to buildings, working capital, personnel, equipment, and tooling," a company executive says. "We're like Howard Johnson—we want our buildings to have a distinct Volkswagen look. Even the interior space distribution is standardized. And we insist on cleanliness everywhere, not just for the customers, but for the sake of the 'grease-monkey,' that much-neglected man whose image is so tarnished. We ask for attractive lunchrooms for the personnel, as well as locker rooms and showers." Dealers receive complete blueprints and floor plans, down to the type of desk and desk lamp the company recommends. The company establishes various specifications, ranging from the smallest to the largest dealerships. It claims these save dealers about $5000 in architects' fees alone. Still, it does not reject an applicant who owns adequate facilities, just because he will not rebuild to its specifications. It is expected, however, that the dealer will sooner or later abandon his present facilities and achieve that "Howard Johnson look" VW likes. In new buildings alone, American VW dealers invested about $25,000,000 in 1966.

New dealers must buy a large parts inventory from the distributor. The minimum parts and accessories inventory for the smallest dealer is worth $7000 retail, representing three months' requirements. A minimum number of work stalls is also prescribed. The smallest dealer must have four work stalls, each two hundred square feet in size. Distributors maintain a minimum five months' inventory. In practice they carry a good deal more. I toured several impressive new headquarters buildings from which VW distributors now operate; not only efficient, these facilities seem to vie with each other for architectural and community awards. The $4,000,000 Capitol Car Distributors' structure in Lanham, Maryland; Arthur Stanton's headquarters in Orangeburg, New York, Carl Schmidt's premises in suburban Deerfield, Illinois.* and several other distributor office and warehouse buildings are really outstanding industrial facilities. All seem to be plagued with the constant need to move to larger space as VW's own growth continues. The millions of dollars' worth of parts and accessories which they need to warehouse for their network of dealers, their growing data processing centers, and their expanding staffs present their managements with ever-mounting growth problems.

Yet these high requirements have proved invaluable. The company was never encumbered with the deadly "lack of parts" stigma which other imported cars bore. Those VW owners who do find parts hard to get generally employ neighborhood garages which do not stock these parts and must send for them. (Even this end of the business is profitable. About 32 per cent of each dealer's inventory is sold to independent garages, repair shops, and body shops.)

VWoA maintains three company-paid representatives at the offices of each of its fifteen distributors. These are zone parts managers, zone service managers, and zone sales managers. They report directly to VWoA and serve as a direct link with company headquarters. "American automobile manufacturers think of service and parts as supporting the sales effort," says Hermann Bruns. "We disagree. They ought to be profitable operations in themselves and act as stabilizing influences. A dealer ought to make a decent living from service and parts if market conditions fluctuate." The dealers' parts business has proved to be profitable: it rose twelve-fold between 1956 and 1963.

"Twenty years ago General Motors and Ford did what we're doing," says Hermann Bruns. "But somewhere along the line they got sidetracked. They began to concentrate almost exclusively on sales. Then they tried to make up for their lack of service by advertising more. Ten years ago, Chevrolet had 11,000,000 cars on the road and today they have more than 21,000,000. But their number of work stalls hasn't increased at anywhere near the same rate. And Chevrolet isn't the only one. Much the same thing has happened to most of the Detroit manufacturers."

Bruns's contention that the early U.S. auto industry had a similarly enlightened policy about servicing its cars is accurate. Like Volkswagen, Ford "sent out traveling agents who taught Ford dealers how to handle stocks of parts, how to

* Carl Schmidt became sole owner of Import Motors of Chicago. In 1967 it was bought by VWoA; the name was changed to Volkswagen North Central.

do repair work, how to use the best tools in repair, and so on," according to Allan Nevins and Frank Ernest Hill. Their Ford history tells of a "not untypical" 1910 dealer in Cincinnati whose mechanics, "drawing on the stock of parts, could build a Model T complete within twenty-four hours." (The feat has been duplicated several times in several VW distributor headquarters, to publicize the completeness of the parts inventories.) This kind of care about service facilities paid off for Ford in those days as it now does for VW. "Nothing that the Ford Company had done pleased the average automobile owner more than its policy with respect to the servicing and repair of cars," write Nevins and Hill.

At VW, service personnel are as much cared for as service facilities, and training programs were started early. Today they exist in each distributorship, as permanent, full-fledged schools. Thousands of service and parts employees have attended them.

Dealers do not seem to mind the company's rigorous standards. The reason, as might be expected, lies in high sales and profits. Volkswagen dealers today vie with Chevrolet for first place among cars sold per dealer. The average VW dealer sells between three hundred and four hundred new cars a year and many sell more. "We can prove that our dealers make twice the average profits of any other car dealers in the U.S. auto industry, yet their profit margin per car is lower and their overhead is greater because of the big investment we require," says Perkins. "When you don't change the model each year, you can afford the extra costs. You can afford to modernize and meet our specifications. Today, eighty-five per cent of our dealers are in buildings less than four years old."

The paradox between unusually high costs and top profits is resolved because VW dealers are not vexed with the built-in weaknesses plaguing their Detroit counterparts. First of all, the demand is still so high that some U.S. customers still have to wait for delivery. This demand eliminates all need for discounts, rebates, price-cutting, and "unloading" at the end of a year. VW dealers do not need to throw in extras, nor sell at cut-rate prices to clear out showrooms for next year's model. As a result almost one hundred per cent of the dealers obtain the full retail price suggested by the manufacturer. In addition, the car's constant design eliminates the need for new tools or new service facilities, or for the retraining of service personnel. Dealers are also not stuck with obsolete parts and accessories.

Almost all dealers sell only the VW, a vital element in

creating the success of VW in America. A very few (fifteen or twenty per cent) also sell Porsches; four dealers also sell Mercedes-Benzes. "But we explained to them that product diversification doesn't mean more profits," Perkins says. "You can't sell a high-powered car in the same showroom with a Volkswagen. Also, if you sell only one car, you can stock fewer parts. Most of our dealers agree."

Each of the fourteen regional distributors maintains a "model retail outlet," or distributor-owned dealership. In part a carryover from the days when some distributors were also dealers, these installations today serve to test and refine new techniques before they are recommended to the dealer body. They also serve to keep distributors in touch with market conditions. The company has successfully discouraged distributors from opening up more than one distributor-owned dealership each, fearing the effect such a move would have on dealer morale. "In a few cases," Hahn says, "we had difficulties in getting distributors to trim down to one dealership. I earned a lot of antagonism at the time, but I instinctively felt it was absolutely essential that a distributor wear only one hat." Today, distributors agree and some say they'd just as soon give up even their one dealership.

Dealer morale is of course a priority item at VWoA, as it is throughout the industry. The company's National Dealer Advisory Council gives dealers a voice regionally and nationally through elected representatives. Local councils supplement the work of the national group. While VWoA is not unique in the attention it pays to its dealers, it does part company with Detroit in the demands it makes on them. For this, the company relies on persuasion. This persuasion has been most effective. It will probably continue to be effective, so long as the demand for VWs exceeds the supply.

"At Volkswagen," says Stuart Perkins, "we don't emphasize sales in our contracts with dealers, as much as Detroit does on the whole. Our contracts are more service-oriented. The dealer who does not maintain our standards is not fulfilling his contract. We keep a very sharp eye on his ability to do so. We know our growth depends almost entirely on how well we continue to service the cars we sell. Consequently, our distributors increase a dealer's allocation of new cars only when they see he can service them. I don't think many manufacturers are that particular. They're quite satisfied if they sell more and more, because next year they have another model to unload."

"We might have sold the first 50,000 or 70,000 Volkswagens on the basis of the car alone," says Guenther Kittel, VWoA's general parts manager. "But all sales after that were due to our organization." Kittel credits the product as first among the reasons for the success and believes the VW paint job is a big attraction. "Only cars in the $5,000-and-up category equal it," he says.

Interest in foreign cars started rising sharply in the early 1950's. In 1955 (when VWoA planned its New Brunswick factory) Volkswagen sales reached 31,000, including 2000 Transporters. In 1956 sales jumped to 50,000 sedans and 5000 Transporters. Headquarters personnel reached fifty-four and moved to a small brick building in Englewood Cliffs, New Jersey, across the George Washington Bridge from New York City.

The Karmann Ghia has also succeeded. It was introduced into the United States in 1955, when five hundred were sold. Today, more than 15,000 are sold annually and it holds first place among imported two-seaters. The Ghia, whose basic design has not changed in more than ten years, is the forerunner of "personal cars" in America. These vehicles, such as the Thunderbird, Mustang, Camaro, and a host of others, emphasize sporty styling and appointments rather than the dual purpose of racing and road driving which marks a real sports car. While other makers issue drivers a challenge to try their sheep in wolves' clothing. VW ads frankly admit that the Ghia is a Pussycat.

Sales ever since have been so good that Volkswagen, in a certain sense, occupies not only first (with its beetles and Ghias), but also second and third places among imported cars in the United States. This is because even VW's Type II's (the bus-like vehicles) and Type III's (the Fastback and Squareback) both outsell all other imported passenger makes. VW today also outsells all U.S. compacts.* A huge gulf exists between Volkswagen and the rest of the imported-car market.

* In 1966, comparative U.S. registrations were as follows (the VW total does not include 15,740 Tourist Delivery sales):

Volkswagen			
		Classic (Rebel)	116,498
Type I	323,998	Valiant	112,360
Type II	34,474	Corvair	88,951
Type III	65,173	American	75,843
		Opel	31,555
Total	423,645	Volvo	25,126
		Datsun	21,726
		MG	21,709
Chevy II	158,968	Toyota	15,814
Falcon	162,113	Simca	12,596
Dart	160,344	English Ford	7,932
Comet	133,533	Saab	6,947

The gulf was widened after Detroit entered the small-car market. The peak year for imported cars in the United States was reached in 1959, with 614,131 sold. Of these, VW's leading share was 120,442 sedans and 30,159 Transporters. Then, when foreign car sales reached ten per cent of total U.S. auto sales, American manufacturers took notice. In 1960, they entered the market with their so-called compact cars.

Of this new competition, Carl Hahn said with delight, "We no longer talk about other imported automobiles . . . They are of minor concern to us. New names are mentioned now —names like Ford and General Motors. We are in the big league now."

Heinz Nordhoff also appraised Detroit's entry into the small-car market in 1960, in an address to his German dealers and distributors. All U.S. compacts, he said, "are interesting vehicles, particularly the Corvair which closely followed our principles. They will all be successful, if perhaps not so completely and not so quickly as their creators had expected. Partly this is a question of time, partly of prices which in some cases are still too close to those of the bigger cars—and for many Americans the big car still has undoubted prestige-appeal, although it is becoming less and less fashionable to display one's wealth by the size of one's car." In March 1960, Nordhoff spoke out again on the subject, at the opening of the International Automobile Salon in Geneva, Switzerland. He noted that American compacts had their "well-earned and sensible success; their share of the market is even bigger than optimists hoped for, or feared, and I am completely convinced that this development will continue." These cars would not hurt Volkswagen, he predicted accurately. He could not resist chiding Detroit for its rigidity. Despite "scientifically advanced market research techniques" which predicted that "it would no longer do to make cars always bigger, always more powerful, it took the example of European imports, particularly of the Volkswagen, to drive the point home to the U.S. manufacturers." His analysis was accurate: VW, as one writer noted that year, was "the pace-setter."

Introduction of Detroit's compact cars had a disastrous effect on most European imports, cutting sales in half, to 378,-622 in 1961 and 339,160 in 1962. Only the VW survived, captured the bulk of the remaining foreign-car market, and eventually outsold the compacts themselves. In 1960, "year 1 of the Compact-Car Age," as one writer labels it, VW imported its 500,000th vehicle into the United States. A year later, forty-six per cent of all imports were VWs; dealers now totaled 550 and employees 8500.

It was at this time that the latest and newest Volkswagen distributorship was opened up—Auto Associates, Inc. (now known as Volkswagen Atlantic, Inc.) of King of Prussia, Pennsylvania, distributing throughout that state as well as Delaware. Raymond A. Vidinghoff, the founder and president, had the courage in January 1961, while the effect of Detroit's compact cars was still being assessed, to dig into his own pocket and purchase a new and efficient distributorship, a big gamble at the time.

Not only were compact cars having their effect, but a nasty "buy-American" campaign had been launched nationally, especially in areas where steel companies were having difficulties. So ugly was it that one VW distributor's son actually was beaten up by his "patriotically" motivated schoolmates and certain midwestern employers had let it be known that workers driving foreign cars would not be permitted into the factory parking lots. That this campaign was as foolish as it proved unsuccessful will be seen in Chapter 12, which deals with VW's worldwide exports and in which the impact of VW sales in and on the U.S.A. is also assessed. As for VWoA, its public relations department countered the campaign by pointing to "the give and take" of world trade; as a matter of fact, a VW film with just that title was issued and has been shown on U.S. television as an unsponsored public service film more often than any other similar motion picture. A VW brochure, *Fair Exchange*, made the point that, if Americans weren't buying such German products as the VW, Germany couldn't "buy American" (which it does far more than the U.S. "buys German"). Such anti-import campaigns continue sporadically even today, especially in the Middle West, but by and large, Volkswagen does not seem hurt by them. VW sales today run over 400,000 a year in the U.S. and keep climbing.

This remarkable sales record applied for a while also to the homely, commercial VW Transporter. By May 1960 VW had grabbed eighty-four per cent of the total import truck market in the U.S. and by 1962 Transporters climbed into second place among all imported vehicles. The company admits being surprised. "The first VW truck to roll over a U.S. road arrived in 1952," said VWoA's *Weathervane*. "That year ten commercials were registered . . . VW drove its truck into America almost unnoticed and in 1958 and 1959 its sales passed some top name producers in our weight class—such as Willys, Dodge, and GMC." By 1962, Detroit was worried enough by the Transporter to copy the boxlike truck. In 1964, however, VWoA was forced to increase the price of its trucks, due to a boost in United States tariffs occasioned by the notorious "chicken war" between Europe and the U.S.A. Tariffs on imported trucks jumped to twenty-five per cent. The VW panel truck now costs $237 more than it did before. "The effect," says Carl Hahn, "has been disastrous to our truck business. It's killed it off in the U.S.A. Selling trucks is already a big job for any dealer. It's real work. But selling a truck which is priced too high is impossible." The reaction of the distributors and dealers to this was at first traumatic. They were well aware that the Type II vehicles were being produced in ever-increasing numbers in Germany. Samuel Weill, Jr., executive vice president and general manager of von Neumann's distributorship (and former advertising manager of *Road & Track* magazine), who doodles in rhyme during distributor meetings, summed up the reaction in verse. His "Ode to Transporters" reads, "They'll build them 'til each dealer is to all intents well-fractured;/They may not sell, but sure as hell they'll still be manufactured!" As it turned out, imaginative salesmanship came to the rescue. Now that the truck market had been knocked out, Volkswagen salesmen throughout the country intensified their sale of this vehicle as a station wagon. Their increased efforts paid off handsomely and the company has by now more than made up its truck losses by means of even greater station wagon sales. Still, there is no question that the increased tariffs continue to hurt, for it can be argued that station wagon sales *and* truck sales would have gone up in tandem over the years.

The impact of the compacts began to lessen in 1963. By this time, VWoA had taken over more than 69 per cent of the imported-car market. As for the compacts themselves, "they got steadily more and more elaborate," the New York *Times* reported. Tom McCahill, probably America's best-known popular automotive writer, put it this way: "When compacts came out several years ago we predicted that the Michigan knotheads would soon be adding size and more power to these jobs and wouldn't stop until they became full-size cars again. They've almost made it."

Not all Volkswagens are sold through the authorized dealers displaying their blue-and-white "lollipop" sign—a round plaque, with VW's initials, on a long pole. A "gray market" operates as well.

No one knows exactly how many cars are involved in the

gray and black markets today, but the company believes it no longer comes to 3000 a month as it once did. VWoA president Perkins is puzzled by the very existence of such a market. "It is amazing to me that customers will pay $150 more for a Volkswagen just to get it immediately," he told me. "I don't see why they'd want to go to fly-by-night operators who do not stand behind what they sell. We don't like to see them do this, not just because our dealers lose a sale, but because customers so often get stung. Of course our dealers end up servicing these cars and we hope they like our service enough to buy their next Volkswagen from us."

The gray market is fed in various ways. Volkswagenwerk employees, for example, are permitted to buy at a discount one new VW a year; and annually (they must agree to keep it for at least a year) the sale of these cars is between 30,000 and 40,000, some of which end up on the American market in private transactions. West German students are another source. For 100 D-marks ($25) they place their names on a VW dealer's waiting list, later turning the car over to the gray market. Another source is the fleet owner who takes possession of several Volkswagens and claims he doesn't wish to register them until his salesmen are ready to use the cars. Travelers are another source. Many buy Volkswagens not for themselves or their friends and families, but rather to resell in the United States. Airline pilots, pursers, stewardesses and others who regularly shuttle between the U.S. and Germany do their share. (On a flight back to the United States after a visit to Volkswagen in Germany, my Lufthansa steward approached me just before landing to ask if I knew anyone who wanted a brand-new Volkswagen, cheap.) According to reliable reports, much of the traffic also originates in the Netherlands, VW's second largest import nation, after the U.S.

Gray market dealers collect a number of VWs and prepare them for export to the United States. "At 'Americanizing shops' . . . the VWs are refitted with American turn signals, safety-glass windshields, sealed-beam headlights and speedometer-odometers that register in miles," says *Mechanix Illustrated* magazine, reviewing the "Scandal of the 'New' Volkswagens" in its February 1964 issue. The "scandal" of course is that used cars are often sold as brand-new in the United States, with their odometers changed to miles (and to a reading of zero). Many gray-market cars are used cars. A Volkswagenwerk employee might buy a new VW and, having held it for the required year, resell it with some profit besides.

There are big profits in these gray-market VWs. There is

no overhead because they are sold out of parking lots and garages. The average one hundred dollars profit brings in $120,000 a year to those who "import" one hundred cars a month.

"In a way the scandal is a tribute to the sturdy little Teutonic beetle, most popular of all foreign cars," says S. David Pursglove, author of the *Mechanix Illustrated* article. "No other auto enjoys such an excess of demand over supply as does the Volkswagen. But it is this very condition, so much envied by other car manufacturers, that makes possible the operation of frauds when it comes to selling VWs to eager customers."

Gray and black markets, as Pursglove uses the terms, overlap, but there are differences. A gray-market Volkswagen *usually* has been driven less than a hundred miles and is often, to all intents and purposes, "new." If the customer does not mind paying a premium to obtain immediate delivery, then he is often not hurt. It is another matter with black-market Volkswagens. The sales of them constitute an actual fraud. "Black-market VWs look new (they must, to be palmed off as new cars)," says Pursglove. "The racketeers who operate the scheme find them more profitable than smuggled diamonds and infinitely less risky. VWs for the black market are rounded up from all over Europe and then go through a face-lifting in well-equipped plants. The extent of the reconditioning and the high quality of the work rule out a hole-in-the-wall operation. A large, well-organized reconditioning layout is indicated."

The two biggest plants feeding this racket were, according to Pursglove, located in the ports of Hamburg and Bremerhaven. "Used and often defective . . . fleet cars are driven into one end of the huge, partly automated former warehouses. Engines are steam-cleaned and tuned. If too many expensive parts are needed, the car is turned back to be merely prettied up and offered frankly as a used car. Seats are removed and placed on a conveyor belt where they are semi-automatically brush-scrubbed, hosed, dried and sprayed with a conditioner-preservative. Meantime, the floor is spray-painted, as are door sills and all areas that show wear. The car is undercoated, an operation which a racket insider says 'covers a multitude of sins.' Dealers point out to their sheep on the way to the shearing: 'And look at this, we've already undercoated the car—free!' " The car then gets new rubber pedal pads, chrome stripping, and new bumpers. Tires which show little wear are blackened or replaced if necessary. After a good wax job, Pursglove says, the car is shipped to the United States "and to Volkswagen fans who are too eager to be prudent."

The United States Department of Justice is aware of the fraudulent black market in VWs, but cannot cope with it, because each violation must be handled separately. Alfred P. Sloan, Jr., discussed General Motors' headaches with the Justice Department in *My Years with General Motors*. "Bootlegging, in my opinion, has been encouraged by an apparently new legal climate established in the late 1940's as a result of interpretations of court decisions later expanded by opinions of the Department of Justice . . . In my opinion the responsibility for equitable cooperation between dealers and manufacturers is not for a legislative body to work out. It is a joint responsibility of manufacturers and dealers."

VWoA takes no public stand on the matter, not wishing to displease a U.S. Government agency. It has resigned itself to living with this gray market against which it is forbidden to act, which undermines its dealer network and often cheats the public. Its own attitude was made clear in its dealer magazine, which editorialized: "The reputation of our product, our organization and our business methods is always under public scrutiny and continually being challenged. We feel that a Volkswagen dealer has a moral obligation to protect his customers' interests on used cars as well as new." This is an obligation hardly shared by those who operate the gray market in VWs under the protection of Washington bureaus. Carl Hahn summed up his annoyance in the following manner: "This black and gray market is as though a man moved his own table and chairs into the Four Seasons Restaurant in New York and set himself up in business, buying his food from the kitchen, but paying no rent and making no investment. The Four Seasons can protect itself against this, but Volkswagen of America can't."

Heinz Nordhoff visited the United States in 1958 to receive the Elmer A. Sperry Medal on his own behalf, for his co-workers, and on behalf of Ferdinand Porsche posthumously. This considerable honor is bestowed from time to time by three American engineering societies to those who make significant engineering contributions in transportation. Nordhoff was the first man ever to receive it for a car. Previous recipients had been Donald W. Douglas, the designer of the DC-3, "workhorse of the air," and William Francis Gibbs, who designed the SS *United States*.

In 1962, Nordhoff returned to America to celebrate the

millionth VW sold in the United States. In New York, he addressed a press conference and delivered himself of some predictions. "The next twenty-five years will be the most significant in history for all those involved in the world's auto industry," he said. "Despite achievements in space, the automobile will continue as basic transportation for the world's millions. There are 127,000,000 motor vehicles in the world today. In the next twenty-five years, the number will double and perhaps triple."

In Englewood Cliffs, New Jersey, he dedicated a new 2.5-million-dollar company headquarters which has since already been expanded. Located on twenty acres, it is a modern gray-glass structure with meeting rooms, lounges, and a cafeteria sporting outdoor tables in the European fashion. It contains offices for VWoA's more than three hundred employees. Its parking lot, designed with VW-size lanes, accommodates 344 cars. Approximately 75 per cent of the employees drive VWs to work. The facilities were planned so as to provide room for growth—and by 1966, the growth had come. A one-million-dollar expansion program added more space, which again was rapidly and fully filled. (If the approximately 375 employees of VWoA are added to the employees at dealerships and distributorships, then the total Volkswagen payroll in the United States included more than 29,000 Americans in 1965—and, counting wives and children, it provided a livelihood for an estimated 100,000.)

From New York, Nordhoff went to Detroit to the Automobile Show. On October 22 he addressed the Detroit Economic Club on the subject of the Common Market, warning that high Common Market tariffs against the outside world "protect obsolescence and inefficiency" and urging more trade between the U.S. and Europe. The second obstacle to such trade, he noted, "is the unpreparedness of many American firms in exporting."

"This has been demonstrated to us during the last half year," he said. "Out of five hundred letters sent to companies in this country producing items and materials we could use, over half were not even answered. Another forty per cent were answered, but stated they were not interested. Only ten per cent seemed to want our business enough to respond positively to our letters." Nordhoff was referring to a situation which continues to trouble business analysts. "Our performance on trade expansion has been mediocre," Sylvia Porter, the syndicated business columnist, has noted. "U.S. exports not tied into foreign aid or our farm disposal programs have been just creeping up. The rise of non-government financed exports in the past three years has been only a meager one per cent a year."

Nordhoff was received enthusiastically at the Economic Club by virtually all of the U.S. auto industry leaders, some of whom were Henry Ford II, GM's Chairman Frederic Donner and President John Gordon, Chrysler's Lynn Townsend, and American Motors President Roy Abernethy. In all, 750 automen came to hear the man whose company had sold a million Americans the car which many of them regarded as unsalable. That evening, Henry Ford II introduced Nordhoff at the Automobile Manufacturers Association's biennial dinner as "my good friend and great competitor." Next morning, Nordhoff and his party visited the General Motors Technical Center and toured its engineering, styling, and research departments. Afterwards they lunched with Henry Ford II and his top aides.

Leaving Detroit, Nordhoff visited VW's Canadian headquarters in Toronto, and from there went to Boston, where he gave the Alexander Graham Bell lecture on communications, on the occasion of the fiftieth anniversary of Boston University's School of Business Administration. Since then, Boston University has awarded Nordhoff his first American honorary doctorate.

In 1964, he called Carl Hahn back to Germany, to take charge of worldwide sales and service, the post which had been vacated a few years earlier through the sudden death of Dr. Karl Feuereissen and the accession of his successor, Fritz Frank, to the Auto-Union board. "We take our promising men and send them out into the field to test them before we bring them home," Nordhoff says. First a deputy member of the Vorstand and now a full member, Carl Hahn brought with him to his new post the experience of five years in the United States, the toughest automobile market of them all, as some automakers characterize it. Those five years have "Americanized" him a good deal and have even provided him with an American wife, Marisa, and three American-born children, the fourth and youngest being the only one born on German soil. While some members of the Volkswagen organization in Germany have questioned the applicability of "American" sales and service methods in Germany, many there and elsewhere in the worldwide VW empire like the infusion of fresh ideas from the States. One of these is Heinz Nordhoff himself. To him, Volkswagen is less a German product than an international commodity, and nationalities

209

disappear when the product one sells is as unusual as is this car.

And so it was also no surprise that Stuart Perkins, an Englishman, was named to succeed Hahn as general manager of Volkswagen of America, Inc. Then, in 1965, at the age of thirty-six, Perkins became president of this U.S. subsidiary. The choice could not have been more logical. Perkins, who was the first man hired by Volkswagen in Canada, had come to New York to be the first man hired by VW in the U.S.A.; he had served as assistant to both van de Kamp and Carl Hahn and he knew and was trusted by every one of the U.S. distributors, as well as by many of their nearly one thousand VW dealers. He was a man with whom the distributors could work effectively and harmoniously; he knew their problems and considered them with understanding. No longer was it true, as one distributor had said of the van de Kamp era, that working in the field for VW was a little like being a States' Rights champion and working for the Federal Government.

It has been fortunate for Volkswagen that Stuart Perkins is presently at the helm, for he has had to reassure the distributors that the recent changes in the distribution pattern of VWoA do not constitute a threat to their legitimate interests as independent businessmen. The death of Hubert Brundage of Brundage Motors and the desire of one of the two partners in the Hansen-MacPhee Massachusetts distributorship to retire have prompted VWoA to purchase the assets of both corporations. Renamed Volkswagen Southeastern Distributor, Inc., and Volkswagen Northeastern Distributor, Inc., respectively, both are wholly owned by Volkswagen of America today. Although the distributors with whom I have discussed this development acknowledge its inevitability and the fact that both acquisitions were forced on the company, several betray a suspicion that it may be the beginning of a trend. They point out that Detroit abandoned independent distributorships years ago, in favor of factory regional offices. As VW "matures" in the U.S.A., these distributors claim, the same development may well take place.*

Stuart Perkins sees no such thing as inevitable and points out that no "take-over" *policy* exists. Each case had been handled on its own merits and according to its own demands. "As long as a distributor runs a profitable, efficient business," he says, "we couldn't be happier to let him continue running it, if he wants to."

* As was noted earlier on page 207, Carl G. Schmidt's distributorship, Import Motors of Chicago, was acquired by Volkswagen of America early in 1967.

Of course distributors assert that the enterprise a man brings to his *own* business—and which every one of them most certainly brought to theirs—assures its success better than would be the case if an "employee" ran it. Yet, on examination, that does not seem entirely true—or, in any case, proven. Eric Sundstrom, under whose leadership Brundage Motors rose to sales of more than 25,000 a year, remains in charge of the same (if renamed) company, with VWoA's corporate secretary, Goetz Grimm, acting as corporate secretary and visiting to consult frequently; Sundstrom is doing as good a job as he ever had done. The same may be said of the man placed in charge of the former Hansen-MacPhee distributorship, Samuel J. Tucker. Skeptical at first, area dealers have since become convinced that Volkswagen of America, Inc., is no less interested in their success than were Tagé Hansen and John MacPhee. If it seems odd that there should ever have been any doubt about that, the fact that there was is a measure of the stresses affecting any large organization.

Stuart Perkins's quiet, soft-spoken, and diplomatic manner seems well suited to dealing with such stresses as exist or may arise. That same manner, as has been noted, has won him the confidence of the distributors over the years. "You can talk with him more easily than with van de Kamp or Hahn," one of them told me. "Both van de Kamp and Hahn tended to tell you what to do, while Stuart will discuss it with you more."

Under him, a continuing interchange of views and opinions has been instituted, with distributor executives attending seminars at VWoA headquarters and feeding it with their own suggestions and ideas. These, in turn, are fed back into the field after the experience and opinions of others have been added and evaluated. The result is a rising flow of information and ideas up and down the network.

The job of raising personnel standards (and salaries, to competitive U.S. levels) also occupies Perkins's time as much as anything. VWoA no longer can afford to rely just on imported Germans or young American eager-beavers; it needs, more and more, experienced U.S. automobile industry men, and Perkins is trying to attract and hold them. An extremely advanced computerized data-processing system throughout the entire Volkswagen organization is being expanded constantly and is already, in this field at least, placing Volkswagen ahead of Detroit. The amount of expert information required by the maturing organization is enormous and has a direct and vital effect upon the profitability of each dealership. Perkins's aim

211

is to make certain that these dealerships remain attractive and profitable, so that the network may continue to expand.

In addition to the management of VWoA-owned distributorships in the U.S., Perkins and his staff are responsible for VWoA's Caribbean Department, advising the VW organization in a host of sundrenched isles and Central American countries.

He is a remarkably young man to run so large and far-flung a corporation. Around forty, slim, and of medium height, he has none of that nervous drive which characterizes so many young men who move up rapidly. What he has achieved, he accomplished by means of calm research and planning. He is horrified at the thought of unpremeditated action or decisions made before research has been completed. Typically, he has instituted a method by means of which VWoA works towards the future. Each job is "programmed" so that each man knows exactly what portion of what job he is to have completed on each day. Stuart Perkins not only has a program such as this for his own work, but he also knows the stage which each of his executives should have reached in theirs on any day. It keeps things moving. Perkins calls it an "Action Program," and it is just this that Volkswagen will need if it is to keep moving ahead in the years to come. Perkins intends to see that it does.

10

A Matter of Taste

IN 1959, Volkswagen of America, Inc., began to advertise seriously—humorously. "What a happy day for Volkswagen it turned out to be," Huston Horn wrote in *Sports Illustrated*. "Volkswagen ads have won a list of prizes longer than an account executive's expense account; they are talked about at cocktail parties, read aloud at the office water cooler, analyzed and dissected in college term papers . . ." *Sales Management* credits the advertising with having "identity and personality . . . like the Bug itself . . . Car and campaign combine to stir comment and wisecracks out of all proportion to the size of either."

"The average American," *Sales Management* said, "may be somewhat confused by Comets, Corvairs, Darts, Falcons, Hawks, Larks, Ramblers, Tempests, Valiants—not to mention such imports as Austin-Healeys, Fiats, Jaguars, MGs, Mercedes-Benzes, Peugeots, Renaults, Saabs, Triumphs and Volvos. But chances are he'll know one little bug by its changeless shape, and even know that its engine is rearward and air-cooled."

Everyone, in short, seems to know Volkswagen's advertisements—and to have a favorite one. There's the "Think Small" ad and the "Lemon" headline, the "Why Won't Your Wife Let You Buy This Car?" ad for the boxlike station wagon, the "Ugly Is Only Skin-deep" confession, and the ad which showed no car at all, but which headlined beneath a blank space, "We Don't Have Anything to Show You in Our New Models." The list has become a long one today and there are Americans who read Volkswagen ads in a magazine before they get down to reading the editorial content itself. Such people seem to have unbounded confidence in the high quality of each ad and they expect to get a chuckle out of each new one that appears. Suzanne Prefect, a teacher at Rye Center School in Rye, New Hampshire, gave expression to general attitudes, writing to Volkswagen of America, ". . . we all think you're tops in the advertising field. The kids 'can't get over your genius' (in their words)."

They are not alone. The average Volkswagen owner, said a firm of motivational researchers in a 1962 report to the company, regards Volkswagen advertisements as "excellent, witty, sophisticated, delightful, truthful, to the point, informative, unique, cute . . ." The ebullience does not belong to the researchers; the adjectives were culled from interviews with Volkswagen owners.

Genius, Emerson said, is the quality of believing "in your own thought . . . to believe that what is true for you in your own heart is true for all men." If VW's advertising has the quality of genius, it derives from the company's decision to be true to itself and true to all men—to be, in short, honest in its advertising.

Will van de Kamp didn't believe in advertising, preferring to use available funds to improve service. In 1958, however, the company placed a few ads via the J. M. Mathes agency but nothing much came of this. The appearance of these ads and the appearance of ever-increasing numbers of Volkswagens on American streets, however, brought on the media representatives—that most persistent gaggle of salesmen ever to infest a corporate anteroom—to offer Volkswagen the pages of hundreds of American newspapers, magazines and trade journals, not to speak of billboards, radio commercials, and television "spots." These salesmen had a hard time at Volkswagen, for the company's executives, knowing they were already far behind existing orders for their cars, often responded with "Who needs advertising?"

The atmosphere changed when Carl Hahn came to the United States, for he suspected that Volkswagen might indeed need advertising, not perhaps to spur the sales, but as a hedge against the future, for Detroit in 1959 had compact cars up their designers' sleeves. Further, distributors were now pressuring their company to advertise nationally and to backstop their own efforts. And so Carl Hahn and a few others began looking into the advertising agencies along Madison Avenue shortly after Hahn arrived in New York.

"This was my first exposure to American advertising executives," Hahn says, "and, frankly, I was terribly disappointed.

We expected great things, but all we saw were presentations which showed Volkswagen ads which looked exactly like every other ad—an airline ad, a cigarette ad, a toothpaste ad. The only difference was that, where the tube of toothpaste had been, they had placed a Volkswagen."

It was hardly surprising, for much of American advertising had by the late 1950's become so banal and its promises so suspect that hardly anyone in the business seemed to have a good idea left. Pink-shirted copywriters who drank only Gibsons were writing beer advertisements which were supposed to appeal to undershirted stevedores; agency art directors vied with each other, not to make their ads more effective, but to win prizes for their portfolios in New York Art Directors Club contests; and the management staffs of advertising agencies whipped the so-called creative group on, urging them "to get down on all fours and look at the problem from the client's point of view." As for the poor suffering public, they were referred to as "the Great Unwashed" and regarded as a herd of nincompoops motivated not by quality, but by saturation advertising. In 1959, nothing much had changed from the situation Samuel Johnson described exactly two hundred years earlier in the *Idler*. "Advertisements," Dr. Johnson wrote, "are now so numerous that they are very negligently perused, and it is therefore become necessary to gain attention by magnificence of promise and by eloquence sometimes sublime and sometimes pathetick."

"Pathetick" was the word all right for most U.S. automotive advertising, and while responsible neither for that nor for its "sublime" counterpart, I watched it being produced while serving a term at one of the medium-sized New York agencies Carl Hahn visited in early 1959. As secretary of this agency's "Plans Board" (a group whose membership seemed to expand in direct proportion to the importance of the prospective client being confronted), I attended one of the presentations through which Hahn suffered. With Hahn on that occasion as on most others were Manuel Hinke, a young German named Helmut Schmitz, and Arthur Stanton, if memory serves correctly. These four men, together with the company's advertising and public relations manager of the period, Scott Stewart, underwent the brunt of the agency assaults. In the smooth but ineffective attack I was privy to, there was an element of pathos. How could our Plans Board know what Carl Hahn was up to? Honesty in advertising? Our men expected, perhaps understandably, that VW wanted the same kind of malarky handed out that every other auto manufacturer seemed to want, the same slippery use of meaningless but allegedly persuasive advertising terms, the same aura of glamour and sex. As one agency art director put it at the time, "Car ads are full of broads, mansions, horses, surf, mountains, sunsets, chiseled chins, and caviar—anything but facts."

It was not this agency which won the Volkswagen advertising account nor for that matter was it any of those which put on elaborate presentations. In 1959, the account was split two ways, that for the sedans going to Doyle Dane Bernbach, and that for the trucks going to Fuller & Smith & Ross.

Edward G. Russell, DDB vice president and account supervisor for Volkswagen, tells the story of how Doyle Dane Bernbach was assigned the account. It began with the famed fashion photographer Richard Avedon, who knew Russell's wife, a model. Avedon had just spent a weekend with his friend Arthur Stanton, who was a member of the VW distributor advertising committee, the very group which was urging VWoA to advertise nationally. Stanton had apparently asked Avedon who did the unusual ads for Ohrbach's, a New York City department store, and Avedon explained that Ohrbach's was the account which had put Doyle Dane Bernbach into business as an agency. One or two other agency names were mentioned by Avedon, and Stanton began looking into them. He then hired DDB to do a Grand Opening ad for his New York City retail operation, Queensboro Motors. While working for Queensboro Motors, they made their presentation to the VWoA group. "We didn't prepare anything special for them," Bill Bernbach says. "We just show prospects ads we've done for other clients. The only thing we try to 'sell' them on is that we are advertising men and know our business. We told VW, 'You know your business better than we'll ever know it. But *we* know advertising better than you do.' "

"When that meeting was over," Russell remembers, "we had the feeling that Hahn thought of us as his kind of agency." Then, however, trouble began, for the advertising trade press, a regular rumor factory, bruited about that "Stanton's agency" had the VWoA account "sewn up."

"The other distributors didn't like that one bit," Russell remembers. "It looked as if Stanton were running the whole show. So Hahn and the others at VWoA continued to interview agencies and these, hearing we were 'ahead,' began knocking us. 'Great artwork they produce at DDB,' they'd say, 'but they're weak on copy.' "

Then Helmut Schmitz visited Russell, to check on DDB's ability to do sales promotional work as well. Schmitz had been assistant to the creative director in the Wolfsburg VW advertising department for a few years and, then in his mid-twenties, was sent to New York to be assistant advertising manager there. Quick, brilliant, and creative on his own, he was just the type of client executive to annoy an agency. "When he walked in, I just happened to have a lot of ads which were heavy on copy, as well as a lot of our sales promotional stuff lying around," says Russell. "It was an eleventh-hour meeting."

At about this time, a minor argument with major repercussions arose about the Grand Opening ad which was slated for a full page in the New York *Times*. Arthur Stanton approved the ad, but as a matter of courtesy to VWoA, asked Russell to take it to New Jersey and show it to Schmitz and Scott Stewart. They also liked the ad, but Schmitz had one objection concerning the copy.

"The second sentence in the ad said something like 'The fender costs only so and so much to replace,'" Russell says, "and the third sentence said that service was quick and easy. Schmitz's point was that VWoA wanted to put the stress on service, rather than on replacement parts, and that the third sentence should therefore come ahead of the second.

"I disagreed," Russell continues, "because I felt we got the idea across by mentioning the low price of the fender first and that it was a logical progression from there to go on and speak about service, once we had established the fact that parts were inexpensive."

The matter was not resolved at that meeting, and a few days later Arthur Stanton telephoned to ask if Russell would have breakfast with him, Hahn, and Manuel Hinke at the Plaza Hotel. "Bring that ad along," Stanton told Russell. "I want you to show it to them."

"We had a very nice breakfast and didn't talk about advertising too much," Russell recalls, "and then, when it came time to go over that ad, we looked around for a place where we could discuss it privately. We finally went into the Palm Court of the Plaza, which isn't open for breakfast. It was rather dark in there and all the chairs were piled up on the tables. We stepped over the ropes and cleared a space on one of the tables and I was literally just taking the ad out of its envelope when who comes racing in out of breath but Scott Stewart and Helmut Schmitz. They'd heard that this was a breakfast with the ad agency and felt they should be there too.

"Hahn asked them if they'd seen the ad and Schmitz answered that he had and that he disagreed very strongly with

217

it. That opening remark started the two of us arguing for forty-five minutes!

"Well, it's very hard to talk about two sentences for three quarters of an hour," Russell says, "and when we were both almost exhausted, I told the group that I would go back and see what the writer had to say about it. If the writer agreed with the change, then we'd make it. If he didn't, I told them, we won't change a line!

"When I got back to the agency, I went in to Bernbach's office and said, 'Well, I either blew it or I got it!' "

The result was not that clear-cut after all. When Volkswagen of America chose two agencies instead of concentrating all their billings at once with DDB, it appeared to some at Doyle Dane Bernbach that Ed Russell had indeed "blown it" at the Palm Court that morning. Some time later, however, Carl Hahn set the record straight. At a dinner in the VW Guest House in Wolfsburg, Germany, he told the DDB agency contingent:

"You know why I hired you people? When we had that breakfast in the Plaza, I'd already seen about four thousand agency people and I had decided that they were *all* a bunch of phonies. Then, after that breakfast and that argument, I had the feeling I'd finally met an honest man in this business and, if he were honest, he'd give us his best advice."

The choice of both F&S&R and DDB seemed advisable to Volkswagen at the time. The former had an exceptionally good record in industrial advertising and so it seemed logical to give them the truck ads to do; the latter was regarded as highly creative—just the type of agency needed to implant the VW "image" and to help popularize the beetle. Further, Hahn and the others at VWoA believed then that having two agencies would prompt each to compete with the other for excellence.

That first year, DDB was assigned $800,000 to promote its passenger cars and F&S&R was given half that amount to advertise the Transporters. About a year later, in November 1960, the two-agency experiment had proved cumbersome and F&S&R's involvement ended. Doyle Dane Bernbach has handled all aspects of Volkswagen advertising ever since.

"When we were awarded the account," says William Bernbach, president of DDB, "the first thing we did was go to the factory in Wolfsburg. A whole team of us went over there. We spent days talking to engineers, production men, executives, workers on the assembly line. We marched side by side with the molten metal that hardened into the engine, and kept going until every part was finally in its place. We watched finally as a man climbed behind the steering wheel, pumped the first life into the newborn bug and drove it off the line. We were immersed in the making of a Volkswagen and we knew what our theme had to be. We knew what distinguished this car. We knew what we had to tell the American public . . . We had seen the quality of materials that were used. We had seen the almost incredible precautions taken to avoid mistakes. We had seen the costly system of inspection that turned back cars that would never have been turned down by the consumer. We had seen the impressive efficiency that resulted in such an unbelievably low price for such a quality product. We had seen the pride of craftsmanship in the worker that made him exceed even the high standards set for him. Yes, this was an honest car. We had found our selling proposition."

Perhaps the first person to write of the Volkswagen as "an honest car" was Arthur R. Railton. Writing in 1956, when he was automotive editor of *Popular Mechanics* magazine, he analyzed the success of the VW in the U.S.A. "Never in the sales history of the automobile," he wrote in the magazine's *1957 Cars Fact Book,* "has so much been accomplished by what, at first glance, seems to be so little." For four years, he said, he had been trying to find out what there is about this car that makes it sell. His answer: "The Volkswagen sells because it is, more than anything else, an honest car. It doesn't pretend to be something it is not. Being an honest piece of machinery, it is one the owner can be proud of. Wherever he looks, he sees honest design and workmanship. There are no places where parts don't fit, where paint is thin, where trim is shoddy. There are no body rattles, no water leaks. Neither, of course, is there overstuffed, false luxury either. There is nothing about the car that is not sincere. One just can't imagine, for instance, a Volkswagen with a fake air scoop or tailfins to make it look like an airplane in flight." (Railton became so enthusiastic about VWs that he joined VWoA in 1960 as public relations manager, replacing Stewart, who opened a VW dealership in Erie, Pennsylvania. In 1965 Railton was named vice president in charge of public relations.)

The "honest car" not only had to have a selling proposition, but advertising guidelines as well. These were provided to the Doyle Dane Bernbach group early in the effort. They are today recognizable elements in all those VW ads which fascinate, amuse, bemuse, and incidentally motivate readers.

DDB's copywriters and art directors found that Volkswagen executives like Hahn and Schmitz were actually serious about insisting on "honest advertising." But just what *was* honest advertising—and did VW's insistence upon it mean that most ads placed by others were *dis*honest?

"Everybody wants to be honest in their advertisements," says Helmut Schmitz, "and a lot of advertisers ask for honesty. But they never seem to take the plunge into a *real* honesty! Honesty isn't just a matter of giving people honest technical data—a lot of advertisers do that—but also of facing up to what people regard as your shortcomings. One of our ads said our station wagon had 'a face only a mother could love.' Well, that's the way people felt about this vehicle, so why not face it?"

Carl Hahn also wanted no drawings or paintings of the cars, to make them look glamorous. "We started using only photographs in all our ads and brochures," Hahn says, "because we believe the car itself looks beautiful." He laughs as he uses that adjective, but does so defiantly. "The beetle," he says, "is simply an acquired taste. Nobody likes oysters when he first tries them." The ads, however, do not call the beetle "beautiful," no matter what VW executives feel about it. "Ugly is only skin-deep," a recent advertisement said, urging another look at the beetle's line.

As another example of VW "honesty in advertising," there is the ad which showed three beetles, each with a different miles-per-gallon figure headlined beneath it. "We simply admitted that there were people who only got twenty-four miles per gallon, that there were others who got thirty-two, and there were even some who got fifty," says a company adman. By contrast, a popular Detroit "compact" advertises that it achieves thirty miles per gallon, although anyone who has driven it knows that this is the case only sometimes, and seldom.

The element of humor was also insisted upon. "We wanted to be not only humorous, however, but also *human*," Schmitz remembers. "We felt that people would take us more seriously if we didn't take ourselves so seriously. We wanted to involve the reader in our ads, not lecture to him. We didn't mind having him argue back, just so long as he was involved. Then, in the last line, we'd try to give the ad a little lift, to make it very relaxing." Says Bob Levenson, DDB writer on the account: "The key to these ads is this person-to-person approach, one person talking to another person."

One other initial rule which VWoA established was not to "knock the competition." "Detroit," says Carl Hahn, "is part of America and we are here as guests. What could offend Detroit could easily offend other Americans." Bob Levenson and Helmut Krone (DDB art director on the VW account) recall two proposed advertisements which never found their way into print because of this consideration. Both dealt with Detroit's introduction of trucks which aped the Volkswagen Transporter. One showed a Ford truck on one half of a double-page spread, with a Chevrolet truck on the other half. The headline: "VW introduces two new models." The other ad showed a picture of a group of white-coated Detroit engineers in a board room discussing a VW truck. The copy underneath: "First thing we do is get this damned VW off it!" Even milder ads which involve Detroit cars have been killed for the same reason. "One which we kicked aside," says Helmut Krone, "showed three compact cars—a Ford, a Chevy, and a VW—coming down the road together. The headline read, 'There's room for all of us.' We didn't do this ad because VW didn't want to be caught coming into the United States and then telling people who lived here that there was room for all of us." Although comparisons have since been made with U.S. cars, VW continues not to attack by name, as several other foreign car companies have done.

The "biggest taboo" on the account, says Krone, "is against lying and exaggeration." Volkswagen ads zero in on one point per advertisement and do not attempt to cover the whole car. "We want the ads to say something meaningful," VW's admen insist. "We don't want words like 'The Quick One' or 'The Car with Youthful Vigor' and fortunately DDB never even considered offering that sort of thing. These are meaningless words and no one reads them."

In 1961–1962, Volkswagen ran an ad which showed no picture at all. The space usually allocated for a photograph of the VW was left blank. Underneath was written, "We don't have anything to show you in our new models"—making the point, of course, that the beetle's design remains the same. Stuart Perkins cleared the ad in his capacity as sales manager at the time, but Wolfsburg was upset when they saw it in print. "How can you buy all this expensive space and not show anything?" they asked. The ad, however, provides an interesting example of how such advertisements do indeed "show readers something." Dealers reported that this ad brought in more inquiries from potential customers than any other that had been run before. "Show us those cars you wouldn't show in your ads," they'd ask the dealers. Wolfsburg changed its mind.

The ads are not "a matter of taste" in that some like VW advertising while others don't; they are a matter of taste in that they are tastefully executed, offering even the most technical data in a way which attracts readers, treats them as intelligent adults, and speaks frankly with them. Such advertisements motivate people, for they reflect the good taste which has been built into the car itself. Columnist William D. Tyler had this to say about Volkswagen's advertisements in a mid-1965 issue of *Advertising Age:*

"VW advertising is so much in a class by itself that it has almost removed itself from consideration by people in advertising." Discussing the "ten top ads," Tyler says, "By that I mean that whereas all other advertising is considered in a frame of competitive reference, Volkswagen's is not. It stands alone, and thus beyond critical comparisons. The excuse for excluding it from comparison with domestic car advertising is that our cars haven't the unusual features to talk about, and thus shouldn't be expected to live up to the VW standard.

"But all cars get painted, don't they? Consider that Volkswagen has done with this less than spectacular feature." He quotes the DDB headline, "After we paint the car we paint the paint." "You know what you are in for," Tyler writes, "but you keep on reading. . . . When did you last read such vivid writing on such a pedestrian (yet significant) subject? And, did you notice, there was hardly an adjective in the lot?"

Volkswagen of America does not buy every ad which Doyle Dane Bernbach proposes. The selection process is a constant one. VWoA's advertising manager works most closely with the agency and is first to see the ads; they go then to Marketing Vice President Michael L. Sanyour. Ultimately, they are approved by Stuart Perkins. At this final stage, the views of a number of department heads are solicited. Service and parts executives, for example, make certain that the ad is technically sound. Those in charge of dealer relations offer their views as well. Doyle Dane Bernbach does, however, have the option of asking for higher reviews if the ads are disapproved anywhere along the line. Occasional ads have reached Perkins after having been vetoed by VWoA executives involved at earlier stages. "If you have no convictions about your ads," says William Bernbach, "then your ads can have no convictions either."

"Cleverness for the sake of cleverness is the worst thing in the agency business," Bill Bernbach says. "When an agency gets preoccupied wtih the techniques of advertising, these get in the way of the message. It's not just words and pictures that talk to a reader. There's a feel and tone to a page. And these too were used in the VW ads to convey honesty. The layouts are utterly simple and plain and clean, the type classic and unadorned, the copy style factual and straightforward: subject, verb, object. Psychologically and creatively everything was done to make our selling proposition of honesty reach the consumer faster and with the greatest impact. We've had five writers on the account and I defy anyone to tell the difference in Volkswagen copy over the years. Once the basic concept is evolved, then the right words follow."

The ads have been called "original, refreshing and effective." Yet there is really nothing "original" about the appearance of a VW advertisement. The company uses one large photograph in the standard position with headline and copy below. What is original and unusual about VW advertisements is that these advertisements actually do say something concrete.

Paul Lee, who had for several years been VWoA's advertising manager, was one of several who helped shape such early policies. He is no longer with Volkswagen of America and others are in charge of working with the agency. Before he left, he delivered himself of some complaints about automobile dealer advertising in general and explained what VWoA tried to do about it. "Most dealer advertising," he said, "is sheer drivel . . . the ultimate in bad taste, in dishonesty, and in bad advertising." Dealers simply are not advertising men, Lee pointed out, and no one tells them what to do. VW early decided they would help their own dealers improve the quality of their local ads.

This effort was not always welcome at first, even in the ranks of the VW organization in the field. Some VW dealers complained that the ads didn't say "Buy one today!" To that, the company answered back that every one of these ads said precisely that—without saying it once. Gradually, Lee reported, the dealers came to understand that soft-sell advertising like VW's is extremely hard-sell advertising after all. There was no need to offer discounts, free trips to Las Vegas, puff up the claims, put in higher mileage figures, or be dishonest in any way. The reeducation process has, by and large, been successful. Today, many of the company's dealers and distributors watch the ads carefully and critically. One distributor advertising manager, for example, objected to an ad which claimed one could get 32 miles per gallon in a Volkswagen because a few of his customers had achieved only 29 mpg, although VWoA's filing cabinets are full of case histories of drivers achieving 50 mpg. When others agreed with this ad manager, VWoA modified the line by adding, "give or take a few miles depending on your driving habits." Such care helps explain just what honest advertising demands.

"Honest advertising sells like crazy," a company adman has said. "Strangely enough, this honest advertising is called 'creative' advertising. And the agencies who produce this type of work are called 'creative agencies.'"

"Properly practiced, creativity *must* result in greater sales more economically achieved," William Bernbach told the 1961 annual meeting of the American Association of Advertising Agencies. "Properly practiced, creativity can make one ad do the work of ten . . . [it] can lift your claims out of the swamp of sameness and make them accepted, believed, persuasive, urgent. Is creativity some obscure, esoteric art form? Not on your life. It's the most practical thing a businessman can employ . . . [But] you've got to have something to be creative about."

As to the question of what credit for the advertising campaign should go to Doyle Dane Bernbach and what to Nordhoff and Carl Hahn, the answer is that Volkswagen's executives "let the ads happen." They did not interfere. Fortunately for DDB's creative group, VW executives like Carl Hahn did not have too much experience in advertising when they began their campaign. They had no preconceptions and were simply looking for a different, honest, attention-getting approach. They were well aware of the fact that their budget could never compete with the budgets of Detroit's Big Three. "We made a rule," Hahn remembers, "not to advertise when Detroit introduced its new models. While Detroit shot off its big guns and rockets, we didn't want to come in with our pistol. We decided to fire our pistol when it could be heard." William Bernbach, whose unusual agency allows writers and art directors to work with no interference whatever from account supervisors or directors, regards Volkswagen as an unusual client. As for Hahn, Bernbach believes, "the company could not have picked a better man at the time." Hahn was no advertising man, he says, but "had an intuitive sense of what we were trying to do when we got started."

Today, Volkswagen's ads in Germany have the same look they have in the United States. The same may be said of VW ads in much of the world, for even where other advertising agencies have been employed (as in the United Kingdom), it is clear that much of their inspiration has come from the ads which are produced by DDB. After Helmut Schmitz left VWoA, he came to be creative director for Volkswagenwerk's advertising division in Wolfsburg, carrying to Lower Saxony the "feel" of the ads produced in mid-Manhattan. He has since left Volkswagenwerk altogether, but his contribution to VW's advertising in Europe continues, for he now heads DDB's office in Düsseldorf. It has even affected other European advertisers. Schmitz's Düsseldorf DDB office handles VW in Germany and it was Schmitz who helped introduce colloquial German into German VW ads, to the horror of many who felt advertisements should speak only the most formal parlor German. The effect has been sensational and VW ads in Germany actually have twice the readership of American ads for the car, because there the ads are so very unusual. In the U.S.A., Starch readership surveys show that VW ads have twice the readership of any other automobile advertisement. "This doubles the value of our advertising budget," the company points out.

The danger of becoming "too cute" worries VWoA as it does Doyle Dane Bernbach. Both feel it is their job to see that each ad makes a very specific point and isn't funny for the sake of humor alone. "But we do like to be arresting," a company adman says. "Take our station-wagon ads, for example. We know perfectly well that no one's going to buy one of these wagons as a surprise for the family and then drive home and be cheered. It takes guts to buy one of our boxes. So we challenge the reader! We ask him frankly if he's man enough to own one. We dare him. We even ask if he's got the right kind of a wife for one of these." Advertisements for the VW station wagon, incidentally, are the only VW ads which consistently appear in color.

Just how responsible are the ads for Volkswagen's growth in the United States? Many Americans tend to credit them with the company's success. Often those who do so drive what *Sales Management* magazine calls "gadgeted Gas-Guzzling Dinosaurs" and encounter the merits of the "bug" only through the pages of *Life* or the *New Yorker*. They tend to believe that the advertising created the car, rather than the other way around. Yet, as Arthur Railton noted in 1956 (before VW began advertising), the car sold "without advertising, without big deals, without fat trade-in allowances and with only four hundred dealers." The company does not believe it is the job of advertising to sell cars. "That's the dealer's job," its admen say. "The job of advertising is to be read and to be believed. And there we've succeeded."

The fact is that at no point in the company's history can one look at the VW sales curve and say with certainty, "Here's where advertising stepped in." The sales have risen steadily, and DDB and those droll ads have done their share. As Carl Hahn put it, "We couldn't rely on word-of-mouth advertising after a certain period. Our campaign created a mass market for us. And Doyle Dane Bernbach's contribution was most significant. After all, it set the tone of all VW ads, not just in America, but around the world." Yet there seems little doubt that what, in addition to ads and salesmen, sold the Volkswagen to Americans was, and is, the Volkswagen and its owners. As Railton wrote in 1956, "Every VW owner is an enthusiastic salesman." The product is exceptional. "It is," said Railton, "a car that, despite its small engine and low power, feels alive. It is nimble. It asks something from the driver. He and the car seem to share a kinship. Volkswagen owners never baby their cars—they drive them mercilessly. But the true Volkswagen owner never asks the car to do something it can't. He shifts gears joyfully because of respect for the car's limitations. There seems to be some of the feeling here that a cowboy has for his pony." Mechanics, even those not trained by VW, often have the same feeling for the car. They find it is easy to deal with, easy to repair. Their respect for its workmanship and the enthusiasm of the owners made the car a success even before advertising began. The company's extraordinarily painstaking service and parts policy was a vital ingredient as well. The advertising merely had to reflect and convey the car's own integrity. To do so was a challenge which probably few advertising agencies could have met.

William Bernbach agrees that it is the quality of the car which is the key to VW's success in America. He regards the company's service facilities as an integral part of the total product, as does VWoA itself. "Our agency looks for good products to advertise," he told me. "We've even had clients improve their products before we'd handle them. Volkswagen was a great product right from the start. We believe our contribution lies in the fact that we helped people appreciate its merits. The car would have succeeded in any case, but we accelerated its success."

It is a different matter with the VW station wagons which, as both DDB and VWoA point out, had no appeal before an advertising program was developed for them. "You couldn't give that bus away," Bernbach told me. "We found that it was women who were against the station wagon. They wouldn't let their husbands buy them. So we faced the problem head on. One of our first ads was headlined: 'Why won't your wife let you buy this car?' By bringing up the objections we had a chance to answer them." The campaign has succeeded beyond expectation.

"The key to Volkswagen's success is simple," said Carl Hahn

in 1961. "An honest product aimed at satisfying a basic consumer need will always sell. This universal truth . . . is our secret. And of course it is no more original than it is secret. The Volkswagen is a well-engineered, reliable automobile. It has engineering features still regarded as advanced by the rest of the automobile industry and, we must add, still being copied. Yet its appearance is so unpretentious, so simple that it would be completely out of character for our advertising to be anything but direct and straightforward. By talking about our product in easily understood language, by describing what makes it the good, reliable automobile it is, we appeal to buyers who have become disenchanted with superlatives and flights of fancy."

"We just aim at being ourselves," another VW executive adds. "By talking plainly, we can't help but be original in our advertising."

The impact of these ads on advertising generally has been substantial. Several advertisers have learned from VW and DDB that it pays to talk sense. Others simply want the identity, without the honesty. According to "The Creative Man's Corner" in *Advertising Age,* its author was "among the first to laud the Volkswagen advertising." He added: "We would also like to be among the first to suggest that it has led the advertising world down the wrong path. The great contribution of the Volkswagen advertising was that it called an ugly duckling an ugly duckling, got the basic sales resistance out of the way thereby, and then proceeded to sell the positive side of the picture. But not all products are Volkswagens. And we wonder how many advertisers who tell their agencies they want Volkswagen advertising own and drive a Volkswagen?"

Volkswagen owners, who read VW ads religiously and regularly, seem to appreciate this advertising campaign more and more. There have been objections to the campaign, some experts arguing that it fails to motivate those who do not own Volkswagens to go out and buy one. The fact, is, however, that one of the biggest functions of VW ads is to train Volkswagen's best salesmen—its present customers. "Each ad provides our owners with additional information about their car," says Stuart Perkins, "so that they have more arguments to use in talking their car up. People who buy VWs like to be reconfirmed in their choice." Motivational researchers have reported the same: "The Volkswagen owner," they said, "is often put in the position of defending his choice of a foreign car and is looking for ways to do so. . . . [A VW ad] confirms owners in the feeling that they made a wise choice and gives them 'narcissistic' enjoyment in that it compliments them on their choice of car."

Some of the research interviews are interesting examples of VW owners' reactions to their beetles. A New York tailor, for example, is quoted as saying:

"No doubt about it; I have a car that's working for me, not I for it. Now I spend $2.50 a week for gas instead of the $7 I used to spend for even less driving. Sure it's less car, but then it's more for the money than what you get when you buy the bigger cars in the first place. And then every week you pay more and more for what? Just to get there. Well, we get there too! Sure, maybe it isn't as comfortable; anyone who says it rides as good as the big cars isn't looking at it right. When I'm old and comfort is important to me, then I'll buy for comfort. Maybe you think it's funny I should like a foreign car so much? Some people say you should buy American. Well, if we bought American only, what would happen to foreign trade?"

A cashier in his thirties claimed that "owning a VW is like being in love. It's a member of the family. You don't hurt it or misuse it, yet you don't baby it either. We're fussier with this one than with any other car we've ever had."

"At first I thought it looked like an anteater," said the manager of a shoe store. "But now that I own it, it begins to grow on me. Now I think it's an adorable car and it keeps on growing on me even more. Also, the looks are constant and I don't have to concern myself with being out of style."

The interviewers asked Volkswagen owners what they thought a comparably priced U.S. small car might look like. One owner from Miami answered, "I'd expect it to be more stylish than the VW, with more cheesecake on it, and it would probably end up costing a lot more. They always say it'll cost less but by the time they get through with it, it's way out—three or four hundred dollars more than you expect to pay. They can't kid me."

These attitudes have taught VW that the "honesty" of the advertising must be carried over into the dealerships as well. Volkswagen salesmen could not afford to contradict by their words or behavior the very ads which bring them prospects. VWoA sales training executives point out that the social rank of an automobile salesman is in general very low in his community. "We want ours to stand out," one of them said. "We don't look for the storytelling, back-slapping kind of salesman. We want one who is heavy on product knowledge and is sensitive towards his customers, so that he knows what the customer's needs are and can think in terms of those needs. Our men are taught to listen, not just talk!"

Listening is in some way the key to the selling effort, whether it is in the ads or in the showrooms. The remoteness of the salesman and the ad agency writer or artist from those they are trying to reach is less a problem at VW than elsewhere. Volkswagen does not think of its customers as "targets," or for that matter, as infantile. This is apparent in every advertisement, each of which compliments the intelligence of the customer. It is apparent also in such minor details of VW showroom decoration as the general absence of cellophane tape, for VW has a rule that whatever is put up must be in a frame, not merely Scotch-taped on the walls. This is a matter of taste and, as everyone knows, VW has it. It is also a matter of intelligence. "What I like about Doyle Dane Bernbach," Carl Hahn has said, "is that their copywriters and art directors look at the product when they are trying to think up an ad. They don't just sit and look out their window at the Empire State Building!" Nor, it might be added, at any "Great Unwashed" out there.

11

Volkslore

ONE November day a few years ago, a raging flood swept Mrs. Mabel Stevenson's Volkswagen down Palmer Canyon, five miles outside Pomona, California. When the torrential rains had stopped, Mrs. Stevenson went to find her car. A wall of water five feet high had tumbled it down a stream bed for a quarter of a mile and it now lay in a graveyard of debris. "Both doors opened at once," she recalled later, "and the interior was bone-dry and undamaged. All the windows were in perfect condition. I'm sure I could have ridden down the canyon in it and been perfectly all right. Neighbors who saw it on its journey told me it rode the waters like a little ship."

That same year, thousands of miles away, a newlywed South African couple rode their VW not only like a little ship, but even like a little submarine. Allan and Rita Esser, both in their early twenties, were returning to Johannesburg from a honeymoon in Durban; a few miles outside Standerton, they suddenly came upon a flooded river and encountered a three-foot flood crest bearing down on them. "We resigned ourselves to certain death," the newlyweds said later. "But miraculously, we did not overturn and were washed down the embankment right *under* the water. We later heard it was twenty feet deep. All the windows were closed and the car was virtually airtight. We bobbed to the surface." Allan Esser climbed out of the window of the floating beetle feet-first and, hanging onto the side, tried in vain to touch the ground. As he clambered back, a little water entered through the open window. Leaning out now, he and his bride tried to grab willow branches as they were swept along. "Then we realized," they said, "that if we did catch hold, the jolt might capsize

230

the car. So we resigned ourselves to our little boat trip . . ." The beetle carried them a thousand yards before it came to rest. They then tried flashing for help, but the headlights were under water. "There was only one thing to do, and that was to wait," they said. After four and a half hours, the police arrived, along with a farmer who pulled them out with a tractor. The only mark the storm left on the car was a small dent on the running board. Soon they were back on the road again.

The stories of Mrs. Stevenson and of the Essers are part of what might be called the global "Volkslore" of the car. In providing an amazing store of legendary exploits, the little VW is a sort of Paul Bunyan of Lilliput.

The fact that the VWs mentioned above floated downriver comes, however, as no surprise to those who know the reasons for the car's seaworthiness: a flat, one-piece steel sheet completely seals and encloses the car's bottom and, as any owner knows, the car is so airtight that one is best advised to roll down a window before trying to shut the door. To prove the truth of an article's title ("The Beetle Does Float"), *Sports Illustrated* lowered a VW gingerly onto the water of Homosassa Springs, Florida, by crane; it remained on the surface for 29 minutes and 12 seconds. In far-off Sydney, Australia, a VW dealer did better than that: he launched a standard VW beetle into Kogarah Bay on the final day of speedboat championships being held there. The driver encountered little traffic as he plowed the car along at a steady five knots, for the race had been delayed because of the rough weather. Yachtsmen admitted the car showed good stability despite the heavy swell, and it even made sharp turns (with the driver archly offering hand signals). On subsequent occasions, the same "Boatswagen" was sent across the half-mile Middle Harbour stretch four times, with the car in water for more than 40 minutes on each occasion. A few modifications needed to be made: a 10- by 8-inch propeller had been fitted behind the rear bumper, driven by the generator drive pulley at the rear of the crankshaft, a snorkel had been fitted to the exhaust, and some grease had been smeared onto standard dust seals. No rudder was required, as the front wheels steered satisfactorily.

So-called "Floatswagen" exploits have become worldwide, especially as dealers from Italy to Australia find that their watertight VWs create attention-getting publicity, yet most of the *in*voluntary downwater rides in VWs seem to occur on the African continent, where Volkswagens regularly seem to encounter heavy floods. The Essers' experience is matched by others, as a few examples will show.

The Reverend Carrol W. Eby of Kenya's Kaimosi Mission reports he was swept downstream in 1959. "I drove my Volkswagen sedan over some of the worst roads in Africa," he says, "and in some places where there are no roads and no bridges. The Volkswagen *will float!* I discovered this when I drove into a drift where the water was deeper than I expected and we floated downstream. It took a long time for much water to seep in at the doors. Finally a group of men carried the VW out of the stream."

In 1962, E. D. W. de Klerk, of Oudshoorn, tried to cross the flooded Grobbelaars River when he discovered that the water over the causeway was too deep for him to get across. The stream rushed over the beetle's hood and dragged the car downstream. De Klerk and his two friends acted coolly and confidently. "I immediately closed the windows and shifted into neutral," he says. "Off we went in a foaming, eddying river!" After fifty yards, they collided with a tree. This impact threw the car back into the middle of the stream and then across to the other side. The beetle drifted on, for a total of two hundred yards, without the wheels striking anything. Finally, it came to rest against a bridge, still bone-dry inside.

More recently, J. M. Gerber of Port Elizabeth, South Africa, credits his beetle with "miraculously" saving the lives of everyone in his family. The Gerbers were driving home when they reached the flooded Kouga River; halfway over the bridge, which they felt certain they could cross, they were swept into the rushing waters. "It was an absolute nightmare," Gerber says, "and a miracle we survived." He reports his children were "panic-stricken" and he had to think and act quickly. He opened a front window and managed to climb out, then tried to push the car to the riverbank, but was instead pulled along after it. Suddenly, he lost hold. As he struggled to dry land, he watched in terror as his wife and four children were swept downstream. He ran along the edge of the river until the VW finally came to a halt in a bush, a full nine hundred yards from the bridge. Gerber courageously entered the river again and once more tried to drag his family to safety in the car. By this time, however, help had arrived; Gerber's brother, who had crossed the bridge safely in a truck and who had watched in horror as the VW was swept off, had raced ten miles to get a cable, and was now back. One end of it was tied to a tree, the other to the car, and along it

Gerber made five trips back and forth, carrying his small children and helping his wife to safety. Later, a tractor pulled the car out; shortly thereafter, the Gerbers climbed into their car again and drove the beetle home.

It is of course, on dry land that the watertight Volkswagen tends to perform to best advantage; in Africa, the very qualities which keep the bug afloat in roaring rivers often help it outperform other cars in difficult dry terrain. Hans Kriess of Swakopmund, South-West Africa, drove his VW along the shifting and, in some places, towering sand dunes of the notorious Skeleton Coast, and through the treacherous Namib Desert, remarking afterwards, "It is unbelievable what it stood up to." Kriess carried a load of over 1000 pounds, yet averaged 23 miles to the gallon (versus 9 mpg averaged by an accompanying Land Rover). "The Volkswagen," says Kriess, "carried 22 gallons of extra petrol, emergency water rations, a complete camera outfit, a tent and all personal effects such as bedding, stretchers, cooking utensils, stores, and so forth. The car was a pretty old model which I had overhauled completely. Through all the sixteen hundred miles of sand and mud along the Skeleton Coast and later through the Kaokoveld Mountains she did not give any trouble whatsoever, except for two punctures. Sometimes the air filter was so clogged up with sand that it had to be cleaned twice a day."

It seems to be just this kind of performance under grueling conditions that has helped popularize the VW in such rugged areas of the world as Africa. Automotive writers and car-buyers in densely populated, urbanized societies may look for something else: maneuverability perhaps, speed, and ease in parking; hence the reputation of the VW (particularly the beetle) as a good "second car" in cities like New York, London, Sydney, Cape Town, or Munich. In such places, owners have come to rely so much on VWs in heavy traffic that they seem to think only Beetlemaniacs cross continents in VWs. Yet Africa and Australia (to cite just two places where the going is often rough) prove them wrong. Not only does the VW there stand up under water and under desert conditions, but, as we shall presently see, in grueling test-drives and competitions as well.

"It's bad enough that some people think the VW should float," says *Small World*, VWoA's customer magazine, which reaches 500,000 U.S. owners each quarter. "Worse still, others feel the engine should fly." There are at least nine airplanes aloft which are powered by VW engines. None of these aircraft are produced by Volkswagenwerk or under license by the company. Indeed, the company takes an officially stern attitude toward them, although *Small World* could not resist commenting: "Certainly the VW is aircooled and relatively light [and] would seem well-suited to use in a plane [but] we don't recommend the practice." *Safer Motoring,* the independent British magazine for VW owners shows photographs of one such plane, the Turbulent, at the White Waltham RAF station; in the cockpit, instructed by an RAF squadron leader, was Prince Philip, Duke of Edinburgh. He flew the plane for thirty-five minutes and apparently liked the experience. The Turbulent, according to the editors of *Safer Motoring,* "is not generally known as a VW-powered job" but is "undoubtedly the most economical plane in the world today." It cruises at 80 to 85 miles per hour, gets 40 to 45 miles per gallon, and costs about $2600. Other VW-powered airplanes include the Bébé Jodel, the Fournier RF–01, the Poussin, the Microplane, and the Pinocchio, all of them French, as well as the Tefft Molecule, Belgium's Tipsy Nipper, Yugoslavia's pursuit-like single-seater, the CA–51, and another single-seater designed by an American, Don Stuart of Michigan. Volkswagen industrial engines, adaptations of the automotive engine and sold by the Volkswagenwerk, have also been used to operate an Alpine ski lift, a boat called the Davie Hydroglider, a hydrovane compressor, and a host of other machinery.

Such adaptions will come as no surprise to Volkswagen buffs who are readers of the many magazines issued for their entertainment. Several of these magazines are unconnected with the company or its distributors, who publish twelve of their own, such as *Small World* in the United States, *Mundo Volkswagen* in Mexico, *Senso* in Brazil, and *De VW* in Holland. In addition to Britain's *Safer Motoring,* other independent publishing ventures include *VW Autoist, Foreign Car Guide,* and *Popular Imported Cars* in the U.S. and *Gute Fahrt* in Germany. The editorial pages of such magazines are filled with uses to which VWs and their engines have been put, as well as with accomplishments newly recorded for the car.

Competing in VWs is one such use. While Heinz Nordhoff in 1962 commented that the Volkswagenwerk had no intention of launching a factory racing team, the fact is that in Australia the VW organization has almost done just that. Allan Gray, until recently head of Volkswagen Australasia Ltd., early put VWs into grueling competition races and endurance runs, in order to convince skeptical Australians that the car was up to the continent-size driving conditions Down Under. The results have been extraordinary.

In the mid-1950's, Australian racing enthusiasts watched in amazement (and amusement) as the beetle for the first time entered the field against cars twice its power (and twice its price). The trials, often referred to as the world's severest tests of cars and drivers, covered thousands of miles of Australia's unmade roads, led through the torrid north and over the wet, tortuous mountain roads of the southern Great Divide. As winners of the 1955 Redex Trial (which included a horror stretch of 143 creek crossings in 82 miles) were announced, amused smiles disappeared and amazement was doubled, for VW had won both first and second place. Even the amazement disappeared over the next several years, for beetles were beating big cars so regularly by then that hearing the winners announced was proving monotonous. In the 1956 Mobilgas Trial of 8745 miles, VWs came in first, third, fourth, and sixth. In the 1957 Ampol Trial of 6000 miles, VWs came in first and second; in the Mobilgas Rally of 10,738 miles, staged the same year, twenty of the fifty-two surviving vehicles were beetles and six of these had captured each of the first six places. Then, in the Mobilgas Trial of 1958, VWs came in first, second, fourth, and fifth. Australians did more than watch now: they also began to buy. In the five years from 1954 to 1959, almost 73,000 Volkswagens were sold in Australia; since then, almost 200,000 more have been sold there.

As sales mounted, the company continued to impress Australians with razzle-dazzle promotions and trials victories. In 1962, drivers Ray Christie and Joe Dunlop, driving a beetle, challenged the nine-day record time in which a competitor had sent a big six-cylinder car around Australia. They completed the 8100-mile run in 7¼ days (76 hours). Between Perth and Ceduna (1400 miles), they *averaged* sixty miles per hour. Their only mishaps: two punctures (one caused by a horseshoe). In 1964, the same men challenged their own record, this time using not a beetle, but a VW 1500 sedan. Leaving Melbourne at midnight, August 23, they slid smilingly back to the same spot after covering 8044 miles in 5 days, 22 hours, 17 minutes. They claimed they could have done better if they hadn't caught a few hours' sleep on two occasions while their car underwent routine servicing.

In Africa, too, the VWs have been entered in competitions with considerable success. In 1958, VWs won first, second, third and fourth place in their class in the Kenya Coronation Safari Rally, reputedly the toughest automobile rally on the continent, in which only half of all competitors finished at all. That same year, five of the seven cars finishing the African Endurance Championship were VWs; thirty-two cars in all had started out over 1500 miles of Angola and Congo. The VWs captured first, second, third, fourth and sixth place. In the 1959 Congo Marathon Rally, only ten cars survived a nonstop, 1500-mile run, although thirty-four had started. Of these ten, *seven* were VWs, which also won first, second, and third place. In 1962, a Volkswagen won first place in the East African Safari, a race covering more than three thousand miles of the roughest terrain imaginable. A record one hundred and four cars were entered, but only forty-seven finished, the others falling prey to mechanical failures or being unable to maintain the 45- to 60-mph average speeds. When the winning Volkswagen romped across the finish line, the drivers announced, "It's ready to go round again!" The car's only malfunction had been a sticking headlight dimmer switch. (Interestingly, the same car *did* go round again the following year, winning first place in its class.)

Formula Vee racing has become popular as well, for those interested in a VW that looks like a racing car rather than a bug. Formula Vee cars, offered complete and ready to race by their manufacturers for about $2500, are one-seaters consisting of a stock VW engine and transmission mounted on a tubular frame and covered with a lightweight Fiberglas body. Unlike the VW sedan, Formula Vee cars have their engines ahead of the rear axle and have replaced the rear torsion-bar suspension system with coil springs and shock absorbers. They use ordinary VW parts and upkeep is consequently low. With do-it-yourself kits for their construction available at about $950, they have given birth to a small, low-cost, lightweight, and relatively low-speed form of racing. They reach a top speed of only 100 mph, but, as one enthusiast put it, "Who cares? All the cars are the same. It's the best driver who wins." At Nassau recently, the winning Formula Vee averaged 73.9 mph, while the fastest stock sedan averaged 65 mph. "Volkswagen, however, does not endorse racing or similar competition," the company clucks, while admitting with obvious pleasure that "the VW-based Formula Vee seems likely to flourish in spite of us." Says actor Nigel Green, who built one and races it, "They're nothing like Grand Prix cars, but they sure are fun to drive. I'd compare it to riding a roller skate at seventy mph!"

A car which can float, fly, and race engenders a great deal of loyalty, even of the sentimental kind. When the Metropolitan VW Club in New York discovered a 1956 Volkswagen corroding in a junkyard, its members rescued it, reconditioned it completely, resprayed it a fire-engine red and then named it "The Orphan." Several Volkswagen dealers assisted "this good work." The sentiment involved is what *Sports Illustrated* calls "America's romance with a Plain Jane."

"The car often winds up in some stickily sentimental situations," Huston Horn wrote in *Sports Illustrated*. "In Florida not long ago, a bride stuck a miniature VW in the confection atop their wedding cake, a Kansas couple sent out birth announcements when their VW was delivered by the dealer, a Long Island man built a house for his, complete with shutters, weathervane, eagle over the door and geraniums in the window boxes, and an Iowa man gave his wife a Mother's Day present of a VW station wagon, which she thereupon filled to capacity with their nine children." In addition, Horn says, Texas cowboys ride fence in Volkswagens, a Nashville man delivers money in a bulletproof VW, Los Angeles bank robbers have made their getaways in a VW, and Senator Robert F. Kennedy has campaigned through the sunroof of a VW station wagon. A North Hollywood drugstore which uses a beetle for deliveries has "Medicine Dropper" painted on its door; the same may be said of a Rexall Drug outlet in Reno, which proves that when a VW fad starts, it gets around. At Ohio University and on other campuses, students have "crammed" Volkswagens as they once used to jam telephone booths (a record 18 collegians have been squeezed into a sunroof sedan and 62 into a sunroof Microbus station wagon). Campus pranksters regularly bury VWs in autumn leaves.

Another collegiate game, apparently invented by the students of Wayne State University in Detroit, is the "Volkstote." The Volkstote has since swept Australia, where university students seem to be competing with their American counterparts for the unofficial world championship. The competition involves carrying a VW one hundred feet and then racing it back to the starting position, with all the bearers having to get inside the car for the drive back. During 1965 Orientation Week, twelve law students at Melbourne University made it in 31.6 seconds, claiming the World Championship. West Australian University students retaliated by breaking the record in 27.6 seconds. The championship next moved to Armidale students at the University of New England, in Australia, who made the trip in 26.8 seconds. Its present location is questionable, as is the permanence of the fad.

Not only has the compact size of the car, which allows it

to be toted about (and rescued from floods), become the subject of good-natured humor, but also the fact that the beetle has not changed its basic design over the years. Sargent Shriver, when he headed the Peace Corps, compared his organization to a Volkswagen. "We continue to improve it all the time inside, but it remains just about the same externally." The same theme is echoed by comedian Jerry Shane, who claimed he met his local VW dealer at the post office one morning, the dealer asked Shane whether he recognized him. "Of course I do." Shane says he answered. "You're exactly the same as last year."

The VW also benefits from that "reverse snobbery" which prompts the rich and glittering elements of American society to avoid flashy cars like Cadillacs. Merriman Smith reports in *The Good New Day* that it was "important to keep down with the Joneses" in Washington during the administration of John F Kennedy. One way to do so, he says, was to drive a Volkswagen. This is an attitude the company has encouraged; a Volkswagen advertisement has even been headlined, "What year car do the Joneses drive?" The "Joneses" include King Baudouin and Queen Fabiola of the Belgians, Britain's Princess Margaret, and two cousins of the King of Siam who operate the Volkswagen agency in Bangkok. Charles Lindbergh, according to *Esquire,* drives a Volkswagen, and Dr. Benjamin Spock arrived at a White House dinner in a rented VW. Society columnist Jane Gregory of the Chicago *Sun-Times* writes that "the snappiest auto we've seen of late was not a Rolls-Royce or a Mercedes-Benz or a Jaguar, but a Volkswagen convertible Mrs. Otis Hubbard drove to lunch the other day in Lake Forest." She reports that "the finishing touch of *éclat* is a discreet monogram lettered in gold on the door." VWs are popular not only in chic Lake Forest, Illinois, but also in society's watering-hole, Newport, Rhode Island. The Boston *Globe* noted that "Rolls-Royces, Mercedes-Benzes and the ubiquitous Volkswagens" were omnipresent at Janet Auchincloss's debut there. The Washington *Post* reports much the same at embassy parties. Clearly, the car is "in," at least in the United States, and driving one has become a sign of good taste. The latest in status symbols, according to *Road & Track,* may be the installation, summer and winter, of a pair of skis bolted on the top of a VW, an affectation on the campus of the University of Colorado. In Beverly Hills, when VW driver Princess Margaret and her husband, Lord Snowdon, were being feted on their visit to the U.S.A., actor Paul Newman and his actress-wife Joanne Woodward emerged afterwards and asked an attendant to bring their beetle. Says Gene Youngblood of the Los Angeles *Herald-Examiner:* "The stars drove off in the tiny car amid the cheers of the crowd who saw some 15 Rolls-Royces, three Bentleys, and scores of Jaguars and Cadillacs in the jammed parking lot." In Rochester, New York, Del Rey told readers of the *Times-Union* that "A woman wearing a mink stole and riding in an automobile driven by a uniformed chauffeur arrived at the Eastman Theater the other day. That's not very unusual, even in the informal Great Society. But the car the uniformed chauffeur was driving was a Volkswagen—and you've got to admit that's different!" The ultimate accolade nowadays, however, comes not from society, but from the royalty of the Big Beat, the Beatles. As one might expect, a Beatle would have to own a Beetle. John Lennon does, although he also stocks a Rolls-Royce and a Ferrari, as well as a chauffeur.

The kind of people who drive Volkswagens strike syndicated columnist Sydney J. Harris of the Chicago *Daily News* "as having what traffic officers call 'the right attitude' on the road . . . They seem sensible people, with decent values, and I would wager a sizable amount that the accident rate is quite low among them." Harris is right; insurance rates are often lower for Volkswagen owners than for owners of big cars. As for their being people with "decent values," Harris seems right too, as the "Police Blotter" column in the Sudbury, Massachusetts, *Citizen* shows. "On Saturday night," it reported, "a VW sedan struck a stone wall on the Haynes property on Morse Road. The next day a young man returned and rebuilt the wall." Stephen Baker, writing in *Advertising Age*, believes, however, that the man who "prefers Volkswagens to Cadillacs" is "an intellectual snob" who "prefers to display intellectual instead of material wealth." Dan Greenburg, writing his "Snobs' Guide to Status Cars" in the July 1964 *Playboy*, sets down ground rules for "how to own a Volkswagen" and, in doing so, somewhat supports the "intellectual snob" theory advanced in the advertising trade press.

"If you're not married," Greenburg writes, "take women who are college graduates to little theater or terribly smart cocktail parties or to a picnic in the country, but don't do anything with them until you're married and then, when you're married, make a slat bench and have at least three children and name them after characters from *Winnie-the-Pooh*. Take out your contact lenses before making love. Use a lot of Freudian terminology in your speech unless you have been through psychoanalysis. Go through psychoanalysis. Own the complete

239

works of Copland or Vivaldi. Read the *New Yorker* and check off all the movies in the front of the magazine after you have seen them. Read *Time* but hate it. Spend a lot of time on your modest hi-fi and leave the components exposed. Enjoy Joan Baez. Tell people you voted for Stevenson the first time he ran but not the second. If you are Jewish and somebody should ask you what kind of a car you drive, say: 'A VW, and I know, but it's a helluva solid little piece of machinery.' Go to any Ingmar Bergman movie and correctly identify Max von Sydow and at least three other actors, telling what roles they played in *Wild Strawberries* and *Smiles of a Summer Night*. (If your Volkswagen is a Karmann Ghia, you should have been able to interpret *The Seventh Seal* on at least three levels.) It is all right to take a Volkswagen to a concert, to an indoor art exhibit, or to a university extension class. It is not all right to take a Volkswagen to a Great Book discussion or to a meeting of the Birch Society. If you have a small sticker on your back window that reads 'Made in der Black Forest by der elves,' you should be driving a Metropolitan."

To be sure, VW owners are something else. As a matter of fact, VW owners on the whole "defy classification by any conventional criteria, according to R. L. Polk and Company, statisticians to the U.S. auto industry. They seem to have all kinds of jobs, "from lawyers to prison guard lieutenants, to bartenders, to advertising executives," Horn writes, and they enjoy the most diverse sports and hobbies. "They like to do everything from skeet shooting to skiing, to gem cutting. They read the *Wall Street Journal* and *Mad* magazine. [They] range from introverts to phony gladhanders."

On the whole, they tend to be more sophisticated than those who buy Detroit cars and most live in urban West and East Coast areas. Asked whether a large number of VW customers are of German extraction, market analysts reply that the company sells more cars in Atlanta, Georgia, where there are few German-Americans than in Milwaukee, Wisconsin, where there are many. Pro- or anti-German sentiment seems to have little influence on VW sales in the United States. To some extent, the economic level of prospects does. "The poor shun Volkswagen," Horn says, ". . . probably because it costs too little to represent status. Owners also tend to have two or more cars, to live in the suburbs, to have college educations, to be younger than the average car buyer and to be slightly more inclined to outdoor sports than to bowling or going to the movies."

A survey of Volkswagen buyers, conducted a few years

ago by a Princeton, New Jersey, firm revealed that 40 per cent of VW buyers are college graduates and 60 per cent attended college. The proportion of VW families in the professions or management is 51 per cent, about twice the ratio of these groups versus semiskilled, unskilled, and service groups throughout the country. More recent surveys report that less educated, less well-heeled Americans have gotten the bug, a development VWoA has devoutly hoped for and encourages mightily.

The attitudes American owners entertain about their cars emerged from another VWoA survey, conducted by *Small World* magazine among five thousand of its readers to determine both likes and dislikes. Complaints were minor and few in number. "The beep horn has no authority in freeway driving," a Californian wrote. Another correspondent from that state complained of the "s-q-u-e-a-ky brakes." The biggest gripe at the time (12.8 per cent) concerned ventilation and heating.* Less than 10 per cent complained of passenger room, but some pleaded for more storage space—a problem many VW owners have solved imaginatively for themselves. A Navy man in San Francisco urged the company to redesign the engine lid to increase clearance with the rear bumper. *Small World* commented, "Maybe you're right," and referred the suggestion to Volkswagenwerk designers in Wolfsburg, who have done just that. Others complained about the lack of a cigarette lighter and about the location of the battery beneath the rear seat.

Most owners were less captious. A Wisconsin woman said, "This car belongs to me—I don't belong to it!" and another owner wrote, "It has to take one hell of an automobile when my mother reminds me to change oil!" A New Hampshire man reported that his current VW was his fourth. Significantly, a large proportion praised the company for its service facilities and seem to agree with Hahn and Perkins that Hermann Bruns has established the "best automotive service network in the U.S.A." Those who reported that they were switching to a Detroit car usually gave their growing families as the reason (VWoA hopes to sell such persons its station wagon, which will hold a family of nine). An Illinois owner warned, "If you ever change the styling of the beetle, I will change to a different type of car." A Kentucky VW owner

---

* In reply, *Small World* suggested that opening a vent window improves the heat flow, that respondents' heater flaps might need adjustment, and that keeping the car in low gear for short runs provides more heat. "This means you'll hear air rushing, but it's a cozy, warm sound." Since then, VW heaters have been improved considerably.

advised, "Let the others load on the gadgets." Finally, a Columbia, California, man proposed, "Every VW owner should be forced to drive a loosely sprung, monstrous, four-eyed car over a narrow gravel road once a year. Call it Appreciation Day."

In 1962 one untypical Volkswagen owner in whom the company took considerable delight was a then seventy-eight-year-old justice of the peace in Oconto Falls, Wisconsin, named Albert Gillis. Judge Gillis bought a bright red 1962 VW sedan after what appears to be three decades of resistance to car salesmen. His first and only other car was a Model A Ford, vintage 1929, which was still in his garage when he bought his beetle. He had kept the Ford "like a barber keeps his scissors," VWoA reports. "When a part looked like it was wearing out, he replaced it." He even jacked the car up every night to save the tires. When Judge Gillis bought his Volkswagen, VWoA's *Weathervane* picked up the story and passed it on to VWoA's ad agency; "33 years later, he got the bug," Doyle Dane Bernbach later headlined an ad. Judge Gillis, it reported, bought a Volkswagen because he "heard they hold up." Otherwise, Gillis was cautious. "Your inspectors sure do a good job of inspecting," he allowed. Then he mentioned that he and Mrs. Gillis took a trip of 6750 miles in the VW for their fifty-fourth wedding anniversary. The judge noted that they spent only sixty-two dollars on gas and fifty-five cents on oil throughout the trip. Then he murmured, "I didn't think they were supposed to burn any oil."

Another VW owner in whom the company takes pride is the man who had the oldest Volkswagen in the United States. In 1959, the company started hunting for him, intending to present him with the 500,000th VW to be imported to the U.S.A. In April 1960 the man was found. He was Harold Kuhn, an Emerson, Nebraska, farmer, who had bought his VW from a U.S. Air Force sergeant named Duane R. Margeson, of Dalbo, Minnesota, who, in turn, had picked it up in Germany. The factory records showed the car had been built on December 30, 1945. Just as the company prepared to celebrate the event, it learned that the farmer never obtained clear title to the car and that both the veteran and the farmer now claimed the reward. Rather than sour the occasion, VWoA presented each man with a brand-new sedan.

As has been noted, it took some courage for men like the Air Force sergeant to drive a Volkswagen in the U.S.A. before the car became popular. Owners then often banded together for self-protection, to bolster each other's courage, and for good fellowship besides. They had, after all, something concrete in common. It became logical for a handful of them to establish the Volkswagen Club of America in 1954, "back in those days when there was something terribly lonely about being the first in your block to own the beetle," as Huston Horn put it. Members kept their eyes peeled for other Volkswagens, and encountering them, they honked and waved joyously and, perhaps, with relief. Those days have gone. Ten years later, driving in a VW with my wife and children, I tested out the responsiveness of U.S. Volkswagen drivers. Despite the fact that we honked and waved at well over one hundred VWs, we got just one return salute. It struck me that the drivers I greeted thought I might be somewhat mad. Certainly they did not seem to know the password, or perhaps they considered the gesture antediluvian. In 1954, matters were more fraternal. Alvin Outcalt, a founder of the Club, says, "Of course a lot of foreign-car owners were waving and tooting in those days, but with us it went deeper somehow. You didn't just wave; you stopped and crossed over and shook hands with the guy and asked him how many miles he was getting and did his heater keep him warm like yours didn't. You felt a kinship, you know?"

Although it wasn't hard for the Club's founders to enroll members, it was difficult at first to convince Volkswagen of America of the Club's merits. "Anyone coming from the outside world today," Heinz Nordhoff had said once, "either wants to harm us or sponge on our work." His cautious spirit then infected VWoA as well. The company at first forbade the Club to use the name of the car in its title, but the Club chose to ignore the order, and ultimately VWoA surrendered completely to the enthusiasts. Today, it supports the Club in sundry ways and staff members rarely miss its conventions. Upwards of 2500 VW owners currently belong to the Club and many of them sport Club insignia on their shirts and car bumpers. They even travel together to Wolfsburg where, they say, "we stand around in that factory like pilgrims in a cathedral and think reverent thoughts." They also meet frequently at events sponsored by local branches throughout the United States. Rallies and VW caravans to races and auto shows bring them together. It is, for example, possible today for a VW owner to attend the national convention of the Club, a May Frolic in the New Jersey area, an *Oktoberfest* in Illinois, and a *Herbst Festtag* in the Philadelphia area.

One of the ties that bind is the Club's official publication, the *VW Autoist,* put out in Springfield, Ohio. "Dedicated to helping the Volkswagen owner enjoy his car to the fullest," as its masthead proclaims, it furnishes members with regional news, technical information, and such services as the Emergency Listing Service ("Stuck somewhere? Check the list and call the names [of Club members] nearest to where you've broken down.") The magazine also sponsors a Club Host Plan, whereby VW travelers can spend the night en route at the homes of other Volkswagen buffs. A typical issue of the publication described the meetings of the Philadelphia club (members had a lively evening discussing cornering, shifting, and driving for economy), reported that cash on hand for the National Volkswagen Club of America totaled $1875.82, offered details on the national convention in Cleveland, Ohio, and announced that a second pilgrimage to Wolfsburg was planned, the first having proved a sellout. Oddly, their enthusiasm seems enduring. VWoA vice president Arthur Railton addressed them in 1964 and told them of his interview at VW before he was hired to head public relations. He was told that VW wanted a "nuts and bolts approach" to its publicity. Railton told the assembled Club members his response: "I said I wasn't sure I knew all the bolts in a VW, but I'd been to a few VW Club conventions and I certainly knew the nuts."

In other countries, too, VW owners not only become VW enthusiasts but also enroll in local VW clubs. Testing the car's economy is a popular club event; at a Seymour VW Club economy run in Australia, a 36-hp sedan racked up 58 miles per gallon, while a VW 1500 Squareback scored 44 mpg. At another event in Australia, a club member returned a figure of 58.3 mpg. Such highs are of course abnormal, but the normal seems good enough for most owners. Richard Bayles of Bairsdale Victoria, is one; he reports that his new "Australian" VW, measured over three thousand miles covered in three months, "averaged 40.2 mpg and up to 45 mpg." Bayles took his car to Cooma in the Snowy Mountains, where temperatures run to below 8°F. "Snow, rocks, rain, dust, sun, mud, cold—all just don't seem to affect this car!" he wrote the company. "This is more than I ever expected."

To drive just this point home—that "nothing" seems to bother beetles—Volkswagen Australasia, Limited, recently made a big promotion out of the standard VW 1200 sedan which spent a year in Antarctica, at Mawson Station, a lonely Australian scientific research headquarters on the coast of MacRobertson Land. Taken there at the suggestion of the head of the research team from among hundreds which had come off Australia's VW assembly line in December 1962, this ruby-red beetle was subjected to smothering snows and 125-mph winds, "competing" against dog-teams and tracked vehicles ("Snow-tracs," "Weasels," and "Caterpillars"). The latter, however, proved slow, cumbersome, and costly to operate, while the dogs had a restricted payload and range and could be driven successfully by one owner only. The beetle turned out to be perfect for running around the station and even up snow-covered hills which had proved difficult to climb on foot because of the sinking snow. Air-cooled, it never froze; tightly sealed, it was immune to the drifting snow (so fine a powder at Mawson that it blows through tack holes). The scientists called it their "Red Terror"; back home, Volkswagen Australasia proudly tagged it "Antarctica 1." After its year was over, and it was replaced by "Antarctica 2," it was tanked up and taken out to the 1964 BP Rally of South Eastern Australia, where it was entered against 42 competitors. All leading automobile firms were represented in this rough-road 2000-mile event, VW by a dozen cars. Predictably perhaps, the beetle bearing number 32 and its "Antarctica 1" license plate won first place.

Across the globe, lying more or less on the same meridians of latitude as Australia, there are those who don't like Volkswagens. Mostly, however, they seem to be elephants, refuting the story that pachyderms love anything with a trunk in front. This, at least, was the conclusion reached by Canadian tourist Peter Hollick and his friend Ian Castleden, driving their VW "Microbus" station wagon through the Wankie Game Reserve in Rhodesia on July 6, 1965. Late that afternoon, they found the road suddenly blocked by a herd of elephants. They halted; then Hollick noticed a sudden movement to his left: a huge cow elephant, her calf at her side, had been startled by the bus. No doubt wishing to protect her calf, she turned and charged the 2535-pound vehicle. Hollick and Castleden beat a hasty retreat out the right-hand front door and into the bush. The elephant's enraged attack lasted ten seconds. She flipped the bus onto its side, turned it on its roof, then flipped it again onto its side. When it was clear she had disabled the monster, the elephant stopped. The "enemy" lay vanquished, with tusk-holes six inches in diameter through its steel sides and floor. Smugly, the cow returned to her calf and, joining the departing herd, sauntered off as nonchalantly as an elephant can.

Hoping for a search party (for it was now getting dark),

Hollick and Castleden built fires, switched on the headlights of their overturned bus, and made a lot of noise to keep animals at a distance. They spent quite a night, their sleep interrupted by new herds of elephants, as well as buffalo and an occasional leopard. They discovered that their station wagon lay beside the trail to a watering-hole—a sort of Times Square of the game reserve. Early next morning, passing motorists took them to a nearby station. The game ranger there was shocked: this was the first attack in thirty-three years! He rounded up a team, accompanied Hollick and Castleden to their bus, righted it, and recharged the battery, which had been drained during the night's long vigil. Hollick and Castleden noted that their bus had been battered brutally; still it started immediately and, says Hollick, "it has run perfectly ever since." As the game ranger assured Hollick, the hostile elephant must have come from elsewhere, for the indigenous version was much friendlier—perhaps even to Volkswagens, today surely as numerous in Africa as elephants, and tamer.

A car that provides as many legends as these becomes, inevitably, the subject of many jokes and stories. One of the earliest and best-known Volkswagen jokes—created before its rear engine became familiar—tells of a stalled owner peering sadly inside the car's front luggage compartment. "My engine's missing," he says to another Volkswagen owner who happens along. "Are you in luck!" the other one answers. "They gave me a spare in my trunk." As Huston Horn says, the car "is the butt of some of the sorriest jokes since they told your grandfather he auto get a horse." Typical of the kind of humor Horn says "convulses Volkswagen owners" is the story of the drunk who was knocked down by a Saint Bernard dog, then was hit by a VW as he struggled to his feet. "The dog didn't hurt so much," the drunk told bystanders, "but that tin can tied to his tail mighty near killed me."

Texans, he adds, claim that local VW ads say, "Take home a six-pack today," and a newspaper dispatch from that state reports that an eagle attacked a Volkswagen, smashed the windshield and clawed two rabbit-hunters inside, apparently under the impression the bug was edible. The story is told of the Texas millionaire who bought himself a big air-conditioned Cadillac—and took his change in Volkswagens. Yet another story has a Texas oilman showing his beetle to two friends, who sneer that it isn't air-conditioned. "No," he admits, "but I always keep a couple of cold ones in the refrigerator." Columnist Dick Hitt of the Dallas *Times-Herald* tells of a local VW owner whose beetle *is* air-conditioned and "who gets 40 miles to the ice cube." Finally, the Phoenix, Arizona, *Weekly Gazette* talks of the Texan who bought a VW to drive from his home to his garage.

The beetle has been called a "humpbacked roller skate" and a "pregnant roller skate," and, more recently, a "pregnant skateboard." Columnist Jack Quinn of the Denver *Post* recently amused his readers by asking them to suggest words defining a group of Volkswagens. A "vainglory of Volkswagens" was submitted along with a scurry, an insolence, a peasantry, a churl, and a batch of beetles. A reader named Burton Beebe told Quinn he liked the sound of "a chuffle of Volkswagens," and wrote that a subspecies known as "the double-throated chortler" gets excited in the presence of "the high-crested overbore."

A few Volkswagen owners still festoon their bugs with special signs such as "Half Car, Will Travel," "Student Porsche Driver," and "Transistorized Roll-Royce," and at least one VW sports a license plate which spells out MYBUG. In Los Angeles, according to Bennett Cerf, there is even a parking lot with a special section for Volkswagens, bearing a sign which reads "The Nursery." And the Indianapolis *Times's* Irving Leibowitz writes in his column that he saw a car parked in town with a sign reading "Conservatism is Americanism." The vehicle, of course, was "a true-blue Volkswagen." In 1964, Volkswagen produced a nonpartisan bumper sticker for national elections. The top line exhorted the public to "Vote November 3"; the second line, as you might guess, simply read "Votes-Wagen". The stickers proved very popular; for the 1966 election, about 45,000 were distributed.

Much of this humor is whimsy. Thus, *Time* magazine, referring to Pasadena, California, said that "for 364 days a year [it is] a gentle cultivated city populated by little old ladies who sit behind lace curtains and, according to legend, knit Volkswagens."

Some of the humor purports to be based on fact. Henry Mullen of Cleveland, Ohio, reported in *Gasoline Retailer*, a trade magazine, that an elderly gentleman drove a Cadillac into his service station, followed by a Volkswagen. "Jumping out and dashing back to the Volks," Mullen writes, "he began hurling invectives at the small car for 'tailing him.' Then he abruptly fell silent. Surmising that something was amiss, the attendant rushed to the scene—only to find that there was no driver in the Volks. At that moment, the police pulled alongside the Caddy in search of the Volks, whose owner had reported it stolen . . ." What had happened, says Mullen, was that "the Caddy had backed into the Volks, locked bumpers and had been towing it around." Columnist Herb Caen of the San Francisco *Chronicle* says he saw a municipal bus and a Volkswagen come "nose-to-nose at [an] intersection and the VW refused to blink." Caen writes that "the bus driver reached under his seat, produced a can of Black Flag insect powder, opened the door and sprinkled some on the Volks' hood." The expression on the VW's driver as he backed off, the columnist says, was memorable.

Jerome Beatty, writing in the *Saturday Review*, commented that "next to a couple of Volkswagen owners trading automobile stories, the funniest conversation to listen to is two people talking about their electric blankets" (or, as a subsequent issue of the magazine had it, about their contact lenses). VW owners like to trade statistics such as the one supplied by the Waterloo, Iowa, *Courier,* which reports that the fuel used to power a Boeing 707 for one hour would drive a beetle two and a half times around the world. They enjoy stories about how easily the car handles, such as one which appeared in the Portland *Oregonian,* telling of a VW whose battery went dead in the wilds of the Northwest. The owner "was in a place where he couldn't coast or be pushed," writes columnist Francis Murphy. Appealing to a neighboring camper for help, he was told to jack up the car and turn on the ignition. "Then the neighbor spun the rear wheel by hand and the car started up with the greatest of ease."

Volkswagen of America does more than smile at all such stories; it collects them in the archives of its public relations department and periodically circulates them to newspapers in mimeographed form. VWoA's *Small World* magazine is probably the only customer publication issued by a major auto manufacturer which lists customer complaints; it is hard to imagine one of Detroit's Big Three circulating gripes to 500,000 owners. The Volkswagen company, however, recognizes that its honesty is appreciated. It also knows that the VW is not just a mode of transportation (which was the only purpose for which Porsche designed it); it knows that the car amuses and delights, as well as transports, its owners.

As increasing numbers of VWs are sold to Americans, more and more of them go to sober individuals, and not to that special breed known as car buffs. Yet there are still several thousand owners who tinker with VWs to an extent difficult to imagine among Americans who own Detroit models, modified largely by hot-rodders.

A glance at magazines which reach VW owners reveals how many items are offered for sale to those who want to glamorize, update, or soup up their beetles. Available are: engine compartment silencer pads; chrome-plated air cleaners; chrome muffler tips; rear axle joint boot kits; rubber-faced bumper guards; chrome-plated vent louver trim; tapered muffler tips; cast aluminum flared tailpipes; black rubber fender flaps; defroster vent trim; polished aluminum top carriers; spring-balanced hood supports; passenger-side sun visors for 1952–1961 VWs; camber compensators and anti-sway bars; nine-piece body molding sets; 1962-style tail and stop lights for 1952–1962 VWs; headlamp visors; chrome door-handle guards; reclining seat brackets; gas gauge kits; sunroof wind deflectors; 12-cubic-foot luggage carriers; driver arm rests; chrome-plated trailer hitches; speedometer "tach" decals; windshield and side window defroster-deflector shields; cocoa mats for VW floors; car plaques reading, "You Have Been Volkswagened—Passed by 40 H.P."; locking handles for motor compartments; plastic grip handles for emergency brake levers; dual-carburetor manifolds; vinyl-covered "super-shelves" to fit under VW dashboards; chrome trunk-handle plates; illuminated oil-temperature gauges; ammeters; automatic backup lamp kits; VW-tailored electric razors; transistorized electric tachometers; VW-size interior fans; dual transistor ignition systems; steel expansion studs to increase rear tread by three inches; reserve fuel containers which snap into spare wheel rims; hinged rear windows; "Travellounger" VW seats; plastic foam headrests; superchargers; and such "Pidgin German" dashboard control labels as *Das Glimmerblinken* for the light switch, *Der Drizzleflippen* for wiper switch, *Die Warmercougher* for choke, *Das Schmokegedunka* for ashtray, and *Der Puttersparken* for the ignition.

This kind of humor (like decals which read "Made in the Black Forest by Gnomes") appeals perhaps only to the less sophisticated of the usually sophisticated Volkswagen owners and was more prevalent in the 1950's than it is now. The bumper-strips have also changed with the times. Bill Fiset of the Oakland, California, *Tribune* says he saw one VW recently which bore two bumper strips: "Support Planned Parenthood" and "Make Love, Not War." More complex is the clowning around of a Broadwater, Nebraska, TV repairman named Bud Hathaway, who installed an electronic system in his VW trunk which allows him to trigger engine and accessory controls from a portable transmitter. Hathaway parks his VW in a crowded place, crosses the street, and watches passersby stop in amazement as the car's engine starts, wipers move, headlights and taillights blink on and off, and turn signals flash, apparently of their own free will. After the inevitable crowd gathers, he broadcasts his voice through the car's trunk.

Not only TV repairmen but also most other Americans with an engineering bent seem fascinated with the car. This fact has resulted in the space age adoption of a good deal of VW references. When astronauts James McDivitt and Edward White spent four days in orbit, the Associated Press quoted Norman Shyken, McDonnell Aircraft Corporation Gemini spacecraft crew engineer, as explaining, "Ed and Jim's living space has about as much room as the front of a Volkswagen." Another Cape Kennedy report, originating with Larry Van Gelder of the New York *World-Telegram and Sun,* said, "The first stage of the Titan engine generates 430,000 pounds of thrust at maximum, or the equivalent of the thrust that could be generated by 219,000 Volkswagens . . ." Astronaut Frank Borman, an Air Force colonel, gets around at home in a four-year-old Volkswagen, reflecting the viewpoint which Ed Ramsey offered in the Trenton, New Jersey, *Trentonian:* "Volkswagen is the most modern of cars, as any observer would agree. It features a fast-back design, bucket seats, and four-on-the-floor manual transmission. Its basic design was formulated 30 years ago . . ."

Does that design prove adequate for today? Roy Newquist wrote in the Chicago Heights, Illinois, *Star* that other cars "have lost ground as status symbols." He says "the Ford which looks like the Plymouth is only a bit different from the Cadillac which resembles the Lincoln. Only the Volkswagen, which resembles a pregnant beetle, and the Rolls-Royce, which suggests a large bank account, seem to have any individuality whatsoever."

David Felts of the Decatur, Illinois, *Herald* reports a news story which appeared on the front page of a Chicago newspaper. The news was that a young mother, en route to the hospital, had given birth to a baby in the back seat of a Volkswagen. "Now who can possibly doubt that there's all the room anyone can need in the back of that popular car?" he asked. The total number of babies born in beetles throughout the world may never be known, but VWoA has handed out forty-five "awards" for such performances in just two recent years. The company, which apparently regards itself as a sort of godfather, presents each family with a savings bond and a letter of congratulations (for "helping to prove there's always room for one more in a VW"). Parents have responded just as graciously. One mother wrote VWoA, "I never knew having a baby could prove so exciting." Another, from Wyoming, Michigan, wrote, "Not only does the VW relieve gas pains, as the ad says, but even labor pains." Volkswagen of America, in turn, announced its offer of Bonds for Babies Born in Beetles, in *Small World* magazine, saying "Act now! This offer may be withdrawn at any time."

While the beetle may have enough room for obstetrics, it is nevertheless no car for the five or six adults who can comfortably get into a full-sized American automobile or into the newer VW Fastback and Squareback sedans. The beetle was designed for four and it was, furthermore, not designed for grouches. Driving one is somewhat like driving a VW "bus" or station wagon. As one U.S. owner says, "You just have to be young—at heart anyway—to drive a bus." It seems encouraging that so many Americans still fit that description.

12

From Wolfsburg With Love

THE beetle and the beetle's "big brothers" are today less German than they are international, for they are not merely exported to other countries but in several cases are built there as well. Those who buy Volkswagens in Brazil, for example, do not buy a product of "fine German craftsmanship" at all, for the VWs sold there are entirely made in Brazil, of Brazilian materials, and by Brazilian workers. Their cars are products of the craftsmanship of their fellow countrymen. The same may be said of a number of other places far away from Wolfsburg, for VWs manufactured in Australia, South Africa, and Mexico are similarly largely of local origin; in some places, the "local content" of the car runs sixty per cent, in others more than ninety. In each, however, the aim and the direction is toward producing a car that is one hundred per cent made locally. Today, there are VW manufacturing plants in the nations mentioned above; elsewhere, local assembly plants put together VWs shipped "completely knocked-down" (CKD) from Wolfsburg; in other places, as in the United States, they are imported "built-up," ready for sale. Volkswagens may be bought today in more countries than are represented at the United Nations and Germany's Volkswagenwerk is today the world's largest exporter of motor vehicles.

Probably the very first foreigner to buy VWs from Wolfsburg for import on a commercial basis was Ben Pon, that extroverted, snuff-sniffing, ebullient Hollander who had tried, in 1948, to interest the U.S. in beetles. These, however, were not the first VWs to leave the Wolfsburg factory for foreign climes; before Pon came the occupation powers. In 1946, French soldiers accompanied a military trainload of 3000 VWs sent to France, and the very first beetles to leave the factory for foreign countries were very likely the fifty which were picked up by the Red Army in March 1946. Wing Commander Berryman recalls that the British contingent at the Volkswagenwerk entertained two Soviet officers in its mess, while the fifty young "drivers" accompanying them were being taught how to drive cars.

Ben Pon, on the other hand, knew how to drive—and had even driven in a VW before the VW factory had been built. Back in 1938, he and his father had read of the German plans to build the factory in Lower Saxony and Ben had traveled to Fallersleben to try and get the Dutch franchise for the car. He met Porsche (he even presented him with ten thousand tulip bulbs for his cottage garden near the factory site), then traveled to "Gezuvor" headquarters in Berlin, where he talked with Porsche and Robert Ley. The Nazis actually assigned him the Dutch franchise then, and Ferdinand Porsche, "wearing brocaded felt slippers," as Pon recalls, drove him around the Berlin Autobahn "Ring" in a beetle. "It was terribly noisy," Pon says, echoing the sentiments of almost everyone, "but I liked the basic design."

A year later, the roar of guns had drowned out the noise of the car. Ben Pon reported that he developed a "violent hatred" of the Germans, and that when the war was over, he wanted nothing to do with the VW any more. Briefly, he says, he tried to get the franchise for a U.S. car; when this failed, his father persuaded him to try for the VW again. The elder man pointed out that, through old ties with GM's Opel, the family had a link with Germany that could not be denied. "He told me not to be a fool and said we might as well do business with Germany again," Pon reports.

Temporarily commissioned a full colonel in the Dutch Army, Pon made his way to Wolfsburg, hoping to impress the British officers who were then running the plant. "I covered my chest with phony ribbons I'd made myself, got a Dutch corporal as a chauffeur for an old Mercedes, and drove into Germany in high style, puffing a cigar and waving at passersby," Pon says.

When this theatrical officer pulled into Wolfsburg, he met Major Hirst and Hermann Münch, but preferred to pose as a high-ranking Dutch officer on a friendly inspection tour, rather than as anyone soliciting a franchise. Then Colonel Radclyffe asked to see him and, hearing that he had been in the automobile business, asked him to help "break a few bottlenecks." These, of course, concerned the shortage of materials, and Pon was asked to trade cars for steel. In October

1947, Ben Pon bought six VWs to resell in Holland. "They were," he says, "the first civilian sales of VWs." As it turned out, he got only five beetles, as the sixth broke down on the makeshift assembly line. Pon hired five drivers and took the cars back by road to Amersfoort, Holland, his home town. From this modest beginning, Pon's VW import operation, its headquarters still in Amersfoort, has grown to a network of three hundred dealers, importing about sixty thousand VWs a year. Holland is Wolfsburg's second biggest import country, surpassed only by the U.S.A.

Other countries followed Holland's lead, once Nordhoff had come to the factory. Denmark, Switzerland, Sweden, Belgium, and Luxembourg came next, and then the pattern was set; franchise after franchise was assigned, as the company's policy of global exporting developed.

The size of this export program today is impressive. The number of VWs shipped out of Wolfsburg each year already approaches one million, the total number exported to date is in excess of six million; and well over five hundred thousand other VWs have been manufactured abroad. To handle this worldwide traffic, the Volkswagenwerk has had to go into the shipping business as well, and today it has more than sixty-five freighters under long leases or "time-charter." Just to supply the American demand for VWs one of these ships arrives at a U.S. port almost every single day of the year, returning to Europe loaded with American coal, timber, grain, and other products. I was aboard Captain Rolf Lüning's 15,500-ton M/S *Carl Trautwein* as the process of discharging VWs took place in New Jersey; it took less than 24 hours to unload more than a thousand VWs and to be underway again. The Volkswagens are stacked in such ships as gently as chocolate-covered creams in multilevel candy boxes; as each deck is emptied, the pontoons which form it are lifted away, exposing another level of goodies. When the bottom has been reached and all decks have been cleared away, a hold for coal or wheat stands ready to receive its cargo. Speed is of the essence, says B. A. Hoeger, head of VWoA's Traffic Department, for a cargo-load of more than fifteen hundred Volkswagens must be ready for U.S. distributors and dealers as rapidly as possible, to cut pier costs.

This international traffic, it should be noted, is not just two-way only in that ships return to Germany loaded with products imported by that country. The American products these ships bring back are minuscule when one considers what impact sales of VWs in America have on a larger scale. VWs are

Germany's biggest export to the United States; they provide the wherewithal which allows Germany to buy from the U.S.A. Those shortsighted Americans who support "Buy American" campaigns would do well to remember that Germany buys a great deal more in the United States than it sells to it; those Americans who buy German Volkswagens are helping Germany to "buy American" on a very great scale.

The impact of Volkswagen business on Germany's economic welfare is far greater than even many Germans realize. Any significant decrease in VW's vast export business (and, of course, the import business it fosters in Germany) would seriously affect all German industry and even its trade relations within the Common Market. The Volkswagenwerk, after all, is the biggest industrial enterprise in West Germany, and one-fourth of its production is sold to the U.S. Americans might ponder what the impact would be if 25 per cent of the business of General Motors, the biggest U.S. corporation, were adversely affected. The results would not only affect most U.S. business, but would send shock waves overseas as those with whom GM traded abroad felt the inevitable pinch. Just so is it with the Volkswagen. It is the single most important product in German-U.S. trade relations and thus is, of course, a major element in Germany's financial stability.

While the beetle's success in the United States has been spectacular, its success elsewhere has been even greater, at least in terms of "percentage of the market." In Brazil, for example, the Volkswagen enjoys the same position that General Motors enjoys in the U.S.A.: more than every second car sold there is a VW!

The man who has made the VW a one hundred per cent Brazilian commodity is a German who has himself become a Brazilian citizen: Dr. F. W. Schultz-Wenck, a slim, handsome, graying executive in his fifties, with the air of a man who seems more at home on a polo field than a production line. He established Volkswagen do Brasil S.A. on March 23, 1953, and started production of Brazilian Volkswagens four years later. Between 1953 and 1957, the company assembled VWs from imported parts, selling a little more than 2800. Today, about eleven thousand Brazilians work in the VW plant at São Bernardo do Campo, producing about eighty thousand cars a year. Schultz-Wenck's organization sells about sixty per cent of all passenger cars sold in Brazil and about a fourth of all trucks. Here Volkswagen has provided an automobile industry to a nation that never had one before and, in the process, helped prove that a VW produced elsewhere than in Wolfsburg can be just exactly as good as a Volkswagen which Germans make.

VWs have been built not only in Brazil but in other countries as well. Another nation in the Western Hemisphere which manufactures VWs is Mexico, where Hans Barschkis, head of Volkswagen de Mexico, has sold more than fifty thousand cars; interest in the car is mounting so rapidly in that country that Barschkis expects to sell another fifty thousand in just a third the time it took him to sell the first batch. Today, well over sixty per cent of the materials in the Mexican VWs he produces in Xalostoc is of local origin, and provides work for almost 2000 local citizens.

Two other VW-manufacturing nations are Australia and the Republic of South Africa. More than a quarter of a million VWs have been sold in the former country and more than 150,000 in the latter. That their owners display the same Beetlemania and provide their own national contribution to "Volkslore" the world over has been shown in the previous chapter.

To tell the story of VW's rise in the aforementioned countries (not to speak of its history in more than 130 nations) would be an impossible task to accomplish within the confines of a book of this length; it would, further, be repetitious, for the problems faced in each country parallel each other, even if they differ in local color. The importance of VW's success in the export market lies in just a few points. For one, the global success proves the universality of the Volkswagen design. It shows that this car has adapted itself to all sorts of local conditions and uniquely local needs: that it is a useful vehicle, not only in crowded New York City streets, but also in African jungles or Australian mountains. For another, it proves that this design is one which lends itself to manufacture and service from Germany to New Zealand, any place in the world. There are today thousands of Volkswagen dealers and service centers the world over; by and large, all adhere to the high standards set globally by Wolfsburg. By and large also, VW executives credit the success of their cars to these high standards. Manuel Hinke, the big gruff Bolivian-born German who has for years headed the Volkswagenwerk's Export Department, gives major credit to VW's worldwide insistence on service first, sales second. (He points out that VW goes so far as to maintain service facilities in Moscow, where no VWs are sold, explaining that these are attached to the West German Embassy in the Soviet capital just to make sure each diplomatic VW is treated in Moscow as it would be back home.)

The car itself, or the service provided for it—which, then, can be assigned more credit? In countless conversations with VW executives, importers, distributors, and dealers, one hears again and again that not any one of these can be credited with the "Volkswagen miracle"; the truth, they say, lies in a combination of good product, good service, and good organization. Yet what I have found so particularly pleasant about VW's organization and about its service facilities is that I have not needed to encounter them often with my own Volkswagen. It may be nice to know VW's mechanics are experts in servicing their cars, but it is surely far better to enjoy the feeling that one will encounter them mostly at lubrication and inspection time. Looked at in this way, the success of the VW traces back to a unique integrity of manufacture. That this can be and is being maintained at a current rate of well over 1,500,-000 cars a year is nothing short of amazing. Yet countless trials and the reports of countless independent automotive journalists attest that this is so. Those who question it need only follow the advice that another auto manufacturer once used: "Ask the man who owns one." There are now more than twelve million to choose from.

13

Craftsmanship and the New Cars

GROWTH throughout the world for Volkswagen has inevitably meant changes back home as well. New Volkswagen models have been introduced (just as years ago, VW introduced its "bus" and truck, together with its Karmann Ghias, to supplement the beetle); corporate changes have taken place; prosperity brought on a contest with those who had saved for KdF-Wagens before 1945, and the little town of Wolfsburg itself has undergone changes of its own. These stories help round out the picture of the car, the corporation, and the city it brought to life.

Wolfsburg, in which the story unfolded, is today a pretty, modern town. Its 100,000 inhabitants live by the factory whistle; they either leave the plant at 2:00 P.M. and go to bed early in the evening or they start working then and quit at 10:30. There isn't even any crime to speak of in Wolfsburg and its policemen, motorized in beetles, lead a life as routine as its mailmen and other civil servants, all of whom drive Volkswagens as well. The town has no tradition and no history. What social life exists, goes on at home and on weekends.

Wolfsburg, however, was far duller under the Nazis. As they originally planned the city, it was to be a mere fungus attached to the factory and work at the plant was to provide the only meaning of life for its workers. Peter Koller sketched a city lying in a semicircle facing the factory, its homes oriented towards a city core consisting of Nazi Party office buildings and assembly halls. Only fragments of this original plan were used in building postwar Wolfsburg, and Peter Koller, who returned after being released from Russian captivity, finally was able to plan a city along human lines. A devout Roman Catholic, Koller also began building churches, which were not included in the Nazi plan. The presence of these churches after the war, and their absence under Hitler, symbolize the changed atmosphere, as do the experiences of Monsignor Antonius Holling.

258

Pastor Holling of Wolfsburg's St. Christopher's Church is today the spiritual head of the town's Roman Catholics (who include Heinz Nordhoff). The day Hoiling arrived in Wolfsburg, March 1, 1940, was the start of a five-year battle concerning freedom of conscience which he waged with the Gestapo. Ultimately, he outfoxed them and outlived them all.

"You won't last one month here, priest!" the Nazi Ortsgruppenleiter shouted at Holling when he first arrived, carrying all his worldly possessions in a cardboard Persil Soap box along the road from the Fallersleben railroad station. He refused Holling a room in which to sleep and a place in which to say mass. The "City of the Kdf-Wagen," he told him, was a model National Socialist community and the only shrines permitted bore a *Führerbild*, a picture of Adolf Hitler. He notified the Gestapo of Holling's arrival, a fact which Holling says ultimately was reported to Heinrich Himmler himself.

Holling was twenty-seven years old at the time, son of a Westphalian innkeeper. He looks less heroic than stubborn and, one imagines, he survived by eroding, rather than vanquishing, the Nazis. He himself does not know how he managed it, unless he had divine protection. "But then," he says with a smile, "I am a believer, professionally you might say." His bishop, Joseph Godehard Machens, had sent him to Wolfsburg from Hildesheim, telling him he would not be able to help him once he got there. "Watch your step—and be clever!" the bishop had told him. Holling proceeded to do precisely that. Without telling his bishop what he was about, he packed up for Berlin after being rebuffed in Wolfsburg. Brashly, he decided to visit the papal nuncio to Germany, Archbishop Caesar Orsenigo.

His request was equally brash. He told the apostolic delegate that there was an Italian labor battalion in Wolfsburg and that these workers were permitted to attend mass, said by an Italian priest. He had gone to see the priest, to ask him whether he could use his facilities (a dance hall) to say mass for the German Catholics in town. While the priest hesitated, the Fascist commander of the Italian workers had attacked Holling, almost throwing him out of the hall bodily. Holling now wanted the nuncio to have both the priest and his commandant recalled to Italy and replaced by two Italians who might be more charitable. What he was requesting, in effect, was that the nuncio embroil the Roman Catholic Church in the municipal affairs of a Nazi German city, as well as involve itself in the relations between Rome and Berlin. Surprisingly, the nuncio agreed to help.

After leaving Berlin, Pastor Holling visited a shrine, where he stayed for a few days, and from where he wrote a bold letter to the Gestapo in the "Auto-City."

"I have been to Berlin, where I visited the highest authorities," he wrote. "As a result of these conversations, I shall say mass upon my return." He ended the letter with a "Heil Hitler!"—which was meant to confuse the Gestapo even more. He did not tell them, of course, that the authority he visited was in fact the nuncio ("They would have told me to go to hell," he says) but he let them infer that he had seen governmental or Nazi Party leaders. When he returned to Wolfsburg, he started saying mass in the dance hall. The members of his congregation, all workers at the VW factory, were photographed by the Gestapo.

Soon Holling was reported to the Gestapo for not having a *Führerbild* in his room, a sign of disaffection apparently tantamount to harboring treasonous sentiments. "So I got myself a picture of Hitler, put it on the wall, and notified the Gestapo," Holling says. "The photograph even showed both Hitler and Mussolini. They were walking down a flight of stairs, heads bowed. It seemed appropriate to me, because I saw clearly that they were both going downhill and I knew instinctively that Mussolini would be the first to be punished, as it showed in the photograph."

The harassment continued throughout the months and years of the war. On one occasion, Robert Ley shouted at Ferdinand Porsche, "Burn the priest's home down and throw him out!" But Porsche, a devout Catholic, ignored the command and actually helped Holling find himself a permanent room. Shortly thereafter, Holling was saved from further Nazi badgering by a German Army officer, Major Bruehl, who commanded the 2000-man Army punishment battalion working in the factory, and who appointed Holling battalion chaplain. Holling bought himself black breeches and boots, and wore these under his clerical collar, black shirt and jacket. "I looked like a warlord (*Feldherr*)," Holling chuckles. He recalls that the Gestapo glowered helplessly, not wishing yet to quarrel with the Army in the midst of the war.

In April 1945, the Nazis moved out and the United States Army moved in. Now services could be held with impunity and Holling started building churches for his flock. Many of these are today strikingly modern and controversial, as though architects who endured the culturally stifling atmosphere under the Nazis sought relief after the war in designing an eruption of bizarre architectural shapes. Not only German architects were used, but Finland's famed Alvar Aalto was brought in to design Wolfsburg's Church of the Holy Ghost, while Peter Koller designed Holling's own St. Christopher's Church, and Koller's son built the jagged, crown-shaped Church of St. Henry.

In 1946, while Peter Koller was still in Russia, urban development became the province of Baurat (town planner) Dr. Heinz Reichow, a man of considerable talent and reputation who, however, found himself without funds with which to do anything. Before he quit in 1948, he developed a new plan for the city, along the modest lines befitting those years. Wolfsburg was to lie like a long rectangle on the bank of the Mittelland Canal, opposite the factory. Even these plans were visionary, for the fate of the factory had not yet been decided.

At the end of the war when Dr. Reichow took over, the city consisted of barracks accommodating 10,600; as well as 2358 apartments, quarters for 550 in the factory's home for unmarried men, and about 50 half-completed apartment houses. When Heinz Nordhoff arrived in 1948, he saw the urgent need for more and better housing. "I called the city authorities to get them to finish those fifty apartment houses, but they said they had no funds," Nordhoff recalls. "When I told them the factory would come up with the money, it took them three months even to reply to the offer. They were doctrinaire socialists who hated to take money from a capitalist." As one citizen remembers it, the town authorities spent those early postwar years wallowing in self-pity and writing lengthy memoranda to higher functionaires, detailing the miseries of the population. Finally, however, they agreed to accept 15 million marks (approximately $3,750,000) over the next three years. More than one thousand homes were built by 1951. In November 1951 the plant's new bachelor quarters were put up at a cost of three million marks.

On the twenty-fifth anniversary of the founding of the city, July 1, 1963, Heinz Nordhoff reminisced about these events. After the city fathers accepted the company's money, Nordhoff says, "we threw overboard all the old plans and began to build a modern workers' city, first modestly and later in broader perspective and dimensions." He said he was "bitterly criticized" when he suggested the town double the width of Porschestrasse (Wolfsburg's main street). "But now we have easily the only European town with no traffic problems, no shortage of parking space, open, light, airy, centrally heated by the Volkswagenwerk, without smoke or soot, a town which

261

offers more than many which call themselves a resort . . . This city of Wolfsburg was planned intelligently, so as to grow not through the mere addition of more streets and apartment blocks, but in almost completely self-sufficient groupings, all closely related to nature, to trees, woods, and meadows."

When Peter Koller returned from Russia, he did indeed scrap Dr. Reichow's plans calling for a rectangular-shaped city facing the factory. Instead, he started building the suburban community which Wolfsburg is today.

The city is laid out in seven distinct areas, each containing its own bank, post office, shopping center, market place, and church, and separated from each other by woodland or parks. Two major construction companies in which Volkswagen has a financial interest do most of the building; one of these, VW Wohnungsbau GmbH, is a wholly-owned subsidiary of the factory. They build mainly three- or four-story apartment houses, many with balconies, and all supplied with central heating and electricity from the VW factory's power plant, which produces all power for the entire city. Interspersed with these smaller apartment houses are a few as tall as nineteen stories, many prefabricated. Private homes are available also, although no one may own land in Wolfsburg. All land is owned by the city itself.

Peter Koller finally left Wolfsburg on October 1, 1960, to become professor of urban planning at West Berlin's Technical University, but he stayed long enough to see the town evolve the way he had wanted it to for over twenty years. It remains his personal monument and is still growing fast. New areas are being developed on the factory side of the canal, which originally was not planned for housing. There is no question but that it is a lovely, sparkling, modern city spotted with ample parkland, pools, and recreational facilities, as unlike the usual "factory town" as one can imagine.

Eventually, the town will hold 130,000. Whether it will ever have a town spirit, however, is questionable—and this troubles its thoughtful citizens, including Heinz Nordhoff. From the start, he has tried to divorce town from factory. The Volkswagenwerk has no factory-run hospital, nursery, or other similar facilities, as the Nazis had planned. Nordhoff believes firmly that the company should be a place in which to work, not a center of life. Despite his wishes, the factory inevitably dominates the life of the town. Wolfsburg is populated entirely by its workers, executives, their families and those who provide services to them. More than 70 per cent of its citizens are refugees from East Germany or from those portions of Germany which are under Polish administration. Their average age is thirty-three, about ten years younger than the national average age. The population of the town increases by about five thousand a year, as new homes are made available in the never-ending Wolfsburg building boom, but these newcomers too will have few roots there. The ties they have in common all originate at the factory in which they work.

About half the Volkswagenwerk's employees commute to the factory from towns surrounding Wolfsburg, simply because the city cannot yet accommodate them. Some 75 per cent drive to work, mostly in Volkswagens, and about 33 per cent of the workers own their own cars, the rest riding in car pools. They are prosperous and live the lives of *petit bourgeois*. The factory parking lot is a brightly colored sea of Volkswagens. All of them belong to the workers who buy them for 950 DM ($275) off list price, irrespective of the model they purchase. Nordhoff showed me more than a dozen empty sheds, east of the lot. "Those sheds symbolize the changing times," he said with pleasure. "When I arrived here, they held the workers' bicycles. Now everybody drives and the sheds are almost completely empty." Porsche's dream of motorizing the factory worker on a bicycle has come true, particularly in Wolfsburg. The town has more cars per capita than any other German city.

Salvatore Salis, a twenty-two-year-old native of Sardinia, arrived in Wolfsburg on January 15, 1962, the first Italian worker to arrive at the Volkswagenwerk since Mussolini sent Hitler three thousand unemployed construction workers. Only three two-story wooden buildings had been erected for the Italians when he arrived, but new ones were being built at the rate of two a week. Ultimately, forty-six were completed, plus two large community halls. Together with trees, lawns, and gardens, the area in which Salis and his compatriots live today is called the "Italian Village." It has its own homes, canteens, administration, post office, hospital, athletic field, chapel, and priest. It is no Italian ghetto, but rather a place in which, the company hopes, these Italian workers can feel at home in the strange, cold, and alien North German landscape.

About five thousand Italian workers have come to Wolfsburg since Salis arrived. They are a symptom of and a palliative for the principal ailment which plagues the Volkswagenwerk, a shortage of workers. The company is not unique;

West Germany as a whole employs more than one million foreign workers in its prospering industries. While the vast majority have in the past come from Italy, that country's growing prosperity has begun to absorb many of its unemployed. The composition of foreign workers in West Germany is now shifting to include more Spaniards, Greeks, and Turks. West Germany today plays host to more than 300,000 Italians, 120,000 Spaniards, 110,000 Greeks, and 200,000 Dutch, Austrians, Yugoslavs, and Turks.

The Volkswagenwerk tries hard to make them happy, hoping they will stay on beyond the end of their contracts. It organizes a special train to take the Italians home in July, vacation month at the factory, and also at Christmastime. Homesickness, more than anything else, is the Italian disease here. Father Enzo Parenti, chaplain to the Italian workers, says "There is no cure for that, neither a full pay-envelope nor medicine from the drugstore." About three hundred Italians—mostly young men from South Italy who felt miserable in the North—were freed from their work contracts and sent home. Still, as Father Parenti notes, most workers return after vacationing at home. Nordhoff is grateful. "We are very satisfied," he told the press recently. "And I think they are satisfied with us too, because only a few have left us. They are capable, flexible, and as good as German workers. We will soon have four thousand of them here."

The acute need for skilled and semi-skilled workers prompted the company to establish four schools for apprentices in its Wolfsburg, Hanover, Brunswick, and Kassel factories. More than 1600 boys and girls (nearly one out of every eight employees is a woman) between the ages of fifteen and nineteen received training here under government supervision. They receive forty hours of instruction a week, in the humanities as well as in one of fifteen specialized trades, and are paid a stipend while attending. At Wolfsburg alone, about 870 youths finish their training each year. Although they are not required to do so, most of them take jobs with Volkswagen.

The company employs more than 105,000 workers in its six West German plants, 49,000 of them in Wolfsburg. The German steelworkers' union represents about half of them, its members electing a committee which meets with company management. Labor troubles are virtually unknown. Nordhoff, *Der Spiegel* claims, won his workers to his side not by offering to meet every demand for a wage increase, but precisely because he rejected such demands when he first arrived.

"The decision which the workers made at that time, to go along with Nordhoff, marked the turning point," says the news magazine. "The workers made up their minds to accept a joint responsibility. The new, hopeful *esprit de corps,* the 'VW Spirit,' was born then." For the first years, Heinz Nordhoff did not represent "capital," stockholders, or the state. "It is our car, our factory, and our town," Nordhoff said when he accepted the Sperry Award. "And everybody is proud about it. This, like Professor Porsche's design, is sound." It is also the reason the workers felt little class-consciousness.*

In 1954, Nordhoff instituted profit-sharing throughout the Volkswagenwerk. This annual bonus has risen from 1954's four per cent to today's eight per cent of annual pay. Workers also receive free accident and life insurance, a VW pension in addition to old age benefits from the government, emergency loans, emergency medical aid (and also, if necessary, several weeks at VW seaside or mountain rest homes), as well as long-term interest-free loans for construction of homes in Wolfsburg. Workers who are transferred to less strenuous (and lower-paid) jobs because of advanced age are compensated. If they are fifty and have worked fifteen years, they get 75 per cent of the difference between the two wages; if fifty-five, one hundred per cent. "Class warfare is dead," *Der Spiegel* quotes Nordhoff as saying, and it adds, "In Wolfsburg, class warfare is as dead as Lenin's mummy."

Just who owns the company was finally settled fifteen years after the war ended, on May 9, 1960. The company had been state property under the Nazis and the organization controlling it, the German Labor Front, had been declared criminal. Allied Military Government requisitioned the factory and placed it under the administration of trustees. In 1949, in accordance with Ordinance No. 202, it relinquished control of the property and empowered the Federal Government of Germany to dispose of it in accordance with Articles 89, 90, and 134 of the Bonn Constitution. The Federal Government took over the trusteeship and then delegated control of the factory to the state (*Land*) of Lower Saxony, in which Wolfsburg is located. For the next several years, Lower Saxony and Bonn argued endlessly over who owned the company. At the same time, a settlement of some sort had to be made with those who had paid for Volkswagens under the Nazis.

* In those days, it was said that in France the government owned Renault; in Italy, Fiat owned the government; and in Germany, nobody knew who owned Volkswagen.

An organization to press the claims of the "KdF-Savers" was formed on October 7, 1948, by one Karl Stolz. Registered in Niedermarsberg as the Hilfsverein ehemaliger Volkswagensparer (Association of former VW-Savers), it quickly gathered a few thousand members at dues of 50 pfennigs (about 12 cents) a month, and on May 5, 1949, began pressing its case in court. The test case demanded the delivery of a factory-new Volkswagen, upon producing proof that the claimant had actually paid 990 marks into the savings program of the German Labor Front. Since the West German government had assumed the obligations of the Nazi Reich, the claimants had a point. From that date on, the case bounced around West Germany's courts. In 1950 a Hildesheim court decided that the Volkswagenwerk was indeed the contractual partner of the "Savers" but could not be held responsible today for the fulfillment of the contract. A year later, another court agreed that the contract was valid, but again refused to charge the company with its fulfillment. In 1954 the Supreme Court (Oberster Bundesgerichtshof) decided that the Nazi Labor Front was the true partner of the Savers, absolved the Volkswagenwerk of all responsibility, and referred the case back to a lower court. Both sides continued to argue. In 1956 and 1958 the company met with the Savers to try and come to an agreement with them, but Stolz rejected the company's offer. Finally, on October 10, 1961, the Supreme Court got them together once more. An agreement was hammered out and approved by both sides, as well as by the court referees. Savers who had completed their payments could receive either 600 DM credit towards a new Volkswagen or 100 marks in cash. By mid-1964, 93,000 Savers had submitted their claims and 87,000 were upheld. About half had decided to purchase cars.

It was, under the circumstances, a generous settlement. Six hundred deutsche marks are worth 6000 reichsmarks, for the reichsmark was exchanged at the rate of ten-to-one in 1948. In actuality, a person who saved the full 990 reichsmarks should have received only 99 of the new, post-1948 deutsche marks. Nordhoff, however, was anxious to settle the long-drawn-out court battle so that he could concentrate on a final disposition of the company itself.

Now the company was transformed legally from Volkswagenwerk GmbH into a publicly owned corporation, Volkswagenwerk Aktiengesellschaft, or Volkswagenwerk AG, which is its status today. Forty per cent of the corporation is today owned by the Federal and *Land* governments, each owning 20 per cent of the shares. The remaining 60 per cent is owned by the general public. A foundation (the Stiftung Volkswagenwerk) was organized to further science and technology through education and research. It received the proceeds from the sale of the small shares and continues to receive all dividends paid out to the Federal and *Land* governments. It also received all profits earned by the Federal Government prior to the sale of the shares, but is obliged to lend these sums back to the Federal Government at low interest for the next twenty years.

The sale of VW shares to the general public created a great deal of excitement in stock-exchange and other financial circles. In 1959 the capital of the company was increased to 300 million marks and in 1960, to 600 million. Then, on June 30, 1960, the upper house of the West German Parliament placed the Volkswagenwerk's shares on the open market. More than 1,500,000 persons applied for the 3,600,000 shares available. The issue was more than 84 per cent oversubscribed and two-thirds of the subscribers received two shares each, while one-third received three shares. VW employees (who totaled 65,000 in spring 1961) shared this enthusiasm; the company has the highest percentage of employee stockholders of any major corporation in the world. Only one thousand VW workers failed to buy shares and these one thousand, Nordhoff among them, failed to qualify because of their high income brackets. Under the terms of the stock sale, only persons in the low and middle income groups were eligible to purchase shares. The law also restricted initial purchases to ten shares and demanded that West Germans and company employees throughout the world hold their shares at least two years before reselling. Each worker bought an average of 4.29 shares. Today, the shares are traded on the open market but the restrictions placed on the initial offering prevented large blocks from falling into the hands of major investors. Only two companies in the world have more shareholders than Volkswagenwerk AG.*

* In the fall of 1966, Volkswagenwerk announced a new stock offering of 3,000,000 shares with a nominal value of 50 DM, each at a purchase price of 112,50 DM per share. Twenty per cent was sold to the State of Lower Saxony and twenty per cent to the Federal Republic (which ceded its offered shares to the VW Foundation). The remaining 60 per cent, 1,800,000 shares, was offered to present stockholders under an option which permitted them to buy one new share for every four old shares they owned. The option period ended early in January 1967, when the offering was made available on the open market. The most significant aspect of the new stock offering was that for the first time all of the capital raised accrued to Volkswagenwerk itself, instead of to the VW Foundation.

For Americans, the most exciting news out of Wolfsburg is the introduction of the "new Volkswagens." They have served to broaden the line which the Volkswagenwerk can offer, though they by no means portend a replacement of the beetle. That ever-flowering perennial, which continues to outsell them all, is still the star attraction in the Volkswagen "salon," at least as far as the automobile-buying public is concerned. Yet, as the 1960's approached, it became ever more clear to Heinz Nordhoff, his market analysts, sales executives, distributors, and dealers that Volkswagen needed more than just the beetle, the bus, and the Ghia if it were to grow into the future. Volkswagenwerk AG is, after all, an automobile manufacturing company and not what everyone has always thought of it as, a "beetle-producer" only. Nordhoff's desire once was to make his factory the largest automobile company in Europe; he has long since done just that and now is looking ahead. The terrific impact of American-owned companies on the European Continent has, in part, compelled him to do so. Germans, who continue to make up his largest single bloc of customers, are more prosperous today than they were in the days when the stripped-down, basic, unchromed bug was a luxury to them. They now wished to "upgrade" themselves and, as their needs became larger, to move on to larger cars as well. The suburban Munich family to whom the German translation of this book is dedicated provides one example of this trend. Robert and Theda Schumann of Starnberg in Upper Bavaria bought their first beetle before the decade of the 1950's dawned; by the time it ended, they'd owned three Volkswagens, trading in each as new improvements on the old model made the next more desirable. Then, in 1960, after a decade of Volkswagening, they switched—with regret. By that time, however, more prosperity, more travel, and bigger children demanded a larger car. Ford and GM in Germany were offering them. Nordhoff was being hit—so he hit back with the 1500. Introduced in 1961, this conventional-looking automobile, which somewhat resembles a U.S. compact car, has moved powerfully into the West German market. There, as *Forbes* magazine put it in 1963, it was the "hot new car . . . which in two years has captured 18 per cent of the medium-sized market."

This VW 1500, which was introduced in 1961, was offered in both a conventional sedan styling and as an American-style station wagon. This latter is rather awkwardly called the VW Squareback Sedan in the U.S. today, to differentiate it from the buslike station wagon which continues to be sold in the U.S. The confusion of names is unfortunate and of interest only to automotive semantics buffs.* But what is of interest is American enthusiasm for the new cars. A black or gray market in the new models developed fast, as might have been expected, for not enough of the new models were being produced in Germany to supply the U.S. distributor and dealer network. More than mere supplies were necessary too, for the Volkswagen company always refuses to sell its car in countries whose mechanics do not yet know how to service them.

The VW 1500 which was introduced in Germany in 1961 was somewhat of a disappointment and a host of refinements had to be made, to answer all objections and bring it to the level of excellence which the beetle had attained over its many years. Sam Weill of Volkswagen Pacific, formerly Competition Motors, penning another verse, expressed the dilemma on both sides of the Atlantic by writing: "We're building now a brand new car; the prospect makes me nervous—in Germany there'll be no sales, in America, no service!" (Weill's reference to "no service" applied solely to the 1500 line, which was not then imported by Volkswagen of America. The cars which arrived here through unauthorized channels posed a difficult service problem for the VW dealer, who was not equipped for them. When the 1500 was sold to tourist delivery customers, service and parts were available.)

Mid-1965 marked the turning point and the introduction of several newer cars, all of which have since proven highly successful. The beetle's engine was then enlarged to 1300-cc and made more powerful and the former VW 1500 sedans and "Squarebacks" are now offered with 1600-cc engines. Most dramatic was the introduction of the VW 1600 "Fast-back" sedan, a racy passenger car which, said *Gute Fahrt* magazine in Germany in its August 1965 issue, has all the earmarks of the "Ferdinand Porsche touch," although Wolfsburg designed it.

For U.S. distributors, dealers, and their customers, the new models mean that those Americans who like Volkswagen quality, service, and resale value can now buy:

* A partial primer for such persons: The buslike Type II, when fitted out as a passenger car, is called the "Station Wagon" in the U.S. and the "Microbus" in Europe and elsewhere. The "Squareback Sedan" (as it is called in the U.S.) is called the "Variant" in Germany and elsewhere, this being a name marketing men in the U.S.A. felt resembled that of Detroit's "Valiant" too closely. The Microbus, when fitted out for vacationtime living, is called a "Camper" or "Campmobile" in the U.S. and Germany, while the British refer to it as a VW "Caravan."

—The Type I "beetle," the VW sedan, with its more powerful engine (boosted to 1500-cc in mid-1966), in sedan, sunroof, or convertible models;

—The Type II station wagon (that familiar "bus"), with a 1500-cc engine;

—The Type III VW "Fastback," powered by a 1600-cc engine;

—The Type III VW "Squareback Sedan," outfitted with a 1600-cc engine;

—The Type I Karmann Ghia, as a coupe or a convertible, with a 1500-cc engine.

Charles Barnard referred in *True* to the Type III VW as "truly the 'Nordhoff VW'" and says this new design silences critics who have charged that "Nordhoff might be a good administrator, but he was not an automotive creator." The truth, of course, is that the Type III's are neither more—nor less—Nordhoff's than Ford's Mustang is the creation of Henry Ford II. Nordhoff is not a designer like Ferdinand Porsche and never claimed to be. He is an engineer, an administrator, and a marketing man with an uncommon feel for what Germans —and people throughout the world—want in an automobile. This "feel" has made him extremely design-conscious. His Technical Development department employs over two thousand people, a large number considering the fact that the basic design of the beetle hasn't changed for a generation and isn't likely to in the future. This department, which has refined and re-refined the beetle ever since Nordhoff took control, is also responsible for the new Volkswagens. Ferry Porsche, under contract as a consulting engineer, works on specific VW design problems, some of which involved aspects of the new cars. As he puts it, "We design in advance, but all cars at Wolfsburg are finally designed at the Volkswagenwerk. Certainly we have been urging VW for years to build a more powerful and more comfortable car, but the designs belong to them."

The new VW models have only a few parts interchangeable with the beetle. Their wheelbase is the same (94.5 inches), but they are longer, wider, and heavier. Oddly, in the new models the more powerful engine actually takes up less space than the beetle's. This may produce a new rash of Volkswagen jokes in the U.S. because the new models seem to have no engine at all, either fore or aft. After hunting, one finds it tucked away under the carpeted floor of the rear luggage compartment. No one will feel particularly conspicuous driving the new models and while the public may well buy these cars in large numbers over the years, owners may never get emotional about them as they do about the beetle. Those who own Volkswagens will welcome the fact that they can continue to do so even after deciding they want a larger, more powerful, and more comfortable car than the beetle. These may make up the primary market, for their loyalty is strong. A recent survey shows that nearly half (49 per cent) of all Americans who bought a Microbus station wagon had owned a beetle before and that 40 per cent of those who bought Volkswagens never even looked at another automobile before taking delivery of their VWs. This is extraordinary "brand loyalty." Now those VW owners who abandoned the beetle because of growing families or incomes can move up a bracket and stay in the family. I myself am one such owner, having bought one of the first VW 1600 Squareback Sedans that came off the Wolfsburg assembly line in August 1965. In it, we logged 20,000 miles in the car's first twelve months, with luggage for a family of five stashed in the front end and in a roof rack on top, while the carpeted rear "deck," meant for luggage, was converted into a "mini-lounge" for children and toys. In it, with five persons and a load of effects, the car hit 90 mph on the (unlimited speed) Autobahn and has maintained close to that speed comfortably for two hours. Aerodynamically, the Squareback Sedan offers even better conditions for speed than the Fastback, as a look at the new racing cars, with their squared-off "Kamm-effect" rear ends, shows. This family car may not be as cozy and as intimate as the beetle, but it provides all the power, speed, and comfort an itinerant family needs.

Those who don't own Volkswagens may ask, "Why bother staying in the 'VW family' when you outgrow the beetle?" As everyone knows, there are several makes of car available to buyers and a host of satisfactory ones. The Swedish Volvo, for example, is a quality car, and no one who buys it will regret the purchase. And there are American cars which will get you around faster and more comfortably than a VW. After all is said and done, the beetle remains a bizarre-looking car and its big brothers are not all that unusual to the casual observer.

The reasons lie in the history of the car and the company. Ferdinand Porsche's initial design was "a sound one," to use Heinz Nordhoff's phrase. It was not rushed through to production, but nurtured in Porsche's brain and on his drawing board for a decade before prototypes were built. These were in turn subjected to extraordinary tests before they were pronounced fit for production. Ten years later, when Nordhoff arrived at Wolfsburg, he proclaimed the car "had more things wrong with it than a dog has fleas." Technology had progressed since 1938 and the version of the Volkswagen being put together in the debris of the bombed-out plant was indeed as mangy as Nordhoff suggests. The factory was, after all, not the spotless and modern one Porsche envisioned. Nordhoff proceeded to "redesign" the car. In the early 1950's, his staff took the beetle completely apart. The 1953 and 1954 VWs which resulted, with their synchromesh transmissions, more powerful and quieter engines, greater comfort, and range of colors, had again been tested exhaustively. "Every improvement was brutally tested to the breaking point and the cars were raced along the Nürburgring day and night for 10,000 kilometers, and were chased along the Autobahn, at maximum speed, for 2000 kilometers," says *Der Spiegel*. "The engineers did not do this out of pride or vanity, but because the British commission which had minimized the value of the car was not so wrong . . . What the Englishmen did not see were the enormous developmental possibilities of this original design. The Wolfsburgers saw it—and brought it about."

The redesigning has continued ever since. In 1960, Nordhoff noted, "Our designers have now been working 12 years on only one job: to perfect the VW technically." Over the years, the company has made well over 2000 improvements on the beetle. Today, perfecting the beetle is still a prime task of VW engineers; but the research and development staff, which numbers about 2350 and uses such sophisticated devices as Europe's largest environmental wind tunnel (located at Wolfsburg), is also looking into the future with experimental models and advanced designs.* To this staff must be added the services of Ferry Porsche and his brilliant Stuttgart team of engineers and designers, who have served the Volkswagenwerk (and many other companies) as consultants. Perfecting the car is almost an obsession at the factory. One out of every ten employees at the Volkswagenwerk wears the green badge of Inspector. His word is law. He examines *each car* as it proceeds along the assembly line, checking that aspect of manu-

---

* Future technical developments at VW were given added resources late in 1964 when Volkswagenwerk and Daimler-Benz announced the establishment of a jointly owned engineering facility, which was set up at Hanover in 1966. It was created when Volkswagen purchased Auto Union from Daimler-Benz, acquiring a technical cooperation agreement in addition to Auto Union's production facilities at Ingolstadt. The Auto Union factory is currently producing VWs and front-wheel drive, water-cooled Auto Union "Audi" models.

facture and assembly which is his province. Before the car may move on, the inspection tag it carries must receive his initials. He can—and does—pull it out of production for the tiniest flaw, simply because the standards are so rigidly high. Nicks which no purchaser would ever see are enough to disqualify a Volkswagen. "Rejects" go into a special hall, where the fault is eliminated by a special staff. Those cars which pass muster go through further tests before being driven out of the plant. At this final stage, inspectors check the work of other inspectors. Here the assembly of all units is examined once again; 115 check points are gone over, as well as the finish and the interior. Here there are no spot-checks. What is important is that the production department has no jurisdiction over the inspection staff; Nordhoff saw to it that both departments held equal rank on the management committee (Vorstand) he heads. He is not exaggerating when he says the beetle is "practically faultless" today, as free of faults as any mass-produced, mechanical product can be. The car, he believes, "comes closer than any other make in the world to being the ideal utility car: cheap to purchase, maintain, and run, and with the highest possible resale value."

Outside observers say so too. John Bond, publisher of *Road & Track* magazine, feels the beetle should be classed along with the Rolls-Royce, Mercedes-Benz, Lancia, Porsche, Lincoln Continental, Rover, and Peugeot as one of "the world's best-made cars." When he offered his list of the seven best cars, however, he decided *not* to include the VW. The reason, as he says in the same article, was that the car cost too little. "I suppose VW should have been on the list too," he wrote, "but I've left it off because it hardly seems appropriate to include a very low-priced car in a list of 'quality' cars even if it is a lot of car for the money."

Britain's *Autocar* magazine, confessing it is "difficult to judge impartially the reasons behind the success of the VW 1200," says that "without question, *it has no superiors in any price bracket* on quality, reliability, and after-sales service."*

The technical reasons for the beetle's "Rolls-rating" are many and I believe they apply to all the new models as well. Four-wheel independent torsion-bar suspension offers an excellent ride (in most cars, only the front wheels are suspended independently, while the rear ones are attached to a solid rear axle). The steering responds to the touch of a finger; no one needs power steering in a VW beetle. The rear position of the engine provides better traction in ice, snow, mud or sand,

* Italics mine.

and the car's gear ratios permit it to climb almost impossible 43° slopes.* (In mountainous Switzerland, where more than a hundred makes compete sharply, the VW has led for years with more than 250,000 sales.) The engine's position also saves power and weight, eliminates the driveshaft, and puts the power where it's needed (an obsession of Ferdinand Porsche since 1900, when he developed the hubcap motor). The air-cooled engine will not freeze up in winter or boil over in summer. It eliminates the need for a radiator, which in turn allows for the slope of the front hood, increasing visibility. The car can be buried in snow, be driven at top speed through deserts, climb uphill for hours or inch along in summer traffic, and its air-cooled engine "couldn't care less," as a VW brochure says. Air cooling is only one advantage of the VW engine. It is low-revving and has an unusually short stroke, which means lower piston speeds, less friction, and longer life, and also explains why the VW's top speed is its cruising speed, which can be maintained for hours. Equipped with the 1500-cc engine, the beetle's pickup has been improved sharply, and it can hit 60 mph in *third* gear. Its gasoline consumption is low, although this varies. As has been noted, professional economy drivers have squeezed almost 60 mpg out of the car; the company suggests that 27 mpg is about average for a 1500-cc beetle.

The paint job "is typical of Germanic thoroughness," as one American trade magazine put it. "[It is] both technically advanced and cautious. Four coats are applied, the first a dip coat that is baked; the second applied by electrostatic spray equipment built in Germany under license from Rahnsberg in the U.S. After a second bake, the body is wetsanded and electrostatically sprayed again. Finally, the color coat is added by machine and hand spray guns, to make sure all inside surfaces are covered too. Good finishes inside and out are not accidental . . ." No bare metal is left exposed anywhere in the car. Inspectors here also check each car after each of the four finishes has been applied. The same attention has gone into every part of the car, from upholstery to the quality of the steel used, and the same procedure is followed in the new models, all being produced under identical conditions.

Robert Wyse, editor of *Safer Motoring*, once wrote, "I cannot pretend to understand the Wolfsburg mentality." He was referring, he said, to the "wealth of wonderful ideas" Wolfsburg designers had put into the new model Volkswagens. A partial explanation of the mentality was provided by *Auto-*

* In first gear, with four passengers, plus luggage.

car magazine when it, too, reported on the Volkswagens of the 1960's. These, the magazine said, had "inherited all the well-known features of excellent workmanship and finish" for which the beetle was famous.

That inheritance, that legacy of "well-known features," constitutes the "Wolfsburg mentality" which puzzled Robert Wyse. It certainly betrays a mentality which is completely foreign to Detroit—and, for that matter, to much of European auto manufacturing. Vance Packard devoted two chapters of *The Waste Makers* to the U.S. auto industry's "planned obsolescence" and sums up what he calls the "Iron Law of Marketing in mid-century America" as: "Maximum sales volume demands the cheapest construction for the briefest interval the buying public will tolerate." This concept, accepted readily by some European automobile manufacturers as well, is rejected out of hand by the Volkswagenwerk. It intends to continue perfecting and producing the beetle for as long as it can be sold. This may be years or it may be decades. Concentration on one car has facilitated the task, of course. It has enabled VW to save redesigning and retooling charges and, with the savings, to buy the most modern, automated equipment available. Nordhoff is fortunate, too, that the factory was so thoroughly destroyed during the war, for while Detroit continues to turn out many of "the cars of the future" with the machines of a generation ago, Nordhoff works in what may very well be the most modern automobile factory in the world. He has set out to produce the average man's Rolls-Royce and to make the VW trademark a symbol of uncompromising quality, and he has succeeded.

One man who regards the VW as an incomparably superb automobile is Arnold Gingrich, publisher of *Esquire* magazine, whose June 1966 article, "Some Dreams I've Driven," is a hymn to his "long and ardent affair with a Volkswagen." (It should be admitted that Gingrich also wrote of other "dreams" he's driven, but as these include a Bentley, a Wills St. Claire, and a 1939 convertible Cadillac, they fall into a rather special category and are not usually competitive with the bug.) Gingrich's VW was a 1947 model beetle, bought through the good offices of a high-ranking British officer, and it had neither much comfort nor a synchronized transmission. Gingrich, like others who bought the beetle in those years, had to "use the gearshift lever almost like a whip." Once you knew how to manage that, he writes, "you could make it run like a rabbit, or more appropriately, like a mountain goat, over the steepest grades ever encountered."

His saga is worth quoting, for it speaks of the basic high quality with which even the 1947 model was endowed and which the models of twenty years later have refined to a far greater degree.

"I put three hundred thousand kilometers on it myself," Gingrich writes, "in the three years I drove it, and did it on so little gas that I could never afterward regard as anything but exorbitant the quite normal thirsts of other cars. Once on its own little tankful of not quite eleven gallons, and the contents of two jerry cans that were all I could get, along with its spare wheel, into the engineless space beneath its hood, I drove from the middle of Budapest up to the English Channel at Le Havre, and back down across France to the Swiss border, where it finally ran out of gas at Vallorbe, conveniently just across the Swiss customs barrier from a gas station to which I could easily push it myself. Even if I hadn't spilled a drop from the jerry cans, it had used at most a scant twenty-one gallons. Afterward I pored over maps with a ruler, trying to convince myself that the route I had covered had not worked out to exceed forty miles to the gallon, but unable to bring the average back down, however much I studied it, to more than a fraction under thirty-eight.

"When I moved away from Europe I left it with one of my sons in Vienna, and I haven't seen it now myself since the Fall of '55, when it had run three quarters of a million kilometers and was still on its third motor. By '59, when he moved from Vienna to Geneva, it had passed a million kilometers and was just ready for its fifth. He sold it to a Viennese cabdriver, and I would love to bet that it's not only still going strong but is one of the best-looking cabs to be found in Vienna today.

"Curiously, I've never owned another, but like the Bourbons who neither forget nor ever learn anything, I could never since be convinced by anything I've seen or read or heard that anything but the Volkswagen can be the best car in the world. Interesting, isn't it?, that Hitler, that stinker by anybody's reckoning, should have come closer than anybody else has, at least yet, both to the unification of Europe and to the realization of that lesser and younger dream, the provision of a truly universal car.

"Even before I left Europe at the end of the Forties there were places, such as one I remember in Munich, where you could drive in and have them take out your motor and stick another one in the back, for an absurdly low price, about as easy and simply as you stop in for a refill of a ball-point pen.

"Before I left, I had learned to drive in all weathers over all sorts of roads, in that trusty Volkswagen in which I had at first had so little faith, so that ever since I have been amazed at the reluctance of most American drivers to push on in the face of uncertainties of terrain or weather. I amazed even the G.I.'s at the checkpoint east of Munich on the Autobahn, one winter night near the end of '47, when I showed up from Salzburg in a blinding snowstorm. They said my little Volks was the only vehicle of any kind that had come through from that direction in over twelve hours, and that not even half-tracks had dared attempt it. I had followed what I had to assume was the route of the Autobahn only by staying between the poles that were staked upthrust through the snow on either side of it, whipping the little wagon on by constant shifting, and remembering that the way to keep it going was by whipping it, with the technique of skipping stones across the water. At that I had never once during that trip been as surprised to find that it would still keep going, when there appeared to be every reason why it should stop, as I had been in a freak blizzard over the Arlberg Pass one night the previous July. Then the snow had packed under its belly until its front wheels would rise clear, and each time I felt the front wheels free of the surface, and sure that the vehicle was about to come to a helpless halt, there would be a pitching toboggan-like drop of the whole front end and the little car would start digging in to climb yet another mound of snow."

Can one blame Gingrich for waxing sentimental? He calls his cars "old flames"; how can one jilt a car so faithful? I confess to just as ardent—or sentimental—an attachment to the VW, and if I do not have the pleasure of owning a beetle at present, I console myself with the thought that the VW I do own is its big brother. The family characteristics are the same; one can sit in the new models and drive them with the same confidence. Like Gingrich, I have owned other cars—British cars, Detroit cars, though none as luxurious as Gingrich's—and have been able to draw the necessary conclusions.

The technical reasons why the VW is "one of the world's best automotive buys" do not, however, fully explain why the car "has no superiors in any price bracket," as *Autocar* puts it. What singles out the VW is simply its *value*. Most of its features are found only in cars which are much more expensive and no car in its own price range comes close to it in technology. The man who buys a VW buys an awful lot of car for very little money. He also can usually count on service of the highest order. Finally, the car depreciates so slowly that, years after it has been bought, it can often be resold for more than

277

can an equally old—but initially more expensive—Detroit model.

Whether all these aspects were part of the original dream of Ferdinand Porsche remains open to speculation. Certainly he built value into his design, but it was modern management and marketing which did the rest. The Volkswagen is fortunate in that it was designed by a technician who proved to be a visionary, and inherited by an engineer who proved to be a master salesman. These two men took the little car a long way from those early days in Vienna, where Ferdinand Porsche first dreamed of his *Kleinauto*. That car has traveled through dramatic years of frustration and triumph, war and defeat, and through a rebirth no other company product can match.

"The only decision I am really proud of is that I have refused to change Porsche's design," says Nordhoff. "It's hard to remain the same. You can always sell cars by being new. But we chose a different course." It is true that Nordhoff has diversified and has added the new models, but it remains a fact that the ever-changing, yet basically unchanged, beetle still remains the star of the Volkswagen "salon," of which we spoke.

The secret behind Volkswagen's success — which other car manufacturers know but do not care to adopt — is a painstaking integrity of design and manufacture. This is the "Wolfsburg philosophy" and it applies to all the company's cars and permeates all aspects of the business, right through sales and advertising. More than twelve million people the world over have responded to that integrity. Because it is apparent that the men in Wolfsburg respect them, they in turn have respected the car. As Nordhoff said, he could have chosen a different course. In an age of planned obsolescence and suspect promises, he chose, however, to be honest.

14

Postscript, 1970:
Transition Toward Tomorrow

SINCE the previous thirteen chapters were written, Volkswagenwerk AG has undergone many crucial changes which are even now transforming the successful producer of a single model of motor vehicle into a multi-line corporation with models in virtually every price class. The past three years have brought events so significant that an additional chapter is required to bring the reader up to date.

As 1966 dawned, the company whose fortunes had been so intimately tied to the West German economy and had contributed in large part to the "economic miracle," found itself facing new problems, as the "miracle" acquired some tarnish. At the beginning of that year, Volkswagenwerk completed wage negotiations, signing its biggest wage contracts yet; these compelled it to raise the prices of its vehicles in April — just as economic thunderclouds were gathering in the distance. The 12,000,000th Volkswagen (there are now more than 15,000,000) was produced that year and rolled off the assembly line as West Germany headed with increasing speed into a recession; as this recession mounted, so did the unsold inventories of VWs in West German dealers' showrooms.

The curtailment of production, which began to seem necessary, was delayed for various reasons: Nordhoff was reluctant to inflict the resulting hardships on his workers; the company was hesitant about jeopardizing an increase in its capitalization; finally, Nordhoff knew a cut in production at VW would make for big headlines and be interpreted as clear evidence that the recession was serious. It might frighten many people and create added difficulties for the West German government, already shaken by the economic distress. Action, therefore, was delayed well past mid-1966, when signs of the coming crisis were already apparent. Despite the unsold inventories, the company continued at record production for months. In August, it introduced the 1500-cc beetle; its Auto-Union subsidiary introduced the Audi 80 squareback ("Variant") and, later, the Audi Super 90.

In early 1967, the company was forced to retrench and, in so doing, was not alone. Ford and Opel, the two U.S.-owned auto giants in Germany, dismissed masses of workers to meet the market slump; Nordhoff characteristically refused to take that step. Instead, he instituted "short weeks"; no worker was dismissed; each, instead, got half a loaf, but it was better than none.

The recession hit hard during the first half of 1967, and until late May that year, the factory chimneys seemed to spew out more gloom than smoke: thirty production days were lost and sales of VWs dropped below the average auto industry decline.

Heinz Nordhoff hoped for energetic governmental action to spur his key industry; instead, he was dismayed when Bonn made it even more difficult for West Germans to buy cars. Gasoline taxes were raised, as were auto insurance rates; worse yet, the government cut in half the tax deduction Germans enjoy if they drive their cars to and from work. Disappointed at the course taken, Nordhoff began to speak out openly in criticism of what he regarded as a shortsighted economic policy. He urged the government to eliminate all vehicle ownership taxes (which cost the average German beetle-owner 188 marks a year, or about $47 at the rate of exchange then prevailing); such a move would make the purchase of automobiles more attractive and give a boost not only to the auto industry but to all who supply it with raw materials and parts, as well as all who depend on it. Hundreds of thousands of workers would have benefited. Meanwhile, in order to maintain VW's position in the domestic (i.e., West German) market, he produced a recession-oriented beetle at the beginning of 1967: a basic version of the 1200-cc VW which sold for about $1100. Quickly dubbed the *Sparkäfer* (budget-beetle) — both affectionately and derisively — this car raised sales as knowledgeable, bargain-wise Germans hurried to buy it. It did not, however, do much for profits. Yet it served a public relations function: it kept the beetle's virtues alive in the public consciousness, emphasized VW's good value, and helped the company ride out the recession.

The fact that Nordhoff criticized the government's policies provoked a counter-blast from that ebullient Bavarian, Franz-Josef Strauss, who had become Finance Minister in the Great Coalition government which entered office in late 1966. Strauss icily rejected Nordhoff's call for tax concessions — and then proceeded to attack VW (and, by implication, Nordhoff himself) for having produced "too many cars and too few ideas" as well as "the wrong models." He criticized the fact that only 30 per cent of VW's production was sold to Germans and asked, "What happens when the Americans stop being amused by the beetle?"

Of course he neglected to point out that less than half (32 per cent) of VW's total exports go to the U.S.A.; in reality, 70 per cent of VW production is not dependent at all on whether Americans continue to be "amused" by the bug. Finally, every Volkswagen owner knows something which then seemed to have eluded Strauss: that the beetle's success in the U.S.A. is *not* based on its "entertainment value," Walt Disney's *The Love Bug* notwithstanding.

It seemed less of a coincidence than part of a calculated plan that a small army of minor Bonn officials soon began bursting into print with the same "Strauss line." In retrospect, it seems clear that governmental policies had helped accelerate the economic slump in the key auto industry and elsewhere — and that government apologists were understandably happy to find a scapegoat and a public whipping boy: Nordhoff.

That this hurt Heinz Nordhoff deeply is a fact of which his friends and associates were all painfully aware. With considerable justification, Nordhoff saw himself as being to a certain extent responsible for the nation's economic miracle. Furthermore, the Volkswagenwerk had been almost unique in West Germany in that it succeeded without ever having asked for or having received any governmental aid. Now that Nordhoff for the first time asked for tax concessions to help his industry (not just VW), he was being slapped down for it. These attacks hit Nordhoff at a time when he was no longer vigorous enough to engage in a slugging match with the redoubtable Strauss: at a time when his health was very much in question. He had been ill since the previous December. Although he continued to work every day, his colleagues noticed a growing irritability and impatience as well as a marked loss of appetite. Even his much-loved wines seemed to have less appeal.

It was at this time that, against his doctor's advice, he went to England at the invitation of the Institute of the Motor Industry, the national association of British automotive companies. On April 18, 1967, at Church House Westminster, London, he was presented the Lord Wakefield Gold Medal for outstanding contribution to the motor industry — the first non-Britisher so honored. At the ceremony he spoke on "Management Revolution: A Broader View." Perhaps as an answer to his government critics, Nordhoff said, "Management today must spend less of its time looking down into the factory, and more time looking out at the world and ahead into the future."

In a wide-ranging speech, he foresaw the need for increased industry concern about the pollution of our environment: "There is a critical need for management to widen its view from the private interest to the public interest. . . . Companies must become more than private enterprises devoted to making profits for the stockholders. Today's corporation must accept responsibilities beyond this. It makes little sense to return a profit to the stockholder at the same time we take away from him, as a citizen, some of his rights to clean air or clear water."

At an intimate formal dinner that evening, the top men of the British motor industry heaped praise upon the man who had created the miracle of Wolfsburg. It was an evening that Nordhoff often recalled during his remaining time.

He returned to Wolfsburg renewed and refreshed, invigorated by the recognition showered upon him in London. Mrs. Nordhoff commented to a friend that the British trip was "the best medicine he had ever taken."

But the effects were short-lived. He suffered a sharp decline in May 1967.

Plans for the eventual retirement of Heinz Nordhoff had been underway since June 1966, when Dr. Josef Rust, an industrialist and onetime aide to Franz-Josef Strauss (when the latter was Defense Minister), moved from deputy chairman to chairman of Volkswagenwerk's Aufsichtsrat, or board of directors. The press came alive with speculation that Rust's main job was to find a successor to Nordhoff (then sixty-seven years old) and comments abounded about the need for new management at VW.

There was certainly a pressing need for a succession — simply because Nordhoff, already well past the customary retirement age of sixty-five, had spent his energies, was aging, tired, and ill. He himself planned to retire at the beginning of 1969, just short of his seventieth birthday. The search for a successor was, accordingly, pressed. The board of directors and Nordhoff's colleagues on the Vorstand all realized it would take an extraordinarily big man to fill the biggest industrial job in the biggest industrial nation in Western Europe.

Just such a man fortuitously became available: one not only big in size (6 feet 5 inches), but big in accomplishments. This was Dr. Kurt Lotz, then fifty-four and head of the West German branch of Brown, Boveri & Cie., a vast Swiss-owned engineering firm and the third largest electrical corporation in Germany.

Rust knew Kurt Lotz, as did Dr. Hermann Richter, another member of the VW Aufsichtsrat, for both Rust and Richter were also members of the Brown, Boveri board of directors. Nordhoff also knew him, for he and Lotz were both members of yet another board of directors. As Kurt Lotz recounted it to me, he and Nordhoff got to know each other particularly well during these meetings — simply because their initials (L and N) were so close alphabetically that they were often seated beside each other. Lotz's company had also been among several which wanted to sell the Volkswagenwerk turbines for a power plant opened in 1962; Nordhoff gave the contract to Lotz partly because he was very much impressed that Lotz had been the only top industrialist among the bidders who had made a personal effort to make that sale.

In 1966, just prior to VW's search for a successor, Kurt Lotz had resigned as head of the Swiss parent company of Brown, Boveri. He continued to be head of the German branch of that corporation in Mannheim, and he seemed to many West German firms to be a man who might now respond to an outstanding offer. A good many such offers had already come to Lotz and more were coming now; it was at this juncture that the Volkswagenwerk entered the picture.

Kurt Lotz describes these events in the following words:

"One doesn't exchange letters about such matters. What happened is this: I got a telephone call from Professor Nordhoff, in which he asked me to meet him at the Frankfurter Hof [a hotel in Frankfurt am Main]. When we met, he told me that he needed to find a man who could succeed him as chairman of the Vorstand. He offered me the job."

Lotz said he'd think it over; when he did, he realized this was the challenge of a lifetime. In mid-April 1967, the announcement was made that as of June 1, Lotz would become deputy chairman of the Volkswagenwerk management board.

As it turned out, Lotz arrived in Wolfsburg not a moment too soon. Nordhoff, as previously noted, had become seriously ill at the end of May and his physicians declined to be responsible for him if he addressed the June 28 shareholders' meeting. That information was communicated to the Auf-sichtsrat on June 27; Lotz was advised at 5:30 P.M. that he would have to fill in for Nordhoff literally overnight: he would have to represent the company at the meeting at 10 A.M. the following morning.

Lotz found Nordhoff's prepared speech "too typically Nord-hoff," "too personal" and, moreover, too peppered with criti-cisms of the government. In order that he might have his own speech to deliver, Lotz assembled a staff in temporary offices in the basement of the company's Rotehof Guest House in Wolfsburg, and he himself checked into a room in the same building. Work on that speech went on throughout the entire night; Lotz snatched a couple of hours' sleep before being awakened at 4 A.M. to be shown a draft. After going over it, he awakened Dr. Rust at 5:30 to show the draft to him; the re-write then went back to the basement for a final typescript — which was thrust into Lotz's hands as he hurried into his car for the meeting in Wolfsburg's Town Hall. "I made my last corrections onstage seconds before I spoke," Lotz remembers.

That weekend, Heinz Nordhoff entered a sanatorium in Zürich, Switzerland; his heart was giving way.

Because Nordhoff would remain in the hospital until late October, Kurt Lotz was again called upon to speak for the company at the Frankfurt Automobile Show in mid-September 1967. There the company introduced quite a line: Volkswagens with automatic transmissions and advanced electronic fuel in-jection systems; a fundamentally redesigned Type II Trans-porter (the VW "station wagon" and/or truck in the U.S.A.; elsewhere, the "Microbus"); the new Audi 60; the Audi 72 and Audi 80, both with technical improvements.

Critics did a *volte face;* suddenly, Strauss's blast of four months ago seemed totally irrelevant. Sales of Volkswagens began to pick up sharply during the second half of 1967: first outside West Germany but, shortly thereafter, within the Fed-eral Republic as well. The automobile industry—and its leader, Volkswagenwerk AG — was pulling out of the recession. Recognizing this, the company decided to enlarge its capacity, at first cautiously by introducing extra shifts and hiring more workers; then more aggressively, by building yet another Volkswagenwerk factory in 1968 at Salzgitter, not far from Wolfsburg.

It had been the custom to stage a New Year's reception for key VW importers and distributors. Despite its title, this affair was not held on January 1 but on January 6, Nordhoff's birthday. Thus, the reception actually became an opportunity for hundreds to honor the man who had made their own success possible — and became an expression of Heinz Nordhoff's deeply personal involvement with the company. The last of these receptions (which Lotz has since discontinued) took place in 1968 and Heinz Nordhoff was there for it, having returned to Wolfsburg late the previous October. Those who attended the January event were dismayed to see that he seemed years older: they feared they might be saying goodbye to the man who had led them so brilliantly for two decades. Then, to everyone's amazement, Nordhoff seemed to improve sharply in the weeks following the reception, almost as though the sight of old friends and associates and the reliving of old triumphs had buoyed him up. Sensing himself stronger, he even insisted on working a more or less normal week.

That improvement proved, tragically, to be an illusion, for a decline soon set in again. At the beginning of March 1968, the board of directors pushed forward the date of Heinz Nordhoff's retirement from January 1969 to May 21, 1968. With appropriate ceremonies, Nordhoff was to be named "Honorary President" of the company.

So very much had Nordhoff identified himself with his company for twenty years that he was understandably reluctant to lay down his responsibilities and retire from active leadership. It was not a fear of boredom that caused him to dislike retirement; as previously noted, Nordhoff was not a man whose world began and ended at the office door. He fully recognized and accepted that it was necessary for him to step down, but what the mind accepts is not always reconciled with old habits. Thus his friends became aware of a painful contradiction: during those months in 1968 when his health seemed to be improving, he repeatedly introduced Kurt Lotz to others as the man he had personally chosen as his successor, but the very presence of *any* successor at all merely underlined for him the emotionally unpalatable fact that he needed to step down. It was a difficult time for "the old man" — and for everyone.

It was in deteriorating health that Heinz Nordhoff exerted himself once too often in mid-March 1968, shortly after the board of directors had communicated to him the painful news that he must step down seven months ahead of his own schedule. He raced south to deliver a speech in Baden-Baden, almost as though he wished to prove to himself and others that he remained as vigorous as he had always been throughout more than forty years in the auto industry. That speech and that trip proved too much. During the flight back from Baden-

285

Baden on March 15, the day he gave his speech, Nordhoff collapsed in the company turboprop and needed to be given oxygen, a supply of which was now never far from his side. On landing at Brunswick, Nordhoff was raced home — and from there to Wolfsburg's city hospital.

It was almost as though fate were setting appropriately solemn dates for these last events: Nordhoff was stricken on the Ides of March and died at noon on Good Friday, April 12. Early that morning Mrs. Nordhoff and her eldest daughter, Barbara, were summoned to the hospital. Nordhoff had suddenly begun to weaken. He was surrounded by doctors and assistants. His old friend Monsignor Holling arrived shortly afterward to administer the last rites.

In a few hours, however, he rallied and asked his wife and daughter to have a glass of champagne with him. The champagne available at the hospital was not chilled, so Barbara quickly drove home and returned with several bottles of his favorite brand. The three members of the family sipped the champagne and Nordhoff appeared to be gaining strength. He felt well enough to spend some time writing Easter greetings on his calling cards and he asked that they be sent with flowers to certain of his friends (who received them after he had died). Later that afternoon he weakened suddenly and died quietly. With him at his death were Mrs. Nordhoff, his wife of thirty-eight years, and Barbara.*

As telegrams from the President and the Chancellor of West Germany, as well as from countless others, poured in, all work ceased for a minute's silent tribute in all VW factories the world over. In Wolfsburg, where forty-five thousand workers silently filed past Nordhoff's coffin in a factory hall, the town fathers declared official mourning — as was done also in São Bernardo do Campo, Brazil, where Nordhoff's initiative had built South America's largest automobile factory. On April 18, his coffin was driven to church on a specially modified VW pickup truck. Its cab roof had been cut away and the flower-bedecked flatbed served as a bier for the coffin as it was driven slowly through the streets of Wolfsburg. Hubert Rommel, his driver for many years, was at the wheel, and seated beside him was Mike Hocke, who had served as Nordhoff's chauffeur years before. A Pontifical High Mass in

---

* Nordhoff's widow continues today to live in the Wolfsburg home she shared with her husband; Barbara, who had left Volkswagen of America, Inc., for a job in Germany, later returned to the U.S.A. and in 1969 married a New York physician (and former Rumanian prince), Dr. Dan Cantacuzino.

Monsignor Holling's St. Christopher's Church followed; when Nordhoff's body was carried from there to Wolfsburg's Forest Cemetery, a guard of honor was rendered by his fellow Knights of the Holy Sepulchre.

The most meaningful honors, however, had not come from those who had delivered the official eulogies. They had come from the men and women in the Wolfsburg factory who had filed past his coffin in their everyday working clothes and from the thousands of Wolfsburg citizens who lined the sidewalks of the town to watch that black pickup truck roll solemnly through their streets. They were not dignitaries, but they all knew they had been his people.

A generation had gone; twenty years after the Wolfsburg factory was turned over to German management all its early veterans were twenty years older. The passing of Nordhoff was followed by the death of that colorful Dutchman, Ben Pon, VW's first importer, and by the death of Joe Werner, whom Ferdinand Porsche lured away from Ford in Michigan to risk his future with VW. With Werner's death, there were now only two left of that original "German-American" contingent recruited for VW before the war: Otto Hoehne, a member of the management board, and Mike Hocke, a driver in the motor pool.

Illness had struck several. The dashing F. W. Schultz-Wenck, who had built up VW's operations in his adopted Brazil, had to step down, incapacitated by a stroke shortly after Nordhoff's death. He remained titular Director Presidente of the Brazilian subsidiary until his death on December 28, 1969. Hans Hiemenz of the Wolfsburg Vorstand, whose VW career began in 1940, also stepped down for reasons of health at the end of 1968.

Retirement further thinned the ranks of the veterans, several leaving the Vorstand because they had reached or passed sixty-five years of age. Julius Paulsen, in charge of procurement and materials, retired at the end of 1968, and was replaced by Horst Münzner, then forty-three years old. Kurt Haaf, personnel chief, also retired at the end of that year, after which the forty-eight-year-old Horst Backmann took his place on the Vorstand. Another veteran, due for retirement at the end of 1970, is Frank Novotny, who had previously withdrawn from day-to-day participation in the company's affairs, though he periodically attended Vorstand meetings. Helmut Orlich, the member of the management board in charge of Technical Development and Inspection, left in April 1969, due to changes instituted by Lotz, who brought into the Vorstand Professor Dr. Werner Holste, forty-one, charged with Research and Development. Yet another new management board position was created by Kurt Lotz for a forty-year-old lawyer, Dr. Gerhard Prinz, to head what is called "Participations, Planning and Organization." Three active members of the Nordhoff Vorstand who remained on Lotz's management team were Dr. Carl H. Hahn (still in his early forties), worldwide head of sales and service; Otto Hoehne (in his early sixties), given enlarged responsibilities encompassing both production and inspection; and Dr. Friedrich Thomée (also in his early forties), who remains the Vorstand finance chief.

When Kurt Lotz arrived in Wolfsburg, Volkswagenwerk AG was being run by a management board whose age averaged in the sixties; Lotz works today with a management team whose age averages in the forties. The way Lotz sees it, that "rejuvenated" board is just what the company needs in order to ensure its continued success in the future.

Concern about the decades to come is not an academic exercise for Kurt Lotz; he really looks and plans ahead fifty years, a fact which became very evident during the long, freewheeling and informal conversation I had with this extraordinary man in Wolfsburg recently. Time and again, Kurt Lotz "returned to the future" as we spoke. Objective evidence of his concern may further be seen in the importance attached today to Holste's "R&D" department and to Prinz's position on the Vorstand, the latter a kind of VW "think-tank" for the analysis of future opportunities.

This emphasis, I discovered, derives in large part from Kurt Lotz's own personal life history — and from what he has learned from it.

"My philosophy," Lotz told me, "is to make the best of any new situation, to invest in the future and to be willing to make sacrifices for that future. My motto throughout life — and my motto now at the Volkswagenwerk — is to pay little attention to the past if it is no longer useful for the future."

That is the approach of a pragmatist, and apparently an approach that works, for it seems to have brought Kurt Lotz an unusual degree of success. While his rise is in some ways a peculiarly German success story (incorporating the climb up after the early postwar hardships), it is so surprisingly fast that it almost strikes one as something that ought to have happened "only in America." Consider these facts alone: The "typical" German industrialist is traditionally only supposed to reach top management positions after his hair has turned a dignified gray, but Lotz made it in his forties (hence, perhaps, his readiness to staff his Vorstand with young men). Lotz attained his success without attending a university (except, briefly, night school): this in a nation in which academic doctorates are not only used in daily conversation and correspondence but where they still create social distinctions and assure many a young man a smooth entry to top jobs.* Furthermore, Lotz's entire business career took place after World War II; thus he had no prewar background nor any prewar connections on which he could rely or lean. Finally, unlike many a West German industrialist, Lotz does not come from an influential family having industrial connections, much less one having influence or wealth. He was one of nine children of a farm family; his father Konrad owned an average, medium-sized farm in Lenderscheid near Ziegenhain. When Kurt Lotz was born on September 18, 1912, he was given what by German standards was practically a "log-cabin" start in life: he was expected to make good on his own, without family help or even a higher education.

He graduated from secondary school just as Germany wallowed in the midst of the severe 1932 depression, when six million Germans were out of work and jobs seemed impossible to obtain. One of his teachers suggested that a police job in such a time was as good as any and more secure than most. Lotz, a pragmatist even then, decided "he had to start somewhere"; this turned out to be a police academy.

Rookie policemen were supposed to be at least twenty-five years old before becoming eligible for a commission; Lotz was commissioned a police lieutenant at the age of twenty-two. A year later, the Luftwaffe searched for young police officers who had already proved their leadership potential, to form a cadre. Lotz was invited to join and accepted, because the prospect of flying attracted him; commissioned a lieutenant in the air force, he was sent to study air reconnaissance. Then he fell ill with the flu and, rather than miss classes by reporting himself sick, brashly attempted to cure himself with quinine — an experiment at self-medication which landed him in the hospital for eleven months, after which he was declared ineligible for flying and reassigned to antiaircraft defense.

He got his first taste of industrial planning and his first brush with industry during the war when he was assigned for a time

---

* Dr. Lotz's own "doctor" title derives (as had Nordhoff's) from an honorary doctorate given him in 1963; he had earlier (in 1962) been honored by ancient Heidelberg University, which named him an Honorary Senator of that institution.

to the Luftwaffe armaments department. By then, Lotz was a captain in the general staff corps and it became his job to convey the air force's requirements to the armaments ministry and German factories.

The war's end found him (by then a major) commanding a flak unit wedged between U.S. and Soviet lines in Czechoslovakia. The months which followed were more exciting than Lotz might then have wished; these events deserve to be recorded in detail someday, but the particulars are not relevant to the story of Lotz the industrialist. Only the fact that he escaped to find the American lines needs to be mentioned — and that only because it helps one to measure the man. His chance of escaping successfully were considerably short of fifty-fifty; he had no maps, help, or resources; even he did not entertain much hope of success. Despite these gloomy facts, he was determined to risk his life to reach his family; in doing so, he discovered resources as well as characteristics in himself which he now believes were essential for his postwar success: a willingness to dedicate himself totally to a goal, a readiness to risk everything, an ability to persevere in his aim, and courage enough to act decisively when all the cards were stacked against him.

After discharge from prisoner-of-war status in November 1945, Lotz found his family on a small farm near Homberg, West Germany. By this time, he had both a wife and a daughter (He had married Elisabeth, daughter of Professor Dr. Gustav Lony, in December 1939). Needing to obtain food for them and himself, Lotz got a job on a farm: the onetime farm boy who had become a major in the general staff corps was back again where he had started life. But the job offered food when money was worthless; indeed, his wages for a time consisted of a sausage per day.

In the spring of 1946, Lotz was offered a small job in the cost accounting department of Brown, Boveri's Dortmund office. This paid 300 marks ($75) a month — at a time when Lotz might have earned that much far more easily on the farm, where one pound of butter sold on the black-market for the same amount. Taking a poorly paid job in industry at a time when no one hoped for an economic miracle would mean sacrificing the immediate well-being of his family. It was a long shot, but Lotz took the gamble.

"The decision to move from the farm to Dortmund," Lotz told me, "was among the most difficult decisions I ever had to take in my life. But I wanted to get into industry when it was just starting up again, at the very hour of its birth, so as to get the jump on others."

He is convinced today that he would never have reached the top so fast had he been unwilling to take the two risky decisions he took during this time: the decision to risk his life in escape; the decision to risk his family's immediate well-being in the hope of assuring a better future.

Having been decisive then, Lotz learned the habit of acting decisively. At Brown, Boveri & Cie., he quickly came to be watched as a "comer." While working as a cost-control expert (having taught himself how to use adding machines), he took evening courses in industrial management to broaden himself. By 1954, his record in the company so impressed management that they promoted him to head of a corporate division.

Four years later, Kurt Lotz was chairman of the entire West German operation. Twelve years after he began work as a seventy-five-dollar-a-month cost accountant, the forty-five-year-old Lotz had reached the very top. He was, in fact, the youngest on the company's Vorstand (of which he was chairman), nine years younger than the next youngest man on his own management board. Then he rose even higher; he was made, in 1961, director, and in 1963 managing director, of the Swiss parent company of Brown, Boveri, while retaining his chairmanship of the German Vorstand. As we have seen, he resigned from the parent company but was still head of that German corporation when he was approached by Volkswagenwerk AG.

Volkswagen could, of course, have chosen an automobile man as Nordhoff's successor: it chose, instead, to do the unexpected. Clearly, the board of directors was convinced that the Volkswagenwerk required a top industrial manager who would feel inclined to make use of the most modern management techniques — and an outsider who could look at the company as a corporate entity rather than "merely" as a motor vehicle factory.

It has already been noted that the VW was fortunate in that "it was designed by a technician who proved to be a visionary, and inherited by an engineer who proved to be a master salesman"; the challenge of tomorrow seems to call for an industrialist who can operate a major industrial enterprise which today encompasses more than Volkswagen itself. Kurt Lotz is even now transforming VW into a vast, international, multi-line corporation whose story is no "small" wonder at all.

Kurt Lotz's confidence in himself had brought success and

success had increased self-confidence, yet in meeting him one quickly becomes aware of a paradox: he speaks of himself and his career without self-glorification, almost as though he were speaking about and analyzing someone else. He did not refer to his managerial abilities when he assessed the reasons for his rapid rise; instead, he harked back to those two crucial decisions he had taken at the end of the war, seeing them as crossroads he had successfully traversed. He seemed less proud at having done so than thankful that he had absorbed the lessons implicit in each, and it was clear he felt that any man of similar background, who had met similar challenges successfully, might have succeeded as well — and in any field, since all careers demand resolution, intrepidity, and a willingness to take calculated risks. The thoughtful self-questioning also becomes apparent in the low-keyed manner in which he discusses his background — and in his hesitancy about conducting the conversation in English, despite the fact that he is almost fluent in that language. When he first visited Volkswagen of America, Inc., some in the American VW team were understandably concerned about the "new boss" and what he might be like; from all accounts, Kurt Lotz disarmed everyone with his relaxed, "American" manner, with his considerable personal charm, with his mastery of English — and with his courteous habit of listening attentively to others.

These are all characteristics I myself discovered in Lotz — and they proved a little surprising in a man who is quite overwhelming physically: 6 feet 5 inches tall and built proportionately, with big powerful hands, a generally large frame and broad shoulders, and a massive head. Twenty minutes of calisthenics each morning (before showing up at his desk at 7:45 A.M.) give him the physique of a man ten years younger; in short, this man with an extraordinarily impressive career comes across very personally impressive as well. One half expects a booming voice and a steely-eyed gaze in a man like this; instead, one finds a quiet manner and eyes which reveal a ready and often ironic sense of humor.

Kurt Lotz lives with his wife and two sons in a large modernistic house built for him close by the Rotehof Guest House.* While Lotz enjoys concerts and the theater, his life centers about his work and his family. His two teenage sons, Christian and Michael, are as much affected by the times as any American boy: Christian, the elder, adamantly refuses to let a barber near him and he and his father periodically haggle

* Helge, the Lotzes' first child, lives in Hamburg with her husband, Edgar Hennigen, and their two children.

292

about just how long he ought to wear his hair. Michael is involved in the big issues of life and occasionally chides his father for being too dispassionate. Thus the generation gap makes itself subtly felt in this Wolfsburg home, as it does in others the world over, but despite Lotz's long service as a military officer, he takes a refreshingly liberal view of it all. The fact that German youngsters today have a much freer relationship with parents and elders than they ever had in the past is something which Lotz finds "entirely positive." As for "external appearances," he believes they don't matter as much as some people suppose. "The freedom these youngsters enjoy," he told me, "is bound to bring in its wake some exaggerated behavior. But, by and large, that's nothing to worry about."

I asked Lotz whether he agreed with other top industrialists that the main job of the head of any company was to find the best men, put them in the right jobs, and give them free rein.

"That's only part of it," he replied. "Outstanding men are just the very ones who need to be coordinated and made into a team. Goals have to be determined and adhered to. My job as Vorstand chairman is, after all, to provide leadership."

Setting goals is a responsibility Lotz takes very seriously; a good deal of his private reading is in books and journals which assess the world of tomorrow. For years, the Volkswagenwerk never needed to concern itself with much more than producing enough cars to meet the existing demand, but that era is over.[*] Volkswagenwerk AG, Lotz believes, does not only need plans for the immediate future or for five years hence, but also needs almost visionary thinking about the "futuristic" future two generations ahead.

"If I had thirty free days at my disposal," Lotz said wistfully, "I'd spend them traveling the world and studying the automobile industry, looking for new Volkswagen markets and particularly researching the Far East. I'd visit Japan again, spending more time there. The day may come when Japan will surpass the U.S.A. in gross national product, if not in per capita income; when that day comes, two-thirds of all the world's motor vehicles may be produced in the Far East."

Lotz has already begun to restructure the VW corporation to meet the demands of the future. On April 26, 1969, the shareholders of NSU Motorenwerke AG approved a fusion

---

[*] The fact that corporate headquarters remained for two decades (and still remains, however incongruously) *within* a factory is one demonstration of this early and long-lasting orientation of the company as a sort of production facility, rather than as hub of a worldwide enterprise.

of their company with the Volkswagen-owned Auto-Union GmbH; this resulted in the creation, during August 1969, of a new corporation called Audi NSU Auto-Union AG. This company, with its headquarters in Ingolstadt, is 59.5 per cent owned by Volkswagenwerk; Kurt Lotz is chairman of its Aufsichtsrat. (The awkward corporate name derives from a wish to retain all three time-honored names.) In November 1968, Auto-Union GmbH (prior to its union with NSU) introduced its luxurious Audi 100, which proved a very big success; Audis are so popular today that they are even assembled alongside VWs at Wolfsburg, as well as at Ingolstadt, so as to meet the demand.

A joint sales corporation was established between the Porsche company and Volkswagenwerk; this came to be called VW-Porsche Vertriebsgesellschaft (sales company) and markets sports cars developed and manufactured jointly by both Porsche and VW. The newest of these is the hot Porsche 914, the first production sports cars with a midship engine, providing roadability and handling characteristics equal to those in race cars. (The joint company also markets the various other models of the Porsche.)

Thus Volkswagenwerk AG already includes two major "divisions": Volkswagen and Audi NSU. (Porsche remains separate from the VW giant, being still a family-owned and family-managed manufacturing company. The newly formed VW-Porsche company is a marketing company only, thus allowing the engineering-oriented Porsche works to specialize in what it does best.) The future trend is obvious and inescapable: the day will come when a complete restructuring of the Volkswagen corporation will take place; it would create a sort of German "General Motors," perhaps with an overall corporate name as vague as GM's. Whether further divisions, to manufacture still other lines of motor vehicles, will eventually be added is of course a corporate secret. Asked if he might diversify to the extent that the company would some day produce home appliances ("beetle-brand" washing machines and the like), Lotz replied with a smile that he intends to concentrate on the motor vehicle industry for the time being. "The wish for such diversification," he said, "and the fulfillment of that wish are two separate things."

Lotz regards all these new corporate moves as logical developments flowing out of the dynamics of the auto industry. Indeed, he denies that he "made a lot of changes" at VW after he took over.

"There was less of a need to change things," he said, "than

to complete. There was a need to introduce additional modern management techniques and concepts, as well as to initiate further technical planning. But this was a fulfillment rather than a change."

Nevertheless, Kurt Lotz admitted that any new corporate chief inevitably introduces not only his own "style" into things, but also a "personal emphasis." This, in Volkswagen's case, did produce some changes — or fulfillments, as the case may be. The biggest may be found in the competitiveness of the new divisions. They compete actively with each other and with the VW itself, are independent of each other, and have separate marketing organizations to sell their separate product lines. This separation was not achieved without creating some anguish; Lotz insisted that free competition required German VW dealers to be divested of their Audi franchises or to set up completely independent Audi dealerships, which for a while did not please these dealers. A complex method has been worked out to facilitate this divestment without hurting the men involved financially; a good many of them are today beginning to agree with Lotz that competition per se is a good thing for all.

Another development initiated by Lotz enlarged Otto Hoehne's responsibilities on the Vorstand and introduced Professor Dr. Holste's R&D post as a replacement for the earlier Technical Development position.

When Lotz joined Volkswagenwerk, he discovered that there often were uncertainties about "who was at fault" when something went wrong. He also felt that VW inspection should not be limited to the production process. A customer whose VW contains a faulty part doesn't care where the fault lies—but the company needs to know. Inspection, Lotz reasoned, ought to be enlarged to control the quality of all key processes at work on a vehicle: product planning, production, and sales-and-service. For example, did the part fail due to a fault in design, in production or in service procedures? Standards for all three, not just for production, ought to be set and maintained.

Accordingly, Lotz established a new staff position called Qualitätsförderung ("Quality Promotion") under a thirty-one-year-old engineer named Claus Borgward, a scion of the defunct Borgward auto company, who has worked for VW since 1963. An energetic young man who speaks intensely and volubly while puffing big cigars, Borgward emphasized to me that his department now works hand-in-glove with both the planners and designers as well as with the worldwide sales-and-service organization, to make sure that quality control everywhere remains as high as it ever was in production. If a part turns out to be defective in Baton Rouge, Louisiana, or in Sydney, Australia, chances are that this part will end up in Borgward's department at Wolfsburg, air-freighted there for detailed analysis.

As for the inspectors within the various VW factories, they remain totally independent of the production staff within those factories, and even of the plant managers themselves; they continue to be able to yank any car off the production line if they spot the slightest flaw. Today, they ultimately report to Otto Hoehne on the Vorstand, because Hoehne is no longer only "production boss" at the Volkswagenwerk; Lotz has given him the additional task of supervising inspection standards.

"His job today," says Lotz, "is to act as referee between the production and inspection people under him."

One vehicle which came in for heavy criticism when first introduced in West Germany in 1968, was the "Type IV" Volkswagen: the VW 411 (since redesignated VW 411E, for electronic fuel injection). For a variety of reasons, that line of cars failed to "take off" in the domestic market when first introduced; in fact, in the early months, the joke goes that they were called "411" because the company only expected to sell 411 of them.

Today, the VW 411E has had the kinks knocked out of it: it has increased horsepower, improved stability, and a reduced noise level. Holste even ventured the surprising opinion that the VW 411 is in many ways today as technically advanced over other contemporary cars as the beetle was in 1939. It is not yet marketed in the U.S.A., but soon will be.

The 1975 Volkswagens are already on the drawing boards in the tall Research and Development building in Wolfsburg in which I interviewed Holste. "Every man here," Holste said, "knows what jobs he has to do right through 1975." R&D breaks down into its component parts: Research, often basic, deals with engine, transmission and other changes well into the future, some twenty years hence; Development deals with the production of VW prototypes.

"It takes about five years," Holste told me, "to develop a car which meets Volkswagen quality standards. We are now designing cars in all price ranges, so as to reach every category of potential buyer; no matter what a man wants to spend on a car, he ought to find one of our cars meeting his needs.

"But our interest is not and never will be to follow Detroit's direction," Holste continued. "We won't bring out cars each year which have been merely restyled; we won't restyle for the sake of restyling. We are interested only in bringing out new cars which are of the highest technical quality and which are really technically new."

Each VW "division" (Volkswagen and Audi NSU, as well as the marketing division, VW-Porsche) is meant to have a *full range* of motor vehicles — and each range is meant to be competitive with the cars produced by the other divisions. Not even a "luxury Volkswagen," says Holste, "is out of the range of possibilities"; indeed, such a car would give the "VW division" a complete line, enabling it to compete, for example, with the Audi 100, which costs about $4000. As for that perennial question about the survival of the beetle, Holste gave the only logical answer: "Who wants to get rid of the beetle when you're selling 5000 of them each day?"

The beetle and its "big brothers" remain very popular indeed in the United States, despite Detroit's sub-compacts. VW's Emden plant today produces *exclusively* for the U.S. market, so great is the demand for VWs in the United States. The record year for VW sales in the U.S.A. was 1968, when 569,292 Volkswagens were sold; that year, VW had a 5.5 per cent share of the entire U.S. auto market and a 55 per cent share of the imported car market. The first half of 1969 saw a general stagnation of the U.S. auto market — plus a three-month dock strike which kept Volkswagens out of dealer showrooms for a quarter of the year. Further, the revaluation of the German D-mark in late 1969 compelled Volkswagen of America, Inc., to raise its prices (though only 2.3 to 2.8 per cent, as against a rise of between 7 and 11 per cent elsewhere in the world).

The enforced price rise does not seem to have cut U.S. enthusiasm for the VW, for sales in the latter months of 1969, directly following the revaluation of the mark, were so good that VWoA hoped to come close to its 1968 record — and this despite losses during the three-month strike. In late January 1970, the 4,000,000th VW was produced for America.

"The big changes at Volkswagen of America," says J. Stuart Perkins, the company president, "are similar to those elsewhere in VW. We now also sell the Audi, the Porsche 914 and the Porsche 911's. Thus, in addition to our VW range, we have moved into selling high-performance cars — and even racing them. Porsche 917 prototypes have raced at Daytona and the Formula Super Vee has been introduced to bring the Formula Vee concept up to date."

297

Changes in Formula Vee racing have been so far-reaching that there may soon be "World Olympics" of this kind, with national champions competing against each other for the world title. A new World Formula Vee (bringing together the old World Formula Vee and the U.S. Formula Vee) has made this possible, thanks to the acceptance of VW-1600 engines. The new Super Vee cars, which can reach more than 130 miles per hour, incorporate Volkswagen components of more recent manufacture. The greatest testimony to the entire "Formula Vee concept" came when the Sports Car Club of America accepted the new Super Vee class without seeing a single car of that kind — despite the fact that a new class normally is accepted only after many cars have been built and raced.

Stuart Perkins restructured his American organization early in 1970, giving VWoA two separate "line" divisions called Volkswagen Operations and Porsche Audi Operations. Both are headed by a vice president. The new head of Volkswagen Operations is Al Breckwoldt, formerly general manager of VWoA's Washington distributorship; John Reilly is the new vice president in charge of Porsche Audi Operations.

Other company officers took over "staff functions" under Perkins. Michael L. Sanyour, for example, became V.P. in charge of Corporate Marketing, while Arthur R. Railton became V.P. in charge of Corporate Relations. "These changes," says Perkins, "make certain that both divisions are completely competitive, while both have available to them all the staff experts they need."

The young company president then adds: "It all amounts to a certain coming of age for Volkswagen in America."*

Perhaps the most American of all Volkswagens is the "dune buggy." 95 per cent of these (and there are more than 25,000 in Southern California alone) are based on the standard VW chassis, cut down about 12 inches. A fiberglass body is then put on it; VW's light weight, air cooling and traction do the rest. "Volkswagen," says Art Railton, "has even become American enough to get into the Sears, Roebuck catalogue." (Sears sells a dune buggy conversion kit.)

The U.S. dune buggies are a far cry from the standard Volkswagens, but even the Volkswagenwerk and its own subsidiaries have recently introduced rather surprising, specialized cars

---

* So much are the two divisions being kept apart and kept competitive that Doyle Dane Bernbach, advertising agency for Porsche Audi as it has been for VW, established an entirely separate "unit" to make sure no PA copywriter would write VW ads, or vice versa. The result, says Perkins, is "a completely different advertising image."

meant for a limited market. One new model is the VW 181 which sells for over $2000 in West Germany and which resembles the wartime "Kübelwagen." Originally meant to meet vehicle requirements of the armed forces West Germany has assigned to NATO, this Jeep-like VW is also sold to civilians who like a rugged car for rough terrain.

The Australian Volkswagen organization has also produced a somewhat similar car (though this does not resemble the Kübelwagen), calling it the Volkswagen Country-Buggy. Volkswagen do Brazil, which also produces its "own" VWs (not sold elsewhere), stuck to a more conventional design in introducing a four-door sedan in 1969. Called the VW 1600 "Brasilia," it is based on a Wolfsburg prototype, of which there were about thirty produced in Germany; these thirty Brasilia prototypes are today used for internal transport in the VW factory.

Not only new cars have been introduced outside West Germany, but new management as well. The Australian VW organization, which today sells about 15,000 vehicles annually and which has to date sold about 250,000 "Down Under," is now headed by Dr. A. Solzer, working alongside Peter Rupp and D. Herzmer, respectively the financial and production directors. In charge of the Brazilian subsidiary since Schultz-Wenck's illness and death is R. Leiding; in South Africa, G. E. R. Eckert has become managing director. In Great Britain, the importer, an independent organization, not VW-owned, is now headed by Alan M. Dix, formerly of VWoA.

This vast, international export organization is run in Wolfsburg by Dr. Carl H. Hahn and, directly under him, by Dr. Werner P. Schmidt, thirty-five, who replaced the retired Manuel Hinke as head of exports. Formerly sales manager for German Ford within West Germany (a post from which he was lured by Carl Hahn's assistant, Dr. Gunther Flüs, also a Ford veteran), Schmidt speaks fluent English (or, more accurately, fluent American), having studied at Kalamazoo College in Michigan when he was twenty. Like Lotz, Schmidt sees a big VW opportunity in the Far East. Already, Japan ranks among the twenty or so nations (out of VW's total of 130 export countries) which buy at least 5000 or more VWs a year. "The Japanese buy six thousand a year," says Schmidt. "That may not seem like much, but it's a day's production — and not a bad start."

The development of such embryo markets will, hopefully, reduce the U.S. share of the Volkswagenwerk's export business — without reducing the upward trend of VW sales in the

U.S.A. New market developments along more coordinated lines and with more centralized information-gathering facilities is a Lotz-era innovation and accompanies a rejuvenation of the export business as a whole. The pioneers, members of the first generation of Volkswagen importers, have retired or, like Ben Pon, have died; even those who do remain active have in many cases turned over day-to-day management to younger men. The effect of this is considerable.

New talents are being discovered, modern management techniques vital to Volkswagen's success in the future are being utilized, and the energy of youth is being brought to bear on an organization which is a quarter of a century old. The Volkswagen era which began with Kurt Lotz seems everywhere to be characterized by youthful, bold ideas and by younger men impatient with past accomplishments; it is this management which will help Volkswagen in its transition toward tomorrow.

Bibliography

Bittorf, Wilhelm, *Die Geschichte Eines Autos* (Limbach, Germany: no date, but c. 1954, based on a series of articles appearing in *Der Spiegel,* West German news magazine).

Buchheim, Hans, *Das Dritte Reich* (Munich, Germany: Kösel-Verlag, 1958).

Frankenberg, Richard von, *Die Ungewöhnliche Geschichte des Hauses Porsche* (Stuttgart, Germany: Motor-Presse-Verlag, 1961; Engl. transl. by Charles Meisl, London: G. T. Foulis and Co., 1961).

Hendrick, Burton Jesse, *Age of Big Business* (New Haven: Yale University Press, 1921).

Hopfinger, K. B., *Beyond Expectation: The Volkswagen Story* (London: G. T. Foulis and Co., 1954).

Horne, Alistair, *Return to Power: A Report on the New Germany* (New York: Praeger, 1956).

Kölling, Fritz, *Ein Auto Zieht Kreise: Herkunft und Zukunft des Volkswagens* (Reutlingen, Germany: Verlag Robert Bardtenschlager, 1962).

Markmann, Charles Lam, and Mark Sherwin, *The Book of Sports Cars* (New York: G. P. Putnam's Sons, 1959).

Molter, Guenther, *German Racing Cars and Drivers,* transl. by Isolde Syben (Los Angeles: Clymer Motors, 1950).

Mönnich, Horst, *Die Autostadt: Abenteuer Einer Technischen Idee* (Brunswick, Germany: Georg Westermann Verlag, 1958).

Nevins, Allan, and Frank Ernest Hill, *Ford: Decline and Rebirth 1933-1962* (New York: Charles Scribner's Sons, 1962).

Nevins, Allan, and Frank Ernest Hill, *Ford: The Times, The Man, The Company* (New York: Charles Scribner's Sons, 1954).

Nitske, W. Robert, *The Amazing Porsche and Volkswagen Story* (New York: Comet Press Books, 1958).

Packard, Vance, *The Waste Makers* (New York: David McKay Co., 1960).

Quint, Herbert A., *Porsche: Der Weg Eines Zeitalters* (Stuttgart, Germany: Steingrüben Verlag, 1951).

Rosenmann, Ernst, and Carlo Demand, *The Big Race*, transl. by E. Evand (Frankfurt, Germany: Nest Verlag, 1955).

Scholz, Hugo, *Herr Seiner Welt: Der Lebensroman Ferdinand Porsches* (Augsburg, Germany: Adam Kraft Verlag, 1962).

Shirer, William L., *The Rise and Fall of the Third Reich* (New York: Fawcett Books, 1963).

Singer, Charles, E. J. Holmyard, A. R. Hall, and Trevor I. Williams, *A History of Technology*, Vol. 5 (London: Oxford University Press, 1958).

Sponsel, Heinz, *Porsche, Autos, Weltrekorde* (Hanover, Germany: Theodore Opperman Verlag, 1953).

Strache, Dr. Wolf, ed., *Wolfsburg: Die Volkswagenstadt* (Stuttgart, Germany: Verlag Die Schönen Bücher, 1960).

Todtmann, Heinz, *Kleiner Wagen in Grosser Fahrt* (Offenbach in Baden, Germany: F. Burda, 1949).

Walker, James Blaine, *The Epic of American Industry* (New York: Harper and Brothers, 1949).

MISCELLANEOUS

Dein KdF-Wagen (Berlin, Germany: Verlag der Deutschen Arbeitsfront GmbH, no date but c. 1938).

German Motor Vehicles Industry Report (Washington, D.C.: United States Strategic Bombing Survey, 1st ed., 3 Nov. 1945; 2d ed., January, 1947).

Handbook of German Affairs (Washington, D.C.: German Diplomatic Mission, 1954).

Um die Zukunft des Volkswagenwerkes (Berlin, Germany: A. V. G. Verlagsgesellschaft, 1958; Schriftenreihe der Gesellschaft für öffentliche Wirtschaft, Heft 6).

Volkswagen-werke, Fallersleben, Germany (Washington, D.C.: United States Strategic Bombing Survey, January 1947).

Wolfsburg and the Countryside Between Harz and Heath (Hamburg, Germany: Hoffmann und Campe Verlag, 1958).

American Machinist/Metalworking Manufacturing, various issues.

Autocar, March 27, 1964.

Barnard, Charles, "He Built the Boom in Beetles," *True*, May 1962.

Cahier, Bernhard, "Targa Florio," *Road & Track*, August 1958.

Car and Driver, April 1964.

Clark, Blake, "The Car That Built a City," *Reader's Digest*, February 1954.

Hahn, Carl Horst, "Nobody Wanted the Bug," *German-American Trade News*, March 1963.

Haniel, Joachim, "German Myth on Wheels," *Living Age*, October 1938.

Horn, Huston, "The Beetle Does Float," *Sports Illustrated*, August 19, 1963.

Langen, Hans Herbert, "Foreign Workers in the Federal Republic," *Magazine of the Federal Republic of Germany*, No. 37, 1964.

McCahill, Tom, *Mechanix Illustrated*, February 1964.

New Horizons with VW, published by Volkswagen Australasia Ltd., various issues.

News of Volkswagen, published by South African Motor Assemblers and Distributors Ltd., various issues.

Porsche, Ferry, "Porsche," *Wolfsburg and the Countryside Between Harz and Heath* (*Merian, das Monatsheft der Städte und Landschaften*, 11th year, Issue No. 7, 1958, Hoffmann und Campe Verlag, Hamburg).

Railton, Arthur R., "Will Success Spoil Volkswagen?" *Popular Mechanics*, February 1958.

Rigby, Robert, "King of the Small Car World," *Sign*, October 1960.

Road & Track, September 1959.

Rowan, Jan. C., "Wolfsburg: Suburb Without a City," *Progressive Architecture*, December 1961.

The Samad Scene, published by South African Motor Assemblers and Distributors Ltd., various issues.

Small World, published by Volkswagen of America, Inc., various issues.

Stern, December 12, 1948.

Time, August 25, 1952; February 19, 1954; April 6, 1962.

VWA Review, published by Volkswagen Australasia Ltd., various issues.

VW Autoist, published by Volkswagen Club of America, April 1963.

VW Informationen, published by Volkswagenwerk AG, Wolfsburg, various issues.

Weathervane, published by Volkswagen of American, Inc., various issues.

Wheels, February 1961.

Wyse, Robert, "The Great Berryman Story," *Safer Motoring*, various 1965 issues.

HOW TO TELL THE AGE OF A VOLKSWAGEN

The only certain way of identifying the year of a particular VW 1200 sedan is to check the chassis number of the car in question and to compare it with the chassis numbers listed below. Until 1955, the Volkswagenwerk did not have any "model year." Before that, a 1953 VW was simply one which was produced between January 1, 1953, and December 31, 1953. Since 1955, model years begin on August 1.

What makes identification doubly difficult is that improvements (both exterior and interior) often were made midway in production. The absence of the Wolfsburg crest on the VW's front hood is the only exterior change which sets a 1963 VW apart from a 1962 model. But this modification wasn't made until November, three months after 1963 production began on August 1.

Basic Changes

1949   **Chassis Numbers: 91,922-138,554**

1. License plate identification on rear deck dropped
2. Inside pull cable release for front hood; formerly locking handle on hood
3. Solex carburetor introduced as standard equipment
4. Dashboard redesigned
5. Starting crank hole dropped (VWs previously could be started by both key and hand-crank)

1950   **Chassis Numbers: 138,555-220,471**

1. Hydraulic brakes introduced; formerly mechanical brakes
2. Ash tray introduced on dashboard and on right rear quarter panel
3. Noise mufflers for heating ducts added
4. Automatic air cooling by thermostatically controlled throttle ring
5. Fuel mixture heating device (heat riser) introduced

305

1951　　　　　　　**Chassis Numbers: 220,472-313,829**

1. Chrome garnish molding added to windshield
2. Wolfsburg crest added to front hood above hood handle
3. Vent flaps added to front-quarter body panels

1952　　　　　　　**Chassis Numbers: 313,830-428,156**

1. Glass vent windows added; formerly vent wings in front-quarter body panels
2. Heating control by rotary knob; formerly pull-knob
3. "T" type rear hood handle introduced; formerly loop-type
4. Two brake-and-taillights: formerly one brake-and-taillight in center of rear hood
5. Window crank makes 3½ turns; formerly 10½ turns
6. Glove compartment gets door; formerly open bin
7. Turn signal control moved to steering wheel from dashboard
8. 5.60 x 15-inch tires replace 5.00 x 16-inch tires
9. 2d, 3rd, and 4th gears synchronized; formerly crashbox

1953　　　　　　　**Chassis Numbers: 428,157-575,414**

1. Oval one-piece rear window replaces split window
2. Lock button added to vent-window handles
3. Brake-fluid reservoir relocated behind spare tire; formerly at master cylinder

1954　　　　　　　**Chassis Numbers: 575,415-722,934**

1. Starter now incorporated with ignition switch; formerly separate button on dashboard
2. Bigger, more powerful engine, hp increased from 30 hp (1131-cc) to 36 hp (1192-cc), 5.8:1 to 6.6:1 compression ratio
3. Oil-bath air cleaner introduced, formerly felt-element filter
4. Break-in driving requirement dropped for engine
5. Automatic three-way courtesy light added
6. Top window in taillight housing dropped

1955　　　　　　　**Chassis Numbers: 722,935-929,745**

1. Flashing directional indicators mounted low on front fenders replace the semaphore "idiot sticks"

1956　　　　　　　**Chassis Numbers: 929,746-1,246,618**

1. Chromed dual tailpipes added; formerly single tailpipe
2. Taillight housings moved 2 inches higher on fenders

3. Bumper overrider "bows" added
4. Sunroof made of plastic fabric; formerly cloth fabric
5. Steering-wheel diameter spoke (horizontal) moved lower, off-center
6. Heater knob moved forward; formerly located in back of front seats
7. Front seat backs now adjustable; formerly non-adjustable
8. Redesigned gas tank yields larger luggage space

1957 **Chassis Numbers: 1,246,619-1,600,439**

1. Tubeless tires replace tube-type tires
2. Adjustable striker plates fitted to doors
3. Front heater outlets moved back to within 12 inches of door for better heat distribution

1958 **Chassis Numbers: 1,600,440-2,007,615**

1. Brake drums and shoes widened for faster, surer stops
2. Rear window and windshield enlarged
3. Front turn-signal lights moved to top of fender
4. Radio grille moved left, in front of driver
5. Accelerator pedal introduced; formerly a roller

1959 **Chassis Numbers: 2,007,616-2,528,667**

1. Stronger clutch springs
2. Improved fan belt design
3. Frame reinforced for greater strength

1960 **Chassis Numbers: 2,528,668-3,192,506**

1. Steering wheel "dished" for safety
2. Door handles become grab handles with pushbuttons; were formerly pull-out lever type
3. Padded sun-visor; formerly transparent plastic
4. Anti-sway bar added for improved cornering, handling
5. Generator output increased from 160 to 180 watts
6. Steering damper added for improved handling
7. Footrest added for front-seat passenger
8. Seat back contoured for greater comfort, reduced driver fatigue

1961 **Chassis Numbers: 3,192,507-4,010,994**

1. Sun visor and grab handle provided for passenger's side
2. Increased horsepower; from 36 to 40 hp
3. Automatic choke and preheater introduced

4. Transmission synchronized in all forward speeds
5. Flatter gas tank yields increased luggage space
6. "Quick-check" transparent brake fluid reservoir
7. Push-on connectors fitted throughout electrical system
8. Pump-type windshield washer
9. Non-repeat starter switch
10. Key slot in doors changed from vertical to horizontal

1962   Chassis Numbers: 4,010,995-4,846,835

1. Spring-loaded hood
2. Large taillights
3. Sliding covers on heat outlets
4. Compressed-air windshield washer
5. Seat-belt mounting points added
6. Gas gauge; formerly reserve fuel tap
7. Worm and roller steering improves handling; formerly worm and sector
8. Permanently lubricated tie-rod ends

1963   Chassis Numbers: 4,846,836-5,677,118

1. Leatherette headliner introduced
2. Wolfsburg hood crest dropped
3. Folding handle for sunroof added
4. Foam-insulated floors
5. Fresh-air heating
6. Nylon window guides

1964   Chassis Numbers: 5,677,119-6,502,399

1. Sliding metal sunroof replaces cloth roof, making car "theftproof"
2. Sunroof crank improvement
3. Horn operated by thumb bar instead of ring
4. Vinyl upholstery discarded in favor of porous leatherette, to improve air circulation
5. Four new colors introduced: Panama Beige, Java Green (dark green), Bahama Blue (light blue) and Sea Blue (same as 1963 Karmann-Ghia). Black, Pearl White, Anthracite and Ruby Red continued

1965   Chassis Numbers: 11-500001-11-5979202

1. Significant increases in window area: windshield increased 11% and slightly curved; door windows, 6%; rear side windows, 17.5%; rear window, 19.5%

2. Windshield wipers improved: blades longer and more efficient; more powerful electric motor added; blades park to left instead of right, wiping more glass in front of driver
3. Slight thinning of backs of front bucket seats provides additional legroom for rear-seat passengers
4. Contouring of backrests of front bucket seats for additional comfort
5. Rear seat backrest now folds down nearly flat onto rear seat cushion, allowing rear compartment to be used as luggage space as in a station wagon
6. Improved braking system; brake master cylinder and brake-shoe supports on backing plates redesigned, reducing lining wear, improving braking, and reducing pressure needed on pedal
7. Control knob for heating system replaced by two levers near parking brake handle, one for front compartment and the other controlling heat entering rear seat compartment
8. Four thermostatically operated flaps added to engine's fan housing now permit air to flow through car's heater and defroster ducts as soon as engine is started
9. Engine compartment turn-handle eliminated and replaced by pushbutton device

1966　　　　Chassis Numbers: 116-000-001-116-1021-298

1. Horsepower increased from 40 to 50 and displacement from 1200-cc to 1300-cc. Number 1300 on engine lid
2. Ventilating slots in wheels; flat hub caps
3. Safety latches for front seat backrests
4. Emergency blinker switch
5. Headlight dimmer switch mounted on turn signal lever
6. Center dashboard defroster outlet

1967　　　　Chassis Numbers: 117-000-001—

1. Horsepower increased from 50 to 53 and displacement from 1300-cc to 1500-cc
2. Glass cover over sealed beam headlights eliminated
3. Dual brake system
4. Volkswagen nameplate on engine lid
5. Two-speed windshield wipers
6. Back-up lights
7. Engine lid redesigned for vertical mounting of license plate

1968   Chassis Numbers: 118-000-000-118-1-016-098

1. One-piece bumpers; bows and overriders eliminated; bumper height raised
2. Head restraints combined with front seat backrests
3. Automatic Stick Shift (optional) introduced
4. External gas tank filler, spring-loaded flap
5. Front hood air intake louver, push-button front hood catch
6. Fresh air ventilating system
7. Collapsible steering column
8. Exhaust emission control system
9. Flattened door handles with built-in trigger release
10. Backup/brake lights and rear turn signals in single housing.
11. Certification sticker on door post that vehicle meets federal safety standards

1969   Chassis Numbers: 119-000-001-119-1-093-704

1. Rear window defogger and defroster, electric heating wires on inner surface of glass
2. Double-jointed rear axle for improved ride and handling
3. Warning lights in speedometer identified by letters or symbols
4. Ignition lock combined with a locking device for the steering wheel
5. Gas tank filler neck flap has lock, with release under the right side of the dash panel
6. Front hood release relocated in glove compartment
7. Day/night rear-view mirror
8. Warm-air outlets at base of the doors moved rearward; remote control knobs on door columns

1970   Chassis Numbers: 11-0-2000001—

1. Air intake slots on engine lid
2. Increased horsepower (from 53 to 57) and displacement (from 1500 cc to 1600 cc)
3. Enlarged front turn signals (combined with side marker lights)
4. Reflectors mounted on rear bumper
5. Side reflectors built into taillight housing
6. Tenths-of-mile indicator on odometer (also appears on late '69 models)
7. Head restraints reduced in size

8. Buzzer sounds when door is opened and key is left in ignition
9. Remote control knobs for warm air outlets discontinued
10. Lock on glove compartment door

Where to Locate Chassis Numbers

Chassis numbers for all Volkswagen sedans (1200, 1300, and 1500) are located in two places on the car's body: (1) under the back seat, stamped on the frame tunnel, and (2) behind the spare tire in the trunk.

New Numbering System Introduced in 1965

Starting with the production of 1965 model VWs, the factory introduced a new serial numbering system, replacing the old chassis numbers listed above. The first two digits of the new nine-number system represent the model (e.g., 11 for Models 113 and 117; 14 for Models 141 and 143; 22 for Model 2212 and 2252, etc.)* *The third digit will designate the model year* (e.g., 5 for Model Year 1965, etc.) The remaining six digits will be used to number the vehicles themselves, beginning with 0 for each new model year. Those who want to ascertain the age of a particular Volkswagen produced after the introduction of 1965 models need only look at the third digit; however, the digits which follow will also be a help in ascertaining age, for a high-number 1965 VW would, of course, be newer than a low-number model.

* Series 100 vehicles (those model numbers beginning with the numeral 1) are beetles and Ghias; 200-series vehicles are trucks and Microbus station wagons; 300-series vehicles are VW 1600's. Thus, Model 113 happens to be the left-hand-drive beetle; while Model 2252, given in example above, happens to be the standard model Microbus station wagon with a sunroof. (This model is unavailable in the U.S., where only the Deluxe model Microbus station wagon is sold with a sunroof.)